The AACRAO
International Guide

A Resource for International
Education Professionals

*American Association of Collegiate
Registrars and Admissions Officers*

The AACRAO
International Guide

American Association of Collegiate
Registrars and Admissions Officers
One Dupont Circle, NW, Suite 520
Washington, DC 20036–1135

Tel: (202) 293–9161 | Fax: (202) 872–8857 | www.aacrao.org

For a complete listing of AACRAO publications, visit www.aacrao.org/publications.

The American Association of Collegiate Registrars and Admissions Officers,
founded in 1910, is a nonprofit, voluntary, professional association of more than
11,000 higher education administrators who represent more than 2,600 institutions
and agencies in the United States and in forty countries around the world. The mission of the Association is to provide leadership in policy initiation, interpretation,
and implementation in the global educational community. This is accomplished
through the identification and promotion of standards and best practices in enrollment management, information technology, instructional management, and student
services.

LIBRARY OF CONGRESS
CATALOGING-IN-PUBLICATION DATA

Names: American Association of Collegiate Registrars
and Admissions Officers, issuing body.

Title: The AACRAO international guide : a resource for
international education professionals.

Description: Washington, D.C. : American Association of Collegiate Registrars
and Admissions Officers, 2016. | Includes bibliographical references.

Identifiers: LCCN 2016021089 | ISBN 9781578581139 (pbk.)

Subjects: LCSH: Student exchange programs—United States. |
Universities and colleges—United States—Admission.

Classification: LCC LB2376.4 .G85 2016 | DDC 378.1/610973—dc23

LC record available at <https://lccn.loc.gov/2016021089>

Table of Contents

Best Practices in International Education

ONE

International Students: A Starting Point to Comprehensive Internationalization 01

Lindsay M. Addington

TWO

Internationalizing Your Campus: Action Steps and Best Practices 09

Jacquelyn D. Elliott

THREE

International Admissions Policies, Procedures, and Practices 19

John Wilkerson

FOUR

Recruiting International Students 29

Liz Reisberg

FIVE

Graduate Student Recruitment and Admissions

Adina M. Lav

SIX

EducationUSA and International Recruitment

Peggy Blumenthal & Kristina Jenkins

SEVEN

Collaboration with Internationally-Based Counselors

Johanna Fishbein, Becky Konowicz & Kathleen Schultz

EIGHT

International Student Recruitment Agents

Eddie West

TWENTY-TWO

The Art of Credential Evaluation 233

*Jeannine Bell, Jennifer Minke, Ellen
Silverman & Margaret Wenger*

Beth Cotter & Jasmin Saidi-Kuehnert

LesLee M. Clauson Eicher

George F. Kacenga

TWENTY-SIX

Vocational Education in Foreign Education Systems: An Overview of Selected Pathways

Alexander Chucklin & Anatoly Temkin

TWENTY-SEVEN

AACRAO EDGE: History, Development, and Future

Gloria Nathanson, Johnny Johnson, William J. Paver & Robert Watkins

Case Studies

TWENTY-EIGHT

In-House Credential Evaluation Services: Lessons Learned at the University of Phoenix 287

Marc Booker, Nathan Cicchillo & Beth Simpson

TWENTY-NINE

Articulation Agreements at the American University of Beirut 301

Hala Abou Arraj

Country Studies

THIRTY-FIVE

Ukraine: Education in a War Zone.............355

Kristina Zaluckyj

THIRTY-SIX

The Korean Non-Formal Education System.............367

Anthony Sabo

THIRTY-SEVEN

Evaluating Credentials from Mexico.............373

Mandie L. Brooks

Appendices

Preface

JACQUELYN D. ELLIOTT, ED.D.

Vice President for International Education, AACRAO Board of Directors
International Liaison Specialist, University of Missouri–St. Louis

What a great time in our history at AACRAO to be producing a comprehensive book on international higher education. I am especially pleased to have been asked to write this preface, as international education is among my most treasured passions. This book was designed for campuses of all sorts across the globe. For some, it will serve as a handbook of best practices here in the U.S. For others, it will be a glimpse into the ways in which we work to connect our institutions globally. Either way, we at AACRAO hope that your copy of the *AACRAO International Guide* will soon have frayed edges and bent corners!

Like most everything in U.S. higher education, our federal agendas—economic and political—have shaped our progress and returns in terms of academic programming, research, and policy. The development of international higher education is a product of such agendas. While to review the history of international higher education would be too cumbersome here, it is important to note that the history does exist.

I will give you a postcard version here—for my fellow historians, forgive the brevity. Following WWII, a tidal wave of new independent nations dotted the globe, with organizations emerging to serve greater cooperation across national boundaries. Higher education was not immune. U.S. international education stemmed from the National Defense Education Act of 1958, whereby centers focusing on language and international research were set up. These programs formed a comprehensive approach to foreign language and world regional education that would help prepare our nation to compete globally. These early programs were an impetus for the Fulbright-Hays and subsequent development of international education.

It is this history in international education and competition that pushes our system of higher education to the forefront. Most leaders in higher education today realize the need for their campuses to be internationalized; but often, they may not know how to develop strategies that will move the effort forward. This is where you, as a practitioner, have a significant and meaningful role. As registration, enrollment, and international affairs specialists, we are armed with information to help make this goal a reality. Our faculty members are eager to push the boundaries of research across deserts and seas, and our students are graduating into a world that truly is integrated in ways never before experienced. This creates vibrant opportunities for global partnerships, international linkages, new research, and entrepreneurship; but, it also creates challenges in understanding different habits, peoples, and work cultures. We must prepare our students to navigate successfully, with both hard and soft skills.

So, I now leave you in the good hands of the authors. As you can see, this book grew out of a collaboration of many people with varying backgrounds in international higher education. From enrollment, credential evaluation, study abroad, immigration, and agreements of good faith, this volume serves as a go-to resource regarding global educational practices. The contributors draw upon a variety of experience both experiential and research-based in an effort to present best practices, research contributions, and implications for practitioners—just like you!

2016 AACRAO INTERNATIONAL GUIDE

XI

Introduction

JENNIFER MINKE

Texas A&M University Kingsville
AACRAO International Publication Advisory Committee
AACRAO International Education Standards Council

I am proud to introduce the newest version of the *AACRAO International Guide* (The Guide). In the introduction to the 2010 edition of The Guide, Robert Watkins stated, "One of the fastest growing sectors of higher education administration in the United States is the field of international education." Today, due to the increased globalization of education, not just in the U.S. but across the world, it is more important than ever that those who serve our students in higher education have the necessary resources. The Guide continues to be one of those resources.

With thirty-seven chapters, divided into five sections, this is the most comprehensive Guide to date and is representative of how the field of international education has grown and has become more integrated within higher education. Whereas the Study Abroad chapter was first introduced in 2001 as a unique higher education experience, now it is fairly commonplace for U.S. students to have at least one study abroad experience during their college years, if not several. A phenomenon that we have been seeing over the last six years, and that will only continue to grow, is the changing educational options being made available in many countries across the globe. If you look at some of the resources in

our field from twenty, ten, or even five years ago, most non-U.S. countries had very clear education pathways from preschool on up through doctoral degrees. And, historically, the distinction between academic education and vocational education was very clear. Now, with the globalization of education, new pathways through these education systems are developing, intermixing with, and in some cases, even replacing what was once the "traditional" educational pathway. This is addressed in several chapters of this Guide.

Two new sections have been added to this version of The Guide. Those are the Case Studies section and the Country Studies section. Again, recognizing how the scope of international education has changed over the years, these sections will allow the reader to have a closer look at situations experienced by their peers in international education and to gain a deeper understanding of how other countries' education systems have changed. With a diverse group of authors, representing many fields within international education and from various entities that support international and higher education, the *AACRAO International Guide* is an excellent resource to aid you with your professional development and expand upon your knowledge of this exciting field.

About the Authors

Lindsay Mathers Addington

Lindsay Mathers Addington is Assistant Director of International Initiatives at the National Association for College Admission Counseling (NACAC). She develops research and designs and implements programs for counseling and admission professionals worldwide who advise, recruit, enroll, and support students in an increasingly global landscape. She regularly presents on topics related to international student mobility at conferences around the world, and is a member of the International Association for College Admission Counseling, NAFSA, and the Association of International Education Administrators. Prior to NACAC, Lindsay worked at the American Council on Education's Center for Internationalization and Global Engagement and at the George Washington University's Office of Undergraduate Admissions. She holds an M.A. and Ph.D. in Higher Education Administration from GW, and a B.A. in Communication from the University of Delaware.

Andrea Armstrong

Andrea Armstrong is the Senior Policy Advisor of Enrolment Services, University of Toronto. In her 15 year career at the university, she has specialized in undergraduate admissions, international credential assessment, and policy development. In addition, she has developed and led training for university staff in areas including client/student service, technology in the admissions office, and foreign educational systems. She holds an Honours B.A. degree from the University of Toronto.

Hala Abou Arraj

Hala Abou Arraj has been the Associate Registrar at the American University of Beirut since 2005. She began working with students in 1995 as a student services officer. Hala Abou Arraj is currently pursuing her Ph.D. in Political Sciences at the Lebanese University. She received her master's degree and her bachelor's degree from the American University of Beirut in 2000 and 1994, respectively. She has served on many committees, including two terms on the AACRAO Academic Progress and Graduation Committee.

Jeannine Bell

Jeannine "Jeanie" Bell is Senior Assistant Director of International Admissions in the Office of Admissions, University of Colorado Boulder. She has led international admissions teams at several universities, including in her current position. She has set standards for international academic admissions, recruited students, and trained staff in credential evaluation and immigration processing. Professionally active in international education since 1986, her accomplishments include presenting and chairing sessions in Asia, Europe, and North America for various profession organizations including NAFSA, EAIE, AACRAO and OACAC. She is currently

Vice-President of The Association for International Credential Evaluation Professionals (TAICEP). She received her Master of Public Administration from the University of Colorado Denver.

Michelle A. Birch

As the co-founder of Global Education Group, Inc., Ms. Birch has served as President of the organization, overseeing all aspects of foreign credential evaluation, work experience evaluation, and translation since 1996. Since 1993, she has completed foreign credential evaluation reports for individuals with applications for immigration status with the U.S. Citizenship and Immigration Services; for professional licensing; for employment in U.S. government agencies; for service with the U.S. Armed Forces; for admission to U.S. high schools, colleges and universities; and for use by a multitude of other public and private organizations and institutions in the U.S. and abroad. She has extensive experience in assisting legal counsel with RFE responses on H-1B, EB1, EB2, EB3, EB4 and EB5 visa cases, and numerous other immigration matters.

Ms. Birch holds a B.A. in International Studies and Spanish/Latin American Studies from the American University and an M.B.A. from the University of Miami.

Peggy Blumenthal

After 25 years at IIE in various management roles, Ms. Blumenthal became its Chief Operating Officer in 2005, transitioning in 2011 to Senior Counselor to IIE's President. Earlier responsibilities at IIE included supervision of its research team, educational services, and international offices in Africa, Asia, Europe, and Latin America.

Before joining IIE, Ms. Blumenthal was Assistant Director of Stanford University's Overseas Studies and Coordinator of Graduate Services/Fellowships for the University of Hawaii's Center for Asian and Pacific Studies. Her earlier international work focused on U.S.-China exchanges, as well as the National Committee

on U.S.-China Relations and the Asia Society's China Council.

Ms. Blumenthal holds a B.A. from Harvard University in Modern Chinese History and an M.A. in American Studies from the University of Hawaii at Manoa. She chairs the Board of Japan Center for International Exchange and serves on the Board of the Hong Kong-America Centre and the Global Engineering Education Exchange. In 2016, she was honored to receive AACRAO's Centennial Award for Excellence.

Marc Booker

Marc Booker is the Associate Provost at University of Phoenix, and most recently served as the Vice President of Admissions and Evaluation at the University. He has worked in higher education for over 14 years in a variety of admissions, training, and student support roles.

Marc is actively engaged in the higher education community serving as the 2016 President for the Pacific Association of Collegiate Registrars and Admissions Officers (PACRAO), and is a named a contributor to the *Transferability of Postsecondary Credit Following Student Transfer or Co-Enrollment* report published by the National Center for Education Statistics. Since 2009, Marc has also been a speaker at AACRAO, PACRAO, and CAEL conferences on various transfer topics including prior learning assessment, international admissions, and articulation.

Marc holds both a B.S. and M.A. in Management from the University of Phoenix, and is currently working on his Ph.D. in Higher Education Administration.

Mandie L. Brooks

Mandie Brooks is the Associate Registrar for Alexander College in Vancouver, Canada. She began her career in international education as a teacher in South Korea before joining the newly-established Alexander College in 2009. She has worked to develop the college's domestic and international admissions and registration policies, practices, and publications.

Mandie lived in Mexico's San Quintin Valley for several years working in support of migrant families and children from the southern state of Oaxaca.

C. Dean Campbell, Ed.D.

Dr. Dean Campbell has served as Assistant Dean for Academic Services at The Graduate School at North Carolina A&T State University (NCAT) since 2012. Campbell participates in leadership and management of the unit with a focus on developing strategic direction and the implementation of admission and enrollment policies. He is also a member of the graduate faculty and teaches as an adjunct instructor in the NCAT School of Education's Adult Education master's program. Prior to NCAT, he worked for over a decade in a variety of professional administrator roles in graduate education, academic affairs, and enrollment services at urban research universities on the East and West Coasts. His research interests include organizational effectiveness in higher education, workplace learning, administrator professional development, and qualitative methods in the study of adult and higher education administration.

Dr. Campbell earned his B.A. in Political Science from Yale University, M.A. in Higher Education Administration and Student Development from Boston College, and Ed.D. in Educational Leadership-Higher Education Administration from the University of Southern California.

Olivia Chen

Olivia Chen Loo is Assistant Director at the University of California Los Angeles Office of Undergraduate Admission. Much of her 10 years of experience has been in international education with a focus on recruitment and credential evaluation. She has presented on international admissions and evaluation at International ACAC, NAFSA and WACAC Share, Learn & Connect conferences.

A native of Panama, Olivia moved to the United States for college and graduated from the University of Southern California with a B.A. in International Relations and an M.Ed. in Postsecondary Administration and Student Affairs. She formerly worked as an Assistant Language Teacher with the Japan Exchange and Teaching Programme.

Alexander Chucklin

Alexander Chucklin is general manager of the North American Educational Group. He lived in Estonia before moving to the United States in 1989. He earned a B.S. in Business Management from Rhode Island College and studied engineering at Tallinn Technical University, Estonia. Mr. Chucklin has been doing language translations for over twenty years and has been evaluating academic credentials since 2003.

Nathan Cicchillo

Nathan Cicchillo has worked in higher education for over 13 years and, since 2011, has served as the Director of Admissions and Evaluation at University of Phoenix. During that time, Nathan has overseen the University's International Evaluation department, which has reviewed and evaluated credentials from thousands of institutions from over 200 countries. Nathan has earned all of his academic credentials from University of Phoenix, most recently receiving his M.B.A. in 2011. Nathan resides in Phoenix, Arizona, where he likes to spend time coaching local Little League baseball and hiking the hundreds of miles of local desert trails.

Beth Cotter

Beth Cotter received her B.A. in German from Wake Forest University and her M.B.A. from Georgia State University. Ms. Cotter has 40 years of corporate experience, including eight years of teaching and administrative experience in curriculum development at the postsecondary level. She has 19 years of experience as an international credentials evaluator. She learned foreign credentials evaluation from her father, James L. Clegg, former foreign student admissions officer at the Georgia

Institute of Technology and past-president of NAFSA Region VII. Beth has presented at the Region VII conference, at the Georgia Association of International Educators conference, the NAFSA Summer Workshop, and at the AICE 2016 Phoenix Symposium. She is a member of NAFSA and the Georgia Association of International Educators, and an Endorsed Member of the Association of International Credential Evaluators, Inc. (AICE). Ms. Cotter is President and CEO of Foreign Credential Evaluations, Inc.

Dr. Steven D. Crow

After graduating from Lewis and Clark College, Dr. Crow received his M.A. and Ph.D. in U.S. History from the University of Wisconsin-Madison. In the 1970s, he taught and did some administrative work at Kalamazoo College, Vanderbilt University, Bates College, and Bowdoin College. In 1982 he moved to Chicago to work with the Commission on Institutions of Higher Education of the North Central Association of Colleges and Schools. Over the next 26 years he rose from Assistant Director to Executive Director/President, the role he filled from 1997 until he retired in June 2008. He provided leadership to the Commission (renamed The Higher Learning Commission) assuring the effectiveness of regional institutional accreditation and representing the organization nationally and internationally. He was instrumental in making regional institutional accreditation responsive to e-Learning, to U.S. education delivered internationally, and to new collaborative and consortial arrangements created in and among several states. Crow has been active in international quality assurance activities, allowing for significant international travel for meetings, training programs, and participation on international quality assurance boards and evaluation teams.

Edward Devlin

Ed Devlin is currently a foreign credential evaluator with AACRAO International Education Services and previously held the position of Director of Special Projects. He has worked in international education for more than 40 years. He has directed the International Student Program at Monterey Peninsula College (MPC), the English language and academic orientation programs at Stanford University, MPC and the University of California Santa Cruz, and has worked in international admissions at Golden Gate University. He has served as a consultant for many schools and programs in the U.S. and abroad.

Mr. Devlin served on the International Admissions Committee of AACRAO and several NAFSA committees. He has given presentations, workshops and training sessions at numerous AACRAO and NAFSA conferences, and has contributed many articles for AACRAO and NAFSA publications. Ed is the author of the AACRAO Country Guide *Australia: Training & Education* and co-author/editor of the PIER workshop reports on Poland and the Czech/Slovak Federated Republics. Ed developed the first model for the AACRAO EDGE (Electronic Database for Global Education) and is a Life Member of NAFSA.

LesLee Clauson Eicher

LesLee Clauson Eicher has been working in the field of international credential evaluation for over 25 years. She has worked at public and private universities, at a private credential evaluation agency, and has spent the last 15 years with AACRAO. She has contributed to AACRAO and NAFSA international education publications, and has presented at many national and regional conferences on international education topics.

Dr. Jacquelyn D. Elliott

Dr. Jacquelyn "Jacqui" D. Elliott is known for her diverse background in higher education, which includes academic affairs, institutional advancement, and enrollment management. Well-versed in management techniques, she has nearly 25 years of experience in higher education. She was formerly Dean of Admissions and Financial Aid at Mary Baldwin College, Associate Vice President of Institutional Advancement at Bridgewater

College, and most recently, served as Vice President for Enrollment Management at Tusculum College. Her current academic appointment is with the University of Missouri—St. Louis, where her primary focus is on developing international collaborative faculty research, student exchange, accreditation, program reviews, and faculty training and development throughout the Middle East. She is also Chief Enrollment Specialist with Marion Military Institute, Marion, AL.

Dr. Elliott received her Ed.D. in Higher Education Administration from The George Washington University, Washington, D.C., where her dissertation, *The American Council on Education's Office of Women in Higher Education: A Case Study of Evolution and Decline 1973–2011,* was the winner of the national Myra Sadker Dissertation Award.

She currently serves as Editor of the *SACRAO Journal* and serves on the AACRAO Board of Directors as Vice-President for International Education.

Otho Allen Ezell, Jr.

Allen Ezell retired from the FBI after 31 years of service. As a Special Agent investigating white collar crime cases, he operated the FBI's DIPSCAM (Diploma Scam) program for eleven years (1980-1991). The program dismantled over 40 diploma mills, convicted 21 individuals, and established a data base of over 12,000 'graduates.' He was then employed as Vice President of Corporate Fraud at First Union National Bank, Wachovia Bank, and Wells Fargo Bank, until his 2010 retirement. He has continued to follow ongoing academic frauds, has co-authored and authored several books in this field, including the AACRAO publications *Accreditation Mills* and *Counterfeit Diplomas & Transcripts.* He continues to make presentations on these subjects both in the U.S. and abroad, and testified before a Congressional committee.

Johanna Fishbein

Johanna Fishbein is a University Advisor at the United World College South East Asia, Dover Campus in Singapore. Prior to this, Johanna was the Head of College and Careers Counseling at the International School of Brussels and the Coordinator of International Recruitment at Barnard College. Johanna holds a B.A. from the George Washington University, an M.S. from Mercy College, and a College Counseling Specialized Certificate from the University of California, San Diego. Johanna has served on the Executive Board of the International Association of College Admission Counseling for the past three years and will be the President-Elect of the organization as of July 2016.

Christy M. Fry

Christy Fry is the Associate Director of International and Transfer Recruitment at Colby-Sawyer College. Christy has been an international education practitioner for nearly fifteen years, where she has held public, private, and government positions in Malta, Sicily, and the U.S. These positions have afforded her experience in immigration and compliance, credential and transfer evaluation, training and assessment, student services, and articulation agreement management. Christy's M.A. in International Education and Advising was obtained from SIT Graduate Institute; her B.A. Honors was completed in Psychology. She enjoys presenting and facilitating sessions, especially on the topic of credential evaluation.

Marshall Houserman

Marshall Houserman is a Senior Evaluator at Educational Perspectives, where he has worked since 2011. His main evaluation interests are in the United Kingdom and Commonwealth-patterned educational systems, as well as Russian and East European educational systems. He is highly interested in international student mobility trends and patterns. Prior to working at Educational Perspectives, he worked in International Admissions at Indiana University. He holds an M.S. in International Public Service from DePaul University and a B.A. in History from Albion College.

Kristina Jenkins

Kristina Jenkins has been with the Institute of International Education (IIE) since 1999, and joined the Global Education USA Services team in June 2015 as Assistant Director. Previously, she has worked with the Hubert H. Humphrey Fellowship Program, the King Abdullah University of Science and Technology Scholarships Program, the International Visitor Leadership Program, the National Security Education Program, and IIE's midwest office. Kristina holds an M.A. in International Development Studies, with a concentration in Education and Training, from The George Washington University and a B.A. in International Relations with minors in Business Management and Portuguese from Brigham Young University.

Johnny K. Johnson

Johnny Johnson's 45 years in international education includes administrative and teaching positions at two-year and four-year colleges and universities, both public and private, in the United States, Asia, and the Caribbean. He has consulted with colleges, universities, government and private sector organizations, and has written or edited 30 publications and made more than 120 conference presentations in the fields of international education and student affairs. Mr. Johnson has served on the following Boards of Directors: the American Association of Collegiate Registrars and Admissions Officers (AACRAO), as Vice President for International Education; the Association of International Educators (NAFSA), as Vice President for Regional Affairs; and California Colleges for International Education (CCIE), also as Vice President. Research, conference presentations, consultations and leisure travel have taken Mr. Johnson to more than 80 countries.

Alexander Jun, Ph.D.

Alexander Jun is Professor of Higher Education at Azusa Pacific University's School of Behavior and Applied Sciences. Dr. Jun is a TED speaker and author of *From here to university: Access, mobility, and resilience among urban Latino youth* (Routledge Press). He has published extensively on issues of postsecondary access for historically underrepresented students in underserved areas. Dr. Jun recently completed a three-year narrative inquiry research project on the educational mobility and academic resilience of Khmer orphans, and is currently completing a book related to his fieldwork in Cambodia. Dr. Jun conducts research on issues surrounding equity, justice, and diversity in higher education, as well as globalization in the Pacific Rim.

Dr. Jun holds a Ph.D. in Education Policy from the Rossier School of Education at the University of Southern California, where he earned a Ford Foundation fellowship to conduct research on college preparation programs for urban youth. Professor Jun teaches courses in diversity and social justice in higher education, comparative higher education, and qualitative research methods. Dr. Jun serves as APU's qualitative research consultant, and joined APU's faculty after 15 years of service as a faculty member and administrator at the University of Southern California.

George F. Kacenga

Mr. Kacenga is the Director of International Enrollment Management at the University of Colorado Denver. He has presented nationally and internationally regarding domestic and international admissions, recruitment, enrollment management, and cross-cultural awareness issues. An active member of AIRC, AACRAO, NAFSA, and TAICEP, he is engaged with the IEM community, having recently authored an article on evolving strategies in global student recruitment for the Institute of International Education. He is a member of NAFSA's International Enrollment Management Knowledge Community as Recruitment, Advising, Marketing, Admissions (RAMA) Network Leader. He is a recipient of the Fulbright Korea International Education Administrators award and is pursuing his Ph.D. in Social and Comparative Analysis in Education at the University of Pittsburgh.

Ann M. Koenig

Ann Koenig is Associate Director of AACRAO International Education Services. Her career in international education spans more than 25 years and includes foreign credential evaluation with IES and other professional evaluation services, campus-based work in international undergraduate and graduate admissions, student records management, and academic advising and transfer credit evaluation. She has worked with Cardinal Stritch University, a University of Maryland University College program in Germany, Golden Gate University in San Francisco, and the University of California, Berkeley.

As a respected expert in academic document review and fraud detection, Ms. Koenig has contributed to several AACRAO publications on the topic and shared her insights and recommendations for best practice at numerous workshops and conference sessions. Her achievements in international education include in-depth research and writing on education in several countries. She has presented at professional development and training events sponsored by AACRAO, NAFSA, NAGAP, EAIE, and several other organizations in the U.S. and Europe. Ms. Koenig has served on the NAFSA National ADSEC committee and the AACRAO International Education Committee.

Becky Konowicz

Becky Konowicz is the Director of International Admission at Santa Clara University (CA) and is currently serving as the Vice President for Professional Development of the International Association for College Admission Counseling. With more than 10 years of experience in the field of International Admission, Becky has worked at small and medium-sized private institutions on both coasts and in the Midwest. Recruitment activities have taken Becky to over 40 countries and she has fostered numerous school-based and independent counselor relationships across the world to best serve students in their transition to university. She holds a B.A. in English Literature from DePauw University and an M.A. in Education

and College Student Affairs Leadership from Grand Valley State University.

Adina M. Lav

As the Assistant Provost for International Enrollment at the George Washington University (GW), Adina Lav works to foster the expansion of GW's international student enrollment across all major divisions. Ms. Lav has nearly 15 years of experience in higher education, primarily in graduate enrollment management. She holds a B.A. in Organizational Communication from the University of South Florida and an M.A. in Organizational Management from GW.

Ms. Lav is also a doctoral candidate in GW's School of Education and Human Development. Her research centers around higher education and social change. She is currently running two research projects on China's brain-gain and returning Chinese students.

Ms. Lav lives in Washington, DC with her two young sons.

Lorianna Mapps

Lorianna Mapps is currently the Director of Admissions Processing at the University of Houston. Having worked in undergraduate, graduate, and law school admissions as well as medical residency program management, Lorianna has a special interest in working with students from underrepresented groups and first-generation students. Lorianna is a member of the Department of Student Affairs and Enrollment Services Assessment Committee at the University of Houston, the Liberal Arts Advisory Council at Texas A&M University and is a former advisor of the Latin American Law Student Association at the Emory University School of Law. Lorianna has presented at the Houston Hispanic Forum Career and Education Day on The Legalization of Immigrant Students—Updates on the DREAM Act. Lorianna Mapps earned a B.A. in English degree from Texas A&M University and an M.S. in Student Affairs and Higher Education Administration from Indiana State University.

Leah Wren McCormack

Leah McCormack is the Director of Eligibility Services at the National Association of Intercollegiate Athletics. Leah graduated with honors from DePaul University with a B.A. in Anthropology and earned her M.B.A. from the University of Missouri–Kansas City. She is an avid traveler, proficient in numerous languages, and has lived for short periods of time in Brazil and France. Leah helped establish the NAIA Eligibility Center's international division and has been a leader in developing credential evaluation standards since the Eligibility Center's inception.

Jennifer Minke

Ms. Minke is Associate Director of Admission in the Undergraduate Admission Office at Texas A&M University-Kingsville. Prior to her current position, she worked in the Graduate Admissions Office at the University of Idaho and in the International Admissions Office at the University of North Texas. Jennifer has been working in the field of international admissions and credential evaluation for 23 years. She has been a member of AACRAO since 1995. She has served as a member of the International Publications Advisory Committee since 2004, chairing that Committee since 2011, and she served as a member of the International Admission Committee. Jennifer is the author of the Belgium and Canada: New Brunswick profiles for AACRAO EDGE and provided the "Resource Organizations, Agencies, and Institutions" and "Publications and Other Useful Resources" appendices for the 2001 edition of The AACRAO International Guide.

Jennifer has also served on the NCAA International Student Record Committee since 2009 and is the incoming Chair of that committee for 2015. She was a member of NAFSA from 1995–2007 and has previously served on both the Physician Assistant Professional Standards Committee and the Credentials Committee for the Commission on Graduates of Foreign Nursing Schools (CGFNS). She holds a B.A. in Anthropology from the University of North Texas and an M.A. in Anthropology from the University of Idaho.

Gloria R. Nathanson

Gloria Nathanson served as Associate Director of Undergraduate Admission at UCLA, overseeing both domestic and international admission, including credential evaluation, operations, public relations, and IT. She spent her entire career of more than 30 years in college admissions at UCLA, her alma mater, before retiring in 2010.

Gloria has been an active member of AACRAO for many years, serving on numerous committees, mostly related to international education. She participated in workshops that resulted in AACRAO publications, and was a member of the AACRAO Board of Directors as Vice President for International Education from 2000–2003. In 2013, she was appointed by the AACRAO Board to serve as Chair of the *AACRAO Task Force on International Admissions and Credential Evaluation*. The Task Force, made up of 28 college and university administrators and other professionals in the international education field from around the country, submitted a report with recommendations for the future of AACRAO activities in international education to the AACRAO Board of Directors in July 2014. She continues to serve AACRAO as Chair of the International Education Standards Committee and participates in the administration of EDGE.

Linda Patlan

Linda Patlan completed a B.A. in Sociology from the University of Houston in 2004. Her career in higher education began as Freshman Admission Counselor at the University of Houston in 2005. During this time she began to work with students, including first generation students and undocumented students. In 2009, Linda transitioned into International Admissions as an International Admissions Coordinator. Her passion for both technical and cultural knowledge, with her training in sociology, have proved integral in working in higher education.

William J. Paver, Ph.D.

Dr. Paver was an Assistant Dean of Graduate Studies and directed the Graduate and International Admission Office at the University of Texas at Austin, where he worked for 23 years before retiring. He has authored and edited numerous articles and books in the field of applied comparative education. He has been a member of the board for NAFSA, AACRAO, SEVIS, and TOEFL. Additionally, he has served as Vice President for International Education for AACRAO and ADSEC Chair for NAFSA. Bill founded the EDGE project after leaving UT and has been deeply involved in its creation and ongoing activity.

Liz Reisberg

Liz Reisberg is President of Reisberg & Associates, LLC, a firm that provides consulting support toward the improvement of higher education internationally. She has worked with government, universities, and international donor agencies throughout the world, including the World Bank and InterAmerican Development Bank. She is also a Research Fellow at the Center for International Higher Education at Boston College, where she has collaborated with international partners and contributed to numerous publications. She began her career in international admissions and was responsible for designing and implementing international recruitment strategy at several U.S. universities. Her recent experience and research have focused on quality assurance, internationalization, improving university teaching, and higher education policy reform and implementation, especially in Latin America.

Anthony Sabo

Anthony Sabo is an Evaluator at Educational Perspectives. He has experience working in U.S. education and evaluating foreign academic credentials while main-

taining a strong interest in Asian, British Commonwealth, and French educational systems. Anthony earned a B.A. in History with a minor in Geography from The Ohio State University.

Jasmin Saidi-Kuehnert

Jasmin Saidi-Kuehnert is the founder, President and CEO of Academic Credentials Evaluation Institute, Inc., a private credential evaluation organization. She has been actively involved in international credential evaluations since 1982 and has provided training and presented at conferences and symposiums in the U.S. and abroad. She is frequently called on by the U.S. government, academic institutions, state licensing boards, private enterprise, as well as institutions and educational ministries abroad for assistance with international academic credentials.

She has published a number of articles and authored the AACRAO Country Guide Series Reports on Senegal (2000) and Cameroon (1995) and co-authored *The Education System of Hong Kong* (1998). She has contributed to the AACRAO-NAFSA Projects for International Education Reports (PIER) on Central America (1987), Canada (1987), and the United Kingdom (1990). She is a regular contributor to the online blog Academic Exchange.

She served as Chair of the Admission-Section (ADSEC) Committee of NAFSA from 1999 to 2001, as Chair of NAFSA's Region XII Southern District committee from 1995 to 1999, on AACRAO's Publication and Reviews Committee from 1990–1993, and as Chair of the International Credential Evaluation Committee on the AACRAO Special Task Force (2013–2014). She is currently the Acting President of the Association of International Credential Evaluators (AICE) and serves on AACRAO's International Education Standards Council (IESC).

Luke David Schultheis, Ph.D.

Luke Schultheis has served as a faculty member, chair, dean, and enrollment management professional and is

also the current AACRAO Vice President for Admissions and Enrollment Management. His scholarship and work are focused upon student success, especially for underserved urban populations. He has an extensive history of national presentations, writing, and is a member of the Editorial Review Board for Strategic Enrollment Management Quarterly as well as the Southern Association of Collegiate Registrars and Admissions Officers Journal. He has spent the majority of his academic career in New York City, Las Vegas, and Richmond, where he currently serves as Vice Provost for Strategic Enrollment Management at Virginia Commonwealth University.

Kathleen Schultz

Kathleen Schultz is a high school counselor at NIST International School in Bangkok, Thailand. Previously she worked as a counselor in Czech Republic, Germany, and Portland, Oregon. Kathleen holds two bachelor's degrees in psychology and human services and an M.A. in Education: Counseling. She currently serves as a Delegate on the International ACAC Executive Board and is a member of the NACAC National Communications Committee. She has previously served on the Council of International Schools Guidance Committee and chaired the European Council of International Schools Guidance Committee. She is passionate about serving the needs of international students.

Garrett Seelinger

Garrett was raised in Morocco and England before earning a B.A. from DePaul University and an M.A. in English from the University of Notre Dame. Garrett has worked for the NAIA Eligibility Center for two years, evaluating documents and processing eligibility for thousands of international student-athletes.

Steven M. Sheeley, Ph.D.

Dr. Sheeley has served as Vice President of the Southern Association of Colleges and Schools Commission on Colleges since 2008, following over 20 years as a college professor and administrator. A native of Missouri, Sheeley holds a B.S.Ed. from Missouri State University, an M.Div. from Southwestern Baptist Theological Seminary, and a Ph.D. from The Southern Baptist Theological Seminary. He completed further study at Indiana University and Yale University, exploring narrative and literary criticism. He is the author and co-author of three books and numerous scholarly articles, reviews, and essays.

Sheeley is a frequent speaker and workshop leader on topics including institutional effectiveness, educational program assessment, and the Quality Enhancement Plan. In addition to supporting the accreditation efforts of approximately 80 member institutions, he continues to pay particular attention to issues related to academic policy and the quality and integrity of academic programs.

Ellen Silverman (author in absentia)

Ellen Silverman is the Coordinator of International Training and Development at the City University of New York (CUNY). Prior to her current position, she was Director of International Evaluations at CUNY and Assistant Director of Admissions at New York University. She has more than 30 years of experience in international education. Ellen has served as a member of the AACRAO International Publications Advisory Committee since 2012. She holds a B.A. in Asian Studies from Eisenhower College and an M.A. in Psychological Foundations of Reading from New York University.

Beth Simpson

Beth Simpson has worked in higher education for sixteen years, and has worked with international students for fourteen years. She earned a B.A. in History from the University of Tennessee, and has engaged in graduate studies at Texas Tech University and the University of Phoenix. Her favorite activities include traveling widely with her family, exploring the Phoenix restaurant scene, cooking, reading, watching Formula 1 racing, and bad movie night with her husband and daughter.

Clayton A. Smith, Ed.D.

Dr. Clayton Smith is Vice-Provost, Student Affairs and Dean of Students at the University of Windsor, where he has coordinated campus internationalization and implemented new approaches in international student recruitment and retention. He previously held enrollment management positions, which included oversight for international student affairs, at the State University of New York College of Agriculture and Technology at Cobleskill, Tallahassee Community College, and the University of Maine at Augusta.

Dr. Smith holds an Ed.D. in Higher Education from Florida State University, an M.A. in Public Administration from the University of Maine, an M.A. in Political Science from Drew University and a B.A. in Political Science from the University of Southern Maine.

Dr. Smith is a frequent conference presenter on enrollment management, student affairs, and internationalization topics and is co-editor of the AACRAO's *SEM in Canada: Promoting Student and Institutional Success in Canadian Colleges and Universities*. He has long been active in AACRAO and currently serves as a senior consultant with AACRAO Consulting where he has conducted consulting projects at nearly 20 colleges and universities in the U.S. and Canada.

Robin Straka

Robin Straka is Associate Registrar at Elon University where she has served since 2000. She works extensively with study abroad and international tertiary credential review. Straka earned an M.A. from Marywood University and B.A. from Lycoming College.

Dr. Anatoly Temkin

Dr. Anatoly Temkin has been a faculty member at Boston University for more than 25 years. From 2000 to 2012, he worked as professor and academic advisor in computer science. Also during this time, Dr. Temkin chaired the admissions committee. He currently serves as the chairman of Boston University Metropolitan College Computer Science Department.

Robert Watkins

Robert Watkins is Assistant Director of Admissions in the Graduate and International Admissions Center at The University of Texas at Austin, where he has been in the field of international admissions for almost 40 years. He has served as a committee member and chair, and has also presented at numerous AACRAO annual meetings. From 2009–12, he served as Vice President for International Education on the AACRAO Board of Directors. Currently, he serves on the International Education Standards Committee that provides the credential advice for the AACRAO Electronic Database for Global Education.

Margaret Wenger

Margaret Wenger has worked at Educational Credential Evaluators, Inc (ECE) since 1990. Prior to joining ECE, Margaret worked in Togo and Japan. She received her M.S. in the Cultural Foundations of Education from the University of Wisconsin–Milwaukee in 1998. As Director of Evaluation Methodology, Margaret leads evaluation policy development, new evaluator training, and coordinates quality assurance efforts. She is the author of *ECE Presents: The Educational System of Tunisia* and *The Kingdom of Saudi Arabia: Its Educational System and Methods of Evaluation*, as well as contributing author of the *NAFSA Guide to Educational Systems Around the World* (1998 and 2009). She has given workshops at a number of conferences, including NAFSA, NAGAP, CGS, and EAIE.

Eddie West

Eddie West serves as the Director of International Initiatives at the National Association for College Admission Counseling (NACAC), supporting admissions and counseling professionals who work with international students transitioning to higher education in the U.S., and with American students aspiring to study overseas. Before joining NACAC, he served as Dean of Counseling and International Programs at Ohlone College in Fremont, California. There he led Ohlone's international students and study abroad programs, and oversaw its partnerships with overseas schools. Previously, he worked in international student outreach and support at California State University, Northridge.

John Wilkerson

John Wilkerson is Director of International Admissions at Indiana University Bloomington, where he leads all aspects of a comprehensive international recruitment and admissions operation. Previously, Wilkerson served as director of international admissions for the University of Missouri. He has also directed study abroad for the University of Missouri School of Journalism, and served as director of admissions for Columbia College in Columbia, Missouri. Wilkerson holds bachelor's degrees in psychology and sociology from Columbia College, and completed his graduate work in education and counseling psychology at Stephens College. He has served in leadership positions with NAFSA, International Association of College Admissions Counselors, and the Council of International Schools.

Thy Yang

Thy Yang is Associate Vice President for International Studies at St. Cloud State University. Ms. Yang has more than 10 years of experience in international studies and multicultural student affairs. She previously served as director of international programs and services at Michigan Technological University, director of multicultural affairs for Dickinson State University, and director of international programs for Benedictine College.

Ms. Yang holds a B.A. in English Literature from Ottawa University and an M.B.A. from Benedictine College.

Kristina Zaluckyj

Kristina Zaluckyj has eight years of combined experience in international education and has worked with international students from multiple countries. Prior to her current Evaluator position at Educational Perspectives, Kristina worked in graduate admissions and as a program coordinator at a J-1 Work and Travel visa sponsor organization. During her undergraduate studies at the University of St. Thomas, Kristina studied abroad in Kyiv, Ukraine. Upon graduation, Kristina earned a B.A. in Broadcast Journalism with a minor in Russian Language. She received her M.A. in International Studies from DePaul University and also completed additional Ukrainian language studies at Harvard Ukrainian Research Institute of Harvard University.

ONE

International Students:

A Starting Point
to Comprehensive
Internationalization

2016 AACRAO INTERNATIONAL GUIDE

LINDSAY M. ADDINGTON | Assistant Director of International Initiatives | National Association for College Admission Counseling

International Students:
A Starting Point to Comprehensive Internationalization

In an increasingly interconnected world, higher education institutions are responsible for educating students with the knowledge, skills, and competencies to live and work in a global community. Institutions must expose students during their academic journeys to the culturally diverse individuals, perspectives, and issues that they will face upon graduation. Many institutions are undertaking this challenge by creating a campus culture where global learning, intercultural dialogues, and cross border exchanges and collaborations are promoted and supported in a strategic and coordinated way. Enrolling international students is a critical element to developing this international ethos, but not the only one.

International Students on U.S. Campuses

In recent years, more U.S. institutions have dedicated increased attention and resources to recruiting and enrolling larger numbers of international students (Institute of International Education 2015; ACE 2012), and enrollment data proves that such efforts are having an impact. In the 2014–2015 academic year a record 974,926 international students were studying in U.S. colleges and universities, representing a 10 percent growth over the previous year (IIE 2015a).

Though this growth is significant, it is important that institutions not perceive internationalization as merely having international students on campus. International student enrollment becomes a quick and readily accessible indicator of an institution's level of internationalization. However, "colleges and universities that … confuse [international students'] mere presence on campus with internationalization are ultimately headed for stormier seas" (Peterson 2014). Without a larger commitment to internationalization and complementary initiatives, the benefits of having international students on campus will likely go unrealized. International students can serve as a starting point for internationalization, but should not be an institution's exclusive strategy.

INSTITUTIONAL MOTIVATIONS FOR ENROLLING INTERNATIONAL STUDENTS

So, why are institutions taking proactive steps to increase international student enrollment? What is an institution's goal in recruiting students from abroad? How are institutions prepared to support international students? How will international students contribute to the larger comprehensive internationalization effort of the institution?

Due to fluctuating student demographics within the United States and decreasing state funding, recruiting international students has been seen as a financial necessity for many U.S. colleges and universities. Institutions are motivated by the tuition revenue gained by enrolling international students, the majority of whom are full fee-paying students funded by personal and family funds (IIE 2014a). With high demand among international students for U.S. higher education, and high-quality college and university options—albeit with a high price tag—there is a logical synergy for recruiting international students.

Furthermore, international students contribute significantly to the local, state, and national economies. The Institute of International Education reports that in 2015 international students contributed $30.5 billion to the U.S. economy. State-by-state analysis of the economic contributions of international students and their families is also provided by NAFSA: Association of International Educators.

Beyond the financial benefit, and arguably more important, international students add a global dimension to campuses, increase opportunities for intercultural dialogues, and enrich the academic experience with their diverse perspectives; if, that is, they are supported by the institution in a way that these benefits can be realized.

International students' success and their ability to contribute to a campus' internationalization goals are largely dependent on whether a campus community is equipped to support them in their educational journeys from recruitment through graduation. Institutions need to be prepared to meet their unique needs, including, but not limited to, new language acquisition, academic and cultural adjustment, religious accommodations, and health and wellness. In addition, intentional opportunities must be developed for international students to develop constructive relationships with their professors and staff, to help educate the American communities where universities reside, and to meaningfully engage with their domestic peers.

A relatively small number of U.S. students are afforded a global education experience. And although sending domestic students abroad is gaining momentum due to several national initiatives, such as the Institute of International Education's *Generation Study Abroad*, less than 10 percent of students study abroad. With growing numbers of international students on U.S. campuses, an opportunity exists for U.S. students to expand their knowledge of—and experience with—other cultures as a result of having international students in their classes, in their residence halls, and at campus events—another motivation for institutions. Data show that with more international students on campus, the odds of U.S. students engaging in substantial international interaction increases considerably (Luo and Jamieson-Drake 2013).

And substantial interaction is key to U.S. students benefiting from having international students on campus. A recent study, *Examining the Educational Benefits of Interacting with International Students*, looked at the influence of interaction with international students on domestic students' college outcomes (Luo and Jamieson-Drake 2013). U.S. students who reported having substantial interaction with international students perceived themselves to have developed more skills than their non-interactive peers in areas that one would expect—such as language acquisition and relating to people of different races, nations, or religions—but also in cognitive areas; among them, formulating creative ideas and integrating ideas and information (Luo and Jamieson-Drake 2013). Ultimately, theory and research show that students—both domestic and international—who are given the opportunity to question their beliefs and values have more positive gains in general education, leadership skills, and intellectual development.

Luo and Jamieson-Drake's (2013) study also underscored the important role institutions have in leveraging greater international diversity, as analysis revealed that a student's college campus was a robust predictor of international interaction. Strong, campus-wide connections will help to ensure that the preparation to host international students is sufficient, the communication is ongoing, the institution is proactive as well as responsive to the unique needs of its international student population, and meaningful interactions among students are more likely to occur.

Building a Supportive Community for International Students

When an institution decides to develop a strategic plan to recruit international students or to expand existing efforts, critical questions must be addressed *prior to* enrollment. The admissions office can take a lead role in bringing multiple stakeholders from across campus together, as a task force or campus committee, to discuss the necessary preparations needed to enroll or increase enrollment of international students.

CRITICAL CAMPUS STAKEHOLDERS

In determining who should be included to discuss an international enrollment strategy, the following offices and individuals that an international student comes in contact with—from the time they are recruited through to graduation and beyond—need to be included, and their roles in the student experience looked at.

* *International Student Services* should be engaged to assess the capacity to advise and support a larger and potentially more diverse group of international students.
* *An existing or new orientation program* can meet the transition needs of international students.
* The *Registrar's Office* can help assess whether sufficient class sections and classrooms will be available to accommodate the anticipated increases in international student enrollment.
* As the dynamic of the classroom may change, *faculty* need to engage in discussions around learning styles and language barriers.
* Is the *English as a Second Language program* sufficiently staffed, and if this program does not exist, how will the institution be equipped to assess and educate second language learners? This may also impact admission requirements, for example, setting minimum English-language proficiency scores.
* *Housing* should be engaged to address such issues as space availability for on-campus housing, opportunities for globally-themed living and learning communities, and break and holiday schedules.
* *Dining services* will need to be involved in conversations around dietary considerations and restrictions for new populations of students.
* *Student affairs officers* can evaluate the capacity of programmatic initiatives to provide opportunities for domestic and international students to meaningfully engage with one another.
* The *Counseling Center* should be engaged to discuss whether counselors possess the competencies to work effectively with people from different cultures and countries.
* *Career Services* should be engaged to advise international students on work opportunities while in school and after graduation.

Though this list is not exhaustive, it illustrates the full campus buy-in needed to support international students. Whether brought together as a task force or campus committee, representatives from these offices or programs can begin to address the critical questions that must be answered before enrolling larger numbers of international students.

STRATEGIC INTERNATIONAL ENROLLMENT MANAGEMENT

The following represent a sample of questions to be addressed by the institution and considerations on strategic international enrollment management:

* **What are the institution's goals for increasing enrollment?** Has or will the institution set enrollment targets or caps? In the most recent data available at the time of publication, 26 percent of institutions reported having a strategic international student recruitment plan with specific enrollment targets (ACE 2012). Considerations should include state legislation, particularly for public institutions, that might potentially limit enrollment of out-of-state, including international, students.

Another aspect to weigh is the time it takes to achieve the desired enrollment growth. It is unrealistic to think that numbers will increase drastically the first year of instituting an international recruitment plan. On average, it takes about three years to see a return on investment when recruiting in a new territory, as it takes time to build the institution's brand and to develop meaningful relationships with students, parents, counselors and other stakeholders. Be prepared to educate those on campus who believe there are ways to get enrollments quickly. This can often lead to recruitment strategies that are not well-thought-out or lack sufficient resources—human and fiscal. Agency-based recruitment, for example, is a strategy some institutions have turned to as a way to meet growing enrollment targets, oftentimes with limited budgets; however, in order for this to be successful a significant commitment of resources is necessary (West and Addington 2014).

✻ **How many international students can the institution realistically support and at what rate should it expand enrollment?** Consider how a significant growth in international student numbers might impact the rest of the campus. Drawing on the expertise of the campus stakeholders will be particularly important in addressing this question. Resource allocation will also be a critical consideration. Joshee, Leventhal, and Weller (2013, 1) note that "while those charged with achieving... international objectives applaud [the] increased attention to the importance of internationalization, many also note that in this economic environment the rhetoric is rarely matched by the budget to achieve these lofty goals." Additionally, ACE (2012) found that "while efforts to recruit international students are on the rise, the data do not show a commensurate increase in the support services for these students, or activities that facilitate interaction and mutual learning with American peers" (24).

Another consideration is the balance of students among different academic programs and majors. International students tend to enroll in business and management and STEM fields, though in recent years this has begun to diversify with significant growth in fields such as fine and applied arts (IIE 2014a). Assessing the institution's academic strengths and programs for which it is well known, as well as the capacity for these programs to grow, will be a strategic exercise.

✻ **How does diversity play into the institution's strategy for increasing international enrollment?** What are the institution's priorities in terms of ethnic, regional, and socioeconomic diversity among international students? In 2011 59 percent of institutions with a strategic plan identified specific geographic targets for their recruitment strategy (ACE 2012). Currently Chinese students represent 31 percent of enrollment at U.S. colleges and universities (IIE 2015a). At many institutions, this percentage is significantly higher. Institutions should consider whether its student body is truly diverse and international if the majority of international students are from one country. Furthermore, consideration should be given to risks of being heavily dependent on students from a particular country if that country's dynamics were to change and impact student mobility.

Questions around diversity should also include economic diversity of international students at U.S. institutions. As many institutions seek full-pay international students to help alleviate budgetary challenges, very few institutions offer need-based financial assistance and therefore are unable to enroll economically disadvantaged international students. Institutions should consider striving to serve low-income international students along with their current efforts to serve low-income domestic students.

If the institution has had a history of recruiting international students, evaluating the international application pool, analyzing current enrollment statistics, assessing brand recognition abroad, and engaging with international alumni networks will be important and informative exercises for determining ideal recruitment territories. For institutions that might have already undertaken internationalization efforts in other areas, it will also be critical to think about international strengths that an institution possesses. For example, do its faculty members originate from certain countries or regions of the world? Does the university offer curricular specialization in certain area studies? Is the neighboring community home to a particular immigrant population? Reflecting on these areas can help determine an international student recruitment strategy that makes sense for the institution.

✻ **How will international student tuition and fees be set and resulting revenue utilized?** Traditionally, there have been two pricing structures—one tuition rate for in-state students and another, higher rate for out-of-state and international students. However, some institutions have introduced a third tuition rate for students coming from abroad (Redden 2015a). Institutions are justifying these expenses by the additional administrative and support services international students require. However, are international students and those who provide services for them directly benefiting from these funds? The answer varies.

One approach has been to use international student tuition dollars to subsidize the education of domestic, lower-income students (Jordan 2015). In California, for example, one-third of money gained from international student tuition is recycled back into financial aid, largely for California residents (Fischer 2015). An alternate model reinvests a portion of the tuition revenue gained from international students into staff, programs, and services that directly impact their experience. A pilot program at the University of Cincinnati provides an example of how money gained from international student tuition was invested into comprehensive internationalization efforts, including creating new scholarships for incoming international students, increasing the size and scope of the International Admissions Office, and funding study abroad scholarships (Joshee, Leventhal, and Weller 2013). In this approach, each institution's reinvestment rate and the activities it chooses to fund will vary based on institutional context and priorities.

Irrespective of how international student tuition is utilized, it is important that the campus community know that international students have earned their spot at the institution based on their academic abilities, as well as additional qualities and perspectives they will bring to the campus—not simply for their ability to pay (Fischer 2015).

Institutions must look beyond recruiting and enrolling international students to ensuring their success once enrolled. Posing these questions can force institutions to be self-reflective in assessing their ability to enroll and support international students and enable

institutions to be proactive in taking the appropriate steps to facilitate their success once on campus. The intercultural training and firsthand insight that international admissions officers have positions them as strong leaders of campus dialogues around international student enrollment growth and the unique needs of the students coming to campus.

STARTING SMALL: CREATING INTEREST ON CAMPUS

If the institution is not yet in a position to create a campus task force around international student enrollment, there is still an opportunity for the admissions office to create a buzz around campus about international students. Consider the following ways to engage critical campus stakeholders on campus. Invite them to:

* Accompany you on international recruitment trips. Though this has budget implications, explore whether faculty or staff already have international trips or conferences planned and collaborate accordingly.
* Read international student applications or participate in admissions decision committees.
* Attend an intercultural training session hosted by the admissions office or other experts on campus.
* Participate in international student orientation.
* Attend a professional conference focused on international student recruitment. Examples include AACRAO and NACAC annual meetings, as well as NAFSA: Association of International Educators, and EducationUSA meetings.

Comprehensive Internationalization: A Campus-Wide Effort

Enrolling and supporting international students can become a great starting point for broader internationalization efforts on campus. Some of the offices and administrators that have been brought together to discuss international student enrollment may be considering their role in an international student's experience for the first time. For others, they may have experience in particular areas of international programming, but might not have previously considered the interconnections of their efforts (Hudzik 2011). This increased awareness could lead to greater advocacy efforts for other changes and improvements related to internationalization. Build on this momentum.

WHAT IS COMPREHENSIVE INTERNATIONALIZATION?

Comprehensive internationalization is "a strategic, coordinated process that seeks to align and integrate policies, programs, and initiatives to position colleges and universities as more globally oriented and internationally connected" (ACE 2012, 3). Comprehensive internationalization is comprised of six interconnected areas: articulated institutional commitment; administrative leadership, structure, and staffing; curriculum, co-curriculum, and learning outcomes; faculty policies and practices; student mobility; and collaboration and partnerships (ACE 2012).

Special emphasis must be given to the *strategic, coordinated process* among the six dimensions included in this definition of comprehensive internationalization. This phrase implies foresight and planning, the involvement of key constituents across the campus—where communication must play a key role. Comprehensive internationalization takes time and it would be unrealistic to think that efforts can be undertaken all at once. However, this model gives institutions something to strive for. It is important to note that each institution's model of comprehensive internationalization will be unique. Colleges and universities need to prioritize their internationalization activities to be consistent with their mission, constituent groups, strengths, and resources.

The following questions should be asked when reflecting on an institution's commitment to different aspects of comprehensive internationalization:

* Is internationalization, global learning, or international education prioritized in the institution-wide strategic plan?
* Are the president and chief academic officer committed to supporting internationalization efforts?
* Is there an office or administrator responsible for coordinating campus-wide internationalization activities?
* Does the institution maintain collaborations and partnerships with institutions abroad?
* Are students provided opportunities in the classroom and through co-curricular programs to learn about international perspectives and global issues?
* Are faculty provided opportunities to build intercultural competencies and teach or conduct research abroad?
* Are domestic students encouraged to pursue education abroad and are they supported in these endeavors?
* Are academic, social, and cultural structures and programs in place to support international students?

If the institution has prioritized recruiting and admitting more international students, but has not considered other critical areas of internationalization as explored in these questions, reflecting on the bigger picture and larger internationalization strategy is an eventual must.

Consider an institution where senior leaders regularly articulate and support the need for global learning and international collaborations, where faculty are trained in intercultural communication and embed global perspectives in their courses, where co-curricular programs are developed to facilitate cross-cultural dialogues, and where returning study abroad students reflect on their experiences with classmates from the countries in which they studied. This experience reflects an institution that has taken a comprehensive approach to internationalization. Ultimately, the more internationalized an institution is across multiple dimensions, the more welcoming, supportive of, and invested in international students it will be.

TWO

Internationalizing Your Campus:
Action Steps and Best Practices

JACQUELYN D. ELLIOTT | International Liaison Specialist | University of Missouri—St. Louis

Internationalizing Your Campus: Action Steps and Best Practices

The topic of internationalizing higher education campuses has been abuzz for quite some time—with early beginnings noted in the 1930s by the American Council on Education (Callahan 2015). Interestingly, however, its popular use in higher education only dates back to the 1980s (Knight 2003). More than ever, college campuses look to internationalizing for purposes of preparing citizens for a global economy, but also, for practical reasons of generating new student revenue streams. Globalization places a premium on education by emphasizing the importance of cross-national communication (Bao 2009), thus propelling internationalization. As a result, higher education must deliver since it is generally understood that in today's *the world is flat* mentality, college students need to develop skills to navigate circumstances that go beyond the borders of their own country.

As institutions grapple with how to impact these outcomes, the real challenge is defining exactly what *internationalization* means. This debate has been going on for nearly three decades (Knight 2004). For some campuses, it means expanded education abroad or student exchange programs. In some instances, it may require a total overhaul of curriculum and student affairs. For others, it means building partnerships with foreign institutions to infuse international literacy and understanding on home campuses.

Jane Knight (2003), a leading expert in the field, defines internationalization as "the process for integrating international, intercultural or global dimension into the purpose, functions or delivery of postsecondary education" (2). NAFSA: Association of International Educators (2011) defines internationalization as "a conscious effort to integrate and infuse international, intercultural, and global dimensions into the ethos and outcomes of postsecondary education". How campuses elect to approach the process, while keeping in mind that it is a *process*, is quite varied.

The purpose of this chapter is to provide practitioners and institutional leaders a brief overview of internationalization on three fronts. First, a historical overview, aimed at understanding its roots; second, implementation techniques and models for internationalizing a campus; and finally, a look at the role of academic affairs in the process. The chapter will conclude with tips from successful institutional cases where internationalization was achieved (as defined by NAFSA) and some best practice applications for consideration.

Historical Overview of Internationalization in Higher Education

The role of higher education has always been international in nature. For example, Altbach (2004a) notes that "from the beginning, universities represented global institutions—in that they functioned with a common language, Latin, and served an international clientele of students" (4). He further indicates that "students have always traveled abroad to study, and scholars have always worked outside their home countries" (5). Many historians share accounts of students and scholars traveling from the U.S. to Europe during the colonial period for both education and etiquette training (Callahan 2015).

Globalization has had a major impact on internationalization in business sectors and health fields, but perhaps the area where it has had the biggest influence is higher education. Globalization gained momentum in the post-World War II era. It was at this time that English became the dominant global language, and the U.S. was positioned as the new center of higher education, becoming a global marketplace for scholars and ideas (Thelin 2011). Internationalization of higher education, however, was controlled by how institutions *responded* to larger issues of globalization (Altbach and Knight 2004).

Stemming from this era emerged the Truman Commission of 1947, which dramatically altered the student affairs profession (Callahan 2015). As a result of the Commission, the 1949 Student Personnel Point of View (SPPV) focused on the development of the student as a whole, highlighting a newfound importance for globalization and internationalization within higher education, student affairs, and the U.S. as a nation (Williamson 1949). Soon after, the 1961 Kennedy administration established the Peace Corps and passed the International Education Act of 1966 (Read 1996). These advances strengthened the internationalization movement in higher education in the U.S., as communication and exchange among scholars and students across the globe expanded (Dalton 1999).

In more modern-day terms, campus internationalization, like retention, is the job of everyone on campus. Faculty members are not excluded, and in many ways, play the most integral part of internationalization if it is to be considered comprehensive and lasting. Institutions must establish a strategic framework to govern these efforts.

Implementation Techniques and Models for Campus Internationalization

There is not one certain way to internationalize one's campus. However, there are some standard practices that have been implemented across multiple institutions leading to success. There are two areas in particular where the work is done—administrative processes and curricular changes. Process is what happens from the top down and involves a plan that is generally over-seen by administration. Curriculum is wide sweeping and is mostly overseen by academic affairs.

Administrative Process

In order to achieve success, the first thing any campus must have is a strategic plan that addresses internationalization—and then budgets to successfully execute it. Within that plan must be strategic goals, performance indicators, and action steps with timelines, responsible agents, and monitoring (Knight 2004). Creating a plan involves a two-step process. The first step is to do an *internationalization review*, whereby the institution catalogs and analyzes what it is doing in terms of internationalization (Hill 2010). This step is critical in knowing where the institution stands at present and where it wants to go in the future. The second step is the articulation of student *global learning goals* and a method for understanding how the institution's activities impact student learning (Hill 2010). The integration of these two steps leads to the development of an insightful internationalization strategic plan.

The internationalization review commonly includes an evaluation of the college's commitment to internationalization in its mission, goals, and vision. Then, a look at the broader environment is often taken to include local, state, and regional commitment to support the institution. Other areas to investigate are the international office structure, portfolio, and personnel. And, finally, does the *institutional* strategic plan incorporate internationalization?

Other areas to consider include faculty international background, interests, and activities. These data should be collected and reported annually to the campus. Concrete structures, policies, and practices for faculty development, travel, tenure, and promotion should also be put in place. Attitudes of the domestic students should be evaluated to help navigate areas where new program initiatives should take place, both within the curriculum and co-curriculum. Further, international students should be surveyed to determine what needs are not being met in terms of their experience, how they feel they are making impact on the campus, and in what ways they are expanding access to new views and cultures of the domestic students.

These are some basic (and non-exhaustive) approaches to be taken within the administrative structure of the campus. In addition, the academic process plays a major role in helping create a wholly internationalized campus.

Academic Process

The division of academic affairs can—and should—play a major role in the development of campus internationalization. Certainly, there are multiple aspects to consider, but for purposes of this chapter, the internationalizing of the curriculum will be the focus. With all the activities reviewed in the administrative functions, there are many reasons to invest in internationalizing the curriculum. To begin, by taking action, the reputation and competitive position of the institution is enhanced. Further, students become prepared for global citizenship and positioning, which is a main purpose of obtaining a college degree. Three other main considerations are to generate revenue, enhance the research agenda of the institution, and to strengthen overall faculty/student engagement.

There are multiple ways to approach internationalization of the curriculum, including the introduction of additional electives, foreign language requirements, international majors and minors, and the addition of cross-cultural comparative elements in existing courses. To take this to the highest degree of commitment, an institution must be willing to incorporate global learning goals across all disciplines, as well as transform course content.

Global learning goals share many of the same outcomes as liberal education. But, what separates the two is the ability for a student to gain a deep comparative knowledge of the world's peoples and problems, as well as generate scientific knowledge needed to understand the "global contexts of critical civic engagement"

(Hovland 2010, 7). With this in mind, global learning goals should consider the following (Elliott 2014):

  ✱ **Knowledge:** Students can demonstrate knowledge of other cultures to include values, perspectives, practices, beliefs, and products.
  ✱ **Abilities:** Students can use knowledge of these cultural frames to better solve problems, think critically, and generate new perspectives.
  ✱ **Attitudes:** Students will appreciate art, religion, music, language, and philosophies of different countries.

In an effort to advance these goals, it is critical that faculty include international content in the curriculum wherever possible.

In addition to global learning goals, the internationalizing of course content is critically important, as the two go hand-in-hand. Essentially, there are three ways this can be done: add-ons, infusion, and transformation (Olson 2010). Add-on changes are the easiest and include aspects such as inviting a guest lecturer to class, adding a reading from an author from a different cultural context, or creating an assignment with an international focus on the subject matter. The infusion approach requires more preparation by the faculty member and involves an international or cultural aspect in *all* aspects of the course. And finally, the transformation approach, the most demanding of all, creates a total immersion experience. The intended outcome is the ability of the faculty and students to move easily between many worldviews, since different ways of seeing and organizing the world are embedded in all aspects of the course. Often, the type of material seen in these courses includes:

  ✱ Books and articles written by scholars from other countries
  ✱ Case studies that are set in non-homeland countries
  ✱ Articles from international journals and newspapers
  ✱ Foreign films, television, and radio broadcasts
  ✱ International and non-country based websites
  ✱ International datasets

It is not clear which approach is right for any given faculty member, but ideally, most would be willing and eager to strive for transformation. One critically important factor to help ensure success is to *reward* faculty who make the commitment to change.

In summary, internationalizing the curriculum is done in two major ways. First, it can be done by creating institutional global learning outcomes to be achieved, and second, by changing the classroom curriculum—through add-ons, infusion, or transformation. The internationalization of the curriculum is about creating change—change for the institution, for us as educators, for our students as learners, and in our business relationships domestically, and globally.

Case Study Reviews of Internationalization

It is evident the role that academic affairs can, and should play, in the internationalization of an institution. Certainly, there are other factors. In this section, mini case study reviews will be provided to show the variances across different campus types in different geographic areas—from the East Coast, the Midwest, and the West Coast. These mini-case studies are not intended to give a complete analysis of the process. Rather, they are intended to provide a bird's-eye view for the practitioner about how different each case can look and still be considered a success. This provides evidence that there is not one cookie-cutter solution to this process called internationalization.

ELON UNIVERSITY

Elon University is located in Burlington, North Carolina and boasts a beautiful 575-acre campus. In its former days, it was considered a small regional college, but now, it is classified as a comprehensive university. Part of what helped make this transformation was Elon's commitment to international studies and global awareness. With two presidents in Elon's history promoting internationalization back-to-back, there was over a 40-year span of seamless vision for an internationalized campus. J. Fred Young was an avid supporter

of study abroad, and Leo Lambert worked to land a major gift that would transform international studies at Elon—a $1 million donation (NAFSA 2007). This gift put in place a new building at the heart of the campus entirely focused on international studies.

So, what did Elon do over these 40 years to make such a transformation? The 4-1-4 calendar helped to propel study abroad in January terms, with everyone given the opportunity to travel. Students, custodians, and faculty all travelled—everyone. This emulated to students the importance of going abroad and learning about new societies. Much of the travel was funded through scholarships, which promoted equal opportunity to anyone who was interested. The study abroad program created a culture where students accepted that it was a normal part of their college experience. Additionally, many courses that had international components did not have prerequisites. This opened the opportunities for students to study abroad at any time during their academic career.

Outside of study abroad, Elon focused its energy on global internships, civic engagement projects, and a freshman seminar on the global experience. It also stepped up the creation of strong exchange programs that were more than just an agreement on paper—they actually produced outcomes.

In Elon's case, what was an early and strong adoption of study abroad turned into an institutional culture from which emerged curricular changes, a focus on fundraising to support the cause, and meaningful exchange programs. Personalized service and care for the students was also a hallmark of the Elon experience.

SHORELINE COMMUNITY COLLEGE

Shoreline Community College is located in Seattle, Washington, just ten miles from the space needle. It opened in 1964. As a community college, Shoreline boasts one of the strongest international community colleges in the U.S. How did they accomplish this? As one might guess, it was not a silver bullet, but a combination of programs and efforts.

In 2001, the college took a bold initiative to create an International Programs Advisory Committee (IPAC) to disburse faculty grants to develop short-term study and service abroad projects (NASFA 2007). Within one academic year, faculty led dozens of students on three-week trips all over the world. Through presidential transition, the commitment to Shoreline's internationalization was unwavering. The administration was focused on programmatic and curricular support. In addition, during the accreditation process, Shoreline strategically embedded and highlighted this aspect of its institutional culture to ensure continued support both monetarily and programmatically. Following its success in study abroad, the college began investing in global service learning projects. Additionally, themed learning classes were implemented that focused on international issues.

These efforts at Shoreline may sound like what most other schools do, but what is unusual is that what one might commonly call a four-year model was implemented at a community college. The fabric of the institution is now known to be international. Strong commitment from the top, buy-in from the faculty, monetary support, and a strategy to embed the international philosophy throughout the accreditation process all led to Shoreline's success in internationalizing its campus.

WEBSTER UNIVERSITY

Webster University, in St. Louis, Missouri, is known for its international brand in higher education. Rooted in a mission from the Sisters of Loreto, the founding order of nuns who opened the college in 1915, Webster continues its mission of *meeting unmet needs*. Webster's first international campus opened in Geneva, Switzerland in 1978. The idea stemmed from its success in educating servicemen at Scott Airforce Base across the river in Illinois, and ultimately, at bases in over 12 states across the U.S.

Spearheading its comprehensive internationalization project, President Neil J. George and other top leaders created a structure of creativity and entrepreneurship that allowed stakeholders at Webster to think strategically and big. Webster was the first U.S. university to win approval for an American MBA program in China and was an early adopter of paying for students' airfare to international branch campuses (NAFSA 2008).

President George, who helped the internationalization of Webster, indicated that campuses should:

"...pursue [international education], but you should enter it for the right motivation. If you have schools that are struggling or looking for a new vein of financial support, that's the wrong motivation. If they are genuinely interested in promoting global perspectives for their students as part of their degree, many different approaches can be used." (NAFSA 2008)

Clearly, being true to the mission of the university is a critical component of garnering success in internationalizing the campus. Additionally, leadership must not only be on board, but be visible players in the process, allowing campus stakeholders the latitude to know they are empowered to get things done.

A case study always provides a direct lens about what to possibly emulate for success. But, as with any study, it does not provide a comprehensive overview. For that reason, a compilation of other best practices, drawn from the literature, will now be provided.

Proposed Best Practices

A best practice may be a particular method or an entire program. Best practices should be measurable, notably successful, and replicable (Rabinowitz n.d.). This section provides some ideas and tips that have been successful at other schools, but it is possible that not every notion is replicable for every school type. It is important to take into consideration the fit with the individual community culture and population. It should be asked if these ideas fit with the structure and philosophy of the institution and if the initiative will lead to reaching a particular goal deemed important. Using best practices has three major impacts: (a) they make the work easier to justify, (b) they can bolster the institution's credibility, and (c) they can make it easier to get the necessary funding (Rabinowitz n.d.). Listed below, in no particular order, are some administrative best practices to consider (Hill 2010; Knight 2004).

* Develop a team and communication plan to engage the broader community
* Clarify institutional goals and language and craft a common vision
* Develop a timetable of the work to be done
* Conduct an internationalization review
* Articulate global learning goals and a method to understand how the activities impact student learning
* From findings, develop a strategic internationalization plan
* Invite a peer review team to assess goals and strategies
* Link that plan to the institution's overall strategic plan
* Appropriate necessary budget
* Assign responsibility and monitor the progress using a work matrix
* Appropriate organizational structures for communication and coordination
* Balance between centralized and decentralized promotions and management of internationalization
* Start alumni-abroad programs
* Increase international recruitment and diversify the portfolio of travel
* Consider student clubs and organizations with global or international focus
* Host international and intercultural campus events
* Liaise with community-based cultural and ethnic groups
* Provide student support services such as orientation programs, tax preparation, passport services, and debriefing programs

Beyond the administrative functions, there are also those for academic services. Listed below are activities and programs to consider reaching comprehensive internationalization of the campus (Knight 2004).

* Create contract-based training and research programs and services
* Create international linkages with other universities for student and faculty exchange
* Support cross-border joint faculty research
* Create new academic programs with international focus, such as languages, business, political science, Irish or Greek studies, etc.
* Increase library holdings related to international studies
* Host faculty development and training
* Ensure faculty know there is an expectation to incorporate international studies in the curriculum
* Embed international learning outcomes in the curriculum
* Make an effort to recruit international faculty
* Reward faculty and staff who make contributions to the international effort, and make it part of the review/promotion process
* Support international assignments and sabbaticals
* Provide funding for international travel
* Create internationally-themed course work
* Ensure study/education abroad curriculum integration
* Provide multiple foreign languages
* Infuse the campus ethos
* Create certificate programs

It is not possible to execute all of these at every institution, but the more that can be integrated, the more fully a comprehensive internationalization plan will be realized.

Conclusion

It has become critical that both students and faculty be armed with global awareness, attitudes, intercultural sensitivity, and knowledge of how this interdependence will impact the future of all societies. The congruence of a number of predictions about global development (technology, the world's middle class, the shift in economic activity) has created a kaleidoscope of realities our graduates will have to face as they work and live day-to-day. Campus internationalization is a bold and necessary step to arm our students with the tools and skills they need to succeed. The decision to internationalize must stem from senior leadership and be executed in both the administrative and academic spheres.

THREE

International Admissions
Policies
Procedures
and Practices

Director, International Admissions
Indiana University

JOHN WILKERSON

International Admissions Policies, Procedures, and Practices

Matias is a student from Bolivia attending a large, public university in the Midwest. He describes his college search experience as overwhelming. "I thought it would be like filling out the same application for each college. But by my third application, I was confused by how many different parts there were to each" (Gallo 2015).

With over four thousand institutions of higher education within its boundaries, it's no wonder that the application and admission processes employed by colleges and universities in the United States are varied. Matias' scenario is not uncommon among the thousands of international students who are welcomed onto campuses throughout the United States at the start of each academic term. These students enrich our campus communities, bringing with them diverse experiences, perspectives, and cultural identities. The process for applying to university can be complicated for students without the cultural touchpoints available to domestic applicants.

Things worked out well for Matias. "The first college that replied to my email also suggested I make an appointment at EducationUSA." He found that advice to be incredibly helpful as he navigated the intricacies of the college search and application process with the assistance of knowledgeable, objective advisors. While Matias eventually chose to enroll somewhere other than the college that provided that advice, he holds that institution in great affinity. "That admissions officer changed my life because he was willing to answer a few questions that probably seemed stupid to him. But for me...it was everything."

Employing empathy when considering each international student application is vital to meeting the goals of both the student and the institution. As admissions professionals working with students who come from beyond the borders of the United States, it is helpful to be reminded of the comprehensive nature of the work that takes place in an international admissions office. Certainly, admissions officers are gatekeepers to their respective institutions, while simultaneously minding the goals and aspirations of the students whom they serve. No matter how similar one student's experience may appear to that of another, the path that each student takes toward university is unique and often deeply personal.

Communication is perhaps the skill most important in the admissions profession. As communicators with students throughout the process, impressions are formed through relationship development between both the institution and the student. The role of both the admissions officer and the applicant is to search for the "good fit" that universities consider when reaching an admission decision. The perimeters of that good fit conversation concern not only the goals and needs of an applicant, but also those of each college or university.

Understanding an Institution

The work of international admissions can be broadly viewed within the context of three institutional objectives: student recruitment, admissions and operations, and student enrollment. While each of these plays a key role in the persistence and success of international student populations on university campuses, the work of AACRAO is largely supportive of the admissions and operations objectives of the field. As best practices are employed at an institution, however, it is important to understand the interplay that exists between each of the three broader objectives.

International admissions officers should have a solid understanding of the institutional imperatives at work in bringing international students to a campus. Knowing the answer to three central questions will help inform the work of an office. These questions involve institutional growth, diversification, and resourcing.

* **What are the growth goals of a university?** Some universities are in enrollment growth modes in which international students may play a vital part in reaching overall student body population goals. Other institutions may be seeking to maintain a stable student population, and some universities may hope to reduce the overall size of the student body. These goals are appropriately institution-specific, and are often a component of a larger mission within a college or university.

In the face of declining high school graduation rates in many states, some institutions now see potential for international students to fill classroom seats and spaces in residence halls which were previously occupied by domestic students. This is a complex and pervasive topic of conversation within the field of international student enrollment management, and many institutions are attempting to balance both the need for increased or sustained enrollment with the need to maintain or develop international diversity within a student body. Just as international student mobility trends are influenced by many factors, so too are the institutional needs surrounding the work of international admissions.

* **What role does diversity play in international student admissions?** Having a solid understanding of a university's goal for student body composition is vital to preparing an international admissions office's structure and training. It is important to know how diversification is defined within an institution, as well. Some institutions will singularly define an international student based upon a student's citizenship. Conversely, universities involved in compre-

hensive campus internationalization are increasingly defining international students based upon experience. At these institutions, an international student body may also include U.S. passport holders who have attended secondary school outside the United States. Knowledge of how an international student body is defined will also be key to measuring the success of an international admissions office's goals.

* **What resources are being devoted by a college or university to obtain the goals established for its international admissions unit and to support the success of international students?**

These three questions combine to address the development of an international strategic enrollment plan (ISEM) at a university. The employment of ISEM on a college campus supports goal-driven, student-centric admissions practices which consider the conversation of good fit throughout the enrollment process, from initial student inquiry through post-graduation student placement. Understanding where an admissions office falls within an ISEM plan allows for more accurate development of admissions processes, strategies, and departmental goals.

STRUCTURAL MODELS FOR THE INTERNATIONAL ADMISSIONS OFFICE

The structure of an institution should be considered when defining the roles and responsibilities of departments in regards to international admissions. Commonly, there are two structural models in which international admissions exists. At some institutions, the work of an international admissions unit is contained within the larger office of admissions and enrollment management. Other institutions imbed international admissions within an international student services office, typically reporting through an international affairs division or through the dean of students. How and where an international admissions unit is located on a campus can have significant impact upon its resources, visibility, and campus integration.

Within an enrollment management division, international admissions may be a separate but parallel entity to domestic admissions. As a standalone unit, it will typically be headed by a director charged with oversight of an operations staff charged with document processing and credential evaluation, and will also generally include a recruitment staff. This structural model benefits from close alignment with recruitment and operations processes employed by domestic admissions staff. This can be helpful in development of student communications, institutional brand consistency, and reduction of duplicate reporting and success measurement.

The challenge of this structural model lies in developing and maintaining close collaboration with the international student services (ISS) and immigration team. Swift and accurate production of immigration documents, and seamless student transitions to advising for immigration and orientation programming, require consistent communication with the ISS unit. Additionally, opportunities for continued interaction with enrolled international students can be limited. This may have bearing upon development of global student ambassador programs for outreach to prospective students and applicants.

International admissions offices contained with an international student affairs division often exist as an independent unit alongside ISS and study abroad programs. The benefits to this structure include opportunities for in-office immigration document issuance which may have significantly positive impacts upon the processing times for immigration documents. There may also be a greater opportunity for collaborative international student programming, creating options for international applicants to interact with current students within a campus' community. There are additional opportunities for staff development as the work of the unit is in tandem with the broader work of international higher education on a campus.

Neither of these structural models exists without risk. Physical separation from the domestic admissions office may result in duplicated efforts in student communica-

tion, reporting, and strategic recruitment planning. Additionally, this separation may further segregate international student programming, forgoing the opportunity for an active, internationally-concerned unit within a campus' enrollment management division.

Regardless of where international admissions take place at a university, it is important to identify campus partners for support and collaboration. Like domestic admissions, international admissions interfaces with many parts of a university campus. Maintaining positive dialog with those units on a campus is vital to developing and maintaining an informed, productive, and collaborative international admissions office.

Aligning Processes

One of the primary challenges faced by international admissions professionals lies in comparing the secondary educational structures and outcomes of hundreds of countries with those of the United States. The key question that is asked when considering a student's application for admission is whether or not the applicant has earned the secondary school credential necessary to pursue a U.S. bachelor's degree. While this may appear a somewhat simple question to answer, it often is not.

Educational ladders, curriculum content, grading scales, and accreditation are a few of the considerations at work in determining a student's readiness for undergraduate studies in the United States. Later sections of this guide will provide insight into these areas. However, the question of student readiness is ultimately the purview of the college or university to which a student has applied.

When developing or assessing admission standards for international students, admissions officers must function within the established review model in use at their respective institutions. Commonly, there are three models of admission review employed by U.S. colleges and universities:

✳ Open admission
✳ Threshold admission
✳ Holistic admission

While many institutions may utilize some combination of the three, it is important to understand the basic tenets of each.

OPEN ADMISSION

The open admission model is utilized primarily by community colleges or higher education institutions with a mandate for student access. This model typically requires evidence of completion of secondary school, but may put aside that requirement at institutions where students are able to earn a secondary credential as part of their college coursework or degree plan.

THRESHOLD ADMISSION

Threshold admission models are often employed by public universities. Applicants are selected based upon a clearly defined and published list of admission criteria. For example, a university may require that students meet a minimum or threshold standardized test score, a minimum grade point average (GPA), and/or a minimum class rank. Universities employing this model can range from moderate to highly selective depending upon the criteria established. Most often, universities and colleges that use threshold admissions have no fixed enrollment caps, and are able to accommodate any student who meets their established standards, and apply by the necessary deadline.

HOLISTIC ADMISSION

The holistic model of admission is most common among private institutions and larger universities with capped or limited enrollment capacity. Applicants to colleges that employ this model will often be assessed upon standardized test scores, secondary school performance or GPA, extracurricular involvement, essay or personal statement, letters of recommendation, or some combination of these.

Assessment of international student applications should align as closely as possible with the assessment practices and criteria in use for domestic applicants. This can be challenging when converting a student's performance on an international secondary school transcript to a U.S. standard 4-point scale. Challenges can also be found in assessing international applicants' performances on standardized test scores in comparison to their domestic peers.

Perhaps one of the greatest challenges in aligning international and domestic student admissions has to do with application deadlines. International admissions officers can benefit greatly from having early, open, and continuing conversations with admission decision makers on their respective campuses. There is great value in discussing the unique needs of qualified students as they relate to an institution's international applicant pool.

Document Collection

Best practice dictates that, with rare exceptions, international applicants should be prepared to submit original academic records in sealed envelopes. These records should ideally be sent directly from the issuing institution to the university to which the student is applying. Universities and colleges may make exceptions or tailor these requirements to accommodate special circumstances, such as students applying from countries of conflict. When possible, such exceptions are made in consultation with colleagues at peer institutions and/or with input from EducationUSA officers who hold expertise in the respective regions.

In recent years, collection of documents required of international applicants has evolved with technological changes. Increasingly, electronic submission of academic records is available to international students. However, many students lack access to online, proprietary software platforms which allow for electronic submission. When available, receipt of electronic documents, whether standardized test scores or academic records, is significantly helpful to both students and admissions officers in the collection and authentication of documents.

There are various models used by universities when collecting financial and support documents necessary to issue immigration forms. Many institutions incorporate financial document requirements into the application process, requiring receipt of the necessary materials in order to mark an application as complete. Other institutions will render admission decisions absent receipt of financial documents, only requesting they be submitted once an offer of admission has been extended. In terms of regulation, either model is appropriate; the former being used as a vetting tool by some universities, the latter being used by universities willing to consider all applications for admission regardless of evidence of funding.

Student Communication

Recalling Matias' experience, the importance of communication with students is evident. Universities and colleges that have successful communication plans are those who have invested time and resources into developing a responsive strategy. The rewards for a well-executed communication plan become almost immediately evident.

For many years, university websites have contained large quantities of text-heavy information. These websites are often the front doors to our institutions. While detailed information is important to provide to students, it is equally important that the key points necessary to complete a university's application not be swallowed by mountains of text that students are unlikely to sift through. Close collaboration with an on- or off-campus website communication team should be considered to ensure several vital components of a web-based communication strategy:

* Mobile friendly website design
* Accessibility of multimedia content
* Consideration for bandwidth limitations

Websites should provide ease of access to information most sought after by international students. Universities can use internal analytics to determine what information is of greatest interest to international site visitors. It most often will include admission criteria, application deadlines, scholarship information, costs of attendance, and a link to the online application.

Beyond the website, active communication strategies with students include email, social media, and telepresence sessions. Any opportunity to provide students with information that helps to further differentiate one university from another allows for continued support of the conversation surrounding good fit.

It is very important when developing a communication strategy to consider the voice of the student. Colleges and universities should contemplate what message is being conveyed through tone, style, and delivery method. Maintaining a status quo can be very appealing in offices where the workload and pace is demanding. However, an investment should be made in communication plan development that includes both automated and customized messages. Communications can have lasting and substantial impact. This can create efficiencies in the quality and timeliness of communication with students.

Filtering student-specific electronic communication through a client relationship management (CRM) tool can provide value. These software platforms assist in communication plan development and implementation. This also may allow for more consistent tracking of student communication. Collaboration within an institutional or enterprise-wide CRM ensures alignment with university branding and communication strategies.

Staff Support

It is often said that it takes one year for an international admissions professional to begin to know what questions to ask about international admissions. As stated, it is a complex and ever-evolving field of work. The specificity of skill and knowledge necessary to perform well as an international admissions professional requires substantial support and development. Unsurprisingly, the pace at which best practice can change when dealing with the world's educational systems calls for responsive strategies.

The development of a cohort of peer colleagues from other universities is invaluable when creating a connected and informed admissions office. An external perspective can provide comparisons that are useful in assessing the functions and processes of an admissions office. Through this, staff also feel more engaged within the broader field of international admissions. Professional engagement is advantageous not only to individual staff, but also to the work of comprehensive internationalization. Engagement with external networks of professionals promote cohesion among operations and recruitment staff by providing a comprehensive understanding of the work of international education.

Internal department communication is also vital in developing team cohesion. Perhaps the most obvious place to start is with a documentation and training plan. Even the development of something as seemingly simple as a glossary of acronyms for both an institution and for international education terminology is helpful in training new staff. Documentation can be challenging to maintain in a constantly changing environment. Digital avenues such as wikis provide an opportunity for staff development in contributing to a platform that is evolutionary and demonstrative of individual expertise and experience.

Mentorship is the capstone of quality staff support. Providing opportunities for staff to interact with one another and with professionals outside of a department furthers the development of institutional expertise within a team. Volunteer groups, professional affiliates, and community-based organizations provide such opportunities, while also increasing a university's visibility.

Using Data

Two key points in consideration of the use of data in international admissions are the need for context and the importance of advocacy. Data provides substance to campus questions surrounding the importance of international recruitment or admissions, and moves the conversation from perfectly framed photos in university recruitment publications to factual information. This influences enrollment strategies, campus learning communities, and student outcomes. Ultimately, the con-

text of international admissions work, when supported by data, allows for effective advocacy for recruitment, admissions, and comprehensive campus internationalization.

Data can be effectively contextualized within three categories. Identifying these is helpful when determining what data to collect, how to collect it, and what to do with it when you have it (Wilkerson 2014):

* External data
* Internal or institutional data
* Experiential data

Each of these categories have a significant impact upon the work of international admissions, and can greatly inform the work of an office.

External data tends to be aggregated information provided by sources involved with international students and scholars. It provides a very broad overview of student trends or influencers upon student mobility. Sources may include AACRAO, the World Bank, Department of State, *CIA World Fact Book*, or the Institute of International Education's *Open Doors Report*. When used in combination, these sources provide considerable insight into the movements of and challenges faced by the international student community at large.

External data may also include regional and community-based sources. State and municipality census information is useful in identifying immigrant or refugee populations within a community. These communities often influence cultural ties from one part of the world to an institution in the United States. The University of Michigan, for example, is located in a region with significant population ties to areas of the Middle East. As such, UM may receive a larger pool of applicants from the Middle East region than other similarly-placed peer universities.

The collection of institutional data from a cohort of peer and aspirant institutions also is valuable to international admissions offices. This activity can afford general insights into the best practices adopted by an institutional cohort. This helps to inform the goals of an admissions office in aligning more closely with stated institutional goals or directives.

The use of internal or institutional data is critical in identifying trends and benchmarks within a university. Enrollment reports, study abroad destinations, international partner universities should each be used to inform admissions officers of the international influences present at their university. Additionally, institutional data identifies quantifiable metrics that can be put to use in measuring the efficiency of an international admissions operation. Such metrics include the average length of time it takes a student to submit all required application documents, the time involved in financial document review, immigration document issuance, and the effectiveness of coordinated communication plans. These are just a few examples of institutional data that is important to the implementation of strategic admissions plans.

Often, institutional data must be collected from various campus bodies. Again, when considering a targeted recruitment or admissions strategy that is country or region-specific, it is very helpful to investigate any ties that your institution already maintains with that region. In creating a country report which outlines known faculty interactions, study abroad programs, institutional partnerships, research collaborations, or alumni connections, universities gain comprehensive insights into what resources are available or what resources could be cultivated within the target region.

The value of experiential data in the daily work of international admissions is difficult to overstate. This is data gained through the experiences and expertise of professionals within an office, a campus, and the broader field of international higher education. This data includes conversations had with colleagues at other universities who are able to share knowledge regarding certain topics, or guidance counselors at professional conferences, and on recruitment trips. Experiential data often employs the realities of a particular situation in determining a best course of action.

Advocacy

The complexity of international admissions work is extensive. It requires a great deal of balance between operational needs, international student recruitment, communication, and understanding many global educational systems. The primary consideration remains the needs of our applicant population. While universities and colleges are increasingly involved in developing internationalized student bodies, the methodology to do so in a strategic, sustainable, and informed manner may not be pervasive on all u.s. campuses.

Professionals actively engaged in the work of international admissions are in unique positions to engage campus leadership. Demonstration of expertise and a student-focused approach to admissions allows for powerful advocacy of international students on u.s. campuses. The best international strategic enrollment plans are those which temper enthusiasm for immediate internationalization with plans that can be adapted to meet the constantly shifting demands of international student engagement. Positioning oneself in a role of expertise in this arena affords opportunities for student and program advocacy important to the development and maintenance of a solid international admissions plan.

The most effective advocacy is one that is proactive. Creating comprehensive expertise within international admissions allows professionals to promote the activities of an international admissions office. In doing so, professionals play an imperative role in building campus visibility and ensuring inclusion of international students.

FOUR

Recruiting International Students

LIZ REISBERG

President
Reisberg & Associates, LLC

Recruiting International Students

Individuals have traveled outside of their home country to study abroad for centuries. Scholars went elsewhere when they had exhausted educational opportunities and resources at home. This remained the primary, if not the only, "push factor" until the 20th century.

Today individuals pack suitcases and board planes for a myriad of motives—knowledge, academic freedom, infrastructure, innovative approaches to education, prestige, international experience, career leverage, and more. In 2014, the Organization for Economic Cooperation and Development (OECD) estimated that from 1975 to 2012 the number of internationally mobile students had increased fivefold, reaching a total of more than 4.5 million (*ICEF Monitor* 2014a).

Universities have welcomed international students for centuries, benefiting from the enhanced perspective of different nationalities and cultures. Yet few universities saw the enrollment of international students as a key part of institutional development or sustainability until the latter half of the 20th century.

The impulse behind this mobility remained mostly passive until fairly recently. Today marketing strategies are more sophisticated, more aggressive, and more targeted. Universities recruit international students to address numerous objectives and to enjoy the many benefits that result from the presence of international students on campus.

The international student marketplace is dynamic. Countries that have historically been exporters of students are now developing national strategies to attract international students. China, Korea, Malaysia, and international hubs in the Middle East are competing with traditional study destinations in Canada, Europe, and the U.S. As one example of this trend, Institute of International Education (IIE) data show that international students in China have increased from 110,844 in 2004 to 277,054 in 2014 (IIE 2015b).

Motivations and the Key Elements of Decision

To market successfully to international students, it is important to understand the factors that motivate people to go abroad and influence their choice of institution. Some recent papers suggest patterns that provide potentially useful insights.

A 2011 study surveyed international students studying in the U.K. to determine what influenced their decision to go abroad and their choice of destination (Wilkins and Huisman 2011). The sample was comprised predominantly of graduate students, with roughly 38 percent from China, 13 percent from India, 25 percent from Europe, and 24 percent from other areas. The choice of country and institution was heavily influenced by the perceived quality of education in the destination country, the reputation of the university, the content of the program, the department's rankings, the quality of the program, and the reputation of the faculty. Other key factors included the ease of application, availability of housing, the opportunity to improve English language skills, and anticipated employment opportunities. There were only slight variations by gender, country of origin, and level of study. Although cost did not have significant influence on choice, concern about rising costs indicate that this could be a more significant issue in the future. Economic volatility and currency fluctuations can certainly have unanticipated consequences on recruitment success.

STUDENT SATISFACTION AND WORD OF MOUTH

The study also found that student satisfaction (or the lack thereof) resulted from the ease with which students adjusted to culture, lifestyle, and dietary differences. International student satisfaction was critically important as their recommendations greatly influence friends and family in their home country who are considering study abroad. A 2007 study also found that word of mouth is extremely influential in the selection of a study destination (Verbik and Lasanowski 2007).

In 2011, William Archer, director of i-Graduate, polled 150,000 international students at 1,200 higher education institutions. Results of the study indicated that for 45 percent of the students, recommendation by friends were the most important factor in their choice of institution, while 41 percent were primarily influenced by the institution's website. Other key influences on destination choice include teachers, tutors, and parents. Archer concurs with the Wilkins and Huisman study regarding the importance of the international student experience on campus (starting with their welcome to campus) and the extent to which an individual's experience will determine whether they will become future unofficial marketers for the school they attended.

Additional research confirms that the quality of the personal experience on campus is of critical importance to international students. Students want to feel connected to faculty and staff and value "friendliness" (McFadden, Maahs-Fladung, and Mallet 2012).

RESPONSIVENESS AND EMOTIONAL FACTORS

"Responsiveness," like friendliness, influences a student's choice of institution. In his study of the class of 2015, Gil Rogers (2015) notes that most U.S. prospective students desire an email response from the colleges they contact within 24 hours, and tailored to their particular query at that. In this respect, international students are likely to share the expectations of U.S. students, looking for quick and personal replies to their questions and concerns from the institutions they are considering.

It is important to interpret the research carefully. If students are asked which institutional attributes are most important to them, they provide expected answers such as cost, school reputation, location, etc. (WES 2015). Although these criteria may influence the initial search, institutional *choice* is based on more emotional factors.

Research tells us that important elements of international student recruitment include reassuring a prospective student that people on campus will care about them, and ensuring the well-being, satisfaction, and success of current international students, as their recommendations are likely to be extremely influential with friends, relatives, and colleagues after they return home (Verbik and Lasanowski 2007; Archer 2011).

Institutional Strategy

Terms such as *marketing*, *branding*, and *competitive advantage* were once unspeakable in admissions offices and actually considered inappropriate concepts to apply to education. Times have clearly changed and today it is difficult to imagine any admissions or enrollment management office where these topics are not discussed explicitly. The challenge is to develop a unique and suitable recruitment strategy for an international audience.

There are both short-term and long-term approaches to recruiting international students. Short-term strategies might include sending a representative or alumnus/a to college fairs overseas or signing a contract with an agent who recruits candidates for a commission. Long-term strategy involves developing region-adjusted strategy based on knowledge and insight, and cultivating relationships and networks. Long-term strategy helps protect against the volatility of the global economy when it involves cultivating a network in multiple countries and regions. Recent decreases in funding to scholarship programs sponsored by the Brazilian and Saudi governments could have serious financial impact for institutions that have become dependent on a single stream of international students (Redden 2015b;

Redden 2016). Social media is important to both long- and short-term strategies but is only effective when integrated with an overall strategy.

Marketing to an international audience can follow different implementation strategies. The question that universities must consider is whether they are marketing to *persuade* or to *inform* (Gibbs 2007). Short-term strategy tends to focus on persuading or selling, while the most effective long-term strategy is a marketing plan built on informing.

SHORT-TERM STRATEGIES

There are a plethora of international fairs throughout the year and around the globe. These events are organized by both private and public organizations and vary enormously in cost and quality. They can attract anywhere from several dozen to thousands of students and parents. Some organizers require that a participating institution be represented by a campus-based administrator, while others will accept alumni or third-party agents. Some limit participation to institutions that are accredited or officially recognized by their host government. Some institutions hand out gifts or food to attract prospective candidates to their stand, while at other events, gimmicks and gifts are not permitted. The composition and criteria that define an event are significant determinants of its potential value as a place to meet appropriate candidates.

To make good use of recruitment funds it is wise to consider these and other factors before committing to participate. For example, is it better to attend fairs that attract thousands of students in order to receive greater exposure or is it more useful when an event organizer advertises to a particular profile and attracts fewer students? What is known about the individuals who have attended a particular event in the past? Can impartial educators in the region (*e.g.*; EducationUSA, British Council) provide useful information about different event organizers?

Some organizers offer optional activities in the city where an event is held. Events might include "briefings"

about the region that provide useful data for developing a targeted recruitment strategy. Other opportunities might include visits to local "pipeline" schools or meetings with individuals and services that provide orientation, testing services, or advising to prospective students. These opportunities leverage the value of attending a fair overseas as they provide critical information and opportunities for developing professional networks that strengthen the development of an institution's strategy.

Success at fairs depends on whether they are used strategically. Trained and skilled representatives can more effectively engage students at college fairs where interaction with prospective candidates can be difficult to initiate and tends to be brief. The odds improve if an institution is highly ranked, in a large city, or promoting scholarships—a "persuading" tactic that may lure new interested parties at a large fair.

LONG-TERM STRATEGIES

An institution-based, multi-dimensional strategy is more likely to produce stronger and more sustainable results, but results may take a few years to materialize.

In a competitive international market, institutions struggle to stand out, especially when the institution does not appear in the top tiers of the rankings. Yet institutions frequently overlook opportunities that can be leveraged to build international visibility. Long-term strategies are built on careful institutional self-assessments—the identification of institutional networks and resources, competitive advantages, and unique qualities. A careful self-assessment will provide the critical elements for successful strategy.

The obvious place to begin is by identifying current and past international students and their families. Collectively, these individuals provide critical data for marketing as well as a key network for international visibility. Additionally, as noted above, one of the most powerful influencers of student choice is the recommendation of friends and family members. Remarkably, this network is often underutilized, as undergraduate admissions offices often overlook international graduate students and alumni, while graduate admissions offices frequently overlook undergraduate international students and alumni. These are the individuals who can speak to the value and benefits that an institution offers and who can make those experiences relevant to prospective international students. International alumni are often the best ambassadors for a university if they are put into contact with prospective students, as they can convey enthusiasm for their campus experience that is not limited to the program they pursued. International students, their parents, and international alumni can be tapped to shape the marketing strategy for their home country, as they can identify what aspects of the campus experience have the most appeal and most relevance in their culture and country.

Another and often-overlooked resource is any international business or organization located near a U.S. campus. There might be international parents who are looking for a university where a child might study or international managers who might help with introductions to potential network connections abroad. These individuals can also provide support to make a lesser-known destination more attractive by providing insights—and perhaps quotes—as to the advantages of the location. Most international students will initially consider major cities, creating challenges for colleges and universities located in less-populated areas. Much like international alumni, international business professionals can help to define the characteristics of an area and a campus that will appeal to prospective students in their home country while simultaneously giving credibility to the value of that particular destination.

A key aspect to long-term recruitment success is distinguishing the institution from other institutions and learning to highlight its unique qualities. It is stunning to wander through a college fair and hear admissions representatives from different institutions saying exactly the same thing—outstanding faculty committed to teaching, small classes, international student office providing support, international clubs and events, excellent liberal arts curriculum, internships, etc. This approach neglects the qualities that research tells us international students value and seek. Here also, international students and alumni can provide important insights and perspective. Stories and anecdotes are key to making a personal connection with prospective students, and admissions representatives should have a generous supply of them.

Finally, the satisfaction of current students remains a critical element of long-term recruitment success. This implies institution-wide initiatives to ensure that faculty, staff, and students are prepared to welcome international students and that the international students receive appropriate orientation to be successfully integrated. Not doing so can have serious long-term impact, as Idaho State learned when hostility from both faculty and students prompted an exodus of students from the Middle East and a loss of more than $2 million in tuition income (Saul 2016).

Third-Party Participation

There are many intermediaries that are involved in the international recruitment process today. The selection of partners and vendors should be made with care, as the potential benefits and risks to both colleges and students are significant. What follows is a summary of various kinds of intermediaries and some of the implications of working with them.

PRIVATE COUNSELORS

In many countries families turn to professional college counselors for guidance and support in choosing and applying to programs abroad. Many of these individuals have earned one or more degrees abroad, or are ex-patriots who are knowledgeable about the process of living and studying abroad. These advisors often develop a relationship with a student and a family over time, and as such are well positioned to help a student match their needs and objectives to appropriate institutions overseas. Their reputation and income depend on providing the best service possible to the student. Most of these professionals are interested in meeting traveling admissions representatives and learning about the unique characteristics of different institutions in order to improve the information they provide to the students they counsel. Relationships with a network of professional college counselors are invaluable to long-term strategy since they have a continuing presence "on the ground" and can be an important bridge between campuses abroad and the prospective student market.

RECRUITMENT AGENTS

In some ways, recruitment agents provide a comparable service to private college counselors as they guide prospective students to destinations overseas. The important difference between recruitment agents and professional college advisors is that agents sign a contract with the institution for the purpose of referring students to that institution. The agent works with a narrower range of institutions, limiting his or her recommendations to prospective students to the institutions that pay them a commission for each international student enrolled. (It should be noted that paying a commission to agents to place American students at a u.s. university is prohibited by laws governing eligibility for federal financial aid.) These options may not always represent the best options for a particular student. Despite a number of mechanisms being introduced to monitor the conduct of agents, it cannot be verified that all agents inform prospective students that they are *not* college counselors, but rather, paid agents of specific institutions.

PATHWAY PROVIDERS

Partnerships with pathway programs are another strategy for increasing international enrollment with limited institutional investment. Like agents, these programs generally sign contracts with specific universities to create a pipeline for international students in exchange for a fee. The pathway programs generally provide English language training, orientation to the college life and academic work, and introductory-level courses that transfer to the college partner. Like agents, these programs channel students to specific institutions, not necessarily the best match for the student's interests or objectives.

There are several reasons to consider working with agents and pathway programs cautiously. These contracts provide a good option to the college or university looking for short-term results, but the long-term return on investment is dubious, as these relationships do little to develop institutional capacity or contribute to organizational learning. When universities work directly with teachers, advisors, local international industries, and other key actors on the ground, campus professionals acquire knowledge, insight, and understanding that inform the recruitment strategy and admissions processes and contributes to addressing the needs of international students after they enroll.

Furthermore, it is difficult to supervise third-party actors who operate far from campus, and thus it is hard to confirm how admissions applications were developed and whether all materials are legitimately the work of the candidate. Unfortunately, there is the risk of ethical compromises when admissions and commissions are at stake.

Finally, there are private companies that provide training and marketing support to institutions to help develop recruitment strategies and build internal capacity. Some of these companies conduct research on an ongoing basis and are knowledgeable about the changing characteristics of the student market, how social media is being used by prospective students, and what factors influence student choice. As a result of working with current and useful data, these companies may be able to help institutions focus their efforts for greater effectiveness and optimize the allocation of their budgets.

Web Presence

A 2011 study found that, while many students indicated that they use Facebook, Twitter, or YouTube, these social media sites did not strongly influence their college choice (Archer 2011). Rather, the most significant element of an institution's web presence is its website. The challenge of designing a college website stems from its multiple uses along with the diverse audiences that it must serve, and international students are frequently left out. Also too frequently ignored is that an increasing number of students are accessing the website from mobile devices, a function not always incorporated into website's design. There is useful research available about how individuals access and scan websites, how eyes move across the screen, and what information needs to be easily found. It might surprise some universities to know that Millennials often bypass homepages through their use of Google search (Hoover 2015).

More institutions are adding an "International" tab to their homepage and including information unique to the needs of international students. On some websites this information is very difficult to find or is incredibly limited (with no more than information about obtaining a visa). Several universities are now providing information on their website in multiple languages. As noted, an influential factor in the satisfaction of international students is the "welcome" they receive. This can certainly start when they are doing their initial research and before they apply. When a website offers commentary and virtual tours in multiple languages, this sends a welcoming message to prospective candidates.

Social media sites are resources that international students certainly use but these channels seem to act as a secondary level of influence. Conversations with current students and friends on social media are important, but not as important as conversations in person or by phone (Pratt, Dalfonso, and Rogers nd).

To Travel or Not to Travel

Recruitment travel is not only enjoyable but extremely valuable in terms of the knowledge it can provide. Despite living in a "connected" world, face-to-face, in-person meetings tend to build stronger relationships. Relationships of all kinds are paramount to successful recruitment, including ongoing relationships with

alumni, with professional college counselors, and with government-supported advising services such as EducationUSA. Travel provides the opportunity to develop key relationships that sustain long-term success abroad.

There is no question that international travel is expensive and, as a result, not an option for many colleges. Still, there are important networking opportunities to be leveraged at domestic conferences, such as NAFSA: Association of International Educators, Overseas Association for College Admission Counseling (OACAC), and Going Global. These conferences provide a central place to meet colleagues from many countries who interact daily with prospective international students.

Colleges and universities often overlook the potential for leveraging international travel by faculty, study abroad staff and students, and service learning groups. Although this kind of travel has a specific purpose unrelated to recruitment, travelers are often willing to schedule meetings with prospective students, alumni, or college advisors to increase visibility for their school. Additionally, these international travelers often have unexploited knowledge of and experience with different world regions and can contribute to the development of successful recruitment strategy.

While international travel may be out of reach for many institutions, the cost of contracting agents can quickly add up. In an investigative report that Chris Havergal (2015) published originally in *Times Higher Education*, he documents that universities in the UK spent a total of $133.7 million in commissions to agents during the 2013–14 school year. This money never appears in budgets because it is effectively discounted from tuition income. Still, this is money that universities are spending on recruitment and that does little to build institutional capacity for effective internationalization. One university alone spent $14.6 million in commissions. This amount could have financed a significant amount of international travel and direct interaction with prospective candidates.

Conclusion

The first phase of any strategy to recruit international students should be "know thyself." A comprehensive institutional self-assessment is key. Why does the institution want international students? What unique experiences can the institution offer that make it a good choice for students from abroad? What resources are needed to ensure a successful experience on campus and after graduation? Who on campus can help convey the message about the strengths and advantages of this institution? What are the local resources to be leveraged for effective international marketing? How broad is the commitment to internationalization on campus?

The next stage is determining how communication with an international audience will take place. Are staff adequately trained to know how and what to communicate to students from different cultures? Does the admissions office know which physical and virtual channels to use to reach an appropriate international market? Is the institution's website conveying useful information and an image that distinguishes the institution from others? Students, at the very least, should be informed about the structure of higher education in the destination country: What will be required to be successful and what are possible opportunities and limitations resulting from their degree upon return to their home country? Are they getting that information? Will communication take place through third-parties? If so, how will that message be shaped and controlled?

Institutions recruiting international students should recognize that bringing international students to campus implies a great deal of responsibility. Not only are students (and their families) making a large financial commitment, but these young individuals are taking an enormous risk in the pursuit of education by leaving support systems behind, immersing themselves in a potentially new and unfamiliar culture, and perhaps using a non-native tongue to further their education. These students present challenges in many areas of campus life, both in the adjustment of international students to campus culture and vice versa.

It is imperative that universities provide prospective students with all of the information they need in advance of enrolling; this critical communication is not always complete or effective when working through third-parties. Finally, international recruitment should not be the work of a single office. International student recruitment should be part of an institution's larger international strategy and should include faculty, staff and domestic students in dialog and activities that ensure that the presence of international students enhances the experiences of everyone on campus.

FIVE

Graduate Student Recruitment and Admissions

ADINA M. LAV

Assistant Provost for International Enrollment
The George Washington University

Graduate Student Recruitment and Admissions

International students have a robust history in the United States, where we pride ourselves on being the number one receiving country in the world for international students. Over 886,000 international students were enrolled in U.S. colleges and universities in 2013–14, an increase of 7.6 percent from the previous year (Institute of International Education 2014), adding approximately $27 billion to the U.S. economy during that year alone (NAFSA 2015).

However, these numbers are still a very small percentage of the potential market. For example, in 2012 China sent 194,029 students to the U.S. but had a university student population of over 23.9 million (Institute of International Education 2012; Ministry of Education of the People's Republic of China 2015). Likewise, India had well over 20 million university students in 2012, but sent just 100,270 to the U.S. While most university students in China and India lack the resources to study abroad, both countries have a strong and growing middle class (Choudaha 2015; Institute of Higher Education 2012; Kharas 2011). Strong middle-class populations translate into more students enrolled in higher education and increased student mobility (ICEF Monitor 2015). China's middle class alone has swelled in numbers far beyond the entire population of the United States (Barton 2013). Likewise, India's middle-class population, which hovered around 50 million in 2010, is forecasted to grow to 200 million by 2020.

China and India are not the only countries witnessing massive growth in their middle-class populations. The African continent is expected to see a continued growth—particularly Nigeria, Ghana, Angola, and Sudan—with a middle-class population well over 1.1 billion by 2060 (Standard Bank 2014; Afif 2015). Mexico and Brazil are both expected to double the number of households with over $50,000 in annual disposable income (Ernst and Young 2015). Indonesia's GDP is rising at about 5 percent per year and its middle class is expected to grow to 85 million by 2020 and 135 million by 2030 (Afif 2015). All of this is happening as the size of the middle- class population in the U.S. continues to fall (Searcey and Gebeloff 2015).

As existing international markets grow, new markets begin to emerge. The possibilities for new international students coming to our shores seem limitless. In other words, we've just seen the tip of the iceberg when it comes to the potential international student market.

International Graduate Students and Their Value

International students contribute greatly to the character of an institution, not simply as additional heads in a classroom. In a country that prides itself on diversity, U.S. higher education institutions value the contributions that international students add to the classroom discourse. Their presence strengthens the graduate experience for U.S. students by providing them exposure to new ideas and different modes of thought. The addition of international students helps both domestic and international student populations better prepare for a global environment. They also bring with them significant talent needed for continued U.S. innovation (Anderson 2013a). Stuart Anderson of the National Foundation for American Policy explains,

International students provide a key source of talent for U.S. employers and are crucial to enhancing the ability of U.S. universities to conduct research and

offer high quality academic programs to U.S. students. (Anderson 2013b)

Recruitment and Admissions of International Graduate Students

While some institutions have become successful in the way they manage international graduate enrollment, many others struggle to grow their international enrollment numbers. For those in the latter category, a variety of hurdles—ranging from lack of prioritization to poorly-designed organizational structures—work against such efforts. Below, several of the current issues related to international graduate student enrollment are explored.

Building an Infrastructure

The most successful international graduate recruitment strategy includes both in-country visits and active engagement through robust digital media campaigns (including email, websites, and social media). Many notable institutions spend significant amounts of time on the road, but take a one-size-fits-all approach to their digital communications, rather than tailoring their outreach to specific audiences. Other institutions build out their infrastructure and then fail to engage meaningfully on the ground, adopting a "build it and they will come" mentality. This approach is rarely successful outside of the most highly-regarded graduate programs in the country.

Special attention should be given to building recruitment infrastructure on campus *before* entering new markets abroad. Responses to the questions raised below will help define institutional effectiveness in keeping international students engaged.

✻ *Is web content provided in multiple languages?* Do you have translated 'evergreen' (information that is always relevant and not time-bound) content on your website and, if so, in which languages? Chinese, Spanish, French, and Arabic are good places to start. Large markets like Korea, Brazil and Indonesia may require that you further expand your foreign language section.

One might ask, "Why bother to translate pages if students are expected to be able to speak English?" Students are not making decisions in a bubble. Parents, faculty advisors, coworkers, and friends all play a role in the decision-making process. The more relevant and complete information is made available in translation, the better the decision-making ability of prospective students.

Translated information is also helpful for foreign governments and NGOs that assist international graduate students through special scholarship programs. For prospective graduate students, translated 'evergreen' content should highlight faculty, research opportunities, and outcomes (centered around career services). It should also provide easy-to-follow admissions and funding information.

✻ *Is the institution's website mobile-ready?* This is critical for effective outreach as much of the developing world is reaching the Web primarily (and sometimes exclusively) through their mobile devices.

✻ *How is traffic driven to the website?* Do you have the resources to handle foreign language social media? Current international graduate students can be very useful in creating content and are usually viewed as more valid sources of information. Existing social media feeds in translated formats can also be used, rather than new content.

✻ *Are communications plans "international-friendly?"* Do they address the needs of this special population of students? Are these plans sensitive to the different stages in the student cycle? Do you allow recipients to opt in and out of target languages? Does each communication include both the target language *and* English? Arguably, more and more English should be used as the prospective student moves through the admissions process and on to matriculation.

Are these plans sensitive to a particular culture's calendar? For example, are you sending critical communications to students in China during Chinese New Year, when 3.6 billion people are in transit around the country with limited access to critical documents and other resources? Or are you working within their cultural norms by encouraging them to submit everything before Chinese New Year?

✳ *How are existing in-country alumni being utilized?* Alumni could host admitted student dinners or hold calling campaigns on their alma mater's behalf. It is important to determine the preferred training, content, and procedures for those individuals that will be representing your institution. Your institution should determine the materials used in their efforts. Alumni engagement is a relatively easy way to build out your infrastructure in a market.

Defining Your Markets

A key aspect of international recruitment is defining your markets. Although markets differ widely from institution to institution, prospective international graduate markets can be segmented into three broad categories: maintenance, growth, and exploratory. All three segmentations house prospective graduate students with varying degree level interests (*e.g.* master's vs. doctoral), varying fields of interest, and varying financial abilities (on a spectrum from full need to full pay).

Maintenance markets are ones from which an institution already receives a bulk of applications with little or no effort. A deep dive into the existing application pool will reveal much. Look at home towns of your student body, and search by previous universities to determine where your transfer students are coming from. Pull out a map and start flagging cities and regions. Look for patterns. We have a tendency to want to spend a lot of effort in these markets; while they must be cared for, it may be a better bet to spend more time in growth markets.

Growth markets have potential. Perhaps one or two of your programs already receive a few applications from an area. Mark that area on your map, in a different color. Perhaps there is a well-respected university just outside of a maintenance market. Mark that, too. Do any of your existing faculty members have contacts there? Perhaps you've heard about a developing foreign government scholarship program at a conference you

attended. What does the scholarship program cover? Which fields? Does your institution excel in that field? Does it have the capacity for more students? What would it take for your institution to get on the ground floor of that program?

Exploratory markets are just that—markets worth exploring, either because you happen to be in a particular geographic area or because your institution has some special connection there. Look at national trends—GDP growth, for example, or consider an exploratory market with a population bubble for those aged 15–24. Exploratory markets are long shots; they receive little attention from U.S. institutions, which will make your college or university stand out even more.

As you consider the differentiations above, be sure to match enrollment efforts with your institution's other international priorities like research collaborations, alumni affairs, and development. Once you've begun to define your markets, keep researching to deepen your understanding and maximize utility of the various markets. Call in existing students and alumni from those markets to participate in focus groups. Bring together existing faculty from those markets for their advice and guidance. Use your professional networks (*e.g.* AACRAO, NAFSA, NAGAP, EducationUSA) to learn more about these areas. And finally, take advantage of tools like Google Alerts to keep abreast of current issues related to your markets.

Once recruitment infrastructure has been built and markets have been defined, it is time to decide how you will work within each market. A general rule of thumb is to spend 30 percent of your resources maintaining markets, 60 percent of your resources growing markets, and 10 percent of your resources exploring markets.

In-Country Recruitment of International Graduate Students

International graduate recruitment is not simply domestic recruitment in foreign lands; what works well in the U.S. does not always translate well abroad. And what works well in one international market may not work well in another. For example, a fair circuit may be the perfect way to explore a potential new market by allowing institutions to throw a very large net out to see what comes back. Fairs may also be a very reasonable and cost-effective way to maintain certain markets by simply acting as a reminder that an institution is there and ready to receive students. However, a more strategic way to build momentum in a market is through partnerships.

Partnerships work particularly well in growth markets. Consider 3+2 or 4+1 schemes to feed into your master's programs and research collaborations to attract potential Ph.D. students from niche areas. Many institutions abroad are eager to partner with U.S. universities. It is important to be selective about the best partner-fit for your institution. Because of varying cultural norms, legal differences, and administrative structures, international partnerships abroad can take more time and energy to solidify than domestic partnerships. Partnerships should be reviewed periodically and discontinued if they fail to serve either institution.

Other cultural differences can impact international recruiting. Site visits can take longer and the logistics of getting from one site to another can be a challenge dependent on local infrastructure. But while your institution's work on the ground is absolutely critical, the majority of your graduate recruitment work happens back home.

Recruiting International Graduate Students from Home

Recruitment efforts at home should begin before leaving the foreign markets. Feeding the work on the ground back into the recruitment infrastructure at home in real time is critical, as students have come to expect follow-ups within hours, not days or weeks. Many institutions track their international travels as a mechanism for content-creation on websites and social media.

Well-timed email and messaging communications make all the difference as application deadlines approach. Many institutions hold webinars at all hours of the day and night to capture each of their interna-

tional markets. Others offer late-night and early-morning one-on-one Skype sessions for interviews and admissions inquiries.

In working with your team back home, allow your institution to stand out by finding creative ways to engage the prospective students using in-country alumni and through your institution's online presence. Finally, be prepared to work with the many new applications your institution will be receiving from new markets.

Getting it Right

Not too many years ago I was in a senior admissions position in my institution's graduate engineering school. Late one evening during admissions season, I found myself sitting on the floor of my office, surrounded by admissions files and in tears. That year, our applications from China had doubled. It was far beyond any reasonable number of students our relatively small school could accommodate. I struggled that year, resolved to honor each and every one of those applicants with a proper and swift admissions review. It was an enviable position to be in, in some respects, but it also highlighted the critical responsibilities we have in our field to get things right.

This is a tall order given the relatively few resources most of us have to work with. And it is a bit of a chicken and egg problem: it is hard to justify the growth of admissions resources and capacities without increased application numbers, and it is hard to handle increased application numbers without more resources and capabilities.

The constant push-and-pull for resources requires creative problem solving and constant tweaking. For example, a strategy we utilized in the engineering school was to bring our graduate student services staff into the recruitment and admissions process where it made sense for their skill sets and expertise. We asked that teams focus on yielding admitted students, verifying official transcripts, and orientating newly matriculated students—all tasks originally handled by the admissions and recruitment staff. This allowed us some space to grow competencies and shift priorities in recruitment until we had enough justification for growth.

Responses to the questions raised below will help define your effectiveness in handling an increased pool of international graduate applications.

❋ *Do you have the expertise to handle international transcript evaluations? If not, are you prepared to outsource these efforts to a third party?* As your institution's international enrollment grows, it may make sense to build internal expertise in international transcript evaluation. This requires constant development and frequent interactions with others in the field to compare and contrast notes, flag trends, and be responsive to real-time changes in higher education systems around the globe.

It is also perfectly acceptable to decide against building this expertise in-house.

❋ *Is your faculty prepared to compare and contrast the capabilities of students from different countries with different educational systems?* Faculty must be trained in different systems from around the world. One strategy is to call upon faculty from different parts of the world to train other faculty. It is important for professors to hear that Iranian universities don't suffer from the same grade inflation as U.S. universities, for example. Or that a 68 percent from an Indian university isn't really a D grade.

❋ *Do you have thoughtful, data-driven English language requirements? Do you have solid policies around these requirements, including how best to handle exceptions to these policies?* How did you develop your current English language requirements and when was the last time they were reviewed? Starting with a general understanding of your current international students' scores—including section scores and bandwidths—can be insightful enough to prompt a more critical examination of such policies.

❋ *Have you extended your "international friendly" communications plans into your admissions and yield communications?* Many institutions have separate plans for students, depending on where they are in the

admissions process. It is important not to forget to review the often dry, action-oriented admissions communications to be sure it takes into account international students. For example, are you asking for transcripts from Indian students or mark-sheets or both? Are you asking students to submit final, official transcripts before they are released in their countries? A sophisticated CRM with conditional messaging can help with this, but a simple plan with extra information posted to a webpage can also serve this purpose well. At the engineering school, we posted detailed information about final, official transcripts by country on a webpage and drove communications there.

Yield activities are those that work to convert admitted students into matriculated students. Have fun with your yield communications. Ask current international students to create 1–2 minute welcome videos in different languages and send them out to prospective students as part of your larger yield communications plan. Revert back to foreign language content for mom, dad, and others. Send appropriate foreign language thank you notes to recommenders of students who have been admitted, encouraging them to recommend more students. Use your in-country alumni to host Admitted Student Days and Summer Send-offs, preparing them with giveaways, foreign language presentations, and FAQs. Encourage faculty and student ambassadors to be available during off-hours via Skype to congratulate students on their admissions and answer any questions they might have. Finally, prepare and deliver online pre-departure orientations.

❋ *Have you factored in the time and resources needed to process I-20 and DS-2019 forms?* Pushing out admissions decisions early simply isn't enough to yield anxious international graduate students. It is absolutely critical to get I-20 forms or DS-2019 forms into their hands as quickly as possible. Having expertise around foreign financial credentials is as critical as having expertise around international transcript evaluation.

Whether you decide to build those capacities in-house or externally, they must be factored into your process.

The ripple effect of growing your institution's international enrollment is enormous and far beyond recruitment and admissions. Orientations and other on-boarding activities must be re-thought; student services and classroom support must be expanded. It behooves recruitment and admissions teams to start these conversations early so that your campus is ready to welcome an influx of new international graduate students.

SIX

EducationUSA and
International
Recruitment

2016 AACRAO INTERNATIONAL GUIDE

KRISTINA JENKINS

Assistant Director
Global EducationUSA Services
Institute of International Education

PEGGY BLUMENTHAL

Senior Counselor to the President
Institute of International Education

EducationUSA and International Recruitment

The U.S. Department of State, through its Bureau of Educational and Cultural Affairs (ECA), promotes the United States as the leading higher education destination for students around the world. Maintaining that #1 position is a priority shared by U.S. colleges and universities, along with many state governments. International students expand the horizons of U.S. students and local communities with unique perspectives and experiences, while enhancing the research and teaching capacity of U.S. institutions and increasing their prestige and position in the competition for global talent. The knowledge and skills that international students develop during their U.S. study period prepare them to become the next generation of world leaders who can work across languages, cultures, and borders to solve shared global challenges. The Department of Commerce estimates that international students annually contribute over $30 billion to the U.S. economy in payments for tuition, room and board, and other expenses, making U.S. higher education one of America's leading service export industries (Bureau of Economic Analysis, U.S. Department of Commerce 2015). International students enrich local communities not just with short-term investment but also longer-term partnerships when alumni return home to jobs in industry, government, and higher education.

ECA coordinates the federal government's activities in support of international education through a wide range of programs—most directly through its EducationUSA network of several hundred advising centers in 170 countries. ECA's mission is to build mutual understanding between the peoples of the United States and other countries. The EducationUSA network supports this mission by helping international students better understand and navigate the U.S. admissions process and connecting U.S. higher education professionals with international students, as well as foreign educational institutions and governments.

EducationUSA Advising Centers

EducationUSA advising centers are located in U.S. embassies and consulates, and in a variety of partner institutions, including Fulbright Commissions, binational cultural centers, U.S. nongovernmental organizations (NGOs), foreign NGOs, as well as foreign universities and libraries. These centers share a common goal: assisting students in accessing U.S. higher education opportunities. They provide group advising sessions, virtual advising, individual appointments, pre-departure orientations, and information about the breadth of U.S. higher education. Table 6.1 provides statistical details on the network's outreach to almost 13 million prospective students annually through center-based and outreach activities, including virtual and social media platforms.

EducationUSA centers are organized by three levels of service: Comprehensive, Standard, and Reference. When searching for an advisor or advising center, it is helpful to know the level of service one can expect. The levels of service offered at different centers are described in Figure 6.1. While most centers generally offer most of the services listed for their level, not all centers provide every single service listed.[1]

---

[1] The locations and contact information for all centers can be found at <EducationUSA.state.gov>.

TABLE 6.1. EducationUSA By the Numbers

Number of In-Center Contacts, by Type	
Individual advising appointments	111,208
Advising by phone or SMS (each conversation)	269,502
Advising by email	606,098
Group advising attendees	183,753
Walk-ins/library/computer users	391,183
U.S. institution representatives	10,721
MOOC camp attendees	4,012
Total	*1,576,477*
Number of Event Attendees, by Outreach Activity	
Education fairs	1,062,535
American corners/centers	52,925
Local universities/secondary schools	383,249
Other fairs/conferences/seminars	154,285
Host government events	22,560
Embassy/consulate events	26,122
Public locations	256,401
Total	*1,958,077*
Number of Virtual/Social Media Contracts, by Type	
Social networks—pages likes and group members	2,651,126
Video channels, views	376,360
Skype contacts and IM advising calls	15,443
Blog follows	591,214
Twitter/microblog follows	195,724
Digital Video Conferences (DVCs) participants	2,151
EdUSA newrow webinar sessions attendees	6,955
EducationUSA interactive sessions	3,170
Virtual fairs—EdUSA booth and session visitors	16,484
Mobile App Users	8,206
Total	*3,866,833*
Total unique website visitors (center and flagship websites)	5,519,342
Total contacts	12,920,729

SOURCE: EducationUSA Global Guide 2015, 6.

about the U.S. higher education system and application processes. These advisors help international students and their families navigate the U.S. college admissions process by providing accurate, comprehensive, and current information about the full range of accredited U.S. institutions of higher education. They promote all accredited U.S. higher education institutions, assist students with the application process, and facilitate pre-departure orientations. They also work with U.S. higher education professionals to increase international student enrollment in the United States, looking for the student's best fit in accredited U.S. higher education institutions.

In addition to providing print and online materials at EducationUSA advising centers, advisors reach prospective student audiences through higher education fairs and outreach events at local schools, universities, and other public venues. Extending outreach beyond personal interaction, the network reaches millions of students through websites, webinars, and social media platforms.

The 400+ advising centers are staffed by EducationUSA advisors, many of whom have first-hand experience studying in the United States and all of whom receive training and support from ECA. All advisors must adhere to EducationUSA ethical standards, abide by the EducationUSA policy to refrain from working with commission-based recruitment agents, and undergo U.S. State Department-approved training

Regional Educational Advising Coordinators

Regional Educational Advising Coordinators (REACs), working under the aegis of the Institute of International Education (IIE), support and enhance the EducationUSA network within their world region to foster international student mobility and advance ECA's public diplomacy goals. REACs collaborate with U.S. embassies and consulates and provide guidance, leader-

Comprehensive

- Maintains up-to-date library of reference books/materials
- Offers individual and group advising, information on financial aid, and pre-departure orientations/information
- Has advising staff with college degrees (U.S. bachelor's degree or equivalent) who are proficient in spoken and written English
- Provides virtual advising and consulting through email, web, social media, instant messenger, etc.
- Maintains computers with internet access for visitors
- Organizes and participates in alumni group activities and college fairs

- Has existing relationships with local high school counselors and university administrators and conducts outreach to them
- Provides briefings for visiting U.S. representatives on the local education system
- Is able to describe and compare U.S. and host country educational systems
- Is able to verify Ministry of Education recognition/certification of local high schools and universities
- Facilitates communication with local secondary and tertiary institutions for visiting U.S. representatives
- Organizes public presentations for visiting U.S. representatives at off-site locations

- Hosts visiting U.S. representatives for promotional presentations
- Organizes general U.S. higher education orientation sessions, often featuring visiting U.S. representatives
- Provides information on local government and foundation scholarships, and other financial aid
- Displays college- and university-provided materials
- Adheres to the EducationUSA Principles of Good Practice

Standard

- Maintains up-to-date library of reference books/materials
- Has at minimum a half-time advisor or sufficient hours to meet local demand at standard service level
- Has advising staff proficient in spoken and written English
- Offers individual advising
- Provides information on financial aid
- Is able to describe and compare U.S. and host country educational systems

- Has existing relationships with local high school counselors and university administrators
- Displays U.S. college- and university-provided materials
- Has access to video conferencing equipment, e.g., internet-based
- Offers pre-departure information/orientations
- Participates in college fairs, hosting the EducationUSA booth

- Provides briefings for visiting U.S. representatives on the local education system
- Is able to verify Ministry of Education recognition/certification of local high schools and universities
- Organizes general U.S. higher education orientation sessions, often featuring visiting U.S. representatives
- Adheres to the EducationUSA Principles of Good Practice

Reference

- Maintains up-to-date library of reference books/materials

- Has no advisor or only minimal assistance is available

- Adheres to the EducationUSA Principles of Good Practice

SOURCE: EducationUSA Global Guide 2015, 8.

FIGURE 6.1 EducationUSA Advising Centers: Levels of Service

ship, training, and assessment for EducationUSA advisors and advising centers to maintain and improve the quality of their work. These regional coordinators also serve as resources to the U.S. higher education community on local educational systems and the development of strategies for increasing international enrollments and U.S. study abroad.

REACs are based in 14 locations worldwide:

- ✳ Sub-Saharan Africa (Ghana and South Africa)
- ✳ East Asia and Pacific (China, Japan, and Thailand)
- ✳ Europe and Eurasia (Hungary, Turkey, and Ukraine)
- ✳ Middle East and North Africa (United Arab Emirates)
- ✳ South and Central Asia (India and Pakistan)
- ✳ Western Hemisphere (Brazil, Ecuador, and Mexico)

Resources and Services to U.S. Higher Education

The U.S. higher education community can look to the EducationUSA network for advice about developing regional and country-specific recruitment strategies, creating programs and products to connect with students, as well as obtaining information about the local education system and admission issues. EducationUSA advisors also use their expertise to help U.S. institutions develop relationships with local universities and schools for recruitment, study abroad programs, and deeper institutional partnerships.

EducationUSA advisors around the world are experts in understanding their countries' national education systems and have long-standing and strong relationships with local universities and secondary schools. If a U.S. college or university is considering establishing or expanding study abroad programs, they can contact an EducationUSA advisor in the target country to explore the information and services they may offer. EducationUSA staff also frequently provides in-person and online student recruitment training sessions (including videos) for regions or specific countries through various education organizations. Additionally, the EducationUSA network facilitates conversations with consortia, works with other government agencies, and offers insight on leveraging scholarships.

One of the most reliable and comprehensive resources on international student mobility is the Institute of International Education's annual *Open Doors* report, funded by the U.S. Department of State's Bureau of Educational and Cultural Affairs. *Open Doors* provides data on numbers and key characteristics of international students and scholars in the United States and of U.S. students studying abroad for credit back at their home institution. *Open Doors* data are used by U.S. embassies, the Departments of State, Commerce, and Education, and other federal, state, and local organizations to inform policy decisions about educational exchanges, trade in educational services, and study abroad activity. U.S. colleges and universities, foreign governments, and the media rely on these annually updated statistics to understand trends in student mobility. The report also provides data on places of origin, sources of financial support, fields of study, host institutions, academic level, and rates of growth of the international student population by state and by leading municipalities, as well as on the economic impact of international students to the state where they study and the nation as a whole. Also included in the publication are sections on international scholars in the United States and Intensive English Programs.[2]

Increasingly, U.S. colleges and universities are exploring collaborative approaches to international student recruitment through state and regional higher education consortia. There are currently more than 35 consortia operating across the United States. These groups, which are independently governed and organized under an array of structural models, can serve as an excellent way to foster collaboration among institutions and promote a city, state, or region as a destination for international students. EducationUSA supports these groups by providing guidance on group recruitment strategies, convening consortia members during the annual EducationUSA Forum in Washington D.C., and maintaining a closed listserv for consortia leaders. EducationUSA can help higher education professionals learn more about the consortia in their state or region and the ways that they can engage with colleagues in their area.

The EducationUSA network maintains close ties with the range of federal agencies that play a role in international student mobility and works collaboratively with them to provide guidance and support for both students seeking to study in the United States and U.S. colleges and universities seeking to recruit them. These include the U.S. Department of State's Bureau of Consular Affairs; the U.S. Department of Homeland Security's Office of Academic Engagement, United States Commercial Service, Office of Postsecondary Education, and National Center for Education Statistics; the U.S. Department of Commerce's U.S. Educational Institutions and Intensive English Programs; and the U.S. Department of Education's International Affairs Office. Coordination of these inter-agency efforts is led by the Department of State's Bureau of Educational and Cultural Affairs (ECA).

There are many foreign government-sponsored scholarship programs for international students seeking to study in the United States. These programs vary widely by country and many focus on specific degrees, disciplines, or types of U.S. study. The EducationUSA network can serve as a resource for U.S. colleges and

---

[2] More information on *Open Doors* data can be found at <www.iie.org/opendoors>.

universities seeking to learn more about these scholarship programs and how to recruit sponsored students. REACs can provide additional information about foreign government scholarship programs offered to students within their respective regions. REAC contact details are in the "log-in" section of the EducationUSA. state.gov website. The annual *EducationUSA Global Guide*, also available on the website, includes information about national scholarship programs.[3]

The annual EducationUSA Forum, held each summer in Washington, D.C., provides higher education professionals an opportunity to engage with EducationUSA advisors from around the world. Approximately 50 advisors from around the world and all 14 REACs, as well as U.S. Department of State and IIE EducationUSA staff, present the latest regional and country-specific trends and tips for strategic international recruitment planning. EducationUSA regional fora, held internationally, bring together advisors from one world region and U.S. higher education institutions to share best practices. U.S. higher education professionals are invited to present specialized training sessions and to network with advisors and REACs during these events.

EducationUSA partners with CollegeWeekLive (CWL) for a virtual international student college fair during International Education Week (International Students' Day) in November. In the 2014 event, over 20,000 students and parents from 206 countries and territories interacted with EducationUSA advisors and representatives from 178 U.S. colleges and universities. Students' interactions with U.S. institutions totaled 68,565 (*EducationUSA Global Guide* 2015). EducationUSA and CWL have also presented additional global International Students' Day fairs, along with regional fairs aimed at markets in Asia, Latin America, Europe, the Middle East, and Africa. EducationUSA plans to continue its involvement in these International Students' Day fairs in the coming year as part of its public-private partnership with CWL.

[3] Additional information on scholarships offered by U.S. and non-U.S. sources is available on IIE's website: <www.FundingUSStudy.org>.

Online Resources and Services

EducationUSA offers a variety of virtual programming and resources to help higher education institutions reach out to international students. These include a special higher education section of the EducationUSA website, the *Higher Education Institution News* monthly virtual newsletter, EducationUSA webinars, and social media platforms to engage potential international students.

In March 2015, EducationUSA launched a new website. EducationUSA.state.gov was built with a responsive design and as a mobile-friendly site. The site has Google Translate embedded, providing automated translation into 90 languages. The site features updated design, functionality, and content. In addition to sections with refreshed content for international students, their parents, and U.S. colleges and universities, there is a new section for foreign governments and foreign institutions of higher education. The integration of Zoomph on the homepage facilitates pulling users' social media posts from Facebook, Instagram, Google+, and Twitter that use the hashtag #EducationUSA to create a more interactive and dynamic site. Additionally, with links to social media on each page, users can share pertinent information about study in the United States with their own social networks. The website also contains a special resource section for U.S. higher education, State Department employees, and EducationUSA advisors. Users can request a login to gain access to key educational market intelligence, including the annual *EducationUSA Global Guide*, 170 country fact sheets, the weekly *Social Media Digest*, and more.

The U.S. higher education section of the EducationUSA website helps institutions develop and refine their international student recruitment strategies. Staff members at Council for Higher Education Accreditation (CHEA)-recognized accredited U.S. postsecondary institutions or at a national education membership association can request a free login. Once logged in, higher education representatives can access recruitment resources and find contact details for Regional Educational Advising Coordinators (REACs), as well as submit financial aid opportunities and campus news stories to raise awareness of their institutions.

EducationUSA publishes the *Higher Education Institution News* monthly. The newsletter is the primary vehicle through which EducationUSA communicates with U.S. higher education professionals. It contains updates from the U.S. Department of State; information about opportunities to collaborate with EducationUSA; interesting and emerging trends in international student mobility; and information about upcoming events, including recruitment fairs, EducationUSA programming, and/or workshops for the U.S. higher education community and international students.

U.S. higher education professionals can volunteer to present at EducationUSA webinar sessions produced either in Washington, D.C. or at the advising centers globally. Webinar sessions typically focus on a topic from EducationUSA's *Your 5 Steps to U.S. Study*. Past topics highlighted researching admission at U.S. universities, applying for financial aid, writing admissions essays, and the like.

Interested individuals can volunteer via the website; however, if someone is interested in assisting with a webinar in a specific country they can also reach out to the advising center directly. All EducationUSA centers globally have access to an online webinar platform, and there are country rooms set up to maximize crowdsourcing of sessions from multiple centers.

EducationUSA, in collaboration with the U.S. Department of State's Bureau of International Information Programs, launched the EducationUSA Interactive series in the summer of 2014. These web chats feature international students, U.S. higher education representatives, and other experts discussing American campus culture, financing U.S. study, and the U.S. visa process. Recent programs attracted more than 3,000 viewers from around the world who watched and asked questions using the program's popular chat feature via chatrooms that are dedicated by language. U.S. embassies and EducationUSA centers participate in the live interactive sessions and feed questions via teleprompter to the studio panel in real-time.

Social media and other virtual communication tools link the EducationUSA network to students and U.S. higher education institutions, and are vital to EducationUSA's goal of promoting U.S. higher education abroad. A newly-launched Study Abroad Office within ECA will help study abroad staff in the U.S. expand their programs abroad, increase the numbers and diversity of their U.S. students going abroad for short-term and long-term study, and widen the destinations to which they are headed.

U.S. institutions can quickly and effectively reach prospective international students through the EducationUSA network's social and virtual media channels. EducationUSA social media channels and webpages reached 9.4 million people in 2014. In addition to popular, dominant social media networks such as Facebook, Twitter, and YouTube, EducationUSA advising centers embrace country-specific social media platforms to better engage with the students they serve. For example, advisors in Russian-speaking countries reach students on Vkontakte, while advisors in China connect to students on the popular micro-blogging site Sina Weibo. In parts of the world like Belarus, Iran, and Syria, where an in-person advising presence is not feasible, EducationUSA advising centers operate exclusively on virtual platforms.

EducationUSA expanded its online presence in 2014. In addition to producing the new *Study in the USA* video, which garnered over 15,000 YouTube views by early 2015, the network launched a new Facebook page (EducationUSA—U.S. Higher Education Professionals) to further share topical information with U.S. higher education professionals. The EducationUSA Facebook page for prospective students had approximately 252,000 likes by May 2016.

U.S. higher education professionals are encouraged to engage with EducationUSA on social media. Institutions can submit content such as videos, financial aid opportunities, and campus news for hosting on the EducationUSA website and on social media platforms. Those interested in localizing their institution's social media recruitment can reach out to the REACs and advisors to learn more about how social media is used in their regions.

Global Recruiting Strategies

Given the wide variety of ways in which EducationUSA can assist in reaching out to international students, below are a few suggestions for how institutions can start working with EducationUSA to enhance their global recruiting strategy.

* Consult Regional Educational Advising Coordinators (REACs), the first point of contact for region- and country-specific advice.

* Ask REACs about connecting with education ministries and scholarship-granting bodies in the region.

* Encourage prospective students to connect with EducationUSA advisors early in the application and college search process to save time and ensure accurate information.

* Demystify the U.S. application and admissions process by directing international students to *Your 5 Steps to U.S. Study* at the EducationUSA website. This resource guides international students through the application and admission processes for undergraduate, graduate, and English language programs, as well as short-term educational opportunities at U.S. colleges and universities. The steps give students a timeline and practical tips to navigate the process.

* Conduct market research to find regions or countries that fit your school's recruiting priorities. Take advantage of *Open Doors*, the regional information in EducationUSA's annual *Global Guide*, and the EducationUSA Center and/or Country Fact Sheets available on the EducationUSA website.

* Visit EducationUSA advising centers to make a presentation and gain exposure. REACs and advisors can help representatives get the most out of their international recruiting trips. Contact the center in advance to arrange a meeting or school visit, present a group session, or attend a college fair.

* Encourage international alumni to get involved with EducationUSA advising centers. Word-of-mouth is an important factor in building institutional name recognition overseas, and alumni can be excellent ambassadors. EducationUSA advisors can assist in setting up alumni presentations.

* Leverage state and regional consortia collaboration with the EducationUSA network to promote your institution to students abroad.

EducationUSA staff around the world stand ready to assist U.S. higher education institutions make connections with potential students, establish study abroad partnerships and programs, and better understand the competitive environment for recruitment of international students. Through the combined efforts of U.S. universities and colleges, supported by EducationUSA centers and other programs of the U.S. Department of State, almost 1 million students from around the world are enrolled on U.S. campuses, and over 300,000 American students are studying abroad each year.

SEVEN

Collaboration

with Internationally-Based Counselors

KATHLEEN SCHULTZ
High School Counselor
NIST International School

BECKY KONOWICZ
Director of
International Admission
Santa Clara University

JOHANNA FISHBEIN
University Advisor
United World College of
S.E. Asia–Dover Campus

Collaboration with Internationally-Based Counselors

Maintaining a high level of ethical behavior is one of the most important aspects of university counseling, whether domestic or international in scope. High stakes admission and pressures to attend particular universities result in additional stressors, thus increasing the importance of fair and ethical action in the face of these challenges. High school counselors strive to act in the best interests of the student at all times and can look to the American School Counselor Association (ASCA) for a set of recommendations that applies to the college counseling realm as well. Counselors should aim to work within their professional expertise and inform students of any limitations in helping them.

Continuing professional education, along with honest, personal reflection, is paramount to providing the most useful assistance to students looking to continue their studies. One must actively attempt to understand the diverse cultural backgrounds of the students they work with in addition to respecting their cultural norms. For example, it is an American value to encourage students to leave the family home after graduation, and some counselors encourage parents to follow this custom in their own families. However, it is important for counselors to try to understand the culture of their students and then evaluate how their own cultural/ethnic/racial identity has an impact on their values and beliefs about the college. In an effort to diffuse personal biases, one can learn some best ethical practices by consulting with other professionals and having a readily accessible support network of such professionals. Joining professional organizations and associations aids in keeping up with the latest ethics trends and research in college counseling. Whenever possible, it is important to exchange ideas with professionals at conferences and regional get-togethers, or via social media or any other appropriate forum.

Defining Roles

Whatever one's role in international higher education, it is vital to understand the various people working within the international education landscape, and the way in which they interact (or do not interact) with one another.

Internationally-Based School Counselors

Many international and local high schools employ school counselors to help guide students through the varied university application processes around the world. School counselors tend to work closely with students in their last two years of high school, guiding them in career exploration and supporting them throughout the university application process. The degree and type of instruction varies widely: in some schools, the school counselor may only manage university applications and university advising, whereas in others they may teach, be a member of the administration, or provide social and emotional support to students. In addition, the way in which school counselors advise students varies from school to school. Some counselors advise students based on their last name regardless of university destination, while in other cases, they advise students based on the country to which they plan to apply. Dependent upon school resources and the other roles a school counselor may hold in the school, a school counselor's role may include sending documents to support student applications, or they may provide support not only with choosing where to apply to university, but also with essay writing, interview preparation, advocating for applicants and all aspects of the university application process. It is also important to note that school counselors are often the first point of contact for parents during the university application process. This is an important position as the counselor provides workshops, information evenings, and is a consistent resource for information.

Although the role of a school counselor varies school to school, the school counselor is an excellent 'point person' for various items including: planning and scheduling school visits in the region, queries related to school curriculum (or local curriculum), general inquiries about the country, and specific queries related to applicants. The international community of school counselors is exceptionally collaborative.

International Independent Counselors

As universities have become more mobile, recruiting around the world, there has been a great increase in international independent counselors. In some cases, these counselors may be located in a school without a school counselor, but in most cases international independent counselors work on their own. An international student may choose to work with an independent counselor because they do not have a school counselor available to them or because they require more attention and 'hand holding' than a school counselor may be able to provide (the availability of the counselor will vary by school). International counselors can be hired to provide individualized support throughout the university application process, and may be hired as early as middle school to provide support with choosing classes, etc. Independent counselors are paid as consultants and their fees vary greatly, depending on their market and experience.

In the current international landscape, there is no regulation of independent counselors. Thus, if choosing to work with an independent counselor, it is imperative

to do one's research to ensure proper accreditation and ethical handling of the admissions processes and that the counselor adheres to the National Association for College Admission Counseling's (NACAC) Statement of Principles of Good Practice (SPGP). Independent counselors should be members of NACAC or the International Association for College Admission Counseling and should also have accreditation from the Independent Education Consultant Association (IECA) or Higher Education Consultants Association (HECA). In addition, independent counselors who have worked as a school counselor prior to becoming independent are often highly regarded. A reputable independent counselor will not write essays on a student's behalf or falsify any information related to university applications.

International independent counselors may be a part of the school counselor network that is often available in many cities and countries around the world. When universities visit high schools, they may also choose to meet with independent counselors as well to network and introduce their university to the independent counselor. Independent counselors are often present at conferences and networking events throughout the international higher education community.

International Admissions Officers

Given the nuances associated with an international student application, universities often commit dedicated resources to international recruitment and admissions for their university. In some cases, an international admissions officer will manage recruitment only and not the reading of applications; in most U.S. universities, the international admissions officer will do both. International admissions officers' scope may include specific geographic regions or they may be responsible for the entire world. These officers meet with students, parents, school counselors, and other advisors or counselors around the world to not only provide information about their own institutions, but in many cases to also provide general information about U.S. universities, the liberal arts, financial aid, and the application process. International admission officers are often able to support international school counselors and their students and parents by running general information sessions for students, parents, and administrators.

International admissions officers are responsible for familiarizing themselves and their admissions colleagues with the schools in a given country and the diversity of educational curriculums that exist internationally. They are tasked with identifying the rigor in a curriculum and the grade scales that are used in international schools around the world. In an admissions committee structure, the international admission office is also responsible for advocating for international applicants that would be considered a 'best fit' for the university. In U.S. universities where financial aid is available to international students, the international admissions team may work closely with the financial aid office to determine candidates for this financial aid.

International Student Advisors

In addition to school and independent counselors, many countries around the world have strategically placed higher education advisors 'onsite' to advise students interested in pursuing a higher education degree in their given countries. An example lies with the U.S. government having established several EducationUSA offices around the world.[4] These advisors can be an invaluable resource to international admissions officers as they generally have an excellent overview of the educational landscape in a country, and these advising offices may have access to a more local population. EducationUSA offices host university visits, provide student visa information, and generally advise students on undergraduate and graduate opportunities in the U.S. Some EducationUSA offices do charge students a small fee for their services. Other countries have similar educational advising organizations, such as the British Council and Canadian Higher Education Commission.

---

[4] For more on EducationUSA, see Chapter 6, Role of EducationUSA in International Recruitment.

International Agents

Some universities employ international agents to represent them in-country. A student should never be charged a fee by one of these agents as they are employed by the recruiting university. If a university is utilizing such an agent, it will be the role of the international admissions officer to educate and train the agency, while also monitoring their ethical practices. (For more on working with international agents, *see* Chapter 8, International Student Recruitment Agents.)

Networking across Time Zones

There are 24 time zones and international-based school counselors may need to reach out to each of them. In the past decade more and more international admissions counselors have increased efforts to travel across these time zones to connect with school counselors face-to-face and their students. In addition, there has been a growth of support for school-based counselors to visit and tour universities. For those international admissions counselors who do not travel or high school-based counselors who do not receive many university visitors, "armchair recruitment" (recruiting students across the world from one's desk) has evolved greatly to allow information-sharing through a multitude of avenues, including but not limited to: email, mailing materials, listserv involvements, webinars, social media, and networking at conferences. Today, many admissions counselors utilize a combination of both travel-based and armchair efforts. It is important to consider strategies for communicating across time zones whether for recruitment travel or armchair recruitment activities. Here are a few tips to keep in mind:

* Patience: delayed responses can occur due to time zone difference, internet connections, mail speed, varied holidays, natural disasters, political unrest, firewalls, and general cultural influences in communication styles and preferences.

* Communication channels: email may not be the preferred communication tool for students, families, and counselors in a particular country.

Researching and being flexible for alternative methods such as social media or print mail may be necessary in some markets.

✳ Relationships with school-based counselors develop over time. Whether in person or via armchair, allow for the time to nurture these relationships.

Useful Conferences

In the field of international admissions there are several conferences that draw school-based international counselors and allow for meaningful relationship-building and professional development. The following list of organizations hosting conferences is not comprehensive, but provides an excellent starting point when considering this avenue for working with international school-based counselors:

✳ International Association for College Admission Counseling (membership required)

✳ National Association for College Admission Counseling (membership required)

✳ Council of International Schools Institutes and Forums (membership required)

Hosting Counselors

Similar to domestic counselor fly-ins or campus visit days, universities should consider hosting international school-based counselors for visits to the campus. Often the only trusted voice for their students and families about university options, a counselor that has toured and experienced a campus significantly impacts their ability to convey the unique aspects and offerings of a particular university. When planning to host one or a group of international school-based counselors there are a few internationally friendly additions to keep in mind:

✳ Jetlag: allow for a flexible schedule or down time for a counselor's traveling across time zones.

✳ Connect counselors with current international students, who can share their perspective of campus life.

✳ Offer a meeting with an international admission counselor to cover nuanced admission require-

ments and financial aid/scholarship offerings for students attending schools overseas.

International High School Counselors as a Resource

International high school counselors can provide practical and important information for the traveling admissions counselor.

CURRICULUM UNDERSTANDING

Many international schools have some "local" students—students who study the national curriculum and then transfer into the international school—or students that study the national curriculum along with their international one. As such, counselors at international high schools have some understanding of the academic content of regional secondary diplomas. These counselors often evaluate student transcripts before students can be admitted, and in doing so they become familiar with grading scales, leaving requirements, and specific courses or programs. They can talk about similarities and differences between the various curricula and demonstrate how these variations develop a stronger student. Because of the strong network of international school counselors, if they do not have the answers, they are able to refer to someone else in the community who does.

VISIT PLANNING

While high schools that have school or college counselors typically welcome university visitors, it can be difficult to schedule visits to schools that are not as well-staffed. International high school counselors can help make recommendations to admissions officers about other schools or counselors to visit in their city or region and the best way to travel between areas. While most schools do not let their students miss classes for university admissions presentations (especially when the visits number in the hundreds!) they often are able to be flexible and some counselors even plan city visits for admissions representatives. It is always worth reaching out and asking a counselor what would be the best way to visit as many schools as possible in a city or where would be an appropriate venue to host a larger gathering. Counselors may also know of schools that have a great number of local students or representatives in an EducationUSA Center.

CULTURAL UNDERSTANDING

As many international high school counselors are also ex-patriots in the countries in which they work, they are well-equipped to promote cultural understanding and awareness. Individuals less familiar with particular regions can benefit from their experience and insights.

International Admissions Officers as Diplomats

International admissions officers are educational diplomats who value the diversity of education systems around the world and work to best serve students' transition into the U.S. system of higher education. Understanding foreign education pathways, grading scales, curriculums, and entrance and exit exams are essential when recruiting international students. World systems do not always align perfectly with one another; thus unbiased scrutiny is required from these officers. It is important to evaluate each student within the context of their own school system—no country's education system is intrinsically superior to another. The hallmark strengths that attract international students to U.S. higher education include the vast choices available among institutions and various admissions requirements. Knowing that many international students come from a system where one exam (exit or entrance) determines their access to higher education in their home country highlights the nuanced and varied application and admission requirements in the U.S.

An international admissions officer is an advocate for deciphering, understanding, and building a bridge between two educational systems. Understanding the challenges and opportunities international students face within the application process can lead to building a more inclusive and internationally-friendly admissions office. Such challenges include admissions and higher education terminology, higher education's structure in the U.S., application requirements, and the diversity of the more than 3,000 institutions. For example, many educational systems refer to "college" as secondary school, whereas, in the U.S. "college" and "university" are interchangeable terminology. Another example is that most international schools do not offer a GPA. Therefore, when using such terminology or benchmarks, offering a converted metric to their own curriculum and grades for the particular international school can be useful. For example, if it is an IB school, one can use the 1–7 range for grades instead of the 4.0 GPA metric.

Building practices and policies within recruitment and admissions that allow for flexibility and accommodation instead of uniform rigidity will best serve the institution and student. Some school-based international counselors work in a school with significant support in terms of resources such as the Naviance software and a high volume of U.S. university representatives visiting. Others may be working with limited resources without hosting any U.S. university visitors. Therefore, adapting practices to unforeseen circumstances and limitations can showcase an institution as understanding of the complicated and nuanced issues an international applicant must navigate. International school-based counselors can be an important resource as an institution's policies and practices are reviewed.

EIGHT

International Student Recruitment Agents

EDDIE WEST

Director of International Initiatives
National Association for College Admission Counseling

2016 AACRAO INTERNATIONAL GUIDE

International Student Recruitment Agents

International student recruitment via third-party agents is a common strategy of universities in the United Kingdom, Australia, and Canada. It is also an industry norm at foreign language schools, such as intensive English programs (IEPs) in the U.S. and other popular international student destinations. However, despite signs of recent growth, the recruitment practice remains far less prevalent when it comes to degree program admissions at U.S. universities.

Agent-based international student recruitment has been the subject of considerable controversy. Some admissions professionals vouch for the practice, believing it both effective and sound. Others remain strongly opposed to it, on practical and sometimes principled grounds. This chapter includes an overview of agents—who they are, who they are not, and what they do. It also provides recommendations to aid institutional decision-making about this international student recruitment strategy.

What is an agency? Who is an agent?

International student recruitment agencies are private companies—or units of larger firms—in the business of recruiting international students. Universities, colleges, and language programs that contract with third-party agencies pay them for their international recruitment services, usually contingent upon the enrollment of referred students. Detailed below, these per-capita commissions payments underpin most agencies' business models.

Agents are individual recruiters, and while they sometimes work alone in a sole proprietorship, more often they serve as employees of a larger firm—the agency. The agency owner may compensate their agents by a salary, by commissions (*commissioned agents*), or both. Agents offer prospective students (recruits) advice about institutions, university application processes, and preparatory language training options. Many also assist students with the acquisition of visas, health and travel insurance, and flight reservations. Some provide pre-departure orientations. To families with minimal familiarity with these processes—and oftentimes limited English language ability as well—the handholding agents provide can feel invaluable.

From an institutional standpoint, agents serve international marketing, promotional, and recruitment functions. Agents provide year-round, in-country representation for the schools they represent. Universities cannot afford to staff and run dedicated offices in all the countries from which they recruit. Thus utilizing agents is seen as a pragmatic, alternative way of raising the institution's visibility among local students and families. Agents also provide institutions with market intelligence, alerting them to changing student preferences and other local trends. And, as with the assistance they provide families, agents can help their partner schools navigate cultural and language barriers.

Though definitive data is scant, estimates suggest that as many as 20,000 to 30,000 agents operate worldwide. While a small but growing number of agents conduct their entire business online, most offer in-person services to prospective students in their home countries. Functionally, they are akin to travel agents before the internet—storefront locations students and families visit in order to obtain help and information about studying overseas. Some agents specialize in recruiting students to certain countries, for example, the United Kingdom. Some specialize in recruiting to specific academic levels, such as high schools. Larger agencies fulfill all of these roles, boasting a diverse partner portfolio as they recruit students to different countries, institutions and programs.

Most agencies are small businesses, employing 10 or fewer agents, while some are far bigger operations, with headquarters in one city and branch offices in others. Particularly in countries with huge landmasses and populations (for example, India and China) larger agents sometimes subcontract with external individuals or smaller firms. These are called *sub-agents*. Sub-agents extend the master agent's recruitment reach to other locales. The subcontracting relationship between an agent and sub-agent involves revenue-sharing agreements.

The business relationship between an agency and a university or college for which it recruits is typically governed by a contract. In some cases institutions agree to pay the agency a specified fee to fund promotional efforts aimed at raising its visibility in the area(s) where the agency operates. Such promotions may be components of a broader business or marketing plan. However, a far more common arrangement is for the institution to pay its partner agency only when a referred student applies, is granted admission, and successfully enrolls. These payments are ordinarily called commissions or per-capita commissions, though some schools use less charged terminology, such as "referral fees," or "marketing support."

Schools send individual commission payments to their agency partners after a referred student has enrolled in classes and the add-drop/refund deadline has passed. Commissions generally take the form of either a flat rate or percentage payment. For example, the contract may call for the school to make a flat payment of $1,000 for every enrolled international student the agent referred. Alternatively, it may stipulate that the school sends the agent 10 or 15 percent of the student's paid tuition for their first term or academic year.

In the Higher Education Act that governs administration of the Title IV federal financial aid program, the term *commissions* is referred to as *incentive-based recruit-*ment. Incentive-based recruitment is illegal with respect to U.S. students who are eligible for federal financial aid. A "foreign student carve out," as it is colloquially known, permits institutions to engage in incentive-based international student recruitment. The relevant language of the statute follows:

> *The institution will not provide any commission, bonus or other incentive payment based directly or indirectly on success in securing enrollments or financial aid to any persons or entities engaged in any student recruiting or admission activities or in making decisions regarding the award of student financial assistance, except that this paragraph shall not apply to the recruitment of foreign students residing in foreign countries who are not eligible to receive Federal student assistance* (20 USC §1094[a] [20]).

The domestic prohibition against incentive-based recruitment of American students came about in 1992 in response to "waste, fraud and abuse" within the federal financial aid program, much of which was attributed to for-profit schools. The fact that incentive-based recruitment of domestic students is against the law in the U.S. is one reason it is controversial, albeit permitted, internationally.

Another source of controversy concerns allegations of recruiting agencies' involvement in international admissions fraud. Over the years, media reports have depicted agents employing ghostwriters for student essays, forging recommendation letters, doctoring transcripts, and helping international students cheat on standardized tests like the SAT and TOEFL. When unqualified or unprepared students gain university admission, they often struggle to keep up with academic requirements once enrolled. Some then resort to plagiarism or other forms of cheating to avoid failing their courses, thus perpetuating dishonest tactics used during the admissions process.

Another controversy involves a practice called double-dipping. Referred to in the real estate industry as "dual agency," this is when both parties to a transaction—the buyer and the seller—pay the same agent. International student recruitment agents that engage in double-dipping receive a commissions payment from a partner school while simultaneously being paid for advising services by the student or his/her family. U.S. state laws mandate the disclosure of such arrangements by real estate agents, given the obvious potential for conflict of interest. However, international students working with third-party education agents lack such statutory protections. Institutions that work with agents can help safeguard students' interests by taking steps to encourage transparency about this practice where it does occur, as discussed later in this chapter.

Campus Impacts of an Agent-Based International Recruitment Strategy

A first step in considering whether to engage third-party international student recruitment agencies is to assess campus readiness and potential impacts. The decision to undertake agent-based international student recruitment or expand its scope will affect many departments and campus officials. These colleagues should be involved in exploratory discussions as well as planning and implementation.

RISK MANAGEMENT

Agent-based student recruitment entails a variety of institutional risks. For example, students and/or the institution run the risk of incurring financial damage. In 2008 Gateway 21, one of the largest recruitment agencies in Japan, declared sudden, unexpected bankruptcy. The firm had collected the equivalent of approximately 9 million U.S. dollars from more than 1000 students, but failed to remit these monies by the time it went under. Legal action by agencies constitutes another risk. For example, a 2014 lawsuit alleging breach of contract filed by a former agency partner of a Canadian university named the president and other institutional personnel as defendants in the case. Still other risks include misrepresentation and damage to reputation, examples of which are illustrated in the Figure 8.1, A Cautionary Tale. Given the potential pitfalls inherent in this recruitment method, it is vitally important to involve risk management officials in related decision-making. Consulting with campus colleagues in the office of risk management or trusted external experts about appropriate risk mitigation strategies is essential. These officials will also want to factor the planned international student recruitment activity into the campus's overall risk portfolio.

There are numerous risks entailed in agent-based international student recruitment, risks exacerbated by insufficient institutional oversight. The experiences of North Dakota's Dickinson State University serve as a compelling cautionary tale.

In the early 2000s, Dickinson State University (DSU) utilized recruitment agents to generate international student enrollments in its international articulation agreement programs. In February 2012, an internal audit of these programs, requested by then-DSU President D.C. Coston, concluded that the operations were "seriously lacking controls and oversight." For example, transcripts from the students' home country were said to be "a basic excel spreadsheet where the student can enter any class or grade

they desire." The investigation concluded that over several years DSU had awarded degrees to hundreds of international students who had not completed program requirements. Consequently, the degrees were rescinded.

The audit cited the involvement of China-based student recruitment agents as one problem. Agents involved were found to have been misrepresenting themselves as DSU employees and, in referring students, were said to be "driven by quantity of student and not quality." The report stated that agents told students that "once at DSU they could change their major and/or take whatever classes they'd like." The auditors recommended that DSU terminate all its agreements with agents, in favor of utilizing the institution's own recruitment personnel.

President Coston, the Interim Registrar, the offices of Multicultural Affairs and Institutional Research, and AACRAO International Education Services collaborated to eventually restore the integrity of the university's international admissions operation, but not before the university suffered grave damage.

These and related events at Dickinson State University were extraordinary. However, institutions would be mistaken to assume serious problems could not happen on their campus. Working with third-party representatives operating in vastly different language and cultural environments requires tremendous care and vigilant oversight.

FIGURE 8.1   A Cautionary Tale

LEGAL COUNSEL AND BUSINESS OFFICE

The institution's office of legal counsel or external counsel should be engaged in the formation and execution of contracts with international student recruitment agencies. These experts can advise about important federal, state, municipal, and campus regulatory requirements. Because third-party recruitment agencies are often considered vendors, prospective contractors will in some cases have to register as such and take part in a formal request for proposal (RFP) procurement process. In any case, an important note: when contracting with an agency, it is the entire institution entering into the legal relationship, not only the campus unit or official responsible for day-to-day interactions. Obtaining advice from trusted legal counsel is imperative. (*See* "Contracting with Agencies" on page 73.)

ACCOUNTS PAYABLE

Accounts Payable will be directly impacted by the decision to initiate or widen the scope of agency-based international student recruitment. Insofar as the activity successfully generates enrollments, this unit will see an increase in commissions invoices submitted by agency contractors. Note that some agencies request or contractually obligate their institutional partners to process invoices and remit payments within a specified timeframe. It will need to be made clear which campus official(s) will exercise the authority to approve payment of invoices, and how this will be determined, documented and communicated.

THE IMPACT ON OTHER DEPARTMENTS

Colleagues responsible for international admissions should be prepared for potential growth in international student applications, enrollment activity, and communications. Agents are likely to inquire, sometimes frequently, about admissions procedures, the admissibility of individual students, and the status of referred applications, among other matters. It will need to be determined who among international admissions staff will be responsible for interfacing with agency rep-

resentatives. Or, will this be the responsibility of another campus unit? Some institutions with long experience and numerous agency partners employ staff dedicated to agency communications and relationship development.

Campus officials who handle application processing and class section scheduling will also be affected. Additionally, if the institution conducts foreign credential evaluations in-house, it may be necessary to consider additional staffing and trainings. Crucially, campus units that provide international student services should be aware of any planned agency recruitment activity and prepared to provide supports commensurate with the anticipated growth and diversification of the student population. These include orientations, academic planning, student visa regulations advisement, and health services. Colleagues in campus housing must ensure additional accommodation space and associated residential life programming and supports. Here too sufficient coordination of campus communications with agents is key. Campus safety and career services colleagues should also be involved in planning and implementation discussions, and kept abreast of outcomes. Faculty and the human resources department need to ensure appropriate cross-cultural training of instructional personnel and staff, so that the campus community adequately supports and meaningfully includes international students. Moreover, many agents serve students who at the time of university application do not possess the English proficiency necessary for success in U.S. university classrooms. Accordingly, IEP or ESL instructors should be closely involved in related planning and assessments.

Identifying and Vetting Prospective Agency Contractors

After determining the institution's readiness to proceed with agent-based international student recruitment, the next step is identifying prospective agency contractors. Sound and thorough agency vetting will help avoid problems and optimize outcomes.

As previously mentioned, some institutions must undertake a formal request for proposal (RFP) process to identify prospective agency vendors. *However, this approach should be considered even if not required.* It can generate equitable and productive outcomes by helping institutions select the most suitable agencies. Other prudent strategies include asking trusted colleagues for introductions. Counterparts at other campuses and state consortia can be good sources of recommendations of agencies with reputations for professionalism and student-centeredness.

Considering agencies and agents who have undergone some form of quality assurance is another sound approach. Examples include trainings, certification, and membership. A number of organizations engage in these activities.

U.S. COMMERCIAL SERVICE
The U.S. Commercial Service is the trade promotion arm housed within the U.S. Department of Commerce's

International Trade Administration. It assists U.S. educational institutions and consortia with overseas promotions and partnership development. Among their services are opportunities to meet international student recruitment agencies via networking events. Although its process of vetting agencies varies by office and country, the Commercial Service strives to involve only those they consider "most reputable". It is also worth noting that the Commercial Service's aims, and thus its perspective on agencies, differ from those of EducationUSA (*see* Figure 8.2).

NATIONAL OVERSIGHT OF AGENCIES
Some countries and cities actively regulate the international student recruitment agencies operating within their jurisdiction. For example, Vietnam's Ministry of Education and Training oversees provincial level departments entrusted with implementing and enforcing the regulation of agencies. Agency requirements include being legally established within the country,

EducationUSA is a U.S. Department of State-supported network of hundreds of advising centers in approximately 170 countries. The network promotes U.S. higher education to students around the world by offering accurate, comprehensive, and current information about opportunities to study at accredited postsecondary institutions in the United States. EducationUSA also provides U.S. colleges and universities services that support their international student recruitment and campus internationalization activities. For more information see educationusa.state.gov.

EducationUSA Policy Guidance
In contrast to the Commercial Service, U.S. State Department-supported EducationUSA advisors are prohibited from partnering with commercial recruitment agents who have contracts to represent specific U.S. universities. A policy guidance document issued by the State Department's Bureau of Educational and Cultural Affairs explains the rationale:

Commercial recruitment agents represent only those universities that pay them a fee, and commercial agents recruit exclusively for those universities. These commercial agents do not represent the breadth of the U.S. higher education system, nor can they represent U.S. universities equitably.

Commercial recruitment agents restrict the options available to foreign students in the U.S., a restriction that may lead students to choose a college or university that will not meet their needs. As a result, these students may have a less than satisfactory experience in the U.S., with lifelong ramifications for their educational and professional activities and views of the United States.

Commercial recruitment agents understandably direct their services to students with the ability to pay. EducationUSA Center association with commercial agents would undermine our public diplomacy message of outreach to well-qualified students from throughout society, including underserved sectors.

Since EducationUSA Centers benefit from U.S. taxpayer funds, they should avoid activities that may favor, or create perceptions of favoring, one U.S. institution over another. We can offer specific services either free or for a reasonable fee, but these services must lead to access to the full range of accredited institutions. Partnering with commercial agents would limit us to representing only those institutions with which the agents have a commercial arrangement.

By adhering strictly to the ethical standards of providing information that is unbiased, objective, and comprehensive, EducationUSA Centers equip foreign students to find the U.S. institutions that are right for them while enabling the full range of U.S. institutions to enroll qualified foreign students. Our goal is to invest in long-term relationships with students and institutional partners.

EXCERPT FROM "POLICY GUIDANCE FOR EDUCATIONUSA CENTERS ON COMMERCIAL RECRUITMENT AGENTS"

FIGURE 8.2

EducationUSA

meeting minimum bank deposit requirements to miti-gate the risk of financial losses, and the adequate education and training of agency personnel. Similar regulations exist in China. Consulting with legal counsel and other trusted colleagues can help the institution be informed about the legal and regulatory environments of each territory where it plans to conduct agency-based student recruitment.

REGIONAL AGENCY ASSOCIATIONS

Agency industry associations exist in a number of countries. These work to uphold and advance certain professional standards. Some have long histories while others are relatively young, and they also vary in what is required of their agency members. Examples include the Japan Association of Overseas Studies (JAOS), the Brazilian Educational and Language Travel Association (BELTA), and the Association of Russian Educational Advisors (AREA). Some of these associations belong to the Federation of Education and Language Consultant Associations (FELCA), an umbrella organization.

BRITISH COUNCIL

Unlike most American colleges and universities, higher education institutions in the United Kingdom have a long history of working with third-party international student recruitment agencies. The activity is also far more widespread in the U.K.; all but the most selective British universities have some such business relationships.

The British Council is the U.K.'s international cultural relations organization. Among its many activities is an agent training program. Individual agents who successfully complete British Council training are listed in the British Council's trained agent database. While the trainings are designed to professionalize and promote recruitment of international students to U.K. institutions, British Council-trained agents demonstrate a general commitment to good practice. They may merit closer consideration as prospective partners of U.S. institutions accordingly.

AMERICAN INTERNATIONAL RECRUITMENT COUNCIL

The American International Recruitment Council (AIRC) is a non-profit Standards Development Organization registered with the U.S. Department of Justice. Founded in 2008, the main thrust of AIRC's quality assurance activity is a program through which agencies can seek certification, based on their conformity with AIRC's certification standards. The standards evaluate organizational effectiveness, integrity of recruitment process, student and family engagement pre- and post-enrollment, institutional engagement pre- and post-recruitment, and the agency's mechanism for processing complaints.

INTERNATIONAL CONSULTANTS FOR EDUCATION AND FAIRS

International Consultants for Education and Fairs (ICEF) is a private sector company headquartered in Germany that runs agency workshops in different countries. The agency workshop is a matchmaking event that facilitates new and continuing relationships between educational institutions and international student recruitment agencies. Prior to each event, participating schools are given access to a list of participating agencies and vice-versa. Schools and agencies assess their potential compatibility and pre-schedule meetings accordingly. ICEF screens agencies as a condition of participation in its workshops via an application form and references. It also runs a variety of agent-training courses specific to recruiting students to different destination countries. The ICEF Monitor is an affiliated market intelligence publication. Besides ICEF, other vendors run similar institution-agency matchmaking workshops and media operations, such as U.K.-based StudyTravel Ltd. and its Study Travel Alphe Conferences.

FINAL GUIDANCE

Institutions that do not undertake a formal RFP vetting process should ask prospective agency vendors to complete an application or questionnaire and conduct a corresponding agency reference check.[5]

Overseas recruitment travel is another opportunity to obtain valuable information about agencies under consideration. When planning international outreach trips, visits to individual agency offices can be scheduled. Doing so will allow a first-hand look at the agency's operations and the chance to get to know their staff.

However the institution gathers information about prospective agency contractors, it is a good idea to establish a campus committee, or involve an existing one, in related deliberations. The committee can evaluate agency applications for a contractual relationship and weigh in on decisions regarding contractual terms. This approach will help preclude conflicts of interest and ensure greater campus buy-in and oversight.

Contracting with Agencies

A formal contract should be signed with any international student recruitment agency before it begins representing the institution. Moreover, it is crucial to engage campus or external legal counsel in the development of the agency contract, sometimes called an "agency agreement." This expertise is necessary to ensure sufficient institutional and student protections. Some agencies might ask to negotiate terms before a contract is signed. Many institutions will decline this request in favor of a consistent approach to their agency relationships and contracts. Institutions willing to negotiate terms are nonetheless well served by utilizing their own contract template, not one the agency itself supplies. The institution should remain firmly in the driver's seat while developing and executing the contract.

The following is recommended content for agency contracts:

✳ Contract governance and interpretation, pursuant to the laws of the specified jurisdiction of the institution.

✳ Contract start date, duration, and processes for modification, review, and renewal.
✳ Material changes affecting the relationship, and the protocol for related notifications.
✳ Prohibition of sub-contracting to sub-agents without the prior written consent of the institution.
✳ Protocol for adjudication of disputes and penalties for violations.
✳ The institution's right to legally terminate the contract subject to furnishing advance written notification of a specified period of time (*e.g.*, 30 days).

Most institutions have contracts with existing commercial partners, and these contain universally applicable clauses and other protections that can be incorporated into a formal agency contract.

It is also important to clearly define the scope of the agency's authority to represent the institution. Schools usually grant agencies limited authority to represent them and provide explicit instructions on permitted and prohibited activities. Agencies are generally authorized to provide unbiased, accurate information about the institution to prospective students and their families. They may also be permitted to assist students in assembling— not creating or embellishing—application materials for admissions and accommodations. Sound contracts also include the institution's responsibilities to the agency, such as the timely provision of important information, including updates on admissions policies, programs of study, and scholarship opportunities, if applicable.

Some institutions will specify the geographical area where the agency is authorized to perform the contracted services. This stipulation better coordinates recruitment agencies' activities in the varied territories where they occur. In some cases agencies request exclusive rights of representation in a given region, to preempt competition. But opinions are divided among institutions regarding the pros and cons of granting such exclusivity. Schools new to agency recruitment are well served by declining such requests, particularly

---

[5] The free NACAC publication *International Student Recruitment Agencies: A Guide for Schools, Colleges and Universities* includes a sample agency questionnaire and reference check questions. Available at <www.nacacnet.org>.

when considering agencies lacking verifiable track records of success recruiting for peer schools.

Good contracts will also help the institution avoid running afoul of the U.S. prohibition against incentive-based compensation for the recruitment of students eligible for federal financial assistance. In the course of its overseas activity an agent may inadvertently refer students whose citizenship status makes them eligible to receive financial aid. Dual citizens are one example. If those students enroll, receive federal aid, and the agent receives incentive compensation for their referral, the institution will have violated federal statute. Legal counsel can ensure that contract language clearly states that the institution will not make commissions payments for the recruitment of any student who is eligible for federal financial aid.

The contract should also address how the institution-agency relationship may be represented. For instance, it should be expressly prohibited for agency personnel to masquerade as employees of the institution. In addition, specify that under no circumstances is the institution obligated to formally hire the individuals serving as its agents. Agencies should also be prohibited from guaranteeing admission to prospective students.

It is best to clarify if and how the agency may use the institution's name, logo, or likeness in marketing activities. Title IV of the Higher Education Act prohibits any substantial misrepresentation by the institution regarding the nature of its educational programs. This occurs when it, *or one of its representatives*, is deemed to have made any "false, erroneous or misleading statement". Legal counsel can ensure that contracts include stipulations that require the agent to comply with the misrepresentation rule. One example of smart practice is requiring institutional pre-approval of all related advertising.

Legal counsel may also wish to include indemnification to cover instances of non-compliance and related financial consequences.

Some agencies will request that the institution supply them a certificate of representation or letter of authorization, to establish legitimacy in the eyes of students

and families. Here, too, legal counsel can advise on whether to provide this documentation and its content.

Of course contracts should also address the details of the financial relationship between the institution and agency. The terms of payment should be clearly delineated, including amounts, conditions, and timing. For information about commissions—the most common compensation arrangement between institutions and international student recruitment agencies—refer to "What is an agency? Who is an agent?" on page 67. It is important to be explicit about what will and will not be covered in remuneration. The institution may also want to specify that all payments be in U.S. dollars, to provide stability in case of fluctuating foreign currency values.

It is generally wise to prohibit the agency from handling student tuition and other monies payable to the institution, and to restrict the agency's ability to bill for any expenses incurred during their work. If reimbursement of certain expenses is permitted, these should be specified in the contract.

Agencies should be required to submit detailed invoices for all student referral-related commissions payments claimed. During the contracting process, the institution's invoicing and payment protocols should be clarified in writing, along with the agency's bank account information and other particulars regarding the transmission of commissions payments. When remitting monies via international wire transfer, per-transfer charges may apply. Whether the agency or institution will absorb these charges needs to be clarified.

An important and related quality assurance measure involves verifying the agency's role in the referral of enrollees. Good practice is to require that an e-mail from a designated agency e-mail account accompany each student application, thus tying the application to the originating agency. For applications transmitted by regular mail, a cover letter on the agency's letterhead should be enclosed. This will allow the institution to substantiate whether an agency partner deserves credit and compensation for having supported an individual student's application.

Many institutions will also include performance indicators in their agency contracts, detailing goals for numbers of students enrolled, and/or their academic performance, persistence, and graduation. It is prudent to incentivize long-term student outcomes, rather than merely application or admission activity. Doing so will encourage agencies to exercise special care in the identification and advisement of students, therefore making them more likely to refer students who will thrive over time once enrolled.

Some institutions with long experience working with international student recruitment agencies opt for a tiered approach to agency contracts and management. Agencies that have demonstrated satisfactory performance over time are accorded preferential contractual terms. Thus the institution may have first, second, and top tiers of agency partners. This earned-trust approach incentivizes good practice by rewarding agencies that meet the needs of students and institutions over a sustained period.

Regardless of the specific terms included, legal counsel should confirm which institutional officials possess the signatory, *i.e.*, legal, authority to sign and execute contracts on behalf of the campus. As mentioned earlier, when contracting with an agency, the entire institution enters into the legal relationship, not merely the campus unit or individual responsible for routine interactions. Legal counsel can also advise on whether and how the agent contract should address other relevant federal legislation, including the Family Educational Rights and Privacy Act (FERPA) and the Foreign Corrupt Practices Act (FCPA). Anti-bribery provisions of the FCPA apply to "foreign firms and persons" working "directly or through agents" and legal counsel may deem these relevant to the exchange of gifts.

Other recommended practices when contracting with agencies concern the beginning and end of the agent-institution relationship. When considering an agent-based international student recruitment strategy, a first step is to conduct an inventory of where agency contracts may already exist at the institution. Other

campus units may be currently engaged in this activity; for example, a continuing education division, or individual academic departments. Coordinating a new agency recruitment initiative with pre-existing contracts and practices elsewhere on campus is fundamental. And centralizing contracts, if not also agency communications, is recommended.

If or when the institution wishes to end an agency relationship before the formal expiration of the contract, this must take place in accordance with contractual terms (*i.e.*, advance written notification). Further, if the institution does not wish to renew an expired contract, it is wise to proactively notify the agency that the formal relationship has ended. Otherwise former agent contractors may mistakenly assume their contract is still valid, continue recruiting students, and make claims for commission upon the referral of enrollees.

Agency Management Services

As an alternative to contracting directly with agencies, some institutions choose to work through firms that provide agency management services. Private sector providers of pathway programs for international students are one example of this model. In effect, these firms act as intermediaries between the institution and a network of third-party agencies deployed to recruit for it.

In these arrangements, institutions are further removed from the recruitment occurring in their name. Thus if considering agency management services, take special care to ensure that the firm's recruitment practices—including financial incentives used, payment protocols followed, and quality controls—meet institutional standards.

Safeguarding Students

The risks of agency-based recruitment are not limited to problems for institutions. Students can also be vulnerable to misinformation, financial risk, and other adverse experiences when working with an agency that does not have their best interests at heart. Indeed, agencies are routinely alleged (or understood, depending upon one's viewpoint) to steer students to the institutions promising the most lucrative commissions payouts rather than those that are a best fit for the student.

Institutions can play an active role in safeguarding students by contractually obligating their partner agencies to ensure certain student protections. Additionally, school officials can send strong signals about the priority of student welfare via written guidelines and other communications throughout the duration of a partnership. The following measures will help strengthen the protection of students' interests:

* **List agency partners and policy** on the international admissions website and/or another international student-facing page. This is standard practice in Australia and the United Kingdom, countries whose institutions have long histories and experience with agency-based international student recruitment. Sharing a published list of the agencies an institution contracts with will help students and families substantiate claims of representation made by agents whose services they may be considering. *See* Figure 8.3, "Sample Listings of Agency Partnerships and Policies," on page 77, for sample website language from universities that do and do not work with agents, respectively.

* **Prohibit "double-dipping" (also known as dual agency). Short of that, require agencies to be transparent about this practice.** When agents are paid commissions for the recruitment of students and also charge students and families fees for advisement, conflicts of interest are likely, if not inevitable. Stipulate that the agency may not charge students for advice related to the admissions process at the institution. At minimum agencies should be required to inform students about their financial relationship with the institution, so that families can make educated decisions about the advice the agency provides.

* **Require upfront disclosure of student fees.** If the agent charges families for services such as help with the acquisition of health insurance or a student visa, insist in your contract that it disclose these fees to

families up front and in writing. Many agents have the families they work with enter into a formal contract for services, to clarify expectations and ensure that terms are mutually understood.

* **Limit involvement in the student's application.** Be clear that all agency employees and affiliated personnel are strictly prohibited from engaging in admissions fraud of any kind. Specify that this prohibition pertains to inappropriate involvement in the student's application, including document fabrication, signature forgery, ghostwriting of essays and recommendation letters, and the doctoring of transcripts. Consider contractually obligating agents to sign a written statement accompanying each application they transmit, attesting to a) having taken reasonable steps to confirm the veracity, authenticity, and completeness of the application materials; b) not having in any way assisted or advised the student to submit falsified or embellished application documents; c) the authenticity of the student's signature; and d) the student fully understanding the terms and conditions entailed.

* **Prohibit guarantees of admissions.** Make clear in the contract and other communications with agents that they may neither promise students admission to the institution, nor imply they are able to influence admissions decisions.

* **Stipulate advisement appropriate to a student's admissibility.** Institutions with campus-based intensive English language or pathway programs can protect families' interests by mandating that students eligible for direct admission into a university degree program not be misled to believe they must begin in the preparatory program.

* **Ensure transparent communications.** Some agents have been known to pose as the students they serve in their communications with overseas universities. This can make it difficult for an admissions officer to discern whether an email or other communication about a student's application truly comes from the student. Similarly, agents often take control of online application processes on behalf of students. Address

these tendencies by spelling out guidelines for institutional and agency communications with students, covering application documents and notifications, as well as fee invoices and receipts. The agent should be required to promptly furnish all documents and communications issued by the institution to the student, without exception. This will preclude the agent from selectively concealing important information the student and family has a right to know.

* **Address discriminatory practices.** Prohibit the agent from discriminating in the selection and service of clients, to ensure equitable student treatment. Specify that this anti-discrimination stipulation pertains to gender, race, ethnicity, color, national origin,

religion, sexual orientation or identification, marital status, age, political views, and disability. Agents should be prepared to adhere to institutional policies that might not accord with existing cultural norms where they are located.

To the extent institutions act on their responsibility for driving good behavior among partner agents, they will professionalize and legitimize this method of recruitment. Fostering transparency, integrity, and accountability is key in all interactions, including the agent-student relationship, the university-agent relationship, and the university's relationships with the students its agents refer. If these best practices are not a

---

Below are examples of institutions that do and do not contract with agents, respectively.

Many institutions that do not proactively contract with agents for the recruitment of international students nonetheless receive applications for students who, themselves, are being assisted by a third-party agent or advisor in their home country. Therefore, whether the institution has contracted with agents or not, it is wise to communicate its policy regarding agency involvement in the international admissions process.

If working with agents, consider posting language like this on the admissions website:

ABC University has relationships with international student recruitment agencies that are authorized to help students consider ABC University as one of their university options. These agencies are compensated by ABC based on the number of students they advise who subsequently enroll at ABC.

Other communications considerations include:

- ▸ Language emphasizing that a student is not required to apply with the assistance of an agent
- ▸ For campuses whose admissions offices do not work with agents

but whose ESL programs do, a statement clarifying this distinction
- ▸ A list of services the student and family can expect from the agent and, by contrast, services the agent is prohibited from offering

University of Cincinnati
On a page titled Overseas Admissions Representatives, the University of Cincinnati states: "UC officially appoints representatives on a commission basis to assist students with the application and admissions process." UC's representative agencies are listed by country. Retrieved from <www.uc.edu/webapps/ucosmic/reps>.

University of Nottingham (United Kingdom)
On a page titled Overseas representatives, the University of Nottingham states that "it places great value on our relationship with agents and we acknowledge the important role they play in supporting applicants and prospective students on their journey to Nottingham." Further on, students are advised that "if an agency charges fees of any kind, detailed, up-front information about these fees should be sought." Retrieved from <www.nottingham.ac.uk/studywithus/international-applicants/meet-us/overseas-representatives.aspx>.

Pennsylvania State University
In a section of its undergraduate admissions website for international students titled Important Message about Agents and Consultants, Pennsylvania State University states: "Penn State recognizes that agents or consultants are retained in many parts of the world to assist students in applying to colleges and universities in the United States. However, Penn States does not partner with agents to help represent the University or to administer any part of the application process." Retrieved from <admissions.psu.edu/info/future/international>.

University of Virginia
In a section of its undergraduate admissions website for international students titled Statement on Agents, the University of Virginia states that the university "does not support the use of a paid agent in the application process. All students are expected to submit their application materials without the help of such services. Please note that we do not work with any agency, so if one is claiming to have a connection to us, that is not the case." Retrieved from <admission.virginia.edu/international>.

FIGURE 8.3 Sample Listings of Agency Partnerships and Policies

priority, this recruitment practice will remain controversial, and the attendant risks to students and institutions will persist.

Agent Training and Communications

Agent-based international student recruitment is not for institutions looking for an instant influx of enrollees, nor is it inexpensive. Institutions have found success working with agents by committing the fiscal and staff resources to ongoing and rigorous quality assurance.

One essential element of agent quality assurance is training. The institution should deliver regular trainings of agency staff to ensure they possess the knowledge needed to appropriately advise students about its programs and requirements. Agencies often contract with many schools worldwide. It can be difficult for agents to keep current with a multitude of ever-changing details and policies, thus it is crucial to arrange refresher trainings and other reliable methods of communicating regular updates. Furthermore, frequent staff turnover at many agencies means that newly hired replacement agents may suddenly assume responsibility for representing the institution to students. It is important to agree to a plan to ensure the adequate preparation of these new agency staff.

A common component of agent training is an agency manual. Institutions committed to supporting effective and ethical agent-based international student recruitment will develop, furnish, and continually update a training manual for the staff of their agency contractors. In years past, institutions would produce and print such manuals in hard copy format and mail at least one copy to each of their overseas agency partners. Today, a more common approach is to house this resource online, publicly or in a password-protected section of the institution's website. This online platform, or portal, approach allows for convenient updates to essential information such as programs of study, tuition and fees, and application or other deadlines. Other elements to address in the agency manual, whether in hard copy and/or digital format, include:

* An overview of the u.s. higher education system and the institution or program's unique place in it.
* Basic facts about the institution, including points of distinction.
* A description of the surrounding geographical area and community, and local amenities.
* Academic programs and calendar.
* Accommodation options and dining services.
* International student support services.
* International student admission criteria.
* Application procedures, calendars, and deadlines.
* Tuition and all applicable fees.
* Payment and refund deadlines and conditions.
* Intensive English language courses and/or conditional admission details, if applicable.
* Student visa acquisition guidance.
* Arrival information, including airport pick-up or related services.
* Required new student orientations and initial enrollment procedures.
* Student visa regulation-related requirements.
* Sample invoice for commissions.
* Dedicated point of contact at the institution.
* Scope of work of agent and institution, respectively, per contractual obligations.
* Frequently asked questions.

The components of the agency manual can serve as the basis of the agent training provided, whether delivered in-person, via web conferencing, or both. Again, initial training and refresher trainings will help ensure that agency personnel represent the institution appropriately.

For agent-based international student recruitment to be successful, however, formal trainings must be supplemented by regular communications with agency staff. Many agents consider communication with the institution to be the single most important element in ensuring a successful working relationship. If agents can rely on responsive, accurate replies to their questions—whether sought via phone call, email, or other channels—they will in turn provide more effective support to prospective students. This benefits all stakeholders. Establishing a dedicated campus contact for all agency questions can prove an effective way of managing these inquiries and relationships.

Finally, another essential aspect of training and ongoing communications involves overseas visits to agency offices. As mentioned previously, visiting agencies "in-country" can be an invaluable way to get to know their staff and better understand their operations. It can also serve as an opportunity to provide agents in-person trainings, which can prove more effective than remote sessions via web conferencing. Moreover, in-person visits to knowledgeable agents afford institutional officials the opportunity to acquire new information about developments in the field. Insights gained can help adjust or fine-tune the institution's approach in the countries where it is recruiting. Similarly, the institution may invite agents to the U.S. to visit the campus individually or as part of an organized agent familiarization group tour.

Ongoing Supervision and Review of Agent Activity

In addition to trainings and routine communications with agents, it is also essential to establish systematic feedback loops. Clearly articulating expectations via the contract is the starting point. However, ongoing quality assurance should continue via regular reviews and reports. And as with the initial vetting of prospective agency contractors, it is prudent to assess agent performance by reviewing multiple sources of data.

Perhaps the most important way to determine how well an agency has met expectations is by asking the students it has served. Student surveys, focus groups, and/or one-on-one in-depth interviews can help to ensure students received appropriate support during the recruitment and admissions processes. For example, if a university expressly prohibits the agent from charging or handling student fees, and an agent-referred student discloses that they were charged a fee to receive their Form I-20, this would be a serious red flag.

A rigorous agency vetting process should preclude such problems. But collecting feedback directly from students, no matter the method, will also help the institution learn about lesser misunderstandings or other areas where agents need greater support and training. Questions pertaining to agents can be incorporated into an existing admitted student survey. If staff or student assistants at the institution have relevant foreign language ability, they can be enlisted to obtain direct feedback from new international enrollees referred by agents.

In addition to direct student feedback, it can be instructive to compare the student profile and success of agent-referred students with students who apply independently or through other sources. And this analysis can be deepened by looking for patterns among students referred by different agents. Did agent-referred students prove to be good fits and thrive accordingly? Did certain agents perform better than others in this respect? These and similar questions can help determine if the time, effort, and budget spent on agent-based recruitment are yielding a satisfactory return on investment.

Affiliating with Independent Educational Consultants

Independent educational consultants, or IECs, are sometimes conflated with student recruitment agents. However, while the services these two categories of professionals provide students and families are comparable, the methods by which they are compensated differ. IECs provide fee-based advisement to students about choosing and applying to programs, schools, colleges and universities, and are paid solely by the students and families they counsel. In other words, IECs are financially independent of the educational institutions they *advise students about*, not *recruit for*.

Many IECs specialize in assisting international students. Some work in the United States and connect with their clients remotely via Skype and other communication technologies. Others live and work in different countries and provide in-person service. Professional IECs avoid accepting payments or other incentives from the institutions they recommend to their student clientele. Nonetheless, u.s. colleges and universities can productively affiliate with IECs, and by doing so progress toward their international student enrollment goals.

Like counselors at international schools and EducationUSA advisors, IECs are another important constituency u.s. institutions should factor into their international outreach efforts. IECs welcome opportunities to learn about institutions they might be unfamiliar with and that might be good fits for their students. Consider inviting IECs on familiarization tours of your campus, and make a point of scheduling visits with them when planning outreach travel in the u.s. and abroad.

Many reputable IECs belong to professional associations such as:

* National Association for College Admission Counseling (NACAC)
* International Association for College Admission Counseling
* Independent Educational Consultants Association (IECA)
* Higher Education Consultants Association (HECA)

These organizations maintain member directories through which one can locate IECs who specialize in serving international students, and/or who are based overseas. They also hold annual conferences and other networking events where you can meet, exchange information and foster professional relationships.

Some institutions may not be comfortable affiliating with any private sector third-party student advisor, be they agents or independent educational consultants. For others, cultivating relationships with professional IECs may feel like a happy middle ground. Affiliating with IECs avoids some of the risks of a commissions-based relationship, while simultaneously raising institutional visibility among a broader pool of prospective international students and their families.

Summary Recommendations

It is unlikely that a consensus opinion regarding the use of international student recruitment agents will emerge anytime soon. The practice will continue to be promoted by its proponents while simultaneously being viewed unfavorably by others. Regardless, all stakeholders can play an important role in improving practice so that the interests of institutions, agents, and, most importantly, students are best served.

Ten summary recommendations follow that should comprise the core of an institution's agent recruitment strategy:

* **Put future and current students at the center of agent recruitment plans by ensuring greater transparency about university-agent relationships and the basis on which advice by agents is given.** A starting point is publishing the list of contracted agents on the institution's website. This will afford students and parents the opportunity to substantiate claims of representation made by agents whose services they may be considering. In rarer cases it will help them refute the same.

* **Develop a productive working relationship with campus or external legal counsel, and consult about contract development and other aspects of agent-based recruitment.** Professional counsel can ensure contracts adhere to campus, local, state, and federal requirements and help with other operational protections. It is extremely important to develop a good relationship with legal counsel.

* **Ensure the sustained buy-in and support of the campus community by including all affected colleagues in ongoing discussions.** When developing an agent-based recruitment plan, involve relevant departments and colleagues right from the start. Few people enjoy finding out about decisions after the fact, particularly about things that impact them.

* **Be proactive in sourcing and vetting prospective agency contractors.** Consider a formal request for proposal process, even if not required. Short of that, reach out to trusted colleagues to ask for referrals of

agents with earned reputations for professionalism and strong student support. Consider giving priority to agencies or agents who have demonstrated their commitment to ethical practice by having undergone trainings or via other examples of substantive quality assurance.

✳ **Safeguard against double-dipping** (also known as dual agency). When agents are paid per-capita commissions for recruiting students and simultaneously charge those same students for advisement services, conflicts of interest are likely—if not inevitable. Institutions can prohibit this practice among its agency contractors, or at minimum stipulate its disclosure.

✳ **Ensure accountability to all stakeholders by implementing an effective feedback loop.** Conduct audits and undertake regular reporting on agent performance, and share findings broadly. These reviews should gauge not just initial enrollment results, but also measures of retention, persistence, graduation, and student satisfaction. Ask students about their experiences working with agent contractors, and make sure what they were told during the recruitment and admissions processes reflect what they experience once on campus. Consider rewarding agents who consistently perform at high standards over an established period of time, commensurately.

✳ **Communicate frequently and responsively with agents.** Communications include visits to agency offices overseas, hosting campus visits, and initial and ongoing training of new and continuing agency staff.

It also includes timely responses to the many inquiries agents need to have answered in order to render their services effectively.

✳ **Be clear about the consequences of application fraud and other examples of potential agent misconduct.** Take swift and decisive action when agents violate contractual terms or otherwise abuse institutional trust, up to and including contract termination.

✳ **Train institutional staff.** Given the important legal considerations and complicated operational details entailed in managing a far-flung network of agency recruiters, institutional personnel should not be expected to simply figure things out as they go along. Review the many excellent resources in the Resources section of this chapter, and make sure to support and take part in related professional development opportunities.

✳ **Assess agent-based recruitment as but one component of a comprehensive international enrollment management plan.** Institutions that expect agent-based international student recruitment to satisfy all their enrollment needs are destined for disappointment. To be effective, this method of international recruitment requires a significant investment of time and resources. It also needs to complement, not displace, the many important other strategies shared in this publication. Furthermore, these collective recruitment efforts should support the institution's comprehensive enrollment management plan and include sustained attention to both domestic and international student success.

NINE

International Student-Athletes

GARRETT SEELINGER

Manager of International Eligibility Services
National Association of
Intercollegiate Athletics

LEAH WREN MCCORMACK

Director of Eligibility Services
National Association of
Intercollegiate Athletics

International Student-Athletes

International student-athletes have a different demographic makeup than the typical international student. Of particular note, a much lower percentage of international student-athletes come from India and China as compared to the numbers of international student applicants in general. Additionally, nearly two-thirds of international student-athletes arrive with a break of longer than one year between the completion of high school and attendance at a U.S. institution of higher learning. This can often be traced to the rigorous process of gaining eligibility and admission to U.S. institutions (college entrance exams, English proficiency exams, sending of records, etc.) coupled with a cultural difference from the U.S.'s norm of attending university immediately following the completion of high school. As a result, students have longer time periods in which athletic eligibility could be affected by university enrollment and athletic competition.

Educational Tracks

Internationally, sport and education are compartmentalized. The concept of university student-athletes is largely unique to the United States. Athletes outside the United States are more likely to pursue their sport outside the context of educational centers, predominantly competing through club teams rather than as a member of a team that is associated with the student's educational institution. Due to the separation of educational and athletic/competitive systems in most countries, high-performing athletes generally look outside of high school or universities for athletic training, competitions, and playing experiences. Instead, organized clubs and youth sport training programs offer the best

opportunities for competitive advancement. As a result, there are complexities related to researching the level of play in these leagues, teams, and structures that do not occur as often when the sport systems are more closely aligned with educational institutions. For example, the student-athlete's amateur status may be affected depending on the setup of the sport's governance system even while the student is still in high school.

In many countries, students intending to pursue an athletic career complete sport-specific high school programs that put them on an athletic track. Some examples include the BTEC in Sport in the U.K., Sport Gymnasiums in Germany and Serbia, and vocational and technical programs worldwide. Tracked educational programs abroad tend to start earlier than tracked education in the U.S. (upper-level bachelor's degree work in the U.S. versus tracked education starting in middle school or high school programs). Tracked high school programs may have a restricted distribution of courses which can result in a deficiency in various core subject areas that could impact admissions or eligibility decisions. In the U.K., for example, a BTEC Level 3 in Sport involves study of the body, health and safety in sport, nutrition, psychology for sports performance, coaching, technical and tactical sport skills, sports injuries, etc. Students from the U.K. are more likely to meet the expected breadth of core courses (such as math, science, or social sciences) at the GCSE-level rather than during their more specialized advanced secondary studies (such as A-levels).

Trends Affecting International Student-Athletes

Online, distance learning, self-paced, and examination-based high school equivalencies are increasingly popular avenues for elite athletes as they merge academics and athletics in the absence of such opportunities in their standard academic high school programs. Examples of such distance learning opportunities include: CNED (France), CEN *Centro de Estudios Academicos a Distancia* (Spain), and CENAPEC (Dominican Republic). Distance learning programs differ vastly in their makeup. Some programs incorporate teacher instruction while others are entirely online; many are self-paced, and in some instances, the programs very closely resemble the U.S. GED program. In the case of the EJA or *Supletivo* program in Brazil, students can finish high school in a consolidated, modular test-based system. The program can bear many titles, including *Certificado de Conclusao de Ensino Medio Supletivo,* distance-learning high school labeled *modalidade de distancia*, or *Educacao de Enseneza de Jovenes e Adultos.* It may be difficult to recognize the program from the diploma title. In that case, one can look for indicators such as multiple years of high school completed in one academic year or the words "distance" or "correspondence" elsewhere on the credential. From an admissions perspective, different institutions treat GED programs differently.

Depending on selectivity levels, GED or high school equivalence may not be considered for admission. The timing of high school graduation can create athletic eligibility issues because the programs are often accommodating an individual student's unusual academic timeline. Completion of high school through one of these methods may result in an atypical high school timeline, either by the student consolidating multiple years of high school or by delaying high school graduation by some time. In either case, the student does not typically receive his or her high school credential with the original graduating class.

Delayed High School Graduation

As discussed earlier, for some students, opportunities to compete may interfere with the standard completion of secondary school. In extreme cases, the student may delay high school graduation. The student-athlete may leave secondary school early to compete in athletics and return to complete school at a later date. More commonly, in educational systems where there are multiple graduation points (such as the U.K. and U.K.-modeled systems, Germany, the Netherlands, and Quebec, Canada), the student-athlete completes an initial level of secondary education in the expected timeline, temporarily delays high school attendance for competition, and later returns to secondary studies at an older age than is otherwise common in their educational system.

There can be eligibility implications for delayed high school graduates. For example, a German student that earns the *Zeugnis der Fachoberschulreife* at age 18 could leave secondary school in order to compete at a high level and return, two years later, to complete the *Zeugnis der Allgemein en Hochschulreife (Abitur)* at age 20. For athletic eligibility purposes in the U.S., the student's high school graduation date must be determined to apply eligibility rules. The student may be considered to have graduated high school at age 18 (especially if the *Zeugnis der Fachoberschulreife* granted access to *Fachhochshule*/higher education), or upon earning the *Abitur* at age 20. However, completing secondary studies at age 20 is considered delayed from the timeline typically seen for students in Germany. There are many examples of delayed high school graduations for international student-athletes, and a variety of athletic eligibility factors can be affected. Students may find that their collegiate athletic eligibility is shortened or delayed because of their unique secondary school timeline.

Non-High School Graduates

The concept of high school graduation abroad can be interpreted differently when evaluating comparability across the variety of educational systems around the world. In the U.S., high school graduation is marked by the completion of various curriculum requirements through teacher-evaluated course grades. In many other countries, secondary school completion is evaluated on the basis of a leaving exam. A student may interpret their own high school graduation as the date when they left school, regardless of whether the final leaving exam was passed or taken. Without the credential that compares to U.S. high school graduation, however, a student will run into hurdles in their athletic eligibility process.

Students from Iceland, for example, can run into issues related to the completion of high school. For eligibility to compete as a college freshman in the NAIA or NCAA, high school graduation is required, regardless of the fact that Iceland's secondary education cycle is 14 years in total versus the U.S. 12-year system (and as a result, students complete high school at around the age of 20). Some student-athletes may seek to leave high school in Iceland after age 18 to come to the U.S. to compete in athletics, but they will not be considered to have earned a credential that gains them admission into university or that is equivalent to U.S. high school graduation.

In the Caribbean, a student may graduate from high school without having achieved the required five exam passes from the Caribbean Examinations Council (CXC) CSEC exams (or the five BGCSE exams for students in the Bahamas) needed to fulfill the graduation requirement for athletic eligibility purposes.

U.S. High School Attendance

The number of directly-enrolled international students in U.S. high schools has tripled from 2004 to 2013 (Redden 2014a; IIE 2014b). It is notable that the number of exchange students to U.S. high schools grew by only 15 percent during that same timeframe, with about 73,000 students studying at U.S. high schools in October of 2013. Increasingly, international student-athletes are among this group. A potential student-athlete (PSA) attending a partial year in a U.S. high school may run into the issue of multiple graduation points, delayed graduation, or even not having earned a high school diploma at all. If a student enrolls at a U.S. high school as an exchange student, the individual may walk in a graduation ceremony mistaking this as having earned a U.S. high school diploma. In fact, many U.S. high schools offer honorary diplomas but are not actually awarding the student a U.S. high school diploma.

The student may have cut their home education short (especially if their home country is on a January to December schedule versus the August to May U.S. high school timeline). In Brazil, students increasingly take their one year of U.S. high school attendance back to the Brazilian government for recognition of an equivalence degree, honoring the one year of study in the U.S. with their two years of *ensino medio* (high school) back home. The student must receive authorization from the Brazilian government confirming recognition of the coursework to earn the Brazilian *Certificado de Conclusao* and thus to be considered in possession of a degree comparable to a U.S. high school degree. Without that official government recognition, the student is not able to receive a completion certificate though they may have taken years worth of studies.

Non-Disclosure of International University Attendance

A trend in international eligibility is the reluctance of international students to disclose their university attendance abroad. For many, there is a cultural misunderstanding that they are coming to the U.S. to start over in new degree programs/majors/postsecondary careers. Furthermore (and unfortunately), many international students are misguided into thinking that it is better to withhold international university attendance. The issue is exacerbated by the numerous ways to interpret the words we generally use to communicate postsecondary attendance (college, university, community college, postsecondary, higher education, etc.). For example, asking a French or U.K. student if they have attended college may lead to a response of "yes" because *le collège* represents middle school in France, and Sixth Form College represents advanced secondary school in the U.K.. Asking a student from the U.K. if they played college sports will also lead to a miscommunication considering PSAs probably played sports while attending Sixth Form College (studying A-levels and/or BTECs, which is considered playing at the high school level in the U.S.). In many countries, university attendance is significantly less expensive than it is in the U.S. (with many countries' postsecondary educational systems state-supported to a greater extent than in the U.S.). Coupled with many international student-athletes coming to the U.S. with larger gaps between high school and U.S. attendance, there are often periods of time that can be accounted for by undisclosed international university attendance.

University attendance can have a major impact on a student's eligibility. In the NAIA, students have exhausted athletic eligibility after ten full-time semesters of university attendance. However, in many instances for NAIA eligibility, university credits can help a student gain eligibility (when a student has used seasons of competition and is required to have accompanying numbers of credit to be eligible). When PSAs withhold their university attendance, significant impacts to a student's eligibility can occur, ranging from major delays in the eligibility determination process all the way to permanent banishment from an entire athletic association based on violating requirements to divulge information.

In 2015, roughly 42 percent of NAIA Eligibility Center international applicants that had a break between high school graduation and enrolling at a member institution had attended some form of international university, up from roughly 36 percent the year before. Yet, the number of students disclosing university attendance on their applications online remains steady. Rather than posing the question outright a single time, asking students about their university attendance abroad is best done through rephrasing multiple questions in various ways. This can help overcome cultural barriers and misunderstandings that may prevent or discourage students from disclosing the full picture of their prior attendance.

Difficulty Submitting Records

There are numerous complexities involved in international students submitting their official academic records. International student-athletes face the hurdle of having to submit official records to the NAIA Eligibility Center and/or NCAA Eligibility Center in addition to institution's admissions departments and credential evaluation companies (if required). Each of these destinations may have different requirements for how records must be submitted. As an institution, it is important to have clear instructions regarding which records are required from each country. Documents that instruct staff or prospective students on record submission requirements should be under constant revision. Every year, changes to educational systems and/or credentials occur, new credentials of high school completion come into being, and student-athletes are often among the first to complete more obscure high school programs that allow them to earn high school leaving certificates or diplomas through more flexible methods that cater to their unique circumstances. As more records move online through various verification methods, more can be done without receiving hardcopy records through the mail and without the risks associated with accepting less official records. For many countries with centralized exam systems or a Ministry of Education, the best receipt method is to have the student order records directly from the examining body. This method can be problematic if there is a deadline and the student has started the process late, as these government offices may take an extended period of time, sometimes weeks or months.

At the NAIA Eligibility Center, the top question from international student-athletes is regarding which records to send and how to send them. Last-minute recruits and rolling admissions deadlines can mean some students are completing the eligibility process later than anticipated, which can create difficulty in obtaining student records from the issuing institution. The best tools for students to deal with complex requirements for the submission of international academic records are to utilize sources made available by each of the recipients (credential evaluation companies, eligibility centers, or specific institutional policies). It is important that students ask questions prior to the submission of records, to ensure the records are sent correctly the first time.

Consistency between Eligibility and Admissions Decisions

Credential evaluation companies and eligibility centers may differ in their evaluation of international credentials. Additionally, transfer credit is not assessed equally by different evaluators, which can cause inconsistent evaluations of different students applying to the same institutions. To best position your institution in the recruitment of international student-athletes, it is recommended to have someone on campus that is familiar with the respective eligibility rules required by the athletics association of which your institution is a part. This in-depth understanding of the eligibility rules will help your institution better understand the application of eligibility rules for incoming international student-athletes, which can help reduce confusion related to the potential differences between assessment of eligibility and credential evaluation companies. To help NAIA members receive consistent credential evaluations with eligibility rules, the NAIA Eligibility Center has developed InCred, a credential evaluation service, to provide an avenue for students to receive a credential evaluation that is consistent with the standards used in NAIA eligibility decisions.

Fraud: High Stakes

Athletic scholarships offer the opportunity for students to compete at a high level and benefit from world-renowned training and facilities, all while completing a university degree. There are high stakes involved in this process for international student-athletes. Many invest a significant amount of money in hiring recruiters or facilitators who strive to gain them entrance into U.S. colleges or universities and a spot on an intercollegiate sports team. The NAIA Eligibility Center regularly encounters fraud related not just to omission of prior athletic or academic experience, but also related to falsified academic records and identity. In some cases, students have changed their date of birth to compete in age-specific competitions (U-17, U-19, U-21, etc.) in their own country or in international competition.

Fraud can be difficult to identify. There are some obvious signs of fraud, such as noticeable changes in the record, different grades of pixilation within a document, incorrect security features, or inconsistent information. Other forms of fraud can be identified by looking at all of the materials at once and piecing together the student-athlete's academic and athletic timeline. Once fraudulent records have been identified from a particular school, country, or region, it is worthwhile to look at other records from the same area already on file and to be alert for future incoming applicants. Fraud can be instigated by a student individually, by a lone recruiter or large recruiting organization, or by others working closely with the student-athlete, including parents and friends. Having established methods for how records must be received and including a review of authenticity for each record received is crucial in uncovering fraud. Questionable records should be verified with the issuing institution or original source for authenticity.

Although fraud exists on a number of different levels (purchasing a diploma, altering grades, falsifying records, omission of information, etc.), any one of these acts of fraud may result in serious implications for a potential student-athlete's eligibility and admissibility.

Tips

Athletic eligibility is administered in different ways across the various national athletic governing bodies. But clearly, there are quite a few complex situations that can arise when applying eligibility rules to international student-athletes. For that reason, it is crucial to advise international students to start the eligibility registration process early. It is also important to rely on the eligibility experts at the respective athletics association (NAIA, NCAA, NJCAA, etc.) for guidance to make sure that the right information is disseminated to the student early in the process.

Asking students the right questions at the onset can facilitate the recruiting process and enable a school to work through nuances earlier. Finding out a crucial piece of information (like attendance at an international university) can mean the difference between the student enriching your campus or staying home. It is important to know the student's story and understand his or her timeline.

It is also important to learn who is helping the student-athlete in their application process. It is acceptable (and often times quite fruitful) for international recruiting companies to help students through the complex process, but there is the potential for mistakes and miscommunication when the student is working with a recruiter that has not done his or her diligence. It may be a red flag if the recruiter handles the entire application process on behalf of the student, the student has never engaged in direct contact, and/or if the recruiter has obfuscated contact with the student (*i.e.* acted on the student's behalf in phone and email communications). Good recruiters should involve students in the process. It is also worthwhile to find out through word of mouth whether others have had positive experiences with the recruiter or recruiting company, and if the recruiting company is in direct communication with the national governing body.

It is generally recommended that schools work to determine a student's eligibility status prior to issuing student visas. This is to prevent situations where a student is ultimately found ineligible to compete after sig-nificant time and money have been invested by the student, their family, and the various admissions and athletic staff at their prospective institution or institutions.

Resources

Ultimately, it is important to rely on the experts in international eligibility when dealing with a unique international background, your first international student, a student from a new country, or even a student with an unusual background or situation. Each country has its own nuances when applying athletic eligibility rules and therefore it is important to engage the governing bodies early in the process.

For NAIA eligibility purposes, the requirements for high school graduation comparability can be found in the NAIA Published Standards.[6] The NCAA Guide to International Academic Standards for Athletics Eligibility[7] provides guidance on the credentials, grading scales, and requirements necessary for NCAA eligibility.

For questions concerning the complexities inherent in analyzing incoming international student-athlete eligibility, it is highly recommended to contact the respective eligibility center directly and early in the process:

✳ The NAIA Eligibility Center: phone: 816–595–8300 (extension "2"); email: ECinternational@naia.org

✳ NCAA Eligibility Center: phone: 317–917–6222 email: ec-international@ncaa.org

---

[6] *See* <www.playnaia.org/page/intldirectory.php>.

[7] *See* <www.ncaapublications.com/searchadv.aspx?IsSubmit=true&SearchTerm=International+Standards>.

Internationalization from a Regional Accreditor's Perspective

2016 AACRAO INTERNATIONAL GUIDE

STEVEN M. SHEELEY

Vice President
Southern Association of Colleges and
Schools Commission on Colleges

TEN

Internationalization from a Regional Accreditor's Perspective

The strategic concept of internationalization takes many names and forms, and an increasing number of higher educational institutions are exploring ways to enter the international arena. Some institutions have modified their mission statements to incorporate an aspect of global or international identity. Others have articulated a desire to emphasize international issues as part of their strategic plan or institutional vision. Furthermore, a significant number of institutions have incorporated global or international competency/citizenship in their statements regarding student learning and the student experience.

Some form of international emphasis has long been a staple of American higher education. Few academic disciplines are contained within geopolitical borders. Academics read, write, and attend conferences—activities that encourage and facilitate collaboration with other scholars. These kinds of collaborations have often been celebrated and supported at the institutional level. Students have also long enjoyed the excitement and benefits of study abroad and international service projects. Such experiences have almost universally been hailed as life-changing, and many institutions have a well-established system and support structure that affords their students a broad range of options for international study and experiences. However, faculty collaboration and study abroad activities are not sufficient to accomplish the sort of internationalization that many institutions consider to be vital.

In *Mapping Internationalization on U.S. Campuses*, the Center for Internationalization and Global Engagement states that "one of the fundamental duties of U.S. higher education is to prepare students for pro-

ductive and responsible citizenship. In the early 21st century, this means preparing students to live and work in a society that increasingly operates across international borders" (ACE 2012, 3). The publication defines "internationalization" as "the efforts of institutions to meet this imperative by incorporating global perspectives into teaching, learning, and research; building international and intercultural competence among students, faculty, and staff; and establishing relationships and collaborations with people and institutions abroad." Finally, the report argues that even though "internationalization has been part of the higher education discourse for decades, the circumstances and demands of the current era require a deeper commitment on the part of institutions, and a far-reaching scope of action." It defines such deep and far-reaching institutional action as "comprehensive internationalization" and provides the results of a survey intended to discover the extent to which the participating institutions are engaging in such a process. A quick review of the data gathered together in the Institute of International Education's (IIE) Open Doors Report (2014a) suggests that U.S. institutions will be exploring international partnerships and recruiting international students to meet those goals, since only nine percent of U.S. undergraduates report studying abroad before graduating.

This chapter explores the intersection between institutional internationalization and regional accreditation. Infusing global perspectives into an institution's curriculum and culture may be an important part of the overall institutional effort, but such initiatives may not directly engage the concerns of regional accreditors. Since regional accreditation is institutional rather than programmatic, those concerns and questions become a part of the conversation when an institution engages in collaborative partnerships—and/or certain kinds of contractual relationships—as part of its internationalization efforts.

This chapter will begin by defining some important terms and providing a general overview of the primary concerns a regional accreditor might have when reviewing collaborative international arrangements. The rest of the chapter will highlight important questions for the institution to consider—from an accreditation perspective—as it moves forward to plan for and implement various types of programs involving international collaboration. These questions are organized by the most common types of arrangements—or by mode of delivery—since the questions may have different emphases or nuances depending on the structure or location of the program(s).

Internationalization and Regional Accreditation: Some Context

Institutions initiate strategies addressing internationalization for a number of reasons. For some, the strategies have an altruistic foundation. Institutional leaders have a realistic view of the global landscape, and they are committed to educating students who can take full advantage of a globally-infused curriculum and co-curricular experiences. For others, the impetus is more pragmatic. Internationalization is viewed as a means to create a more culturally and ethnically diverse campus environment. Other institutions hope to raise their own reputation by engaging reputable international partners or seek to offer faculty and students high-profile opportunities for study and research in collaboration with such partners. Finally, many institutions, whether or not they will admit it, view internationalization as a means to increase enrollment and enhance revenue.

Institutional personnel across many departments will play some role as these arrangements are envisioned, planned, and implemented. Accomplishing such initiatives effectively builds on considerable expertise found across the institution. Unfortunately, sometimes the

person(s) whose responsibilities and expertise include academic records, admissions, or financial aid fail to be included until the conversations turn to initiation and implementation. By this point, the discussion may already have advanced to the point where raising questions about academic quality, student preparation, and academic and student support might be seen as an impediment. In addition, the process of developing an institutional infrastructure to manage and support such internationalization initiatives may identify a need for increased communication between offices whose responsibilities would normally be kept separate. For those reasons, if for no others, those on campus who deal with such questions on a daily basis should participate in the conversation from the beginning, since these questions will likely be raised in the peer review accreditation process.

Accreditation in the United States

Institutions in countries other than the United States usually obtain accreditation through a governmental agency or department. Such accreditation offers a level of legitimacy and often governmental approval to operate and confer academic credentials. This legitimacy and approval to operate is determined in a significantly different fashion for institutions of higher education in the United States, where accrediting agencies were developed with the purpose of gauging academic quality—either at the program or the institutional level. In addition, states are responsible for conferring approval to operate. Over the past few decades, institutional accreditors have been tasked with serving a gateway function for Title IV federal financial aid: in order to be eligible for this aid, sufficient academic standards must be maintained. As a result, many institutions view their relationship with institutional accreditors primarily through the lens of determining eligibility for aid, although accreditors maintain a primary focus on educational quality and improvement.

There are three types of accreditation organizations in the United States. Regional agencies accredit the entire institution, including all of its educational programs, wherever and however they are offered. Programmatic (or specialized) accreditors accredit programs, and their focus is usually discipline-specific. Many institutions hold membership in both regional and programmatic accreditors. Some accreditors have more of a hybrid identity. They are able to be either (or both) an institutional and a programmatic accreditor, depending on the nature of the institution. These accreditors operate in areas such as theology/religious studies, medicine, and law, disciplines which have historically created some self-contained and independent institutions. A third type of accrediting agency is a national accreditor. These national agencies usually have very specific requirements regarding institutional type and/or philosophy.

Accreditation Standards and Internationalization: Overarching Concerns

An accreditation agency's standards are formulated by its membership. The standards are founded on the twin concerns of compliance and improvement, with educational quality always in the foreground. Each regional accreditor has its own unique character and set of emphases— evident in the language and organization of its standards. But the common foundational concerns of educational quality and improvement are easily discerned from these standards.

While an institution is expected to be able to demonstrate compliance with all accreditation standards at any time, an institutional decision to initiate and implement academic programs somewhere other than its main campus usually requires some form of notification and approval from its accreditor(s). This is particularly true when the location is international. Questions raised by accreditors fall under the general categories of control, quality, and support.

CONTROL

Accreditation is an institutional asset, but it cannot be transferred. One of the realities of collaborating with

international institutions is that some of these institutions may be looking to capitalize on the "asset" that is American accreditation. For that reason, accrediting agencies carefully review the language of agreements involving their institutions and international partners. In such collaborative arrangements, the U.S. institution will need to maintain a sufficient level of control over the curriculum, faculty, facilities, learning resources, and support services to be able to demonstrate that the quality of the coursework and credential earned through the partnership or at an international location is appropriately equivalent to those offered on its main campus. At the same time, the U.S. institution must ensure that the international partner does not take advantage of the partnership to suggest that it is now accredited by the U.S. accreditor. This may only reflect some cultural differences, but it has been enough of an issue for the Southern Association of Colleges and Schools Commission on Colleges (SACSCOC) that its policy on "Agreements Involving Joint and Dual Academic Awards" contains specific disclaimer language and a prohibition against the use of the SACSCOC logo.

In essence, the accrediting agency would be looking for evidence that its member institution maintains an appropriate and sufficient amount of control over the academic program(s) to warrant putting the institution's name on the transcript (including individual courses) or diploma.

QUALITY

Issues of institutional control are inextricable from questions about program quality. Depending on the specific nature of the collaboration, the accrediting agency expects to see evidence that the institution's faculty members have remained appropriately involved in evaluating the quality of any coursework included on a student's transcript. This is true of both work taken in transfer and work provided as part of the collaborative arrangement. In addition, the accreditor seeks to ensure that the institution has evaluated the qualifications of the faculty teaching those courses. This is particularly crucial for any courses taught for the institution at an international location, whether the faculty members at that international location work full-time or part-time for the institution or are employed by an international partner. Other questions likely focus on the ways that the U.S. institution plans to incorporate the assessment of the educational quality of its international program(s) into its institutional effectiveness processes.

SUPPORT

Activities related to internationalization usually encourage students, faculty, and staff to engage with unfamiliar environments, especially when students and/or faculty go to an international location or come from an international location to study on the institution's home campus. Since academic quality and student success are significant concerns for accrediting agencies, many questions posed during a review of international off-campus sites or collaborative arrangements with international institutions will focus on academic and student support structures. The institution will be asked to demonstrate that it has structures and personnel in place to provide appropriate and sufficient support in areas such as library/learning resources, information technology instruction and support, advising, academic support and tutoring, counseling, and admissions/recruitment, among others. Additionally, reviewers will expect to see evidence that the institution has an administrative structure in place to ensure the sustainability of these support networks.

SOME IMPORTANT DEFINITIONS

Agency staff and peer reviewers often note that institutional representatives use terms on their own campus that assume a different denotation when they communicate with their accreditors. For example, institutions may call their distant locations "branch" campuses but those sites may not actually meet the formal definition of a branch campus. The director of financial aid will certainly point this out when he or she has to address

any questions concerning the eligibility for financial aid raised by the U.S. Department of Education. Additionally, collaborative arrangements between institutions take many different forms. Sharing common designations and institutional definitions with the accreditor(s) should make the process much smoother from the beginning. SACSCOC staff and reviewers have identified the following as examples of terms that need careful definition.

Dual and Joint Degrees

The SACSCOC policy ("Agreements Involving Joint and Dual Academic Awards") provides the following formal definitions of joint and dual degrees:

* An agreement by two or more institutions to grant dual academic awards is one whereby students study at two or more institutions and each institution grants a separate academic award bearing only its name, seal, and signature.
* An agreement by two or more institutions to grant a joint academic award is one whereby students study at two or more institutions and the institutions grant a single academic award bearing the names, seals, and signatures of each of the participating institutions.

Madeline Green's helpful review of the relationship between accreditation and internationalization in the United States suggests that these are "commonly accepted definitions" (2015, 13). The initiation and implementation of such programs is usually a significant departure ("substantive change") from the programs currently included in an institution's accreditation; as such, they usually require that the institution report them to the accreditor and provide sufficient information for the accreditor to review and approve them prior to implementation. Depending on the nature of the collaboration and the location of the program(s), a substantive change committee may also be authorized to conduct an on-site review.

Branch Campus

Institutions with multiple off-campus instructional locations sometimes refer to those locations as "branch" campuses, particularly when the "campus" is also an international location. Such designations often make perfect sense within the institutional community, but the off-campus location may not actually meet the federal definition of a "branch" campus. The SACSCOC policy contains the following definition of a branch campus:

A location of an institution that is geographically apart and independent of the main campus of the institution. A location is independent of the main campus if the location is:

* permanent in nature,
* offers courses in educational programs leading to a degree, certificate, or other recognized educational credential,
* has its own faculty and administrative or supervisory organization, and
* has its own budgetary and hiring authority.

Many off-campus instructional sites meet the first two criteria of this definition. Others—particularly in international locations separated geographically from the main campus—meet the third criteria. But a "branch" campus must meet *all four* criteria to demonstrate that level of administrative "independence" from the main campus. That is not to say that an institution cannot continue to refer to the campus as a "branch" campus, but documents submitted to the institution's accreditor(s)—and the U.S. Department of Education—should use the appropriate definition and designation.

Joint Venture

Some arrangements between institutions result in a formal structure that can be succinctly termed a "joint venture." In these cases, the institutional partners form a third entity, which often looks like an educational institution. Such arrangements respond to legal and governmental requirements for operating in some international locations, particularly those, such as China, where the government requires a certain level of participation by local administrators in order to allow the award of an approved credential.

Internationalization and Regional Accreditation: Modes and Questions

Even at the same institution, internationalization takes a variety of forms. Each of these efforts is a strategic response to an institutional desire to prepare students to succeed in a diverse, multicultural global society. Every "mode" these activities might take comes with its own nuances. The questions of control, quality, and support central to the concern of a regional/institutional accreditor are slightly different for each mode involved in internationalization.

This section will discuss internationalization and accreditation concerns using three modes: academic program collaboration, institutional collaboration, and international students.

These three modes are often inter-connected. For example, program collaboration is often location-specific; collaboration at international locations will necessarily involve more than one academic program. Additionally, student mobility is often one of the most desired outcomes from such collaborative activities. Collaboration between institutions—particularly when one or more institution is an international partner—will involve many considerations on all sides. Not all of those considerations, though, are pertinent to the concerns of the U.S. accreditor(s).

ACADEMIC PROGRAM COLLABORATION

As noted above, most academic disciplines are not confined within a specific country. In the international academic community, faculty collaboration across international lines is a well-established practice. Academic program collaboration seems to be the most prevalent mode of institutional internationalization and a good place to begin. Proposals for joint and dual degrees are often well-received by institutional administrators, especially since they may meet some of the strategic goals related to internationalization without requiring tremendous new fiscal and human resources on the part of any of the institutional partners. Conversations take place, faculty members agree on curricula, memoranda of understanding are signed and executed, and students are admitted to the program(s).

Dual degrees may offer the easiest answer to the questions of control, quality, and support, since each institution maintains control of its own portion of the curriculum. Students enrolled in the program are usually required to meet all of the curricular requirements for each degree awarded. They are often considered to be a special category of transfer or transient student, and decisions about how to articulate the credit from each institution into the partner institution have been negotiated by program faculty as part of the planning for the collaborative program.

In contrast, joint degrees (and dual degrees where the instruction only occurs at one of the partner campuses) present slightly different challenges, since they often require a higher level of collaboration to initiate, implement, and sustain the program. Program faculty at each partner institution may need to cede some curricular and instructional control in order to achieve true joint ownership of the program and the credential. Each institution must consider how to vet and approve such a credential through its degree approval process, including what role the institution's academic committees and governing board need to play in that process. The institution should be prepared to demonstrate to its accreditor(s) what formal steps it has taken to ensure appropriate control over the degree that will bear its name and reputation.

Accreditation reviewers may pose questions similar to the following:

Control

✳ Who "owns" the degree? Is it completely controlled by the U.S. institution? Or is it jointly owned? *(Note: the more partners there are to the agreement, the more difficult it is to demonstrate institutional control over the degree.)*

✳ What institutional process approved the collaborative academic arrangement? How did that process conform to published institutional policies and procedures?

✳ How will the collaborative program be managed and reviewed? Are the structures at the institutional level, at the program level, or integrated? How often and when will the collaborative arrangement be formally reviewed?

✳ How will the program appear in the institution's formal external documents (diploma and transcript)? How will these documents reflect the collaborative nature of the academic program?

Quality

✳ What kinds of curricular conversations took place in planning the collaboration? How involved were program faculty from the U.S. institution? What documents "govern" any articulation of credit from one institution to the other?

✳ How will the U.S. institution evaluate the qualifications of faculty teaching at the partner institutions? Will those faculty members be considered adjuncts for the U.S. institution?

✳ Will the program be evaluated primarily based on the language of the memorandum of understanding (MOU) or other formal documents? Do those documents address issues of academic quality and compliance with the accreditor's standards? What evidence will the institution need to demonstrate that the MOU is being honored by both (all) partners?

✳ If the curriculum needs revision, how will those conversations take place and when? Who will be involved?

✳ How will assessment of student learning in the collaborative program be accomplished? How will that assessment interface with the U.S. institution's program-level assessment of student learning outcomes?

✳ Are admissions requirements clearly articulated and appropriately published? Are there structures in place for students whose barrier to admission may be largely language-related?

✳ Are curricular requirements clearly published in formal institutional documents made available to both prospective and current students in the program? How will the institution demonstrate that these requirements are being followed?

Support

✳ Who is responsible for hiring faculty and staff to support the collaborative program(s)?

✳ Who is responsible for scheduling classes and recording grades? Will the collaborative program(s) require modifications to the typical processes for advising, registration, and records? If so, have published policies and affected academic publications been revised?

✳ How will students studying at a distance have access to appropriate and sufficient library/learning resources? How will such students have access to training and professional staff?

✳ What academic and student support services are available for students in the collaborative program? How will students studying at a distance have access to professional staff and suitable facilities? Does the U.S. institution have appropriate and sustainable structures to support students as they cope with cultural and/or language differences?

INSTITUTIONAL COLLABORATION

With this second category, there is a slight distinction between the kinds of questions that have been asked about academic collaboration—no matter where it is located—and additional issues that arise when the collaboration between institutions also involves an international site. These questions are similar, though not identical to those asked regarding any off-campus site, since those locations rarely offer immediate and direct access to the institution's primary facilities, library/learning resources, and support structures. International locations usually involve their own additional layer of questions and concerns.

OFF-CAMPUS SITES/BRANCH CAMPUSES

The only substantive difference in the kinds of questions reviewers may ask will relate to the branch campus' level of independence from the institution's main campus. Reviewers need to confirm that the branch campus meets all of the criteria necessary to be classified as a branch campus within the accreditor's records. Otherwise, the concerns will be those similar to distant locations. Reviewers might pose the following questions:

Control

✳ What legal and/or governmental arrangements have been made regarding the institution's operation of the site? Does the institution own or lease the property, and is that relationship clearly demonstrated by the MOU?

✳ Does the institution operate the site with an international institutional partner? Is the arrangement collaborative, or does the U.S. institution lease/borrow the facilities from the international partner? Is the site a partnership between the U.S. institution and a partner which is not an institution of higher education? How do legal agreements/documents demonstrate control by U.S. institution personnel over such things as a safe and secure environment and the quality of the physical facility? Do the documents provide the U.S. institution with the ability to demonstrate continued compliance with relevant accreditation standards?

✳ How are faculty and staff hired? Who employs them?

✳ What specific financial arrangements are in place with these programs at this site? Who receives tuition and fee revenue? Has the U.S. institution found it necessary to invest significant amounts of fiscal resources to initiate and implement the program and site? Is the program/site projected to break even or produce positive revenue? If so, what is the projected timetable?

Quality

✳ Does the site have sufficient classroom and laboratory facilities?

✳ Does the site have appropriate library/learning facilities?

✳ Does the site have suitable academic and student support facilities?

✳ Has the institution set equivalent admissions standards for the international site? Are exceptions being made? If so, are these exceptions regular or sporadic, and why?

✳ If the curriculum replicates an academic program at the institution's main campus, have any changes been made in the curriculum for the international site? If so, have those adjustments materially changed the program or general education curriculum? Does the program or general education curriculum continue to comply with the accreditor's standards?

Support

✳ Do students at the international site have access to library/learning staff?

✳ Do students at the international site have access to academic support and student support staff?

JOINT VENTURES

As noted above, U.S. institutions have begun exploring joint ventures with international partners. These often arise as proposals from the prospective international partner, with the joint venture (the third "entity" or institution) offered as a way to receive financial support and official recognition from the international government. Such support and recognition appear to depend on an institutional structure that can only be achieved by creating a separate higher education entity that will hire the personnel (including faculty), provide the coursework, and confer the degree. Many U.S. institutions have been exploring these joint ventures as a means to gain more significant access to international markets that have, heretofore, been relatively unavailable.

As one might surmise, this immediately raises questions of control and quality. The U.S. institutions, to their credit, have generally been asking these questions early in the conversations, before the involvement of anyone from an accreditation agency. The legal, political, and quality issues involved in such international partnerships are difficult; aside from the general concerns just raised, each situation will contain issues that will need to be handled and addressed individually. Some institutions accredited by SACSCOC have deferred conversations with their prospective international partners or explored ways to create an off-campus site on or near the campus of the international partner, making the issues of control and quality far more manageable.

INTERNATIONAL STUDENTS

Normally, the international students on campus will not receive special attention from the institution's accreditor(s). After all, international students have long been a relatively stable part of campus life at many U.S. institutions. Data suggests that student mobility across international lines is increasing. The National Association for College Admission Counseling (NACAC) notes that, "Worldwide, international student enrollments at institutions of higher education have more than quadrupled over the past three decades, from 1.1 million in 1985 to approximately 4.5 million in 2012" (NACAC 2014, 4). They suggest that the number will exceed seven million by 2025. Some international students coming to study at U.S. institutions arrive via collaborative arrangements, with a recent ACE/CIGE study indicating that almost "two-thirds (63 percent) of programs enroll only students from the partner country" (Helms 2014, 4). This "heavy skew toward enrollment of non-U.S. students draws attention to the intended purpose of international joint and dual degree programs.... The data suggest—and when interviewed, a number of respondents agreed—that JDDPs (Joint and Dual Degree Programs) may be serving primarily as a mechanism for U.S. institutions to recruit international students" (Helms 2014, 18). The study also noted that "language issues" were among the most significant challenges facing such programs, since many of the students participating were "likely to be non-native English speakers" (Helms 2014, 22). Unfortunately, the 2012 study noted that, "While efforts to recruit international students are on the rise, the data do not show a commensurate increase in support services for these students, or activities that facilitate interaction and mutual learning with American peers" (ACE/CIGE 2013, 24).

When the presence of international students on campus results from some type of collaboration with international educational partners or a contractual arrangement with a third party to aid in their recruitment, reviewers will probably focus some attention on this group of students. The questions raised might include the following:

Control

Since the students are studying at the main campus, using its curriculum, faculty, and resources, most of the questions about control of the program may pertain to the recruiting and admissions process.

* How does the institution maintain control over the recruitment and admission of international students?
* Are exceptions made for international students in meeting admissions requirements? To the institution? To the program? If so, what types of exceptions are made, and via what process?
* Does the institution contract with international recruiters or with a third party to recruit international students? If so, how are these parties compensated? How does the institution maintain compliance with federal law and accreditation standards in these arrangements?
* Are academic and student support services provided to international students through arrangements with a third-party provider? If so, how does the institution ensure the quality of such services?

Quality

* How does the institution ensure that international students possess the language skills to take full advantage of the program(s)?
* How does the institution ensure that international students have the requisite academic preparation to take full advantage of the program(s)?
* How are transcripts of international students evaluated as part of the admissions process?
* If an admissions exception is made, how does the student receive the academic support necessary to succeed in the program(s)?
* Are international students initially taking non-credit courses? Will any of these courses be eligible for conversion to credit coursework? If so, how will the institution ensure the quality and equivalency of such coursework?

Support

* What types of institutional structures support the language and cultural needs of international students?
* Does the institution provide official structures dedicated to the academic and student support of international students?

Conclusion

Internationalization is likely to capture institutional attention for some time. While such strategic efforts do not always intersect with the concerns of accreditation, institutions can benefit from including those questions from the very beginning of the planning efforts rather than waiting until plans are close to fruition. Most accreditors—through their standards and policy statements—already have resources in place to help their member institutions navigate the intersection between internationalization and accreditation. Madeline Green's publication, *Mapping the Landscape: Accreditation and the International Dimensions of U.S. Higher Education,* offers a good and accessible overview for both regional and programmatic accreditors (2015). Her work may be particularly helpful in providing the location for such standards and policies.

In closing, it it worth noting that the campus professionals who provide expertise in admissions, financial aid, academic support, and academic records are often brought into these types of conversations when they turn toward actual implementation. By that time, the collaboration may have progressed to the point where some of the concerns that will be raised by accreditors have already been missed, at which point those conversations often become awkward. An institution may avoid some of the more awkward conversations—both with international partners and with its accreditor(s)—by considering these questions and bringing these professionals to the table from the start.

ELEVEN

Promoting International Student Success

CLAYTON A. SMITH

Vice-Provost, Student Affairs and Dean of Students
University of Windsor

Promoting International Student Success

This chapter, with a focus on North American postsecondary education, identifies international students as a strategic enrollment management institutional priority, presents themes in the international student success research literature, and describes related best practices. It also presents the findings from an in-depth Canadian study which identifies the factors that contribute to attrition of international students. Suggested areas are offered for future improvements to enhance institutional international student success.

International Students: A Strategic Enrollment Management Priority

Students from abroad are increasingly choosing to study at North American colleges and universities. Currently, 1.2 million international students study at North American postsecondary educational institutions, with 336,000 choosing Canada and 886,052 enrolling in the U.S. (Canadian Bureau of International Education 2014; Institute of International Education 2014). Between 2012/13 and 2013/14, international student enrollments grew by 8.1 percent in the U.S. and by 10.5 percent in Canada. Globally, the U.S. is currently the top destination for study abroad while Canada ranks seventh. Top countries of origin for the U.S. and Canada include China, India, South Korea, and Saudi Arabia. The Organization for Economic Cooperation and Development (OECD) projects that the number of students who choose to study abroad will more than double by 2020 (OECD 2014).

This has led many institutions to adopt internationalization as an institutional priority. Knight (2003)

identifies internationalization as a process "of integrating an international/intercultural dimension into the teaching, research, and services elements of an institution" (2). Dr. Paul Davidson, president of Universities Canada, suggests:

> Globalization has become a pervasive force shaping higher education. Today almost all institutions in Canada and around the world engage to some degree in activities aimed at forging global connections and building global competencies among their students, faculty, and administrative units. Developing such activities at many levels within universities is now a central part of institutional planning, structures and programming—a phenomenon known as the internationalization of higher education. (Association of Universities and Colleges of Canada 2014, 3)

The presence of international students at a postsecondary institution adds to the multiculturalism and diversity of the general student population and reinforces a global perspective and exchange of ideas. Mutually, international and domestic students develop global cultural skills necessary for success in an increasingly global environment and diverse workforce. In addition, the retention of international students represents a cost benefit for the institution and the destination country as a whole. According to the Institute of International Education, in 2014 international students contributed more than $27 billion to the U.S. economy. Roslyn Kunin & Associates, Inc. (2012) report that $8 billion is spent by international students who study in Canada. In this environment, the recruitment and retention of international students has become a prior-

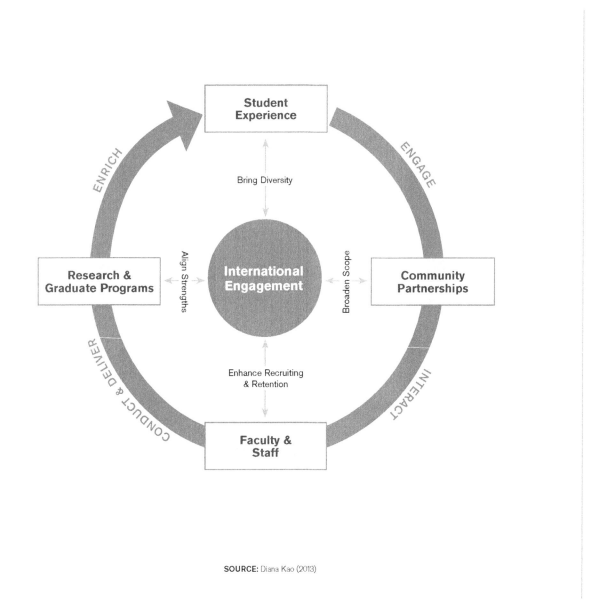

SOURCE: Diana Kao (2013)

ity for many institutions. Figure 11.1 shows how internationalization activities have become central to institutional planning.

Fee and colleagues (2011) suggest that the rise of international recruitment in Canada is being driven by a number of colluding factors: a downward trend in domestic student numbers, increased skilled immigration, less money from the public purse for operational costs, prodding from governments to be more entrepre-

neurial, and a monumental rise in global demand for higher education, particularly from countries with emerging economies. U.S. institutions of higher education have increasingly viewed international students as a source of tuition revenue (Stephens 2013). Accordingly, international students are afforded places on campus as an essential resource to foster cross-cultural understanding based on their academic ability and their ability to contribute to financial stability and sustainability.

The Student Voice

Student satisfaction is one of the major goals of universities. A satisfied student population can translate into a competitive marketing advantage fostering positive word of mouth communication, student retention, and loyalty. The creation and the delivery of excellent customer value is important in creating a sustainable advantage in the highly competitive international education market place (Kotler and Fox 2002).

Satisfaction among international students studying in North American colleges and universities is high. Richard Garrett (2014), the North American director for i-Graduate, found that international student satisfaction and willingness to recommend the institution at both Canadian and American institutions was higher than the average reported by international students globally. This was in comparison to the *International Student Barometer*, which targeted satisfaction toward students' academic experience, friendliness of school, attitude of professor, local atmosphere, and quality of learning. High scores on another survey were also reported at Canadian institutions, with 90 percent of international students being either very satisfied or satisfied with their educational experience (Canadian Bureau of International Education 2014).

While international students are generally very satisfied with their experience, a 2004 study at the University of the Incarnate Word in San Antonio, Texas outlines that international students reported experiencing difficulties and challenges in 14 areas: social adaptation, college services, finances, cultural and social activities, student government and voice at the university, health care and wellness services, the orien-

tation process, dorms, university value system, various university offices, dealing with authority and bureaucracy, receiving accurate information before arrival, being understood, and the geographical location of the university (Tas 2004). Table 11.1 identifies nine reasons students gave for leaving the university.

Other studies identify an integration challenge. A Canadian Bureau of International Education (2014) survey reported that 56 percent of international students surveyed indicated that they have no Canadian friends, and 36.6 percent said it is difficult to know Canadian students. Similarly, a recent U.S. study (Gareis 2012) found that almost 40 percent of international students in the U.S. indicate that they have no close American friends and would like to have more meaningful interactions with Americans. Students highlighted internal as well as external factors for their lack of social bonds. Internal factors included shyness and lack of strong language proficiency. External factors included what is seen as a lack of interest in other cultures on the part of U.S. students.

In Australia, the issue of international student integration has been studied for many years. In a 1973 study (Weiss), two-thirds of international students reported feeling loneliness and/or isolation during their studies.

TABLE 11.1: Reasons International Students Gave for Leaving a University (Tas 2004)

Reason Given	Specifics
Making friends and interacting with domestic students	Language barriers; difficulty making domestic friends; felt discriminated against by domestic students; made friends mostly with other international students; more difficult in this environment to belong
Food on campus	More expensive, less diverse, not as tasty as off campus; lack of sensitivity to religious restrictions and traditions; mandatory meal card plan
International student office	Lack of assistance; feelings of discrimination
Academic assistance	Lack of dedicated and approachable advisors and administrative staff; can't find advisors because they're not around; international students need more assistance because they are making a greater adjustment than domestic students
Cultural and social activities	Inadequate network; isolated; lacking social support compared to home country
Housing	Too many restrictions; frequent and short notice relocations
Incorrect information prior to arrival	Lack of trust in recruitment and orientation process
Availability of courses and flexibility in scheduling within degree plans	Courses not available; little or no flexibility in scheduling process
Other reasons	Social and academic adaptation within a new environment; availability of resources and research opportunities

TABLE 11.2: Faculty Perceptions of International Students' Academically Detrimental Behaviors and International Students' Perceptions of Most Difficult Adjustment Areas (Tompson and Tompson 1996).

Faculty—Academically Detrimental Behaviors	Students—Perceptions of Most Difficult Adjustment Areas
▶ Not participating in class ▶ Not asking for clarification ▶ Sitting only with international students ▶ Studying only with international students ▶ Breach of ethical standards of scholarship	▶ Social isolation ▶ Language skills ▶ Knowing norms, rules and regulations ▶ Overcoming stereotypes ▶ Transportation ▶ Clothing norms ▶ Weather differences ▶ Food differences ▶ Oral presentation assignments ▶ Personal finances

In a 2011 (Gresham and Clayton) study, many students indicated that they have only superficial interactions with Australian students.

A 2004 survey jointly conducted by the British Council, the UK Council for Overseas Student Affairs, and the Council for International Education found that two-thirds of international students have few or no British friends (Curtis 2004). The survey revealed that most international students befriend students from their home country or other international students. In fact, nearly 60 percent of international students said that their friends were other international students only, including students from their home country; 32 percent said they have a mix of UK and international friends; and seven percent of international students said that the majority of their friends were British.

While most international students feel welcomed and at home on their college campuses, many in the U.S. have a low sense of belonging and face challenges in making the transition to American culture (Schweitzer, Morson, and Mather 2011). These same students voice concern over the lack of support from the institution in making that transition.

The Faculty Voice

The faculty perspective gives a different view of the issues and challenges international students face at a postsecondary institution. Carter and Xu (2007) describe nursing faculty perceptions of program ade-

quacy related to culture differences and identify language as a significant barrier to ESL students' progression, testing, learning style, and communication. The challenges ESL students face may be related to patient safety, time demands required for the instruction of ESL students, and various psychosocial issues such as the ability to form relationships with peer groups, isolation, loneliness, and poor social supports. Furthermore, faculty expressed frustration that due to employment restrictions and the subsequent inability to earn an income as a student, international students could not resource a tutor to assist them in academic difficulties. Three concerns identified include language and communication barriers, clinical probation due to communication difficulties as unnecessary humiliation, and competing for attention and time of faculty with other students.

Tompson and Tompson (1996) asked business school faculty at two universities in the southeastern U.S. to identify behaviors exhibited by international students they consider to be academically detrimental. Similarly, international students were asked to identify adjustment areas they perceived as most difficult. Each group identified very different factors. The results are summarized and compared in Table 11.2.

An In-Depth Look

Building on research findings that suggest international student success is at least partly a local matter, a mid-sized public Ontario-based university engaged in a year-long study to identify the factors that contribute to attrition of international students. In the study, the university looked at what might be done to improve the success and persistence of international students academically through support initiatives and by way of student recruitment (Smith and Demjanenko 2011).

The research design included both a full-year cohort qualitative study using both undergraduate and graduate international students, and a two-part interview process and survey of faculty who teach large numbers of international students and staff who provide international student services. The collected data was coded and analyzed for themes, patterns of similarity, and/or difference. Participants in the study were recruited from four sample populations: international students, international student groups, international student service providers, and faculty who instruct international students.

TABLE 11.3: Survey of Contributing Factors to International Student Attrition: Summary of the Emergent Themes by Participant (Smith and Demjanenko 2011).

International Students	Faculty	Service Providers
▸ Culture	▸ Language	▸ Language
▸ Frustration, disorientation, and confusion	▸ Culture	▸ Culture
▸ Facilities and services	▸ Racism and discrimination	▸ Racism and discrimination
▸ Racism and discrimination		

EMERGENT THEMES

Emergent themes were consolidated by international students, faculty members, and service providers, and showed consistency across the groups for culture and racism and discrimination. The faculty and service provider groups also identified language as a contributing factor to international student attrition. The international students added frustration, disorientation, and confusion, along with facilities and services. Table 11.3 provides a breakdown by participant category.

✳ **Language:** Both faculty members and service providers reported on the difficulties international students experience in daily language and communication. A language problem often signals a mal-ability to function in English and/or comprehension issues, which may result in poor communication not only with professors but also with domestic students. Underdeveloped English ability affects the entire education experience for international students.

✳ **Culture:** All three groups identified culture as an obstacle that international students experience. Faculty members reported that some international students are "lonely, tired, and haven't made friends" and said that international students need to adjust from a strict and disciplined environment to a university environment which expects students to be autonomous and responsible for their actions. Service providers said they needed to be "guarded,"

"on," or "engaged and sensitive to a great many factors including language, customs, and comprehension around international students." International students said that it is generally difficult to make friends with Canadian or domestic students and that some international students "don't have Canadian students as close friends."

✳ **Racism and Discrimination:** All three groups identified racism and discrimination concerns. Faculty members reported that they had observed "classmates of international students frequently are rude to international students in group work" and that "students experience discrimination when renting accommodation, when looking for prayer spots, and when forming heterogeneous groups." Service providers responded that incidents of racism and discrimination were isolated incidents and occurred "mainly based on assumptions made about members of a certain race and attaching stereotypes to the membership." Some international students reported experiencing racism and discrimination on campus and that it "just made it difficult...just made the day completely bad for me."

✳ **Frustration, Disorientation, and Confusion:** International students who attended orientation reported that the program was "very helpful" in getting oriented to the new environment while those who missed orientation reported feeling "lost," "disoriented," "confused," and in general uninformed about the tacit knowledge within higher education.

✳ **Facilities and Services:** International students reported that a number of facilities were very helpful (*e.g.*, international student center, library, recreation facilities). Others were not what they anticipated.

Some of this was due to cultural issues around food and faith needs.

The results of the study point toward the idea that in order for students to be retained there must be a fit between student, institution, and sociocultural environment (Conrad and Morris 2010; Mallinckrodt and Sedlacek 1987). Where possible, the institution must meet varying needs of a large number of individual international students. As Conrad and Morris (2010) point out, "the devil really is in the details of each student's experience" (13).

International Student Success Factors

Broadly speaking, numerous cognitive and non-cognitive variables have been identified as impacting the academic success and retention of international students.

Academically, the international student population experiences language difficulties (Barron, Gourlay and Gannon-Leary 2010; Carter and Xu 2007; Fitzgerald 1998; Hansen 1993; Tas 2004; Zhang and Zhou 2010), culture-related learning differences (Carter and Xu 2007; Rice *et al.* 2009; Tas 2004; Tompson and Tompson 1996), academic support issues (Fitzgerald 1998; Sandeen 2004; Tas 2004), and adjustment to a new educational system (Andrade 2009; Boyer and Sedlacek 1988).

Equally important are non-academic challenges international students face while enrolled in postsecondary institutions. These challenges include cultural differences (Carter and Xu 2007; Fitzgerald 1998; Hansen 1993; Tas 2004; Zhang and Zhou 2010), isolation (Carter and Xu 2007; Hansen 1993; Van Nelson, Nelson and Malone 2004), relating to and identifying with the campus community (Carter and Xu 2007; Hansen 1993), social issues (Fitzgerald 1998; Mallinckrodt and Sedlacek 1987; Tas 2004; Van Nelson, Nelson and Malone 2004; Zhang and Zhou 2010), and finances (Beane 1985; Fitzgerald 1998; Tas 2004; Van Nelson, Nelson and Malone 2004).

Figure 11.2 (on page 111) shows how academic and non-academic challenges dynamically impact international student success.

Some of the major international student success factors are summarized below.

✳ **Proficiency in English:** English competency prior to admission is a critical part of international student success (Beane 1985; Carter and Xu 2007; Van Nelson, Nelson and Malone 2004). However, the ability to predict academic success using the Test of English as a Foreign Language has been and is being disputed (Beane 1985; Tompson and Tompson 1996; Van Nelson, Nelson and Malone 2004; Wait and Gressel 2009). Researchers argue that language proficiency is difficult to measure because communication depends on grammatical competence, sociolinguistic competence, discoursed competence, and the verbal and nonverbal dimensions of a language (Van Nelson, Nelson, and Malone 2004).

✳ **Study Discipline:** Discipline of study or major is closely linked to the academic success of international students (Bean 1985; Van Nelson, Nelson and Malone 2004). Beane (1985) found that retention of international students is more closely related to majors than English proficiency. For example, engineering students had a high retention percentage as a result of a high GPA, a sense of identification with students in that department as a result of being admitted into the program as first-year students, and previous engineering experience at the high school level.

✳ **Finances:** Finances impact the ability of international students to do well in postsecondary education (Beane 1985; Boyer and Sedlacek 1988; Tas 2004). Unreliable financial support by the country of origin due to political or economic instability as well as the inability to budget appropriately impact the financial situation of international students (Beane 1985). Similarly, Tas (2004) reported that less than 40 percent of international students responding to a survey identified finances as the main factor for leaving the university.

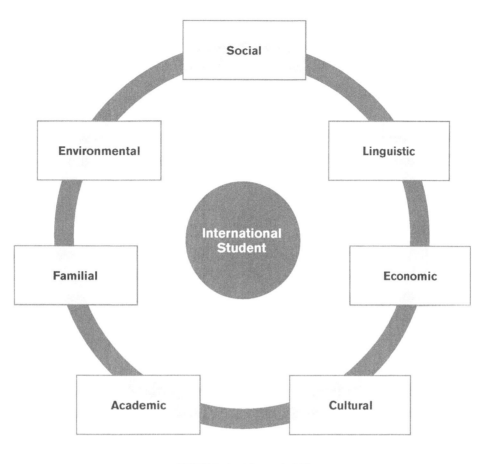

FIGURE 11.2

Factors Influencing Perseverance Beyond First Year

SOURCE: Smith and Demjanenko (2011)

✳ **Cultural Adjustment:** Cultural adjustment permeates and affects most aspects of student life: living arrangements, community participation, socialization, communication, eating practices and food consumption, learning styles, and education system, to name a few (Andrade 2006). It is probably the most difficult issue to define as well as the most persistent because it can affect all aspects of an international student's life.

✳ **Social Supports:** Although difficult to measure and evaluate, the availability of social supports impacts the academic success and retention of international students (Simpson and Tan 2009). Social support has been shown to reduce stress, promote positive health outcomes, and moderate the effects of stress on mental health symptoms (Rice *et al.* 2009).

✳ **Self-Confidence:** Boyer and Sedlacek (1988) found that "[s]elf-confidence and availability of a strong support person consistently predicted GPA" (220). Considering the numerous academic and social adjustments international students must make, "feeling confident, determined, and independent, and having another individual to whom to turn in crisis were important determinants of adjustment to academic demands and attainment of academic success" (Boyer and Sedlacek 1988, 220).

✳ **Community Service and Understanding of Racism:** Boyer and Sedlacek (1989) found that "community service and understanding racism significantly added to the prediction of persistence" (219).

Generally speaking, international students engage more often in effective educational practices than their American counterparts, especially in the first year (Zhao, Kuh, and Carini 2005). International students report greater academic challenge and higher levels of active and collaborative learning, interact more with faculty members, engage more in diversity-related activities, perceive the campus environment to be more supportive, and report greater gains in personal and social development, practical competence, and general education.

Despite the increased focus in recent years on variables linked to academic success and retention of international students, retention rates have not seen any significant improvement (Andrade 2009). The literature indicates that programs targeting retention rates must be suited and tailored to individual institutions. Increased retention of international students depends on the culture of the institution, which must influence the experiences of international students at the level of integration with domestic students, with faculty, and with the larger community.

Best Practices in Supporting International Student Success

Colleges and universities can provide a wide range of international student supports, including academic, financial, health and wellness, social and cultural, transition, immigration, accommodation, and employment support.

ACADEMIC SUPPORT

Academic issues are of considerable importance to the success of international students. Various differences in learning impact the success of international students. Students from China, for instance, were found to have difficulty in learning how to cooperate and collaborate with other students and group members (Zhang and

Zhou 2010). Some of the key academic supports needed by international students include:

❋ **Academic Advising:** Advising should be academic and professional. Peer-advising can also be effective with international students. A 2010 Dalhousie University study found that international students benefit from early and frequent advising; better preparation for students in meeting expectations in the classroom and in workplace internships, placements, and co-op terms; and help with communication skills (The Chronicle Herald 2011).

❋ **Academic Integrity:** International students often have a different understanding of academic integrity from those educated in North America. This can result in international students being over-represented in academic conduct violations. Many universities have gone to considerable length to inform international students early in their academic career of the institution's academic integrity standards.

❋ **Verbal and Written Communications:** Language barriers, especially oral communication in English, are critical for additional language students. Verbal communications support provided by additional language teaching assistants will ensure new international students develop effective English verbal language skills. Graduate students whose second language is English will also need support associated with the writing of their theses.

FINANCIAL SUPPORT

The issue of financial support for international students has always been a contentious one since the admissions and recruitment process is based on the premise that they have sufficient resources to support their choice to study abroad. However, international students often find financial matters particularly overwhelming. A 2009 survey conducted by the Canadian Bureau of International Education found that international students are pressured by financial considerations. One in five students calls for lowering tuition fees for international students and one in ten suggest that institutions provide scholarships or bursaries for international students.

Student support services should help walk students through financial services—from financial aid and student bursaries to banking sources in the community—and other financial decisions including setting up a household, phone and web services, etc. It is important that institutions have a competitive fee schedule, fair access to scholarships in recognition of academic achievement, and programs better able to respond to students who face unexpected financial pressures due to extreme circumstances.

HEALTH AND WELLNESS SUPPORT

International students are often some of the biggest users of campus health and wellness services. The challenge of becoming a student in a new country coupled with a change of diet and lack of knowledge about how to acquire health care services can result in increased illness or distress. Moreover, some international students arrive with untreated health concerns. This is often true for mental health issues and blood-borne illnesses, such as hepatitis B. An additional factor is the number of international students who are accompanied by family members who require support during the student's period of study. Mirwaldt (2010) suggests that "for campus health services, the challenge is to communicate effectively, to provide culturally sensitive care, and to learn from these students an expanded view of health, self, and family responsibilities" (138).

SOCIAL AND CULTURAL SUPPORT

Culture shock is common among international students. Zhang and Zhou (2010) found that international students from China found it difficult to make friends with other international students and domestic students. They concluded that:

The cultural differences set up barriers for their willingness and attempts to make friends with native English-speaking friends, share residences with them and become fully involved in group work. Although language proficiency was mentioned by many participants as one factor that influenced their full engagement in the academic and social life on and off campus, it was often cultural differences that thwarted their efforts to be a part of the large community. For these participants who were able to manage the culture differences and enjoyed friendships with native English speakers, they felt significantly more satisfied with their experiences at the university and more confidence with their ability to finish their programmes. (131–2)

International students often seek a space where they can engage with students from their home country and access services. To meet this need, some institutions offer international student resource centers that serve as the hub for the international student support network, providing a central point for international student services, counseling and referrals, and cross-cultural activities.

International students often form fast and strong ties with international student organizations. These organizations help transport new students to and from the airport, help them during move-in, and introduce students to campus and community resources. Such international clubs and organizations are often supported by the campus international student advisor.

Although systemic racism is not the defining characteristic of the international student experience, isolated incidents of racism leave deep emotional scars and sour the experiences for affected students (Smith and Demanjenko 2011). Colleges and universities need to work proactively across the institution to enhance a sense of community to reduce incidences of racism or cultural misunderstanding.

TRANSITION SUPPORT

International students often do not bring family members with them, and thus many experience more severe adjustment issues than domestic students who can travel home more frequently. Transition, while a concern for all students, is especially relevant for international students who have travelled from another part of the world to be part of their academic communities. A recent study (Chen 2011) suggests that approximately one-quarter of Mandarin-speaking students encounter adjustment issues. Transition programs and services need to be specifically designed for international students. These supplements should address any number of topics, including international student support services, academic expectations, and cultural differences. This should be an integral part of the institution's general orientation events, although it is also important to offer a standalone program focused on international students' unique needs. Late orientation should also be provided for students who arrive late or start their programs mid-year.

IMMIGRATION SUPPORT

International students inevitably must, at one time or another, apply for (and often renew) their immigration documents. Students often have questions regarding the processes, and may need assistance in dealing with more complex circumstances. Immigration advising and support, most often provided by a central international student office, is important in ensuring students are able to successfully navigate government processes and that they maintain the appropriate status during their studies.

ACCOMMODATION (RESIDENCE LIFE) SUPPORT

International students benefit from a variety of residential life opportunities on campus, off campus, and through homestay initiatives. Some campuses accommodate specific international communities with residence floor themes and married housing opportunities. Homestay, where students live with domestic families in private homes, is becoming more common.

EMPLOYMENT SUPPORT

One way students manage their finances is by finding employment both on and off campus. Students are not required to have a work permit to work on campus, but one is generally required to work off campus. Postgraduate work permits are also available, particularly in Canada where many international graduates begin or continue their working career. According to the Institute for Competitiveness and Prosperity (2010) Canada leads OECD countries in international graduate retention at 9.7 percent.

While the literature and supporting studies suggest that there are many factors influencing international student retention and success, the solutions offered appear to be both universally applicable and locally appropriate. Table 11.4 (on page 115) shows possible strategies for increasing international student persistence within the influential reach of postsecondary institutions.

While we know much about the strategies that increase international student persistence and success, there remains a gap between implementation of these strategies and student satisfaction and usage of the related services.

The Ontario Ministry of Training, Colleges and Universities collaborated with six Ontario universities to administer the *International Student Barometer* (ISB) over a three year period, through i-Graduate, beginning in fall 2010. The ISB tracks decision-making expectations, perceptions, and intentions of international students from application to graduation, providing global, regional, and customized benchmarks.

Overall, the participating universities found the international student experience similar from campus to campus. However, when compared with the international index, reflecting all participating institutions, results showed some noticeable gaps. Looking across the areas of support, levels of satisfaction across the Ontario cohort were 5.2 percent lower than the ISB cohort, which suggests some possible areas of improvement (i-Graduate 2011). When usage is factored into student satisfaction (Smith *et al.* 2013), the areas where there appears to be the most potential for improvement include health center services, student accounts/finance department services, and campus food services.

A Look Ahead

Most institutions have developed strong student recruitment initiatives with the number of international students enrolled growing at many campuses. It is clear that colleges and universities should also work to enhance the success of international students.

Looking ahead, we need to ensure that these students are supported to reach their educational objectives while enrolled at our institutions. In particular, we need to find ways to create consistent interaction and socialization with domestic students. This will require us to pay more attention to the international student success factors.

Efforts to increase the retention rate should involve a paradigm shift in how postsecondary administration conceptualizes the efforts exerted to retain each international student. Conceptually, administrators should focus their thinking away from the retention rate and toward retention risk factors (Conrad and Morris 2010). In other words, the institutional view would ideally shift toward early prevention and efforts to assist international students in real time as the challenge(s) to remain at the institution occur.

The outlook for increasing international student success through North America is very good.

TABLE 11.4: Strategies to Increase International Student Persistence

Area of Support	Strategy
Academic Support	▸ Monitor international students' progress through the academic program and years) (Andrade 2009; Van Nelson, Nelson and Malone 2004) ▸ Develop culturally appropriate approach to meet the unique needs of ESL students within the classroom (Andrade 2009; Carter and Xu 2007)
Admission Policy	▸ Establish a minimum (English language proficiency and/or GPA) entry criteria (Beane 1985; Carter and Xu 2007)
Advising and Counseling	▸ Provide individual counseling to meet needs of international students (Andrade 2009; Boyer and Sedlacek 1988) ▸ Establish a mentor program for one-on-one support (Boyer and Sedlacek 1988; Carter and Xu 2007) ▸ Use an asset-based approach that comes from the field of positive psychology: connectedness, academic culture, resourcefulness, capability (Canadian Bureau of International Education 2014)
Cultural Awareness	▸ Increase sensitivity toward cultural differences within departments (Sandeen 2004; Beane 1985) ▸ Help international and domestic students understand and work against racism in the community (Boyer and Sedlacek 1988) ▸ Encourage domestic students to access the cultural knowledge and perspective of international students (Canadian Bureau of International Education 2014)
Organizational	▸ Develop strategies of cooperation and coordination among offices accessed by international students (Goff and Snowden 2015; Sandeen 2004; Beane 1985) ▸ Consider a more integrated approach to student engagement where international student offices and student life coordinators work collaboratively to create and facilitate more inclusive opportunities for international students and Canadian students, fostering greater multi-level exchange (Leary 2012)
Orientation	▸ Orientations which introduce international students to the facilities and services available to them (Mallinckrodt and Sedlacek 1987; Van Nelson, Nelson and Malone 2004) ▸ Quality enhancement interventions and non-cognitive elements of a student's experience such as daylong workshops (Carter and Xu 2007) ▸ Provide international students with pre-arrival information to decrease the first semester learning curve (Andrade 2009) ▸ Re-conceive student orientation as an ongoing, non-linear process for all students, and strategize around how to address barriers to participation for international students, especially at the beginning of the term (Canadian Bureau of International Education 2014) ▸ Develop a pass/fail acculturation class for new (undergraduate and graduate students separately) international students to make the transition by providing support and feedback over the course of a term (Leedock 2011)
Social Integration	▸ Help international students with community involvement (Boyer and Sedlacek 1988), interaction with faculty members, (Andrade 2009) and domestic students (Andrade 2009) ▸ Encourage group work between international and domestic students (Canadian Bureau of International Education 2014)
Study Abroad	▸ Establish an exchange program (Carter and Xu 2007)

TWELVE

Pre-Arrival Events for International Students

Vice Provost for Strategic Enrollment Management
Virginia Commonwealth University

LUKE DAVID SCHULTHEIS

Pre-Arrival Events for International Students

It is common practice to provide new student orientation to incoming students with an estimated rate of 96 percent of colleges and universities providing such services (Barefoot 2005). International students may be at some disadvantage when compared with domestic students in receiving the services provided at an orientation event. They often arrive on campus in time to begin the semester, but too late to prepare for their academic journey. If class registration is part of orientation, they often find that classes fulfilling degree requirements have already been filled by domestic students, leaving them with what's remaining. Additionally, they may not have had the opportunity to socialize or begin relationships with peers. One can imagine the anxiety related to studying in another country, being taught differently, and trying to quickly acclimate to a new culture.

Other chapters in this book focus upon recruiting and enrolling international students. The focus of this chapter is to outline services and support which can be provided to international students *before* they arrive on campus, at a pre-arrival event in their home country. This activity provides an introduction to the institution and those who work there—something which, when agents or other intermediaries are involved, is absent. Additionally, pre-arrival activity can have a profound effect upon student retention, something which can be difficult to prioritize and coordinate in institutional enrollment management efforts (Schultheis 2013).

An overview of the organizational characteristics of a pre-arrival orientation event will be reviewed, followed by the logistical aspects to planning the event and an outline of staff who are critical to the planning and execution of the events. Additionally, tables are presented which note potential areas of focus for the event, including a timetable for planning and scheduling the event and a sample agenda for the event.

Many institutions hold international pre-arrival events. The Ohio State University and Virginia Commonwealth University (VCU) host events in China while Monroe College in New York has held events in the Caribbean. These institutions recognize that students may not be able to afford to travel and participate in traditional campus-based orientation events. Over time, orientation has become a yield activity and it is common for families to attend such events at multiple institutions before finalizing enrollment. While hosting such events is expensive, they can provide an opportunity for multiple activities. The annual trip to Beijing by VCU includes a visit to feeder high schools and to universities which have academic partnerships with VCU, as well as trips to government offices to discuss higher education and an event to which alumni are invited.

Types of Orientation Structures

Mayhew, Vanderlinden, and Kim (2010) recommend three organizational structures at orientation. The first structure is academic, which will focus upon objectives and learning; the second structure is social, within which students create peer networks for the purpose of studying; and the third structure is functional, within which the rules and policies of the institution are outlined so that students and their families can navigate the institution.

ACADEMIC STRUCTURE

International students may not be accustomed to the academic structure of U.S. universities and colleges—a system which coincidentally is not wholly bound to uniformity. In general, U.S. higher education tends to focus less upon rote memorization and more upon workplace skills including good written and verbal communication, problem solving and teamwork, as well as leadership. Depending upon the home country and culture of the students, these areas of focus may differ greatly and it is important to understand the nuances relative to the students' background. New students and their families at pre-arrival events should receive instruction on these differences, as well as the structure of majors, minors and concentrations, the credit hour format, standards of academic progress, and the means by which faculty teach classes.

Mamiseishvili (2011) found that students who participated in student study groups and met frequently with academic advisors to ensure adherence to a degree plan performed well academically during their first year. Students should be encouraged to be proactive and take advantage of these important resources. The classroom experience and faculty expectations for student learning should be outlined as well. Lecture style halls with large numbers of students who may have little opportunity to participate outside of using clickers should be noted. Some professors utilize flipped classroom methods, assigning extensive readings and expecting students to think about the topic deeply and to be prepared for lively classroom discussion.

Some faculty use the Internet as a supplemental means of instruction and may ask students to participate via course management systems as well as in class. Furthermore, there are academic resources which may be new to the students. Academic advisors and their role should be outlined. Writing and math centers and centers of supplemental instruction should be highlighted. The role of the library requires deliberate attention as well (Cope and Black 1985; Hoffman and Popa 1986).

SOCIAL STRUCTURE

It is important for students and their families to feel a connection to the institution that extends beyond their relationship with administrators. Mamiseishvili's (2011) study found a negative correlation to persistence with social engagement in his study suggesting that the focus upon *fun* activities at orientation be replaced with academic-based socialization. In other words, development of peer networks who share a focus upon academic success will be more beneficial to students. This parallels a study of doctoral students by Curtin, Stewart, and Ostrove (2013) who found that international students did not expect to become acculturated, as they knew they were only studying in the U.S. for a finite period of time. Rather, their focus was upon optimizing their academic experience at the institution and surrounding themselves with those who shared that focus. Mayhew and colleagues (2010) found that international students who participated in orientation reported that it did not help them with social integration. They attributed this to the institution's inability to design socialization activities, which were more reflective or sensitive to the culture of the international students.

While it may not be feasible to design socialization activities independently for each country to which a pre-arrival team travels, a focus instead may be upon developing a supportive network of parents and students from the region. A level of comfort may exist in knowing that there are other students from the same area who will be traveling together to the U.S. institution. The students will have, once they arrive at the college or university, a number of peers with whom they can contextualize their new experiences within that of their culture. This is not meant to discount Tinto's (1975) model of social and academic integration. He noted that students were more likely to persist and succeed at an institution if they became attached to the intellectual life of the institution as well as to develop relationships with students in social settings such as clubs, in housing, and at events. Often, a focus at orientation is to help students to begin this process.

Pre-arrival events are not meant to diminish the amount of on-campus activities designed to integrate students into campus life and expose them to American culture and students. There is great value in diversity for all students, and certainly the exposure to U.S. culture is a reason why many students choose to study there. However, with the limited amount of time and resources likely available for the pre-arrival event, it may be preferable to focus upon the development of an academic socialization activity instead of socialization efforts geared toward friend development.

There are many ice-breakers one may find at a campus-based orientation, designed to develop such social relationships. However, cultures vary internationally and those activities may not be readily embraced. Some examples of academic socialization which may engender friend-making include small group discussions on career trajectories or conversations which encourage students to divulge why they decided to enroll in specific academic programs. These discussions may become more beneficial if the institution is able to include alumni. While there may be disparity between the major from which an alumnus graduated and the interests of the small groups, a focus upon academic resources at the institution will enrich the conversation and enable participants to contextualize their own upcoming experience.

FUNCTIONAL STRUCTURE

A quick glance at the international student websites of nearly fifteen colleges and universities indicates an emphasis upon the functional aspects of attendance. Most sites outline activities related to checking in with international officers at the institution, maintaining student status, and general policies associated with being able to remain at the institution. The terms used on these sites often refer to specific immigration policies and terminology related to processes at the institution. For

example, add/drop deadlines, evidence of medical insurance, and the difference between students' and scholars' vernacular and business related policies may not be completely familiar to many international students. Additionally, the sites generally list the documents needed for entry into the United States, types of visas, and acronyms for campus-based offices. The functional aspects related to being able to study in the United States are of great importance and thus deserving of prominence in materials. Institutions need to provide this important information in a way which can be understood by people from across the world.

Functional aspects of attending an institution should be highlighted well prior to the student's arrival on campus. A pre-arrival event provides an opportunity for attendees to clarify policies and engage in transactions. Some areas of emphasis, outlined in Table 12.1, include registering for classes, securing room and board, getting acquainted with the academic calendar, understanding the transportation to and from campus and

TABLE 12.1: Selection of Potential Topics to Address at Pre-Arrival Event

Academic	
Instruction	▸ Lecture based—large scale especially in lower division classes; smaller upper division courses
	▸ Graduate assistants in large lecture classes; professor in more specialized courses
	▸ Learning management system—[Insert brand name] houses notes, lectures, videos and provides space for interacting with other students via bulletin boards
	▸ Participation is expected in online formats as well as in lecture classes
	▸ Group work is used extensively, leadership roles rotate among students, groups earn grades collectively
Academic Integrity and Honesty	▸ Students do not collaborate on exams or homework
	▸ All citations or ideas which are derived from others must be attributed to those individuals
Social	
Study Groups	▸ Informal study groups may be available in the residence halls
	▸ Writing and math center study groups meet daily and are assisted by tutors
	▸ English conversation groups meet regularly and schedules are posted in the [insert office name]
Functional	
Academic Calendar	▸ Semester dates, holiday breaks, summer and mini-terms
Credits	▸ Number needed for degree, number to earn each semester, satisfactory academic progress
	▸ Repeat policy
	▸ Add/drop and withdrawal policy
	▸ Registration timeline
	▸ Declaring a major

within the campus, checking in with the appropriate officials at the institution, maintaining active student status, safety protocols, and the availability of campus resources. A pre-arrival team would not want to review every policy at the event but would be well served to focus upon policies which they have found international students struggling with over the years.

Assembling the Team

Hosting an international pre-arrival event is an expensive endeavor; however, the anticipated returns vis-à-vis retention and academic success make it a worthwhile activity. The team needs to be able to perform multiple duties and to represent several campus constituencies. In addition to the pre-arrival event, there are opportunities to visit with partner institutions, delegations from the government, alumni, and potential feeder schools. These activities all require a high level of decorum and respect for the host country's culture.

The team needs to be able to speak to students and parents, to the academic, social and functional structures of the institution, as well as be good general ambassadors who are not afraid to perform functions which may otherwise fall to others. Some academic structure areas to be covered include degrees, programs, minors, areas of concentration, and how one progresses through a curriculum to earn a degree. Social functions may be presented to include clubs, intramural and varsity teams, affinity groups, and general social activities. Functional structures may be presented as including administrative and academic areas such as departments, programs, and schools, as well as student affairs, enrollment management, and student government. Some offices which may provide good representatives include orientation, student affairs (in particular an individual from student life or housing), admissions, academic advising, and international student services. If possible, recent alumni who have returned to the country and who are willing to help at the event should be sought out.

It is wise to scan the institution for existing relationships already developed in the host country and to inform the appropriate stakeholders of the trip asking for support. This should be done 6–12 months before the trip so that appointments can be made well in advance. It will also be important to provide the team with training on the culture of the host nation so that introductions, meetings, and the exchange of gifts or other pleasantries are adhered to properly. The lead individual for the team should ensure that all members secure their visas or required travel documents in advance and that all members are aware of their respective duties prior to and during the event. Additionally, an individual should be designated as the spokesperson for any media inquiries and another individual on the team should be assigned as the site manager and be charged with ensuring that the rooms, menu, Internet, and signage are all set up properly.

Planning the Visit

There are multiple logistical issues that will need to be considered, including travel documents, immunizations, a calendar of appointments, shipping or onsite printing of promotional material, securing and paying for space at an appropriate venue during an optimal time for the target market, choosing food and beverages, arranging for media coverage, creating the agenda, and establishing a marketing campaign to inform all relevant parties well in advance (*see* Table 12.2, on page 123). Additionally, it is very important to establish a set of measureable goals for the event that will be assessed prior to the next visit. Reviewing the plan with members of the travel team as well as some others at the institution such as the international student's office, admissions, advising, housing, and new student orientation will likely be beneficial. Six months prior to the event can be a particularly good time to engage international alumni for their insights on venue, timing, and communication of the event. This enables the institution to secure a site and make travel arrangements early enough to appreciate any potential discounts and to reduce the chance of not being able to finalize arrangements because it has already been secured by others.

The Agenda

It is important that the students and families be informed of expectations and be aware of what they may need to bring or what type of business will be conducted. The pre-arrival event will provide for many their first exposure to and impression of the institution. While a structured agenda will be made, one may wish to anticipate the need to arrive early and stay late in order to deal with the unexpected. Some agenda items are presented on Table 12.3. The location should be chosen carefully and checked with alumni to see what type of impression the venue may send. The institution does not want to seem as if it uses excessive funds on properties which are overly formal, nor does it want to hold an event at a site which has local repute as a low budget enterprise. An alumni contact will be able to provide insights into what type of menu will draw attendees as well as what would be tasteful. In some areas, families may be traveling via train or bus and the event could be hosted near a train or bus hub. Parking arrangements should be outlined for those who will arrive by car. The chosen date should not conflict with any national holidays, testing day, or other events which could reduce the number of attendees. The schedule should allow for ample time to meet with families individually as well as to conduct a more formal presentation to the entire group and to participate in media interviews.

Speakers should limit speech time, keeping in mind that the families will expect to hear highlights about the prestige of the institution, the attractions of the area, and some of the important policies and associated deadlines. Engaging an alumnus to provide a brief pre-

TABLE 12.2: Limited List of Activities to Be Conducted Several Months Prior to Event

Scan institution for international partnerships and solicit opportunities to support those on the visit
Make appointments with international partners
Establish the team members and ensure team secures necessary visas, passports and travel documents, reserve flight and hotel
Check with alumni on preferred venues and times to host event
Reserve space, menu, audio-visual, signage, parking at venues; make payment arrangements
Notify media and secure additional marketing to cover event
Secure printing of materials in host country or make shipping arrangements
Communicate event to target market via multiple channels, establish reservation system and monitor
Order any giveaways which are additional to informational materials such as clothing, USBs, gifts
Verify that all students from host country have had admission applications acted upon and financial aid packaged
Discuss goals of event, measureable outcomes
Assign event duties to each team member
Develop assessment tool for participants to measure effectiveness of event
Establish communication plan for post-event but pre-semester time frame
Review student academic records, placement test scores, outline a tentative academic schedule for them
Establish meeting schedule with team, leading up to event

TABLE 12.3: Sample Internal Agenda for Event

Activity	Timeframe	Team Member
Welcome and explanation of the agenda	5 minutes	
Meal—sit down style	45 minutes	
Brief overview of the highly ranked programs and some prestigious notes on the institution	10 minutes	
Alumnus speaker—to endorse the education received at the institution	10 minutes	
Review of academic structure	15 minutes	
Socialization activity to engage families and students	30 minutes	
Review of functional structure	15 minutes	
Transactions and individual questions—at stations around the room (may include class scheduling, room and board, finances, immigration issues, general questions)	1 hour	
Distribution of materials and gifts; pictures with students	20 minutes	

sentation can help establish additional credibility with the institution, but the talking points should be reviewed well prior to the event.

Speech topics should be centered on the academic, social, and functional structures of the institution. Written materials which reinforce the messaging should be provided at the event. If English is not the native language, a bilingual approach should be considered, especially as families will consult these materials. An opportunity for students to form informal conversational groups to discuss some of the aspects of the event could generate long-term supportive academic relationships (Sherry, Thomas, and Chui 2010).

Attendees should be provided the opportunity to conduct transactions and to ask questions specific to their situations in a more intimate setting. This may take the form of team members sitting at separate tables, each with Internet access to the student information system. Any financial transactions should be conducted over secure sites—never with cash, something attendees should be made aware of prior to the event. If possible, students should also be provided the ability to secure housing and board as well as prepare their class schedule. These may have a profoundly positive effect upon students as they see this as a commitment to attending the institution.

Once the agenda has been established, it is important to communicate it with the target market regularly and through the appropriate channels. One may find that email alone will not suffice and phone calls, even though they may need to be made well outside of business hours, are an effective means of communication. Consider providing extensive information on the Web with which students and families can become familiar. This may help reduce the number of questions and provide much needed background on the three structures. It may be worthwhile to have students complete an assessment of the information found on the online component, prior to the event, to learn if they have understood the information. Wojciechowski and Paler (2005) found that students who participated in online orientation related to their online classes performed much better academically. This suggests that having students access the learning system for the orientation materials provides dual benefits: making them familiar both with the important information as well as the system they will be using once they arrive on campus. Additionally, students should be encouraged to access their records through the student information system portal so that they become familiar with the site struc-

ture. Proficiency in the online environment will prepare students well for academic activities (Cho 2012).

Goals and Assessment

Goals will vary by institution, but they are important to establish. Activities which can be assessed include the number of those admitted who confirm attendance at the event and then attend the event. Choosing important outcomes will aid in establishing these measures. Some measures of success may include having students complete online placement tests prior to the visit to aid in the registration process, registering students for classes, students paying deposits on housing and committing to board plans. There may be actions which need to take place on campus prior to the visit, such as updating student accounts and scholarships as well as posting all advanced standing into the student record. Regardless of what goals are established, they should be measurable, with staff who are accountable for them. It is especially important to gauge progress prior to the trip, as falling behind in meeting goals could have a residual and negative effect upon attendance and desired outcomes.

In addition to assessing goals for the team, participants should be assessed to better understand what they learned. Several formats could be developed including pre- and post-event surveys. It may be beneficial to examine the assessment tools in place for on-campus orientation and to modify those according to the specific needs and information shared at the pre-arrival event.

Throughout their time at the institution, student performance should be assessed, remembering that the purpose of the pre-arrival event is to better prepare students to succeed at the institution. Some indications that the pre-arrival event, in tandem with other services of course, are contributing to student success may include: more timely bill payment, improved satisfaction with room and board arrangements, improved yield of international students, decreased time-to-degree, decreased attrition, fewer issues related to academic integrity, and increased interest in the institution from various entities in the host country.

Conclusion

Pre-arrival events can provide students who are unable to attend on-campus orientation with an introduction to staff, resources, and the culture of the institution. Colleges and universities spend significant amounts of money recruiting international students and it is wise to invest in their preparation prior to their arrival for the beginning of the academic year. Students and families who are able to have a clearer understanding of the institution will be able to spend more time engaged in activities which contribute to student success. These trips also offer the institution an opportunity to further develop partnerships established previously by the academic units and to expand networks which can lead to increased enrollment and partnerships. They also enable the institution to re-engage alumni who may otherwise feel as distant from the institution due to their geographic location.

THIRTEEN

Dual Degree
Programs

2016 AACRAO INTERNATIONAL GUIDE

THY YANG

Associate Vice President for International Studies
St. Cloud State University

Dual Degree Programs

The establishment of sister-school relationships between institutions from two or more countries is an established practice within higher education. Formal agreements have been used to document the interests of both parties to explore mutually-beneficial partnerships and collaborations that will internationalize their campuses. More often than not, these agreements serve as precursors to formal exchange agreements for both students and faculty.

More recently, universities are turning to dual degree programs as a formal means of establishing partnerships and linkages to institutions outside of the United States. In fact, the dual degree program may be the first initiative that brings the two schools together. It is not uncommon for universities to find other programs and initiatives to collaborate on after they begin working on a dual degree. For this reason, dual degree programs can serve as a catalyst for comprehensive internationalization and should be considered a viable means to creating more opportunities for students and faculty. Because dual degree programs require the engagement of a larger network of parties and individuals—from curriculum design to conferring the degree—the number of issues to be examined is also larger. A larger network of stakeholders requires a more comprehensive set of questions and deeper complexities which campuses must consider.

Definition of Dual Degree Program

Although some universities may use the phrases dual degree and joint degree interchangeably, for the purpose of this discussion, the definition of dual degree adopted by the American Council on Education will be used: "A degree program that is designed and delivered by two or more partner institutions in different countries. A student receives a qualification from each of the partner institutions. Such programs are also referred to as 'double degrees'" (Helms 2014).

Mechanics of Dual Degrees

Just as there are differing views on how to define dual degree programs, differing views exist on how to deliver them. There remains no standard approach, neither in the United States nor across international borders, to the way dual degrees are delivered, assessed, and conferred. Even parties to the same agreement can agree to follow different principles for selecting the courses, determining the credits, and awarding the degree.

In general, what dual degree programs have in common is the mutual understanding between the participating universities that students will receive two degrees upon completion of courses. This determination has been made jointly. Frequently, both universities will agree to transfer all or most of the coursework completed at the other institution or alternatively recognize those credits as their own. Another way to approach dual degrees is to model them after agreements commonly established between two-year and four-year institutions (*i.e.*, articulation agreements).

Ultimately, the credential awarded may differ from institution to institution, despite participation in a dual degree program. Various options include receiving the same degree in the same major from both universities, the same type of degree but in a different major, or there may be two degrees in two different levels of educational achievement. For instance, in a 3+2 program, students can earn a bachelor's degree from their home university while completing a master's degree from the partner university (Helms 2014).

Lack of standardization adds to the challenges of promoting the program to prospective students (as well as colleagues) effectively. This can erode the confidence of the campus community as well as prospective students. Senior administrators at both institutions must be able to address the differences in how courses are delivered, graded, accounted for, and used for the final degrees.

Stiegler (2015) makes a case for universities to follow preexisting academic policies established by the institution; in other words, referring to the established policies for granting a degree using credits earned from an outside institution. Some questions to ask include: Are there minimum requirements that must be earned in the final semester on the campus? What is the minimum number of upper-division credits that must be earned at the degree-granting university? What are the restrictions for recognizing upper-division credits taken within the student's major? When awarding degrees that combine both transfer credits and credits earned at the home university, one should follow the established policies and procedures to alleviate any faculty members' concerns about the legitimacy of the dual degree program. Another strategy is to only work with international universities who share common accrediting agencies, particularly in professional programs such as business and engineering. This simplifies the process of articulating courses taken at the other university.

Dual Degrees and Their Role in Comprehensive Internationalization

An observation made about dual degree programs is the lack of student mobility from the U.S. side. In *Mapping International Joint and Dual Degree Degrees: Program Profiles and Perspectives,* respondents to the ACE survey indicated that dual degree programs are designed primarily to recruit international students to study in the U.S. This is noted in conjunction with the criticism that universities engaged in dual degree pro-

grams are not fully realizing the purported benefits of the international partnerships, including study abroad opportunities and curriculum internationalization.

However, since 84 percent of survey respondents stated that their programs require international students to enroll in courses on their campuses, a case can be made that dual degree programs are not just about increasing enrollment and revenues. Dual degree programs serve as a catalyst for enlarging a university's capacity to serve students from outside of the U.S., as well as force the campus to address issues related to cross cultural teaching and learning. Take the examples of Northampton Community College (PA) and Appalachian State University (NC). Both institutions saw a need to create faculty exchange opportunities first as a way to ensure effective engagement. Over time, the exchanges allowed for faculty on both sides to have greater understanding of the cultures and complexities required when engaging partners from outside of one's own country. Prior to the launch of its dual degree program, Northampton hosted four faculty members from its Chinese partner institution, Jinzhou University, for six months, and sent three of its own faculty to China for a summer. Appalachian State and its Mexican partner, Universidad de las Americas, have also utilized faculty exchanges as a means to develop their joint programs. These exchanges allow for faculty to become familiar with the curriculum of the other institutions, study the differences in teaching methodologies and student expectations, refine course equivalencies, and build relationships. All of these are essential to securing the commitment required by the faculty for long-term sustainability (Helms 2014).

For the State University of New York (SUNY), the decision to engage in a dual degree collaboration with the Turkish Higher Education Council (YOK) has yielded many benefits aside from increased enrollments. For instance, preparing for the students' arrival required system-wide conversations about campus readiness to support international student success. The initiative led to the doubling of study abroad programs with Turkish partners. Most notably, the collaboration gave SUNY universities the confidence and experience to pursue additional collaborations with other institutions in other countries (Lane, Krebs, and Thompson 2015).

Cost Structure and Revenue Models

Because most dual degree programs are designed to recruit international students, generating net revenue can be one of the most important outcomes of the initiative. Depending on the partner institution, universities may follow any one of the following models:

❋ **Direct Enrollment.** Using this model, students pay the host university directly for all costs associated with the program. Fees may include tuition, course and lab fees, books and supplies, international student health insurance, and room and board. Both universities may charge a nominal administrative fee to recover costs associated with establishing (initial costs) and coordinating the programs (ongoing costs). It is not unlikely that a student would be charged a fee by the home university as well as the host university in order to be enrolled in the program.

❋ **Reciprocal Exchange.** This model requires both universities to commit to sending a balanced number of students each way. Under this model, the student pays tuition and fees to their home university and only pays the host university for course and lab fees, books and supplies, international student health insurance, and room and board. This model is common for programs that enroll a limited number of students. It is also a good model to use if the institution wishes to engage a partner institution located in a country with limited student mobility. It could also be considered for use with partner institutions located in countries which are a popular destination from the home university. Due to the high demand to attend the foreign university, the partner may require the dual degree as an incentive to waive their tuition for students from the U.S. school. This is also a popular model to use with partner schools who charge very little or no tuition to their own students.

Other cost considerations might include the use of scholarships (*e.g.*, discounting or granting out-of-state waivers). Some universities may dedicate funds to support institutional work-study positions for participants in the dual degree program. Some universities have allowed academic departments to claim parts of the tuition to offset their own expenses or to entice faculty engagement in the creation and execution of such programs. Other universities have dedicated some or all of the revenues generated from the programs to re-invest in other globalization initiatives such as scholarships to support study abroad, professional development funds to support international faculty travel, or the administrative costs associated with having an international student support center.

Challenges Faced by the U.S. Campus

After making the decision to offer a dual degree program, the campus must prepare itself for some unique challenges. It is important not to underestimate the total amount of time required to launch a new dual degree program: 70 percent of the respondents to the ACE survey reported that the development period was one to three years. Other challenges include establishing course equivalencies, addressing language and cultural differences, as well as identifying various teaching and grading/evaluation methodologies (Helms 2014).

Stiegler (2015) suggests that universities can minimize many of the stresses by carefully offering limited degree options. For instance, the degrees that will be the least flexible with regard to curriculum matching must be identified in advance, along with any degrees which require accreditation or licensure; these programs may not be ideal as both universities would need to have the means and opportunity to address the rigid requirements.

Universities should also be careful not to choose degree programs or majors which may not be appealing to students. While a Liberal Studies degree may have the most flexibility in terms of how the programs are constructed, the target student group may find that the degree is not relevant for their future academic or professional goals. Students may desire the name of their degree to match what the marketplace requires. In some instances, U.S. universities are able to build in minors or certificate programs to satisfy this demand by the partner university.

Another challenge faced by U.S. campuses is the need to increase the amount of time spent at their institutions due to English language limitations, especially for programs designed to be completed within a certain time frame (e.g., 2+2). The additional cost of attendance can be an unpleasant surprise to program participants who will look to their home university to advocate on their behalf.

Lastly, universities must recognize that all program participants may not be as academically prepared for the program. A critical mass of students not academically prepared to take upper-level courses taught exclusively in English pose a threat to the entire program's success. Faculty as well as the other students taking courses alongside the dual degree participants may become frustrated. As universities negotiate their agreements, both should consider how to accommodate students who are not able to follow the sequence of courses due to lack of English proficiency or academic preparedness (LaFleur 2015).

Successful Partnerships

LaFleur (2015) writes that, "identifying appropriate partner institutions is a critical first step in program development. The partners involved should fully commit to evaluating the respective degree programs and discuss the desired outcome of creating the joint or dual degree."

Some institutions select partners with whom they already know and have developed a solid relationship. The two institutions may have engaged in student and faculty exchanges for years prior to the establishment of a dual degree program. However, it is becoming increasingly common for universities to actively seek new partners solely for the purpose of creating dual degree programs. In some instances, the U.S. institution is

responding to a solicitation from a non-U.S. institution. In other cases, the U.S. institution makes a concerted effort to seek out and choose from an array of universities that will best suit their needs. In either case, the success of the program will always mirror that of the partnership.

As universities develop their programs and partnerships, they must be attuned to the needs and wants of students, specifically what incentivizes a student to select the proposed program. Examples of incentives include the ability to enroll in a program not normally offered to them at their home campus, gaining access to a new job market or research field, funding otherwise not available, or the ability to study alongside students or faculty mentors not available at the home university (LaFleur 2015).

While the schools may not need to mutually agree on how to best market the program, it is essential that the universities agree on the substance and intention of the program. In addition to granting authority for the non-U.S. school to use their name and logo, the U.S. school must agree with how the admission policies and procedures are being presented. Students and families will not only have questions about the program being delivered, they will also need to know information such as housing options, safety, program duration, and estimated costs of living. Successful partnerships require constant and ongoing communication throughout all stages of the initiative.

Unexpected Rewards

Dual degree programs have been historically designed to benefit university campuses in terms of increased enrollments and global diversity. Occasionally, universities will see a slight uptick in U.S. students wishing to study abroad in the countries represented by the dual degree participants. They may also see modest demands for additional foreign language or cultural studies courses to be taken by U.S. students whose interests become piqued after prolonged exposure to a particular culture. But what many universities do not expect are the following increases: engagement from their newest group of international alumni, enrollment of full studies international students, and the campus' appetite for larger groups of students from outside of the U.S.

While dual degree program participants may not have spent the same number of years on campus as other students, it is very likely that their affinity for the university matches the intensity of traditional students. Universities should develop those relationships and connections. Because dual degree participants often come from the same country or partner university, it is quite easy to coordinate large gatherings. In time, these alumni can be critical to fundraising or recruitment initiatives.

Universities who offer dual degree programs can see an increase in their overall international student enrollment. Program participants may recruit their friends or families to study at the university in areas not offered through the dual degree. Degree recipients may wish to stay and earn a second degree or pursue an advanced degree upon completion of their dual degree. Another benefit contributing to an increased international stu-

dent population is the familiarity that international admissions offices have with students from a particular country. This can translate to traveling to the home country more regularly to recruit students directly. Another unexpected reward is the enhanced reputation of the U.S. university in these new markets, which may translate into additional enrollments.

Lastly, universities can see an increased appetite among faculty, staff, and students for more campus internationalization initiatives. There may be increases in the number of dual degree programs offered as well as the number of countries represented. Students may demand more courses with an international focus in their disciplines. Or better yet, students may desire the same dual degree opportunities they see afforded to their international classmates and peers. Overall, while there are many challenges to consider, campuses should anticipate that, in time, they will derive many benefits from these initial international partnerships.

FOURTEEN

Professional Development

for International Admissions Officers

2016 AACRAO INTERNATIONAL GUIDE

Senior Policy Advisor
University of Toronto

ANDREA ARMSTRONG

Professional Development for International Admissions Officers

In the field of international admissions and credential assessment, the diversity of applicants, constant changes to education systems, and technological change makes ongoing professional development a must. The benefits of a commitment to ongoing professional development are varied and are shared among the staff who participate, their institutions, prospective students, and the broader international admissions and credential assessment community. Professional development activities come in many forms: attending conferences, courses, and workshops; participating in webinars and online discussions; and in the acts of reading, writing, and reflecting. In this chapter, the benefits of professional development to the different participants in the admissions process will be discussed, as well as development opportunities and activities designed more specifically to benefit the international admissions specialist.

Although one may often think of professional development as 'career development'—that is, as activities that individuals participate in primarily as a means to bettering their own career—it in fact has a much broader meaning. It may be true that, at its core, professional development serves to advance the knowledge and skills of participants, but the benefits of professional development go well beyond the individual.

Admissions officers who demonstrate a commitment to ongoing training benefit in a number of ways. Ongoing learning builds confidence in decision-making, gives staff increased credibility among their peers and managers, exposes staff to 'best practices' for increasing productivity and efficiency, and provides a framework for assessing institutional policies related to

international admissions. At a more personal level, participating in professional development activities can provide the practical skills, knowledge, and networking opportunities required for career advancement. Indeed, the act of taking time to participate in a professional development activity—whether it is an hour-long training session or a weeklong international conference—can help keep staff engaged in work by providing a new perspective on day-to-day activities. It can also provide an opportunity to stop and reflect on current practices in a way that may not be possible in a typical workday at a busy, resource-challenged admissions office.

Colleges and universities that support staff in ongoing professional development also benefit significantly from these activities. From a human resources perspective, offering development opportunities to staff serves two distinct functions: it increases employee retention and it serves to support succession planning. Succession planning is a particularly important consideration for outward-facing units like university and college admissions offices. In the event that the international admissions specialist at the institution were to leave their role unexpectedly, would there be other staff members equipped to preserve the institution's service to—and reputation among—prospective international students and their supporters? An institution that commits to the ongoing professional development of its staff may be in the best position to meet this kind of challenge.

Two other tangible benefits to the institutions that provide professional development opportunities to their admissions officers are increased efficiency and increased quality. It stands to reason that staff who are equipped with the latest information about international education systems are the best positioned to be able to work efficiently through volumes of application files and to be able to make reasoned, equitable admissions policy decisions on behalf of their institutions. In addition, well-trained staff are also in the best position to identify application anomalies, including incidences of fraud. As has been well-documented elsewhere, there are real costs to institutions—and to their reputations—when international students are admitted on the basis of inauthentic documents. Application-related fraud can present itself in many ways, and the techniques used to perpetuate fraud are constantly changing (*see* Chapter 19: Fighting Fraud in the Admissions and Registrar's Offices). Therefore, it is critical that institutions support their staff in obtaining the most up-to-date information possible about this aspect of admissions.

Finally, a less tangible—but still important—benefit is in how the institution's reputation among prospective students and their supporters (including their families, schools, teachers, and others) is impacted by their interactions with the institution's admissions office staff. When a telephone call from an international student who has detailed questions about the institution's admission policies is responded to with a detailed and accurate response, it can only serve to increase the possibility that this student will apply to—and hopefully join—the institution. Similarly, guidance counselors at international secondary schools may steer their students to apply to institutions with whom they have had positive experiences in the past, and particularly if they have confidence in that institution's ability to fairly interpret their student's academic credentials and grades. In the competitive world of international admissions and student recruitment, reputation matters. Institutions can help to enhance their stature by taking steps to ensure that their international admissions staff only add to that reputation.

Perhaps most importantly, prospective students benefit when international admissions officers are able to incorporate the most up-to-date information about education systems and admissions 'best practices' into their work. As noted above, well-trained staff may be able to work through applications for admission more efficiently. They will know which documents to ask international students to provide, and be able to communicate these requirements clearly, saving the applicant unnecessary confusion. Optimally, this will allow applicants to receive their admission decisions earlier than they would otherwise, which may help lessen some of the anxiety that many applicants feel throughout the admissions process. Moreover, admissions officers applying current best practices to their admissions work will be able to evaluate applications for admission in the most fair and equitable way possible. They will draw upon the right resources and use a well-considered process to evaluate applications.

Professional Organizations

There are several volunteer professional organizations dedicated at least in part to supporting and advancing the knowledge of international admissions and credential assessment professionals. Membership in these organizations can offer significant benefits, including access to publications, online newsletters, conferences, training courses, and other networking opportunities. To further skill development, membership can lead to opportunities such as presenting at conferences, writing for publications or newsletters, and leadership opportunities. There are many other relevant professional organizations than are touched upon below. Those listed below are among the most prominent in the field, however.

AACRAO

Founded in 1910, AACRAO is a non-profit, voluntary, professional association of more than 11,000 higher education professionals with members in more than 40 countries. Its mission is to provide professional development, guidelines, and voluntary standards for best practices in records management, admissions, enrollment management, administrative information technology, and student services. Professional development is a main focus for AACRAO. Among its professional development offerings are yearly conferences, workshops, and online training courses. In the field of international admissions and credential evaluation more specifically, AACRAO has long been a leader. Its print publications on foreign education systems, first introduced more than fifty years ago, include the World Education Series, the Projects for International Education Research (PIER), and AACRAO country studies. In addition, AACRAO provides the comprehensive subscription-based online Electronic Database for Global Education. The AACRAO annual meeting typically includes dozens of presentations by leaders in the field of international education and credential evaluation. The association also offers a yearly Summer Institute for International Admissions, a weeklong training program designed for those relatively new to the realm of international academic credential assessment, as well as a Winter Institute for International Transfer Credit.

NAFSA: ASSOCIATION OF INTERNATIONAL EDUCATORS

NAFSA: Association of International Educators was founded in 1948 to promote the professional development of U.S. college and university officials responsible for assisting and advising foreign students. This organization has grown to include a membership of more than 10,000 higher education professionals from more than 150 countries. As with AACRAO, professional development is a key focus for NAFSA. The organization offers an annual conference billed as the largest in the field of international education, as well as additional career and learning opportunities, including courses, workshops, and other colloquia. It also maintains online 'knowledge communities' and conducts and shares research related to international education.

EAIE: EUROPEAN ASSOCIATION FOR INTERNATIONAL EDUCATION

EAIE is the European center for expertise, networking, and resources in the internationalization of higher education. This organization has a membership of nearly 3,000 international education professionals from over 80 countries. It places significant focus on international academic credential evaluation, and offers a variety of training opportunities, including twice-yearly training institutes held in European cities, conferences, and webinars. It also has a notable publishing program, which includes a magazine, a series of professional development publications, and occasional papers on topics in international education.

TAICEP: THE ASSOCIATION FOR INTERNATIONAL CREDENTIAL EVALUATION PROFESSIONALS

Founded in 2013, TAICEP is a new professional organization dedicated to meeting the unique goals of international credential evaluation professionals. As with the other organizations discussed previously, TAICEP has a mandate to provide professional development opportunities to its members and to date has developed webinars, a member newsletter, and an annual conference, including presentations on many specific credential evaluation topics. In addition, their website provides a considerable amount of information on resources for international credential assessment and a compendium of global professional development opportunities for practitioners.

In addition to these national and international organizations, there are many other local and regional professional associations dedicated to the needs of admissions officers, including State and Regional ACRAO groups in the U.S. and Regional/Provincial Registrars' Associations in Canada. Internationally, there are also other professional associations for admissions officers and credential evaluators that may offer professional development opportunities of interest.

Credential Evaluation Agencies

A unique aspect of the field of international admissions and credential assessment is the degree to which information is shared among the many actors in the field. Although universities and colleges compete, in a sense, for the best and brightest international students, they also participate readily in information-sharing with competitor institutions. Similarly, credential evaluation agencies, including for-profit agencies, contribute greatly to the knowledge of the admissions and credential assessment community as a whole. They offer a variety of services to international credential assessment professionals, including in-depth training sessions, and also publish excellent volumes on topics of interest to admissions officers. Often, these services are provided to the broader assessment community at zero or low cost.

In the United States and Canada, there are approximately 25 well-recognized and professional credential evaluation services. Three of the most active and well-known are World Education Services, Education Credential Evaluators, and International Education Research Foundation. World Education Services produces frequent newsletters on timely topics, offers workshops and online seminars, and provides a number of excellent online resources, including country profiles and the *International Grade Conversion Guide for Higher Education* tool. Education Credential Evaluators has published extensively on international credential evaluation with its ECE 'Insights' series of country guides. ECE also provides training sessions and webinars, and is host to an online community of international credential evaluators known as 'The Connection' (and its subscription-required companion, 'The Connection Advantage'). The International Education Research Foundation offers training sessions and has published a series of well-regarded publications including the *Country Index* and the *Index of Secondary Credentials*. A Canadian credential evaluation agency, the International Qualifications Assessment Service of Alberta, has also produced a series of informative Education Overview Guides on over a dozen countries and made these available at no charge on their website.[8]

National and International Government Agencies

In response to an increasingly mobile international population, many governments and their affiliated organizations have directed significant resources to issues in credential evaluation. Ensuring that international academic credentials are fairly recognized by the employers and educational institutions that receive them is of critical importance to countries that seek to attract high numbers of international students and immigrants, and also to countries that have entered into mobility agreements with neighboring countries (as in the European Union). Some of the national agencies that support international education and admissions professionals in interpreting foreign academic qualifications include EducationUSA, the Canadian Information Centre for International Credentials, and the ENIC-NARIC/National Information Centres in most European countries. Although the mandate of many of these organizations is to serve the needs of the country they were established in, many of these organizations make their publications and resources available to practitioners in other countries. EP-NUFFIC, the ENIC-NARIC centre for The Netherlands, provides an example of this: their excellent 'extensive descriptions of foreign education systems' (previously known as country modules) are made available at no charge on their website.[9]

Professional Development on Campus

The human resources/staff development (or similar) departments of most universities and colleges offer a variety of courses, programs, and other training opportunities to help admissions officers perform their roles more effectively and prepare them for career advancement. Staff development units often offer courses around workplace essentials—time management, software, team-building and the like—but also around issues that may be of more specific interest to international admissions staff such as: maintaining the privacy and confidentiality of applicant information, diversity, equity, and inclusiveness.

Many higher education institutions also administer mentorship programs for their staff. These programs

---

[8] See <http://work.alberta.ca/immigration/12638.html>.

[9] *See* <www.epnuffic.nl/en/#tab-foreign-education-systems>.

have many benefits for the institution, the mentee, and also the mentor. Mentorship programs provide mentees with a way to explore and define their career goals, to expand their networks, and to improve their confidence and skills in the workplace setting. Participation as a mentor represents an opportunity to show leadership and to reflect on one's own professional goals and accomplishments. For institutions, these programs can serve as a way to improve staff retention and support succession planning initiatives, and have the benefit of being accessible and low-cost to administer. (It is worth noting that mentorship opportunities and programs exist within professional associations as well.)

In addition to courses and programming that may be offered by institutional HR departments, professional development courses and programs are often offered by other campus organizations. For example, the campus library may offer useful 'how to' courses to assist staff in accessing library resources, or be able to provide one-on-one training to an admissions officer looking to conduct research into a specific topic. Similarly, the international student center on campus may offer training to campus staff on issues related to immigration or intercultural communication.

Some colleges and universities also offer institution-wide conferences or professional development days, which offer an opportunity for information exchange and networking within the institution. At larger institutions, particularly those that have more than one admissions or enrollment services office (for example, a university with multiple campuses), this type of event provides a valuable opportunity to meet face-to-face with other admission professionals who work with the same administrative systems and are encountering similar opportunities and constraints in their work environment.

Staff with an interest in international admissions might also wish to attend lectures, symposia, or other informational events offered through campus faculties and academic departments. For example, a scholar at an institution's faculty of education may present lectures related to a particular education system, or a graduate student returning from a period of field work might present preliminary research findings of relevance. Although this type of programming is not strictly designed for university administrators, it has the advantage of being low-cost and easily accessible.

At many institutions, student recruitment and admissions are two separate functions, carried out by separate offices or staff groups. However, there is considerable overlap in the knowledge required to effectively perform each function. Ideally, international admissions officers would periodically have the opportunity to visit jurisdictions from which they receive frequent applications, to visit schools, and to speak with school officials, prospective students, and their supporters first-hand. This experience would allow them to gain a level of insight into that country's education system they might not be able to otherwise. At the personal development level, participating in international student recruitment activities can serve as a great way for an admissions specialist to improve public speaking skills, develop cross-cultural awareness, and expand their network of education contacts.

Within the admissions office, there are many different ways in which international admissions officers can continue to develop their knowledge and skills. There may be periodic opportunities to participate in training on a variety of admissions topics, or to arrange less formal, one-on-one training sessions with experienced colleagues. Opportunities often exist for more experienced admissions staff to lead training sessions on topics of particular interest, create documentation and training materials, and participate in project work. They can also show initiative and ambition by requesting a 'stretch' assignment: a project or task that goes beyond their level of skill and expertise or beyond the usual scope of their role. Although the professional development opportunities available within the office may be relatively small in scale, they can provide staff with the skills and confidence they need to move into more challenging roles.

Formal Education as Professional Development

According to the NASPA—Student Affairs Administrators in Higher Education Graduate Program Directory, there are more than three hundred graduate degree programs in fields related to higher education, student affairs, and related fields in the United States alone. Graduate programs in higher education are also offered at a number of Canadian universities and in many international jurisdictions. These programs can provide a solid foundation in education theory, comparative education, and research methodology that can be valuable to international admissions officers and those looking to move into management and planning roles within admissions and enrollment management. It is worth noting that in addition to the many specialized graduate programs available in education, there are a number of other areas of undergraduate and graduate study relevant to the work of international admissions professionals, including language studies, political science, regional studies (for example: Latin American Studies or Central European Studies), information studies, and geography.

Many postsecondary institutions also offer credit and non-credit continuing education programs and courses to their staff, often at a reduced rate. The number and types of courses available will vary by institution, but a typical offering includes courses on topics such as information technology and new media, professional skill development, administration, finance, and communications.

Staff at postsecondary institutions should also be sure to consult with their human resources departments to determine whether they may qualify for tuition assistance should they participate in educational opportunities at other institutions.

Community Resources

An often overlooked source of information and partnership for staff working in international admissions are local or regional government and community agencies that work primarily with immigrants or newcomers. Employees of these organizations are often terrific sources of information about what is happening 'on the ground' in many foreign jurisdictions. They can assist in interpreting the true meaning of a translated document or a course description, or suggest follow up points of action. As an example, it is not uncommon for a prospective student who studied previously in a country in distress to submit an application for admission along with a letter stating that they are not able to provide copies of their transcripts from their previous institution(s) due to political instability. In some cases, there is little or no published information available to corroborate this kind of claim. In the absence of published information, contacts at a local government or non-government service organization that typically receives immigrants from that part of the world can be immensely helpful. Although they may not be able to specifically corroborate a particular applicant's story, they may be able to verify at least some part of it, either through their own network of contacts and experience or via other sources of information. As admissions officers working in the field of international education, it is worth remembering that there can be great value in building networks close to home.

Professional Development in the Online World

As technology has continued to shape all aspects of professional life, there has been a decided shift in the way international admissions officers conduct research into foreign academic qualifications. Although print publications remain an important tool for credential evaluators, online sources are now an indispensable asset. Where once one would need to consult a print publication to confirm the name of a foreign institution and the date that it first received government recognition/accreditation, a simple search on a trusted Ministry of Education website can provide this information. Similarly, where one would previously have needed to search through hardcopy admission files to find a sample transcript from a foreign jurisdiction, this work can now be effectively—and efficiently—completed from almost any location with the use of document imaging software and virtual private networks. Indeed, many academic credential evaluators no longer work together with their colleagues at a specific office, but work remotely from disparate locations. The ready availability of online resources are a key reason that this shift has been able to take place.

International Credential Databases

In recent years, a number of organizations have developed comprehensive and excellent online databases of information related to admissions and credential assessment. For many international admissions officers, databases published by reputable organizations have replaced print publications as their most frequently-used resources. Three well-known subscription-based databases are AACRAO EDGE,[10] the United Kingdom's NARIC online information bases,[11] and Australian Education International's Country Education Profiles database.[12] The International Association of Universities also provides a free online database, the World Higher Education Database.[13]

The News and Social Media

As mentioned at the onset of this chapter, international education systems change frequently, particularly in countries where there is economic or political instability. Information published about an education system online a few years earlier may no longer be accurate. One of the key challenges of an international admissions officer is to balance the need to stay abreast of these changes while fulfilling their administrative obligations to their institution and their applicants. However, to ensure that officers are making the most

fair admission decisions possible, staying up-to-date on current global events is an absolute must, and efforts to stay up-to-date should rightly be considered as part of their ongoing professional development.

There are a number of international news organizations that devote significant resources to covering issues related to education. For example, the *New York Times* is an excellent source of information on developments in higher education, and in particular on trends in the U.S. admissions process. In the United Kingdom, the *Guardian* offers extensive coverage secondary education and university admission, and the *Times Higher Education* magazine is considered the leading source of information on higher education issues. The list goes on. International admissions officers should identify reliable news sources in, and about, those countries from which they frequently receive applications and review those sources weekly or monthly.

Many of the organizations that offer professional development opportunities that have been mentioned earlier in this chapter (including AACRAO, Education Credential Evaluators/The Connection, and the Canadian Bureau for International Education) maintain an active social media presence and frequently post links to news items, research reports, and other information of direct relevance to international admissions officers on Twitter, Facebook, and other social media sites. Subscribing to a reputable organization's social media feed is a quick, simple, and no-cost way to help admissions officers remain current in their practice.

Listservs and Forums

Sharing information through listservs and online message boards is a long-standing tradition among international admissions professionals. Among the most well-known listservs are the inter-L (Yahoo Group), the AACRAO International Activities list, and the NAFSA knowledge communities. In Canada, the Association of Registrars of Universities and Colleges of Canada and the Canadian Information Centre for International Credentials also administer listservs that specialize in

10 *See* <edge.aacrao.org>.

11 *See* <www.naric.org.uk/naric/Organisations/Product%20Catalogue/Online%20Databases.aspx>.

12 *See* <internationaleducation.gov.au/Services-And-Resources/services-for-organisations/Pages/Services-for-organisations.aspx>.

13 *See* <whed.net>.

admission and enrollment management topics. A great benefit of listservs and online forums is that a single action—posting a message—can elicit multiple responses, and often in a very short period of time. This is a huge advantage for an admissions officer faced with a question that requires a quick response, or who does not have a resource at hand (whether it is a reference book, a website, or a trusted colleague) that is able to assist. Another benefit of posting questions on listservs and forums is that the responses are shared among all users of the list or forum; in a sense, by posing a question, the poster is in fact adding to the broader community's knowledge of the subject. A third benefit of lists and forums is that in receiving multiple responses to a query, one is likely to receive responses that reflect differing positions and perspectives on a particular issue. Although all admissions professionals seek to adhere to best practices and accepted standards, international academic credential evaluation is not an exact science. Not every experienced admissions professional that responds to a query will have the same perspective, and there can be great value in receiving and considering these different perspectives.

Summary

As has been illustrated in this chapter, the opportunities for continuing professional development for international admissions officers are many and varied. Professional organizations, credential evaluation agencies, and other national and international organizations offer a range of opportunities to the assessment community, including conferences and workshops that offer admissions professionals the invaluable opportunity to network with, and learn from, some of their most experienced peers. Many postsecondary institutions (and other employers) have made staff development a priority, and the options available for advancement and career exploration on campuses has continued to expand. With advances in technology, training and networking opportunities are now more accessible than ever. For many, it can be challenging to find the time (or to secure the funding) required to participate in ongoing learning activities. But as illustrated here, professional development comes in many guises. It can be obtained by participating in an event as dynamic as a weeklong workshop, or as low-cost as attending a lunchtime lecture on campus. For international admissions professionals, staying engaged and current is a requirement for career success, and the rewards of participating in ongoing professional development activities are well worth it.

FIFTEEN

Undocumented Students

2016 AACRAO INTERNATIONAL GUIDE

LINDA PATLAN | International Admissions Coordinator
University of Houston

LORIANNA MAPPS | Director, Admissions Processing
University of Houston

Undocumented Students

Although undocumented students have the legal right to a free, public education in the United States at the K-12 level, this right has its limitations once the student graduates from high school. These limits are evident at the college level primarily due to financial restraints, but may also be caused by family obligations and a sensed lack of support from the institution. With the inception of the Deferred Action for Childhood Arrivals (DACA) program and in-state tuition policies, a few of these concerns may be alleviated. However, it is important to acknowledge and understand the challenges and opportunities faced by the undocumented student population in order to better serve this unique group of learners.

Undocumented

The readily-used term of *undocumented* refers to immigrants who do not have authorization to stay in the United States. Undocumented immigrants generally entered the U.S. by either entering with a valid visa but staying past the visa expiration date or entering without valid documents.

As of 2014, there were an estimated 11.3 million undocumented immigrants in the U.S. (Passel and Cohn 2015). Undocumented immigrants make up 1.4 percent of the overall population in K–12 (2012). Although the entire population of undocumented immigrants only makes up 3.5 percent of the overall U.S. population, it is estimated that undocumented immigrants make up 5.1 percent of the entire U.S. workforce. As the total population of undocumented immigrants has stabilized, there has been a decline in the number of undocumented immigrants below the age of 18 (Passel and Cohn 2015).

Many undocumented immigrants entered the U.S. as children. In 2012, after the height of the growth of the undocumented immigrant population from the 1990s and many failed attempts at immigration reform, President Obama issued an Executive Order to provide deportation relief to protect undocumented immigrants who had entered the country as children. This Executive Order, referred to as Deferred Action for Childhood Arrivals (DACA), is administered through the Department of Homeland Security. Under DACA, individuals who meet specific age requirements at time of entry into the U.S., have proof of residency, and good citizenship criteria qualify for deferred action.

Approval of deferred status through DACA provides two years of deferred action and a renewable two-year work permit (Employment Authorization Card) with a Social Security Number. It must be noted, however, that DACA does not provide lawful status for undocumented students.

To be considered for deferred action under DACA, undocumented students must apply and submit proof of their qualifications to the United States Citizenship and Immigration Services office (USCIS). Since the inception of DACA in 2012, as of June 2015 USCIS has received a total of 770,873 initial requests with 681,345 approved. Since DACA only lasts two years, requests for renewals began in 2014. As of June 2015, 435,806 renewal requests have been submitted, with 377, 767 approved (USCIS 2015).

Historical Precedence

The history of undocumented students and the higher education system in the U.S. begins in 1982 with Plyler v. Doe. In the Plyler v. Doe Supreme Court ruling, it became unlawful in the United States to deny free public education to undocumented students. The Court upheld the equal protection for a free public education by declaring that undocumented children should not be prevented from an education due to the parents' choice to migrate to the United States illegally. The application of this ruling is used in K-12 schooling. Thus, the right to a free public education based on Plyler v. Doe ends once an undocumented student graduates from high school.

In 1996, two bills were passed that prohibited federal financial aid to undocumented students: the Personal Responsibility and Work Opportunity Reconciliation Act and the Illegal Immigration Reform and Immigrant Responsibility Act. Although each bill does not forbid the enrollment of undocumented students in institutions that receive federal aid, the obstacle of not receiving federal aid can provide a great hindrance to undocumented students who seek to attend college.

In response to this financial burden that undocumented students face, 20 states allow undocumented students to pay in-state tuition rates through either state legislation or state university system policy: California, Colorado, Connecticut, Florida, Hawaii, Illinois, Kansas, Maryland, Minnesota, Nebraska, New Mexico, New York, New Jersey, Oklahoma, Oregon, Rhode Island, Texas, Utah, Washington, and Wisconsin (Mendoza and Shaikh 2015). Additionally, five states—California, Minnesota, New Mexico, Texas, and Washington—offer state financial aid to undocumented college students. Conditions for receiving in-state tuition and state financial aid usually include a residency requirement as well as graduation from a high school within the state that provides the tuition benefit.

First introduced in 2001, the Development, Relief and Education of Alien Minors (DREAM) Act is federal legislation that seeks to provide a pathway to citizenship for undocumented persons who entered the United States before the age of 16, have lived continuously in the United States for at least 4 years, have graduated from a U.S. high school or earned a GED, and can demonstrate good character through rigorous background checks. If these requirements are met, undocumented persons would be granted a conditional status for six years. To continue on the path to citizenship after those six years, DREAMers must have attended college or served in the military for at least two years. Although it was reintroduced in 2009, 2010, and 2011, efforts to pass the DREAM Act legislation have not succeeded.

Institutional Considerations

IDENTIFICATION

With the DACA program, it has become easier for undocumented students to provide positive identification using Social Security numbers and drivers licenses. However, there are a substantial amount of potentially eligible individuals who do not apply for deferred action under DACA due to not being able to provide necessary documentation, economic concerns regarding the application fee, and mistrust of sending identifying information to the federal government (Gonzalez and Bautista-Chavez 2014). For the students who cannot provide identifying information, it can be a burden to open a bank account, secure housing and utilities, obtain a university ID card, and participate in educational programs such as internships or study abroad/student exchange programs, all of which require legal identification.

Institutions of higher education can assist undocumented students with identification issues by first becoming aware of institutional, state, and federal policies that impact students without identifying information. Through this awareness, colleges and universities can understand what boundaries or limitations students may face as they attempt to secure identification.

Creativity is key when developing ways to help undocumented students navigate through their college careers without Social Security numbers or identification cards. By partnering with Career Services offices, institutions can direct undocumented students towards unpaid internships that may not require Social Security numbers. Practicums are also a valuable way to gain experience in a student's area of study without the necessity of a Social Security number. In addition, undocumented students can explore reciprocal or exchange programs within the United States as an alternative to studying abroad.

FINANCIAL AID

Unless a college system or state provides state financial aid or offers in-state tuition to students who meet certain criteria, the requirement of having to pay out-of-state tuition without any assistance can be implausible for students and their families. While considering that undocumented students cannot seek employment without Social Security numbers, paying tuition out-of-pocket can be impossible.

Institutions should be prepared to deal with the financial concerns of undocumented students by being able to provide a list of private scholarships, facilitating tuition payment plans, or assisting with navigating the state aid application process available in some states.

TRAINING AND STUDENT SUPPORT

Although the number of undocumented students may be small on any given college campus, it is imperative that university staff and faculty understand the struggles that undocumented students face at the college level and be able to help undocumented students navigate through the application, enrollment, and academic processes in an institution. An unfamiliar process for students can only be more daunting when staff are unaware of how to assist undocumented students or where to send them for more information. Creating a training session for advising, enrollment services, and student support staff may be essential in learning the unique challenges that undocumented students face. Developing a task force that deals with special student populations, including undocumented students, and

their experiences in the college setting, may serve as a resource for other university staff when dealing with issues as they present themselves. In addition, creating a group of staff and faculty allies for undocumented students can create a network of support and resources for students who may not know how to seek assistance for both academic and social concerns. Finally, initiating and fostering relationships with external groups such as community organizations and referral agencies that can help with citizenship, DACA, and immigration issues is an essential practice for helping undocumented students with issues outside of the college environment.

LEGISLATIVE UPDATES

As legislation is created and passed, institutions must remain knowledgeable on current and imminent changes in federal and state laws and mandates as they relate to undocumented students. Understanding current and proposed legislation is imperative so that policy and programmatic changes can occur as soon as needed. It is good practice to seek assistance from institutional legal counsel on immigration matters and other areas of uncertainty.

ENROLLMENT

The implications of approval under DACA offer undocumented individuals an increased opportunity to advance economically. Due to being able to work legally in the United States, DACA students may also present a higher likelihood of continuous enrollment as, historically, undocumented students are five times more likely than their peers to have a break in attendance at the college level (Terriquez 2015). Because undocumented students tend to stop-out due to finances (Terriquez 2015), the implications of employment may mean increased continuous college attendance.

Furthermore, undocumented students approved through DACA do not have to face the possibility of legal action for two years, thus removing the burden of worry and stress that accompanies many undocumented students through their college years. Although this span of time does not cover the entire length of study, students can apply for DACA renewal.

Student Considerations

CHALLENGES

Undocumented and DACA students are faced with a myriad of challenges during their college process, such as navigating the federal, state, and institutional policies. Albrecht (2007) identified seven central challenges experienced by undocumented students. These challenges were: struggling to succeed, feeling the pressure of being a role model, coping with frustration and uncertainty, managing life as a "hidden" member of society, missing out on opportunities, perceptions of self as compared to other students, and complications faced in utilizing campus services. Although these challenges were identified for undocumented students, they can be extended to student under DACA.

When seeking information or services during the college process, undocumented students and DACA students often have to identify their legal status in order to receive the information or service that is pertinent to their circumstances. For undocumented students the fear of sharing personal information relates to the risk of deportation. DACA students are deferred from deportation only while their DACA status is valid. While the risk of deportation is not an immediate concern for DACA students, it is a concern they may experience in the future.

OUTLOOK

Undocumented students and those under DACA still face uncertainty regarding their future legal status. DACA is a renewable two-year program but efforts have been made to legally challenge the executive order that authorized DACA. In the current atmosphere of calls for immigration reform, uncertainty about future legal status can challenge the high financial and personal investment in higher education. Not securing legal status may mean that pursuing and attaining higher education is futile if in the future they are unable to practice or be employed in their profession.

Conclusion

Immigration continues to be a central focus in U.S. political, economic, and educational affairs. As undocumented students pursue higher education, it is imperative to be continually aware of legislation at the federal, state, and institutional level that impact this population. This includes a clear understanding on the difference between undocumented students and DACA students and how the similarities and differences impact institutional policies and student support systems.

Although there are inherent differences between practices in community colleges, four-year universities, and graduate and professional institutions, the common ground for undocumented students includes issues with finances, identification, and stopping out. There are opportunities to provide enhanced support for undocumented students, specifically in the form of encouraging undocumented students to apply for deferred action through DACA, finding alternatives to traditional financial aid programs, study abroad programs and internships, and acting swiftly to initiate change when legislative updates that impact undocumented students arise. Equally impactful are campus taskforces that can address the plight of the undocumented students from a policy standpoint as well as campus ally groups that can support undocumented students with both compassionate and encouraging perspectives. Although this network of assistance will not wholly resolve the concerns that undocumented students face, the aid provided to undocumented students by college campus administrators and staff demonstrates to this group of students that both their educational experience and degree attainment are worthy of concentrated and deliberate attention and action.

SIXTEEN

The Bologna Process in Its Second Decade

2016 AACRAO INTERNATIONAL GUIDE

ROBERT WATKINS

Assistant Director of Admissions
The University of Texas at Austin

The Bologna Process in Its Second Decade

In 2019, the Bologna Process will celebrate its twentieth year of existence. As stipulated by the June 1999 meeting of 29 ministers of education and finance in Bologna, Italy, the European Higher Education Area (EHEA) was to be created by 2010. Since that meeting, not only was the EHEA created, but the Process has grown to include all of Europe (with the 2015 approval of the inclusion of Belarus as the 49th member) and the passing of higher education laws in each of the signatory countries that have created the three-cycle degree structure that has transformed higher education in Europe (with Belarus given a five-year roadmap to match the others by 2020). In the Bologna Process, the educational experience is transparently showcased by the issuance of the Diploma Supplement upon graduation, revealing the accumulation of European Credit Transfer System (ECTS) credits and resulting in the award of the degree. Quality assurance mechanisms at national levels are in turn linked at the European level.

The dream of June 1999 has indeed become largely a reality in 2015. Though two members of the Council of Europe (San Marino and Monaco) chose not to join the Process and students and educators in various countries continue to express concern that problems remain or have not fully been addressed in the EHEA, much work has been completed. Most countries are now embracing the new degrees with the old traditional degrees receding into the past. Before examining the current state and the prospects for the future, it will be helpful to review the basic tenets of the Process as laid out in the Bologna Declaration at the first meeting in 1999.

A Review of the Bologna Process

The Bologna Process proposed a system of new degrees based on an accumulation of credits, with each cycle leading to the next to replace the traditional long degrees found in most European countries. It did not dictate the degree names or their length, except for the minimum duration of three years for the first degree and the need for the ensuing higher degree to complete a five-year total experience. Whether that first degree would be three or four years was left to individual countries to decide. Therefore, countries exhibit a mixture of 3+2 and 4+1 degree structures. The third, terminal cycle was added at the 2003 Ministerial meeting in Bergen. These degrees would be awarded in conjunction with a document called a Diploma Supplement that would explain in great detail (both in English and in the indigenous language) not only the credential, the entry qualification, and the study it would then lead to, but also the entire educational system of the country.

The European Credit Transfer System (ECTS) was adopted from the Erasmus Mundus' higher education mobility programs. The possible combination of credits could be 180+120 ECTS in a 3+2 structure or 240+60 ECTS in the 4+1 model. Finally, the picture was made complete with the creation of quality assurance (QA) mechanisms at the national level that would link to a super QA structure within the European Higher Education Area. That process would entail the construction of national qualifications frameworks (NQFS), which would enumerate the educational 'cradle to grave' chronology in each signatory country.

In terms of nomenclature, many educational systems opted for the English titles of "bachelor" and "master," though indigenous names were also retained in some countries. For example, France chose a mixture of both with the traditional title *license* reserved for the first degree while the English term "master" is used for the second-tier degree in the three cycle L-M-D structure (D denoting the doctoral degree adopted from the English word for the terminal academic degree).

While the credit system was mandated, the grading scale associated with that system (ECTS Grading System) was not; thus, most countries kept their traditional grading scales, though, for mobility purposes, sometimes providing it along with the ECTS grading scale. The ECTS grading scale, first promulgated in 1989, has evolved over time with the latest incarnation introduced in 2014, endorsed by the Bologna Follow Up Group (BFUG), and presented for approval at the Yerevan Ministerial Meeting in April 2015.

Quality assurance has improved among the countries by virtue of more members having completed construction of the NQFs. This is a vast improvement over the situation just five years previously when the EHEA was implemented and only six countries had NQFs. Despite the 2009 Ministerial Meeting in Leuven extending the deadline, only ten countries had completed their NQFs by 2012. By the Yerevan meeting in 2015 that number had increased to 22 completed with 14 more near completion. Completion is attained when the national qualifications framework of a given country has progressed through the ten implementation steps set by the EHEA, linking the individual NQFs to the Area-wide framework known as the European Qualifications Framework for Lifelong Learning (EQF) adopted in 2008.

Once the ministers adjourned and the communiqué for the latest meeting in Yerevan was archived with the others dating back to Bologna in 1999, the focus shifted to the Bologna Follow Up Group (BFUG) where the real work of assessing implementation and compiling stocktaking reports for the next meeting takes place. The BFUG meets every six months and deals with specific topics in more detail, receiving input from various

sources including the Bologna Seminars, which are special meetings held by the various actors within the EHEA.

The BFUG consists of all countries of the EHEA and the European Community, Council of Europe, European Universities Association (EUA), European Students Union (ESU), European Association of Institutions of Higher Education (EURASHE), UNESCO, Education International, European Association for Quality Assurance in Higher Education (ENQA), and Business Europe. Meetings are co-chaired by the EU Presidency and a non-EU country. Actual work between the ministerial meetings is overseen by a Board consisting of EHEA chairs, vice-chairs, European Commission representatives, and four consultative members: Council of Europe, EUA, ESU, and EURASHE. A Bologna Secretariat supports the work of the BFUG and consists of people assigned by the country hosting the next ministerial conference (Armenia in 2015 for example). The Secretariat maintains the archive between conferences.

The work plan assigned to the BFUG for the period between the Bucharest (2012) and Yerevan (2015) meetings outlined three major tasks: to provide quality higher education for all, enhance graduates' employability, and strengthen mobility as a means for better learning. Clearly these tasks get to the root of the social dimension of the Bologna Process, an underlying concern of educators, in addition to the physical construction of the Process in each signatory country. The entire *raison d'être* for the creation of the EHEA was to enhance student mobility within Europe. This was also the reason behind the creation of the Erasmus Mundus program in the 1980s—to enhance European student mobility within and outside of Europe. However, the result was not seen as sufficient within Europe itself where one country's traditional first long degree may or may not enable a student access to the next level of higher education in a neighboring European university. The harmonization of European degrees along the lines embraced in the EHEA, upon full implementation in 2010, facilitated that movement. Similar length degrees based on an accumulation of the same credits and with common quality assurance underpinnings promised an easier articulation method when students moved from one country to the next.

Concerns Regarding the Bologna Process in Europe

Once the EHEA was fully in place in the majority of countries, the movement between institutions became easier, although the social dimension and 'fallout' threatened at times to assail the system. Student protests at several Spanish universities broke out in 2008, due to the claimed de-valuation of first degrees. Spain opted for four-year first degrees, but other countries did not, and the students became concerned that the Spanish educational authorities would move to a three-year first degree. German student and educator concerns were expressed almost from the beginning of the introduction of the new first degree with the students worried about lack of employability for three-year degree graduates in a country traditionally accustomed to long five-year (and more) first degrees. That concern also manifested in the corporate sector where mistrust of a three-year degree compared to the former long degrees traditionally held by prospective new hires was rampant. Most agreed that the former long Magister or Diplom simply could not be 'jammed' into the new 3+2 bachelor/master structure.

In a more drastic attempt to disrupt the new standards, in March 2010, Austrian students attempted to crash the victory party for the Bologna Process held in Vienna. Quick action by riot police enabled the party to go on after a delay. Again the protests centered on the time-to-degree issue emphasized by the educational authorities. The three-year degree structure and accumulation of a full load of ECTS credits each year made students feel pressured to finish before they were ready. In contrast, German educational authorities appreciated and welcomed the new pace of degree attainment; the traditional university degree system in Germany historically facilitated long study times for students whose benefits in terms of food, housing, and medical care were substantial and costly.

In the case of the United Kingdom, the old line universities were not too keen to institute such radical ideas as degrees based on the accumulation of credits when centuries of historical practice had seen the degrees awarded through success on exams following year-long courses. The newer universities (former polytechnics) quickly adapted to a credit model (Credit Accumulation and Transfer Scheme, or CATS), finding no problem in the introduction of mandatory use of the ECTS credits. Lengthy and extensively detailed Diploma Supplements, on the other hand, have not been popular at most British universities, new and old.

While more time and improved implementation has helped to ease the concerns of students and universities somewhat, they have not completely gone away. The European Students Union (ESU) has been vocal in its criticism of too much emphasis on commercialization in the global marketplace with respect to the EHEA and also voiced concern about the lack of more direct involvement by the ESU in the ministerial meetings. The ESU has also repeatedly emphasized its fear of the EHEA incorporating any sort of ratings system into its quality assurance aspects. Finally, the concern about true mobility between institutions within the EHEA has been raised by both students and the ministers (most recently in the Yerevan Communiqué). Too many first degrees are not being fully accepted at second degree levels between higher education institutions in different countries. This, of course, was one of the major reasons behind the creation and harmonization of the new degrees.

The future of the EHEA is not in doubt. The Process has continued for 16 years and every outward sign indicates it will continue to move ahead. The ministers and the Bologna Follow Up Group as well as the satellite entities to the Process will work to improve mobility, employability, and quality assurance. Efforts will continue to better define the scope and nature of the third/terminal cycle of the new degree structure in each country so that doctoral level degrees are folded into the Process, whether with ECTS credits, pure research, or other aspects of advanced research degrees. While some individual national adjustments to degree structure (change from three to four years or the inclusion of short-term study programs at higher levels) will take place, the basic conceptual structure is in place and simply needs continued refinement.

The View from the USA

The higher education community in the United States has struggled with the Bologna Process from its inception. Initially, the greatest concern voiced by U.S. higher education professionals, particularly those involved with graduate-level admission, was how to handle the Bologna-compliant three-year first 180 ECTS degrees. Most followed placement recommendations by the National Council on the Evaluation of Foreign Educational Credentials (The Council) that reviewed almost all publications in the field of international education and assigned recommendations, advisory in nature, from 1955 to 2006. This inter-associational committee, made up of the key players in international education (AACRAO, NAFSA, Institute of International Education (IIE), College Board, Council of Graduate Schools (CGS), the American Council on Education (ACE), and the American Association of Community Colleges (AACC)), had their placement recommendations printed in the back of the books published by AACRAO or PIER (Projects in International Education Research) so that readers could see what experts in the field recommended for the credentials described in the text of the publications. All too often readers simply used the placement recommendations section and did not read the text. The Council's philosophy essentially followed the quantitative (year counting) approach in determining comparability to U.S. higher education credentials. Such an approach meant that a three-year first degree would not be found comparable to a U.S. bachelor's degree for purposes of graduate admission (unless preceded by a 13-year primary/secondary system as is the case with the U.K.). The Council never actually addressed the Bologna Process specifically except to issue a recommendation that ECTS credits be converted

to U.S. semester credits following a 2:1 ratio (2 ECTS credits =1 U.S. semester hour).

In 2006 the Council was dissolved upon agreement of most of the participating organizations, which left a void in credential comparability guidance. National conferences such as the AACRAO annual meeting continued to provide advice on credential comparability in conference sessions on country educational systems; however, no inter-associational entity like the Council existed. To remedy this, then-AACRAO Vice President of International Education Gloria Nathanson of UCLA sought and obtained the Board of Directors' approval to create the International Education Standards Council (IESC), a permanent council under AACRAO aegis to review new publications in international education research.

As funding for print publications on foreign credential evaluation (frequently provided by the U.S. Government) dissipated, a project began under private auspices by interested experts within AACRAO to create a database that would replicate the level of research previously seen with the AACRAO and PIER print publications. This culminated in the EDGE (Electronic Database for Global Education) database of some 232 educational systems around the world complete with credential advice for subscribers. AACRAO acquired EDGE as the project neared completion and became available to subscribers. The IESC was then given the task of providing the credential advice in EDGE that would replace the defunct Council. In addition to numerous institutional subscribers, EDGE is now used by the United States Citizenship and Immigration Service (USCIS) of the Department of Homeland Security which adjudicates petitions for H-1b work visas.

In dealing with the Bologna Process, EDGE and the IESC took a two-pronged approach. As the IESC tends to follow the same quantitative approach to international credential comparison, the initial credential advice for Bologna-compliant three-year degrees is found in each of the signatory country's entries. Here the advice is generally (absent a 13-year primary/secondary education system) to recommend three years of credit toward a U.S. bachelor's degree. However, in a separate entry for the Bologna Process, the IESC supplied a more nuanced and holistic statement. Acknowledging the difficulty of truly comparing a first degree that is broad (U.S. bachelor's degree) with one that is deep and very subject-intensive (European first degrees), the IESC offered some circumstances under which three-year Bologna-compliant degree holders may be admitted to U.S. graduate programs. This opened the door for institutions to examine the degrees closely and make a decision based on factors other than simply duration of study. At the same time, however, the difference between sufficient preparation for graduate study and what truly constituted a U.S. bachelor's degree remained stark. The USCIS needed a definitive statement that the credential in question was, in fact, comparable to a U.S. bachelor's degree or not.

Other entities in U.S. higher education involved with international education have entered into the three-year versus four-year degree discussion. The Council of Graduate Schools (CGS) publishes frequent surveys on international admission statistics and in 2006 conducted a survey of its membership regarding the acceptance and/or suitability of three-year degrees for graduate admission. The survey indicated that of those graduate schools responding, 56 percent found three-year degrees "not to be an issue." This was up from 41 percent in previous surveys just the year before. In 2009 the Institute of International Education (IIE) published as part of its 90th anniversary observance a monograph entitled *Three Year Bologna-Compliant Degrees: Responses from US Graduate Schools,* which found some two-thirds (68 percent) of graduate programs either accepted the three-year degrees as comparable to a U.S. four-year bachelor's degree or had a policy of case-by-case review by individual graduate programs on campus, leaving only some 32 percent indicating the degrees were not comparable to a U.S. bachelor's for graduate admission purposes. The report went on to suggest that as international admissions professionals gained more knowledge about the three-year Bologna-compliant degrees, they tended to place less emphasis on equality or comparability to U.S. bachelor's degrees, instead emphasizing "compatibility" with U.S. graduate programs requirements (IIE 2009, 3).

Unquestionably, attitudes toward the Bologna-compliant degrees have evolved within the U.S. higher education community. Now more than ever, U.S. colleges and universities look more closely at best practices, degree comparability policies, suitability in terms of academic preparation, test scores, and other factors in the graduate admission process, rather than simply looking at the length of study to obtain a degree. Many allow their individual graduate programs to examine the academic background of the applicant with a three-year degree as opposed to rejecting the applicant out of hand. Inevitably some programs will find the degree provides insufficient background (engineering for example), while others will find the depth of study in the subject more than sufficient for acceptance.

The problem of consistency poses a challenge to international education professionals. If the European three-year degree is deemed sufficient for admission, what about the three-year degree from India, Pakistan, Australia, or South Africa? In terms of recruitment and admission, the significant question regarding three-year degrees centers on India, which, along with China, represents the vast majority of international applications to any U.S. campus. And, of course, factors other than simple program fit surface. Declining enrollments at some schools may generate a willingness to enhance international numbers in order to offset a loss in revenues, especially for public institutions increasingly faced with less state budgetary support. However, trends in international student recruitment demonstrate the risk of over-reliance on a specific country, as this could radically change overnight based on any number of local factors.

Consistency and fairness in the handling of three-year degrees is important. When a three-year degree does not unequivocally and universally lead to admission to the next higher (graduate) level degree in its country of issuance, it should not be equated to the degree that does routinely allow access. For example, the Ontario three-year Ordinary degree does not lead to admission to a master's program in that Province. The four-year honours degree is the entry qualification for graduate study in Ontario universities. Conversely, the three-year Bologna-compliant first degree is designed to provide access to the next level of higher education.

Another consideration when faced with the comparability of three-year degrees is the quality of the degree. For example, while the Indian three-year degree is sufficient for master's admission in that country, its quality is largely not comparable to the three-year degrees from Europe. While three-year degrees from excellent universities in India exist, there are almost 650 universities in India and perhaps as many as 30,000 constituent colleges and institutes. Quality oversight for the Indian Government is extremely challenging to say the least. The European Higher Education Area, on the other hand, has made quality assurance a vital aspect of the new degree structure. While the individual signatory countries have their national quality assurance bodies monitoring the degrees, the EHEA and its quality assurance supra-national body, the European Association for Quality Assurance (ENQA), oversees those bodies. This is relayed to the Bologna Follow Up Group, and eventual reports are made to the representatives at the ministerial meetings. Presently the conclusion is that the Bologna Process contains an inherent level of transparent quality assurance that the Indian quality assurance mechanisms lack. Many institutions in the U.S. that accept Bologna-compliant three-year degrees also accept those from Indian institutions that receive high marks from governmental accrediting bodies, and this appears to be a reasonable compromise.

Conclusion

As the second decade of the Bologna Process progresses toward its conclusion, it continues to strengthen its hold on the signatory countries. Early prognostications

of failure of the Process have proven false. While much tinkering remains to be done in refining and improving the overall Process, the experiment appears to have been successful. This success has resulted in avid interest outside the EHEA, including from countries such as Australia, Israel, and China. Former colonies of Britain and France with systems of education adopted from colonial times have adopted a mixed approach to the Bologna Process reforms. Anglophone countries like those in West Africa have moved away from the British model, replacing it with an indigenous model that borrows from the past, but also reflects features of other systems such as the U.S. educational system. Francophone countries, on the other hand, have almost all enthusiastically embraced the L-M-D (Licence-Master-Doctor) structure found in post-Bologna France.

The positive aspects of the Bologna Process, such as faster time to completion offered by the three-year first degree, have inevitably led to discussion in U.S. higher education circles of the attractiveness of a three-year degree. However, this discussion invariably takes the form of faster time to degree through various means such as year-round schooling or heavier loads per semester, better articulation of transfer credit allowing seamless transition to degree programs, or heavy use of advanced placement testing or concurrent enrollment in high school and college. So far, no three-year degree advocates speak of a 90-hour degree or one that in terms of overall content lacks some aspect of the program content now found in the standard four-year degree.

The Bologna Process represents nothing less than a radical transformation of the higher education landscape in Europe. Its effects are worldwide in scope, though its initial intent was parochial. Towards the end of its second decade the good news is that the Process is less mysterious, more improved, and better understood by U.S. international education professionals. This has enabled them to build more informed policies regarding the individual aspects of the process, including degree comparability, credit conversion, documentation recognition, and understanding of the quality assurance methodology built into the Process. All this makes transatlantic educational cooperation much more exciting and innovating.

SEVENTEEN

Trends in Quality Assurance

STEVEN D. CROW

Past President
The Higher Learning Commission

Trends in Quality Assurance

Not that many years ago, faculty and administrators in U.S. colleges and universities had only a vague idea about the academic quality of most universities located in other countries. Major research and historic universities might have been fairly well known, but outside of those few institutions—largely, but not solely European—a lack of awareness clouded American understanding of academic quality beyond its boundaries.

AACRAO has made major efforts to provide dependable guidance and assistance to U.S. educators, both through the Electronic Database on Global Education (EDGE) and its International Education Services. Over the past few years many organizations have emerged to provide credential evaluation services, sizeable enough in scope and enterprise to form two umbrella organizations, the National Association of Credential Evaluation Services (NACES) and the Association of International Credential Evaluators, Inc. (AICE). It is fair to say that a U.S. educator faced with making a decision about the credibility and comparability of a foreign credential and/or credits now has several options for help.

Today the diverse scale and scope of international higher education suggests it is still wise to seek assistance from organizations and professionals who specialize in interpreting international higher education credentials. However, it is important to understand two things: across the globe educators have been engaged in significant efforts to build networks addressing the issue of credibility and comparability of educational credentials, and transformations in higher education quality assurance have been central to these efforts. Over the last 25 years, many countries, new and old, have created government-financed but non-ministerial agencies to establish and apply standards for academic quality across institutions within a country. Most governments have adopted a "qualifications framework" broadly defining the credentials awarded by higher education institutions within a country and then calling on the new quality assurance agencies to evaluate how well a given institution's educational programs and credentials maps to the framework. Parallel to these new national endeavors, groups of countries have endeavored to obtain cross-border recognition of the stamps of quality assurance provided in each country. There is not a single story to be told in all of this, but almost all display similar goals even as they illustrate the many different paths followed in attempting to achieve them.

The brief history of the International Network of Quality Assurance Agencies in Higher Education (INQAAHE) illustrates the speed and scale of this development. In 1991, leaders of eight national quality assurance agencies (and only a few more existed at that time), together with a few other people concerned about international higher education—the U.S., for example, played a leading role through the involvement of Dr. Marjorie Peace Lenn from the Center for Quality Assurance in International Higher Education—founded the organization at a meeting in Hong Kong. Today INQAAHE counts over 250 members, a large majority of which are quality assurance agencies. In fact, INQAAHE has served as the training ground for many agencies to offer effective higher education quality assurance across a country or to specific higher education components within a country. Ultimately INAQQHE created a very useful set of guidelines for good practices for quality assurance agencies, as well as an "alignment" process through which, on invitation, an INQAAHE team measures an agency against those guidelines. The 2007 INQAAHE Guidelines of Good Practice for Quality Assurance highlights practices and procedures well-known to U.S. educators: an institutional self-evaluation report provides the basis for an on-site review by objective peers who write a report open for institutional review before final submission to an independent body that reviews and makes decisions.[14] In the U.S., this process is called accreditation, but that is not the case everywhere.

U.S. regional accrediting agencies were a little late to join INQAAHE, but most now hold membership and participate within the organization, as do several specialized agencies headquartered in the U.S. INQAAHE hosts a biennial international conference and alternating biennial forums that focus on narrower topics of interest. The network serves as an effective collaborative for disseminating and encouraging best practices in higher education quality assurance. Perhaps its largest challenge is passing the vision of its founders to another generation of leaders whose skills and insights have been shaped by their own work in higher education quality assurance during the past 25 years. The motivation behind INQAAHE has been to stimulate effective agency-led higher education quality assurance, while expecting that competent quality assurance will figure prominently in bridging national and regional borders.

Other organizations have also shaped the emergence of quality assurance, but often in larger political contexts affected by the globalization of higher education. The Organization for Economic Cooperation and Development (OECD) has explored the international higher education landscape, proposing for its 34 members and key partners strategies to address national needs, even while responding to new global and regional opportunities. The United countries Educational, Scientific, and Cultural Organization (UNESCO) has made global access to quality higher

education one of its key goals. It holds international conferences, publishes reports, and issues guidelines that focus on quality and access in higher education regionally, as well as globally. Both OECD and UNESCO have, over the past decade, promulgated guidelines related to many of the issues of higher education quality in the rapidly changing environment of globalization. The 2005 UNESCO-OECD Guidelines for Quality Provision in Cross-Border Higher Education pays particular attention to cross-border delivery of education, particularly in the new Internet age, and the potential for higher education to become defined as "goods and services" falling under international trade agreements.[15] U.S. higher education voices are a part of these discussions, even though sometimes filtered through diplomats or others invited by diplomats to speak on behalf of U.S. interests.

After several years of annually hosting a small international gathering in Washington, D.C., the Council of Higher Education Accreditation (CHEA) announced in 2012 the launch of the CHEA International Quality Group (CIQG), aimed at drawing on a broader set of participants than INQAAHE, but a somewhat different set of participants than found at OECD and UNESCO meetings, and offering its own meetings and publications. In 2015 it introduced its "International Quality Principles," which it hopes might shape many discussions about the role and purpose of higher education quality assurance around the world.[16]

The importance of quality assurance in globalizing higher education is a hot topic, and while these international organizations often seem to draw on the same people and agencies, they each claim to address the basic drivers and subsequent challenges in bringing some order—coordination, even—into the myriad of higher education quality assurance providers around the globe. As this chapter aims to make clear, the most focused and productive effort to address cross-border higher education quality assurance is occurring in

14 See <www.inqaahe.org>.

15 See <www.unesco.org/education/guidelines_E.indd.pdf>.

16 See <cheainternational.org>.

Europe. The Bologna Process, which started in 1999, has built part of its endeavor on the effectiveness of new national quality assurance agencies in evaluating student academic achievement.[17] But the Bologna Process has spawned a wide variety of programs—some under the direction of quality assurance agencies and others led by universities—that have moved into detailed program-by-program evaluation in an effort to strengthen a sense of trust—across institutions as well as borders—in the consistency of learning and the comparability of certifications that purport to attest to that learning.

While many of the trends in international higher education quality assurance barely touch many U.S. colleges and universities, it remains useful to understand what is happening and why. The systems for evaluating international credentials ought to take into account the impressive endeavors made by international colleagues. Many of the challenges they confront are not new to U.S. educators, for they have had a significant impact on U.S. higher education over the past fifty years. Experience, therefore, ought to be helpful in understanding both the importance of these international developments and the potential for them to inform the realignment of quality assurance processes in the U.S. One word of warning: it is extremely easy to get confused by the myriad of acronyms for organizations, agencies, agency networks, higher education networks, and regional agreements. This becomes even more difficult when names and titles in other languages with their own acronyms are translated into English and then given another acronym. Rather than despairing over this confusion, it is vital to appreciate the key drivers fueling the global focus on quality assurance in higher education and learn from the efforts of others to find solutions to similar challenges.

Access (Massification)

Across the world public policy makers have come to recognize that the economic and social strength of a country depends in large part on providing education to a larger number of its citizens. Traditional elite universities have strained to respond—sometimes balked at the changes expected of them—to the public policy demands that higher education not only reach more people but also provide programs supporting national development objectives. To achieve this end in a relatively short time and without a massive infusion of capital, many countries have turned to other types of institutions, including private and for-profit entities that promised to provide both the capacity and the programming options considered necessary to rapid development. Some countries have handled this expansion with care, but many have unintentionally unleashed an entrepreneurial wave of educational and training enterprises, quickly discovering that while some provided a model for the changes they sought in higher education, others exploited the situation by charging high costs and providing low educational quality. Most education ministries lacked the legal basis and the regulatory tools with which to deal with anything other than public institutions. In several countries, then, the emergence of a new quality assurance agency was in fact an effort to regain some regulatory—but not ministerial—control over the disparate players in the higher education market. The goal to increase access never changed, but the methods of regulating a newly competitive academic marketplace did, and the newest tool was a higher education quality assurance agency.

Accountability

Although many in the U.S. assume that countries with an education ministry provide a centralized model of control—"federal" and "ministerial" are often used interchangeably in political discussions in the U.S.—in many countries, either through constitutional mandate or long practice or both, public universities often exercise exceptional academic autonomy. The national "system" is in fact fairly decentralized. Moreover, in several countries the universities themselves operate with a decentralized system of academic governance largely controlled by the

[17] For more on the Bologna Process, see Chapter 16, The Bologna Process in Its Second Decade.

faculty and departments or schools. Decentralized national systems combined with decentralized institutional governance structures can make for extraordinary confusion about who is accountable for what, and in particular who is accountable for education to meet the needs of an internationally-competitive country.

Confronted by the growing lack of fit between the time-honored culture of the university and the changing educational needs of the country, policymakers have turned to new quality assurance agencies to serve as advocates for and evaluators of a university's efforts to be accountable. Some of the questions posed by these agencies include: Does the university educate its students to an acceptable level? Does it graduate enough of those students? Will those graduates ultimately contribute to the country's economic and social development? While very familiar to u.s. educators over the years, such questions have been new to universities in many countries. This new quality assurance has led to a more direct correlation between public funding for higher education and the public's impact on shaping institutional priorities and outcomes.

Central to all quality assurance programs is the principle that institutions—not governments and not even quality assurance agencies—are responsible for the quality of the education they provide. It should not be surprising, then, that quality assurance agencies have played an important role in shifting the higher education culture from isolation toward responsiveness and accountability. This new matrix of accountability poses the questions: Can students, their credits, and their degrees help the country? Moreover, can they, with reasonable ease, cross borders?

Mobility

One of the major aspects of globalization in higher education is the movement of students across borders, those engaged in studies but moving, those holding degrees or other national certifications, and those wishing to study abroad. Certainly this recognition of and support for mobility played a major role in the massive shifts taking place in European higher education. Fueled by the Europeanization efforts of the European Common Market, 29 countries signed the Bologna Accord in 1999, establishing the European Higher Education Area (EHEA) and committing participants to create and implement processes that would ensure comparability of higher education qualifications across borders. The implicit, if not explicit, challenge in the Accord was for higher education leaders to take hold of this process. If they chose not to or failed, ministers themselves stood ready to create structures and process to achieve these ends. The leaders of the nascent national quality assurance bodies as well as prominent chancellors and other leaders in education rose to the challenge by shaping major components of that initiative. The member ministers set goals and a calendar for their achievement and periodically reviewed and approved the progress made through multiple working groups.

Over the past 15 years, meetings in Prague (2001), Berlin (2003), Bergen (2005), London (2007), Leuven (2009), Budapest-Vienna (2010), Bucharest (2012), and Yerevan (2015) have resulted both in a growth of participating countries (now 49) and the adoption of many large and small programs aimed at coordinating higher education in Europe. These have included agreement on the structure of European academic degrees that have either replaced or complemented curricula and programs already being delivered. Unsurprisingly, several national "qualification frameworks" are mapped to the emerging consensus on the nature of learning to which each new European credential should attest. Universities have adopted new systems for summarizing learning through the European Credit Tracking and Accumulations System (ECTS) and the Diploma Supplement. Many participate in "tuning" efforts to align courses and programs across borders. Moreover, in Bergen, the agreement included naming the European Network for Quality Assurance (ENQA) as the agency responsible for setting and administering standards for quality assurance agencies working in EHEA. For someone outside Europe, this huge endeavor has been remarkably transformative within most EHEA countries and across their borders, while for many Europeans, achievement of real mobility still remains a somewhat distant goal. Within countries, regional differences, traditions, and institutional distinctions often trump efforts to "harmonize" higher education. National agendas are not always aligned with Europeanization efforts. Nonetheless, the Bologna Process is bold and innovative in the age of globalization of higher education.

Mercosur, the free-trade endeavor of Brazil, Argentina, Uruguay, and Paraguay (with participation from Chile and Bolivia among other Andean nations) concluded in the 1990s that movement of professional credentials across borders should be addressed. Working groups drawing on national high education quality assurance agencies in those countries devoted years to create strategies for mutual recognition of selected professions. However, Mercosur—together with the larger Ibero-American networks such as RIACES (translated to English as Ibero-American Network for Accreditation of the Quality of Higher Education)—have yet to resolve the cross-border issues as effectively as have the Europeans.

The Asian-Pacific Quality Network (APQN) is even less well-developed, but its goals are somewhat less ambitious than other regional plans to facilitate the international movement of professional credentials. That Network serves a region defined as "all Pacific island countries and territories, New Zealand, Australia, Papua New Guinea; all island and mainland countries and territories of Asia, including Russia, Afghanistan, the other central Asian 'stans and Iran."[18] Several African states have also created a network, as have the Gulf Arab countries. With the encouragement of INQAAHE, many smaller regional networks have emerged, with most seeking to enable mobility across regional borders.

----

[18] See <www.apqn.org>.

Cross-Border Delivery

Without exploring the exact cause-effect relationship, it is important to note that the groups advocating for national higher education quality assurance agencies also have been responding to the phenomenon of foreign colleges and universities setting up branch campuses and/or delivering their programs through franchises, contracted partners, and, ultimately, over the Internet. While some countries had very strict and enforceable laws about foreign providers, many did not, and immediately the locus of responsibility for quality assurance for these enterprises needed to be addressed. Ministries with responsibility limited to public institutions sought some review of these new private ventures, many from not-for-profit institutions at home, but operating through a for-profit business in the host country. It took U.S. regional accreditation agencies some time to fully appreciate the problems these international ventures caused, but even their stepped-up practice of visiting and evaluating international sites failed to address a given country's concern not only about academic quality but, more importantly, the fit of these international offerings to national needs and goals. For many years, conversations at INQAAHE meetings revolved around if and how quality assurance responsibilities could be shared between a home country (the location of the delivering institution) and the host countries (the location of students). As new quality assurance agencies gained strength and credibility, they typically determined that the host country's quality assurance program must be honored.

Institutional Autonomy and Self-Regulation

In some countries, international financing served as the impetus for limiting ministerial authority, while demanding greater institutional accountability fostered through an external quality assurance system. In fact, in several developing nations in the 1990s and 2000s, the design for this reform to higher education came from international funding groups, particularly the World

Bank. The international lenders concluded that too many national systems had become so unaccountable for meeting the true educational needs of the citizens that a major restructuring of accountability was needed. Components of this reform include self-regulation as well as competition, so laws were changed to allow for new players in the national educational marketplace. While the u.s. model of self-regulation through accreditation could not be transplanted overnight, the overriding sense was that something like it needed to emerge if developing nations were to unleash the power of higher education for the good of the country. In some countries, then, external financial economic development programs incentivized the creation of new quality assurance agencies. The ultimate objective: to develop robust support systems of self-regulation that link institutional autonomy to accountability.

Nation Building

With the collapse of the Soviet Union, many nations—new or restored—suddenly had responsibility for managing and adapting higher education to their new needs. And in many of these new countries the opportunity for private education, considered a good reform, brought on such an onslaught of providers that some kind of regulatory environment, short of the old rigid ministerial authority, needed to be developed. Whether prodded by the World Bank or European funders, these countries rather quickly turned to a government-supported but independent higher education quality assurance. In Central Europe in particular, any country that sought to be part of the European Common Market reformed its higher education to fit the expectations of the European Higher Education Area, and a national quality assurance agency had become a European necessity.

When NATO helped to carve Kosovo from Serbia, it wrote into foundational documents for that country-in-development the requirement that the government would license higher education institutions while a separate body, the Kosovo Accrediting Agency (KAA), would provide quality assurance. If an institution failed

to gain KAA accreditation twice, it would lose its license. Relying on the assistance of international funding and international expertise, KAA came into existence and, borrowing heavily from the u.s. and European quality assurance agencies, promulgated standards structured around accountability and internal quality assurance processes and began the task of bringing some order into the higher education market. Over 30 not-yet-accredited universities vied for students, but even as KAA used its site evaluations and accreditation recommendations to diminish greatly the number of poorly-developed and inadequately-financed programs, it never lost sight of its main goal: to use accreditation to lift Kosovo higher education to meet the tougher European standards. With more youth than available jobs in Kosovo, the mobility of its graduates was critical. KAA mapped its standards and its evaluation programs to European practices, and measured its efforts by seeking ENQA recognition, which it gained in 2014.

The Limitations of Recognizing Legitimate Quality Assurance Agencies

Staff of u.s. institutions know that although all federally- and/or CHEA-recognized accreditation agencies in the u.s. operate similarly and have standards that address similar matters; they do not, in most cases, believe that the learning achieved at one institution is equivalent to the learning achieved at another one. In fact, mobility of degrees and credits, while eased considerably by accreditation of institutions and programs, continues to be slowed by policies and practices at the national, state, and institutional levels. It is, after all, one thing to establish best practices for an agency providing higher education quality assurance and to measure how well a given agency meets those standards or expectations. It is a large leap to claim that effective accreditation ensures comparable academic achievement. It should hardly be surprising that most international efforts to increase student mobility through regional recognition of national accrediting agencies also run into problems. It is impossible to isolate the development and management of higher education quality assurance agencies from the political contexts in which they exist.

In the U.S., for example, both CHEA and the Department of Education provide recognition processes, one voluntary (CHEA) and the other somewhat less so if the agency wants to serve as a gatekeeper for federal funds. In Europe, the Bologna Process determined that ENQA would bear responsibility for evaluating the effectiveness of national quality assurance providers in EHEA. But ENQA had barely received that mandate when it chose to partner with other higher education bodies (organizations of students and institutions, in particular) that wanted to review quality assurance agencies. They created the European Quality Assurance Register (EQAR) that uses the same standards used for ENQA recognition, but reaches its own decisions. Recognition by ENQA does not automatically translate into being listed by EQAR. As will be shown below, an even smaller group of European countries have joined in a mutual recognition pact, yet another winnowing step in alignment and comparability. In short, it is crucial to appreciate the third-party evaluation processes of quality assurance agencies, but understand that in and of themselves, they do not guarantee comparability.

✳ Understand Tuning. As part of the Bologna Process, the Tuning Process addresses comparability of curricula, not only in content, but also in publicly-stated learning outcomes. The goal of this effort is to influence the reforms marking the EHEA without creating a uniform, required European curriculum. Universities, not quality assurance agencies, have been the key players in this process through which several disciplines have identified content and learning objectives that should be similar across degrees wherever they are offered. National quality assurance agencies support these efforts and typically include them in their evaluations. The tuning processes have been powerful enough to catch international attention and promote replication. Europeans have introduced the process in South America, Russia, China,

and Japan even as it refined its implementation in Europe. In many respects the Lumina-supported U.S. "Degree Qualifications Profile" draws heavily on the Tuning Project. The U.S. project is located with the National Institute for Learning Outcomes Assessment. The participation of an international institution/program, particularly one in the EHEA, in a tuning process ought to figure into a determination of its quality. Tuning is a process worth studying, especially focusing on efforts of collaboration regarding alignment and comparability.

✳ Consider the Efficacy of Cross-Border Mutual Recognition. Europe, in particular, displays a further refinement in the development of higher education quality assurance. In 2003, several of the most established agencies created the European Consortium for Accreditation (ECA), the core purpose of which is mutual recognition of accrediting decisions across borders. Currently, only 15 European QA agencies hold membership. In 2014, ECA transitioned from a network to a formal organization embracing internationalization and intercultural learning as another major component of its activities. In international gatherings, talk swirls around the possibility of a U.S. accrediting agency entering a mutual recognition network and, if it did, what impact that might have on the broader higher education community. For several years ABET, the agency that accredits engineering and computer science programs, relied on the Washington Accord, a mutual recognition agreement to ease portability of professional training and credentials. But ABET ultimately chose to extend its own accreditation to international programs. Perhaps mutual recognition will only be achieved through institution-to-institution agreements, but even then the hurdles of state and federal rules and licensing will undoubtedly trip up those who seek more transparent and efficient mobility. It is interesting to note that the United States Department of Education makes mutual recognition across regional agencies difficult, for it demands that each agency apply its own set of standards in reaching an accreditation decision rather than honoring a decision made by a different agency.

* **Make the Most of Public Disclosure.** In the United States, only the WASC Senior College and University Commission and one or two specialized agencies disclose evaluation reports. Almost all other agencies have argued for years that effective peer review processes require confidentiality. In most of the rest of the world, including Europe in particular, accreditation is assumed to be a form of public accountability. Therefore, publication of team reports is expected and required for ENQA recognition. In many countries, the reports are either written in English or translated into English and placed on the agency's website. In the U.S., while accreditors fret about the unevenness of reports, some European agencies turn to staff or paid secretaries to write them, while others, such as Kosovo, simply publish what they receive from a team, no matter the differences among reports. Because the quality of reports even in the same country might vary significantly in their insight and quality, a team/expert report might be an interesting supplementary resource for a U.S. educator but should seldom be considered determinative of quality. Nonetheless, a third-party evaluation report is probably a more dependable source of information than some of the informal word-of-mouth reports accepted as evidence even today.

* **Interpret International Expansion of U.S. Accreditation.** Historically, all regional institutional agencies extended accreditation to international sites for programs or branches of regionally-accredited entities. Some extended accreditation to franchised delivery of programs or to freestanding international entities, often ones that were affiliated with a U.S. institution at some time in the past. The effectiveness of U.S. peer review processes, even for English-language institutions, has been somewhat "hit or miss" as those institutions are inevitably shaped to some extent by a political, social, and education culture different from that assumed in most U.S. stan-

dards. But over the past thirty years, regional agencies have become more sophisticated in their work. Perhaps the greatest expansion of "U.S. accreditation" internationally has occurred in some specialized/program agencies that have responded to market demands for extra stamps of quality. Some professional groups continue to hew to a largely U.S.-defined set of standards, but a few have reconfigured their agency to be truly international in scope and activities. They draw on an international body of peers to make reviews adjudicated by a body more international in its composition. CHEA, not the USDE, has been most proactive in tracking these developments in the agencies it recognizes. However, it presents an interesting conundrum for U.S. education when a student from an international institution accredited by a national agency presents a degree from a program accredited by a U.S.-based specialized agency.

Escape the Diploma Mills[19]

Unfortunately, little progress has been made in halting fraud in higher education. Over the years CHEA has turned a spotlight on diploma mills, now truly an international phenomenon. The Internet has only exacerbated the longstanding confusion between legitimate and illegitimate players. Visiting the website of a mill institution or accrediting agency can be enlightening if for no other reason than to see the sophistication of the operation. It is altogether too easy to be misled by their efforts to use legitimate accreditation as a cover. They often provide links to well-recognized sites such as the United States Department of Education, CHEA, or ENQA, leading to the assumption that they have permission to publish that link. Frequently, in their list of "accredited institutions" or "accredited programs," mill accrediting agencies bury the mill(s) among legitimately accredited entities that have no knowledge of the misuse of their names. They might also claim membership in recognized groups that do not conduct a

---

[19] For more on diploma mills, *see* Chapter 18, Diploma Mills and Fake Degrees.

thorough review of membership. This is particularly true for groups with the primary purpose of stimulating a culture of sharing good practices, for even their membership requirements can be rather loose.

For those institutions and programs that claim the U.S. as the primary site of operation, the best starting point in determining credibility is to research the lists of accredited institutions provided by regional and national accrediting agencies. Although each agency provides its own list, CHEA attempts to combine them.[20] When dealing with an institution using an international address, one can verify its authenticity via the quality assurance agency for the specified country. CHEA, INQAAHE, and ENQA list their member and recognized agencies on their website. This kind of search not only answers the question of whether the institution is legal, but whether it has undergone any form of external review.

Mills change names so easily and frequently that efforts to maintain a dependable and current list is almost impossible. Potential legal challenges further prevent most agencies from actually identifying even known mills. The United States Department of Education provides useful information on diploma mills.[21] The Dutch also write to the challenge of identifying mills.[22] All of these efforts focus largely on identifying legitimate institutions and quality assurance agencies, assuming that if an institution or agency does not appear on those lists, it is probably a mill. But it is true that in the mishmash of acronyms around the world, it is very easy to slip in yet one more name or agency that sounds real enough to believe.

Conclusion

In the future, globalization of higher education will only increase in its impact on U.S. higher education. As other parts of the world, particularly Europe, overcome deeply entrenched traditions and customs to work out collaborative ways to address mobility and comparability, the U.S., through its very decentralized system of quality assurance, needs to adjust. A desire to cooperate and coordinate will be critical to these efforts. The mystery is where the guiding vision and leadership will emerge, for although the U.S. would benefit greatly from its own Bologna Process, it lacks the collective sense of urgency necessary to drive it. It just might help to pay better attention to what our international counterparts are doing and learning.

---

[20] *See* <www.chea.org>.

[21] *See* <www2.ed.gov/students/prep/college/diplomamills/diploma-mills.html>.

[22] *See* <www.diplomamills.nl/index_engels.htm>.

EIGHTEEN

Diploma Mills and Fake Degrees

JASMIN SAIDI-KUEHNERT

President and CEO
Academic Credentials Evaluation Institute, Inc.

Diploma Mills and Fake Degrees

The Higher Education Opportunity Act (2008) defines a diploma mill as follows:

The term 'diploma mill' means an entity that—(A)(i) offers, for a fee, degrees, diplomas, or certificates, that may be used to represent to the general public that the individual possessing such a degree, diploma, or certificate has completed a program of postsecondary education or training; and (ii) requires such individual to complete little or no education or coursework to obtain such degree, diploma, or certificate; and (B) lacks accreditation by an accrediting agency or association that is recognized as an accrediting agency or association of institutions of higher education (as such term is defined in section 102) by (i) the Secretary pursuant to subpart 2 of part H of title IV; or (ii) a Federal agency, State government, or other organization or association that recognizes accrediting agencies or associations.

Diploma mills are bogus institutions—selling printed diplomas at all levels, from bachelor's to doctoral, to individuals who may or may not know that the schools are fake and thus the credentials are worthless. These degrees and transcripts require little or no academic work and/or they may claim life experience as the basis for the diploma. Diploma mills have names similar to well-known recognized schools and universities and profess their accreditation by citing equally dubious accreditation agencies (mills) that they may have set up themselves.

An important distinction to keep in mind when discussing fraudulent credentials: diploma mills should not be confused with counterfeit degrees. The former are illegitimate institutions, while the latter are forgeries of documents bearing the name of legitimate and respected institutions.

Today's current economy can incentivize some workers to seek additional educational qualifications in order to be more competitive and relevant in the global marketplace. There are many barriers which can prevent workers from easily pursuing this goal including but not limited to lacking the time, money, or opportunity to continue their education. Taking advantage of this situation, diploma mills offer a quick fix to interested people for a fee—significantly more affordable than the growing cost of higher education at traditional colleges.

Diploma Mills in the United States

Diploma mills are not a 21st century phenomena; the earliest record of domestic diploma mills date back to the colonial era. In fact, the passage of the Morrill Land Grant Acts in 1862 and 1890—which led to the founding of many new colleges—gave birth to a market of bogus diploma providers to meet the demand for degrees (Council for Higher Education Administration). The diploma mill industry grew even more in the 20th century with the Servicemen's Readjustment Act of 1944, also known as the GI Bill, where millions of returning war veterans were given the opportunity to receive a college education funded by the federal government. The prevalence of diploma mills prompted Congress to include a provision in the bill that such education had to be carried out at accredited institutions in order for the students to receive federal financial aid (Council for Higher Education Administration). Although the requirement for accreditation helped curb the epidemic of diploma mills, it simultaneously helped give rise to its sinister companion: the accreditation mill. In an effort to retain their bogus market from being usurped and undermined by government regulations, the diploma mills set out to create an illusion of legitimacy through their own fraudulent accreditation agencies.

Today, diploma mills survive by operating in states that lack strict and explicit laws regarding institutional accreditation. By assuming identities of well-known institutions or marketing themselves as religious schools, they can avoid a fair bit of scrutiny. U.S. constitutional safeguards that guarantee separation of church and state are exploited by these diploma mills to protect themselves. Most states are reluctant to pass laws that restrict the activities of churches or church-like institutions including their right to grant degrees; diploma mills are aware of this and take full advantage for their purposes. They may also operate from multiple locations, which helps protect them from the stringent laws of one state or country while benefiting from the lax laws of another jurisdiction.

Fake Degrees and Senior Government Officials

A degree from a diploma mill has no value unless those in positions with hiring authority fail to vet a candidate's academic qualifications. Regrettably, most employers only carry out a criminal background check, but fail to verify the candidate's claimed educational credentials. Consider the following case: In 2003 an employee at the Department of Homeland Security called into question the legitimacy of the credentials of a fellow employee, Senior Director Laura Callahan, specifically questioning her educational accomplishments. Prior to her employment at the Department, Callahan had served as the Deputy Chief Information Officer (CIO) of the U.S. Department of Labor and a senior information technology manager at the White House. The investigation of Callahan revealed that she had obtained not one but three academic degrees, including a Ph.D., from a diploma mill, helping her

secure a six-figure salary. She had purchased the degrees from Hamilton University, a diploma mill operating out of Wyoming, a state with very weak laws concerning diploma mills. Callahan resigned in 2004.

The Callahan episode prompted the Government Accounting Office (GAO) to begin an in-depth investigation to determine whether any government funds were used in securing fake degrees. The GAO's narrow focus was on the misuse of federal funds—not the existence of fake degrees and holders of fake degrees within the federal government. The GAO was able to conclude that the number of employees claiming degrees from diploma mills is higher than expected—463 government employees were identified as using diplomas from these mills (Cramer 2004, 2). A report by CBS News Correspondent Vince Gonzalez on May 10, 2004, found employees with diploma mill degrees at the Transportation Security Administration (TSA), the Defense Intelligence Agency, and the Departments of Treasury and Education. At the time of the CBS report, Renee Drouin, who sat on an advisory committee at the U.S. Department of Education, was found to have degrees from two diploma mills.

The fact that individuals holding fake degrees have been able to infiltrate our country's security infrastructure should be disconcerting. It is alarming that high-level employees are successfully representing their fraudulent credentials as legitimate degrees. Not subjected to rigorous screenings of their educational backgrounds, the only penalty for discovery is discipline or termination. These examples clearly highlight the appeal of using fake credentials to advance one's career.

A Global Problem

On May 19, 2015, the *New York Times* reported on Axact, a software company based in Karachi, Pakistan, suspected of running a global diploma mill along with a series of accreditation mills set up to garner legitimacy for its fake institutions and degrees. On May 27, 2015, Pakistani investigators raided the company's headquarters and arrested its CEO and four other executives after discovering a storage room filled with blank fake diplomas. Following these arrests, investigators also discovered another building next to Axact headquarters and found a trove of certificates and diplomas from fake schools and universities under a slew of familiar sounding but misleading names such as Columbiana University, Sterling University, Mount Lincoln University, Bay View University, Nixon University, Oxdell University, and Cambell State University. Axact did not limit its diploma mills to academic credentials alone; it was also issuing U.S. State Department authentication certificates that bore Secretary of State John Kerry's signature. The raid on Axact and arrests of its executives has brought to light one of the largest diploma mill scams in history. Axact's market was far-reaching: they ran a global scam providing bogus diplomas with the majority of their customers in the U.S. and Persian Gulf. (For more on this story, *see* Chapter 31: Axact: A Diploma Mill Case Study.)

Even though investigators in Pakistan were able to close in on Axact and its illegal operations by bringing charges of fraud against its executives, similar entities continue to exist around the world. While the problem of bogus degrees and diploma mills is recognized as serious, research on the damage they have inflicted is limited. Grolleau and colleagues state, "…it is difficult to estimate their full impact because it is an illegal activity and there is an obvious lack of data and rigorous studies. Several official investigations point to the magnitude and implications of this dubious activity. These investigations appear to underestimate the expanding scale and dimensions of this multimillion-dollar industry" (McLemee 2014).

In 2003, Allen Ezell, who investigated diploma mills in the 1980s, stated, "[Diploma mills] used to be mom-and-pop outfits. It's now a professional criminal operation. It's gone high-tech and global in nature. That's something we've never had to deal with before" (Armour 2003). The worldwide expansion and degree of penetration into the global market creates an untenable situation that must be resolved.

A Supply and Demand Chain

As stated earlier, falsifying documents and producing fake diplomas and degrees is not new. However, the Internet has made buying bogus degrees easier than ever before, which has helped diploma mills become a booming industry. Advancement in technology makes it nearly effortless for diploma mill operators to set up impressive websites, to create home pages for bogus universities, and to generate fake diplomas. If employers demand more advanced education than one already possesses, people competing for jobs in today's global economy may look for an edge to set them apart and may resort to buying a fake degree from a diploma mill to help them secure the job.

Identifying bogus institutions has become even more difficult now that a higher proportion of legitimate universities have started offering online courses. It is hard for a prospective student to distinguish a legitimate education from a bogus one when searching for online degree programs. Names similar to bona fide universities are commonly used in an effort to dupe prospective students. Many who fall prey to diploma mills and their scams tend to be citizens of countries looking for a cheap degree from a "Western" institution. They may be deceived by the similarity of the name to that of a recognized and respected institution. This unfamiliarity with the U.S. higher education system and accreditation regulations may make those outside the U.S. more likely victims of a diploma mill.

In AACRAO's 2005 *Guide to Bogus Institutions and Documents*, John Bear describes diploma mills as a $200-million-a-year criminal industry comprising villains and victims. According to Bear, the villains which help sustain this criminal industry include "the people who run the dreadful schools; the media; the world of law enforcement, and the people who buy and use fake degrees" (Bear 2005, 60–68). Bear sees the victims as "those buyers who aren't villains, the employers, the public, and the legitimate schools" (Bear 2005, 68–70). Hunting and pursuing these sinister organizations create abundant headaches given their litigious propensity.

Bear himself has been sued several times by schools operating as diploma mills, however, only one suit made it to court and was dismissed by the judge as frivolous. Essentially, these institutions do not have legal standing to contradict a focused assault against them.

A License to Operate

In the U.S. some states will issue licenses to institutions to operate even if they are not accredited, while some states still only license institutions with accreditation from recognized accreditation bodies. These varying standards of operation create a stage for confusion that facilitates opportunities for deception.

In order to offer the unsuspecting public the illusion of legitimacy, some diploma mills will go as far as having live phone operators answering calls by employers to verify fabricated graduations of their so-called students. They often include toll-free numbers on their bogus transcripts just so that employers seeking verification can call them directly. Some will even release "official" transcripts to employers on request or sell laminated student ID cards, class rings, and other paraphernalia with their bogus school's logo and name to further legitimize their lack of a campus or physical buildings. Having high-tech equipment at their disposal, diploma mills can issue counterfeit degrees that resemble those of legitimate universities. They also issue degrees for large sums of money based on "life experiences."

Investigations into Diploma Mills

From 1980 to 1991, the Federal Bureau of Investigation's Operation DIPSCAM conducted a series of investigations against individuals involved with diploma mills and successfully brought charges against them. According to research conducted by Verifile Limited, a United Kingdom firm, the United States "holds the dubious title of most popular location for diploma mill providers; 1,008 are known to have operated or currently operate from the country, an increase of 198 providers (20%) [in one year]. A closer look at the number of mills by state indicates that California still tops the

leader board, followed by Hawaii, Washington, Florida, Texas, New York, Arizona, Louisiana, and District of Columbia" (Cohen and Winch 2011, 24).

Europe comes second to the U.S. with a total of 603 diploma mills. The UK leads the pack, followed by Italy, Belgium, Netherlands, Switzerland, Ireland, Germany, Spain, Austria, and France. The popularity of the U.K. as a base for diploma mills may stem from the country's lax regulations on foreign institutions operating on U.K. soil, although it is illegal for an institution to claim status as a recognized U.K. institution. These diploma mills adopt names similar to those of legitimate prestigious U.K. universities, but may circumvent legal entanglements by incorporating their businesses in offshore locations (*e.g.* on an island in the Caribbean or the Pacific).

Signs of a Diploma Mill

Basically, if the degree is obtained without doing any work, receiving instruction, attending classes, or taking final examinations, and simply paying a fee, then it has come from a diploma mill. Signs of a diploma mill include:

* It may have a poorly designed website bearing claims of recognition by several so-called accreditation boards.
* It has the same IP and physical address as other bogus universities: they share the same server and are operated by the same person or group of people.
* The accreditation board has the same address as the diploma mill.
* The website mentions accreditation by an accreditation body in another country or a micronation other than the country where it is based or registered to operate. For example, several diploma mills claim to be approved by Hutt River Province, a self-styled state in Western Australia, which is not recognized in any way by the Australian Government.
* The website is littered with advertisements by other online vendors.
* It uses a name similar to that of legitimate respected institutions—for example, Standford

University, not to be confused with Stanford University; Hartford University, not to be confused with University of Hartford; LaSalle University (Louisiana), not to be confused with La Salle University (Philadelphia); and Atlantic International University (Hawaii), not be to confused with Atlantic University (Virginia).

＊ It has no coursework, no instructions, either online or in class, and no final examinations to assess an individual's learning.

＊ It has no minimum timeline required for completion of a course or program, and the degree is issued within a very short period of time.

＊ It offers the individual a choice of graduation date.

＊ It has a flat fee to purchase a specific type of diploma.

＊ Pushy sales people contact the prospective degree grantee with aggressive spam and advertising tactics.

＊ It promises a degree based on life experiences only for large sums of money (while some legitimate accredited schools might grant credit for life experiences, diploma mills do so only for hefty fees and award an entire degree).

Stopping Diploma Mills

A collective effort needs to exist on the part of legitimate academic institutions, companies, and organizations involved in education and education-related services to work together in combating diploma mills. A unified voice and coordinated legislative effort, independently passed in individual countries and globally recognized, is needed in order to address this problem. Bear offers additional suggestions including: alerting state representatives and the media when a legitimate school finds its name maligned by a bogus school; boycotting advertising or threatening not to advertise in print or online media where bogus schools are also advertising; pressuring the Federal Trade Commission to act on its 1998 ruling that regulates the use of the word "accredited" and enforce it against those that are not; notifying the editor, publisher, or Internet site provider of magazines, publications, and websites in which bogus schools advertise and inform federal, state, and local authorities; and educate the public. Remaining passive and hoping the problem will go away will only enable it to continue to fester and grow.

With today's porous global network and the communication and mobility of people from one continent to another, academic institutions, employers, credential evaluation service providers, immigration officers, and state regulatory boards cannot afford to be victims of diploma scams.

In combating accreditation mills, Allen Ezell recommends collecting as much information on the mills as possible and turning it over to the State Attorney General, The Consumer Protection Agency, and even contacting the local newspaper. The more examples of these mills are collected and presented, the better the chances of having someone at one or all of these agencies take action. As the country with the greatest known number of diploma mills, the United States must lead the effort to subdue these organizations.

The public at large, the person looking for a fast way of earning, or, in reality, of buying a degree should take heed of this warning on the FTC's website: "Most employers and educational institutions consider it lying if you claim academic credentials that you didn't earn through actual course work. If you use a so-called "degree" from a diploma mill to apply for a job or promotion, you risk not getting hired, getting fired, and possible prosecution."

NINETEEN

Fighting Fraud
in the Admissions and
Registrar's Offices

2016 AACRAO INTERNATIONAL GUIDE

EDWARD DEVLIN

Evaluator
AACRAO International Education Services

ANN M. KOENIG

Associate Director
AACRAO International Education Services

Fighting Fraud in the Admissions and Registrar's Offices

The education sector is no stranger to fraud. Although professionals in the field of education prefer to think that this sector is safe from fraud and misrepresentation, the reality is that fraud involving our institutions has occurred, is about to occur, or is in progress. Fraud in education takes many forms among students, instructors, administrators, and other members of the institutional community, including cheating, plagiarism, academic and professional misconduct, misuse of the institution's name, misrepresentation of the institution, and credential fraud. AACRAO has published several resources on fraud as it relates to the admissions and enrollment management environment (*see* "Resources on Fraud" at the end of this chapter).

This chapter identifies some of the common types of fraud encountered in the admissions and registrar's offices and presents suggestions for best practices in admissions and student record review processes. The goal is to help institutions become proactive about fraud and develop procedures and policies to minimize its occurrence and protect the integrity of the institution.

Types of Document Fraud

The most common types of document-related fraud seen by the admissions and registrar's offices are incomplete or misleading applications for admissions; altered or fabricated academic documentation; intentionally misleading English translations; counterfeit transcripts and documents from real educational institutions; documentation from fictitious or bogus universities or colleges that sell "degrees" (so-called diploma or degree mills); and documents from bogus accreditation bodies

that often operate in tandem with degree mills. Other offices on campus that require students, faculty, or administration to present academic credentials, such as the human resources department or research and development units, might also encounter problems with document fraud, including misleading, incomplete, or fraudulent résumés.

Misrepresentation of the Institution

Every vendor that sells an institution's name on fake documents is misrepresenting the institution and degrading the value of its reputation. But misrepresentation extends beyond the sphere of fraudulent documents. Other examples include the unauthorized use of an institution's or organization's materials, products, and services; false advertising that implies the involvement or endorsement of an institution; unscrupulous recruiting agents gaining unwarranted financial benefits from an institution's international student applications; and bogus entities such as degrees mills and accreditation mills including an institution's name in lists of its members, associates, etc. without the institution's knowledge or consent. Registrars and admissions officers are sometimes shocked to discover such cases of misrepresentation.

The Roots of Document Fraud and Its Growth

The value of any product reflects the demand for that product. In an environment in which education or a degree is seen as a product, the market value of education increases as demand grows. When access to education is limited or removed, or when authentic academic documentation is not available, an opportunity for fraud arises.

Such things as natural disasters, war, political crises, economic disasters, and social upheaval can limit access to education or authentic educational documentation. It is crucial to keep abreast of current events so that informed and careful consideration can be given to applications from individuals affected by such conditions. The list of countries and regions experiencing disruptive conditions changes with world events. International professionals need to be familiar with resources that can confirm these conditions and give suggestions as to how to handle these cases.

However, careful attention must also be paid to other factors that create an opportunity for fraud. One common example is countries or regions with high rates of corruption or very complex bureaucratic systems that make it difficult for the average person to navigate. Other factors may relate to an individual student's academic history: for example, a student with outstanding education-related debt who cannot get official transcripts; an applicant who has completed coursework requirements, but not other types of additional graduation requirements; an applicant to a graduate program who may have insufficient undergraduate coursework in a particular discipline or an insufficient grade average to be eligible for the program; or an executive who has advanced professionally without commensurate formal education. All of these situations might lead an individual to present fraudulent credentials.

The thread that connects all of these scenarios is the desire to gain access to education. Academic credentials have become a commodity in the world market. The proliferation of fraudulent documents has, of course, been fueled by the development of the Internet and e-commerce. Be it counterfeit transcripts from real institutions, "replacement" transcripts and diplomas from replica services, or "novelty" degrees from degree mills "accredited" by bogus accreditors, it's the "commerce" in *e-commerce* that drives the growth of this industry. Degrees are equal to dollars (or any other currency in the world). What sells in this milieu is the name recognition and reputation of any school whose name or logo appears on fraudulent documentation or that becomes a victim of this type of fraud.

High School Documents and Fraud

Fraud in education is not limited to the higher education sector. The answer to the frequent question of whether fraud in higher education also applies to the high school level is, unfortunately, a resounding "yes." Although it appears less fraud is connected with high school level documentation, when it comes to the possible benefits of presenting fraudulent high school transcripts, diplomas equaling dollars remains the standard. Consider the case of any individual who has not actually completed secondary or high school in the United States or abroad, thus finding him or herself shut out from many types of jobs or education/training programs. Or the person who completed secondary school in a different country, but is constantly asked for a high school diploma or GED by people in the United States and is not aware of the existence of foreign credential evaluators. Or the high school athlete who possesses talent in his/her sport, but does not have the academic ability for college admission. Imagine the results of one of these scenarios when the individual discovers the possibility of buying a high school diploma or GED online. It may seem farfetched or desperate to those who work at the level of higher education, but high school documentation has a market value, too.

Due Diligence is Essential

There are many flags that might alert an international admissions officer to the possibility of fraudulent, altered, or misleadingly translated documents, including academic records, test results, letters of recommendation, and financial documents. So why is due diligence essential? Why should an institution bother to request verification of suspicious documents? Why is it not enough to think that the document is probably okay or that *surely* the international applicant will not get a visa if the visa officer is suspicious about the document too? What is the harm in admitting a student with altered documents? The answers fall into three categories: ethical, legal, and practical.

＊ **Ethical Considerations.** The ethical imperative is simple enough. If a school admits students on the basis of suspicious or incomplete documentation, while denying admission to students who submit authentic documents, the institution is supporting and rewarding fraud. Good practice and simple fairness require that a school take care to ensure that its admission and transfer credit practices reward only real achievement, for all applicants, both international and domestic.

＊ **Legal Considerations.** The legal issue is also straightforward. Institutions that receive state and/or federal funding, as well as those certified to accept international students, have entered into legal agreements with legal obligations. Not practicing due diligence is a clear violation of the public trust granted by state government support, as well as the partnership with the U.S. government that the institution has undertaken by applying for and receiving the right to admit international students.

＊ **Practical Reasons.** The ramifications of ignoring due diligence are also rather clear-cut, although the interpretations may be more subtle and have long-lasting consequences for the reputation of an individual institution. On a larger scale, if an institution admits international students based on suspicious or incomplete documents, the reputation of U.S. higher education suffers worldwide. The same warning applies more obviously to an individual institution. It is common practice in many countries to sell and buy bogus documents, from marksheets and transcripts to complete degree dossiers, including U.S. immigration forms. One single ill-gotten I-20 form from a U.S. institution that is not alert to document fraud can be reproduced and sold indefinitely. That institution's reputation is then tarnished. The reputation of an institution as an "easy mark" for questionable application documents is a hard one to repair. Once this reputation is public, excellent students will stay away. Weak ones will apply, fraudulently or not. Additionally, once word gets out about lax admissions standards, the number of fraudulent applications will skyrocket. The campus then has fraudsters in its midst and must deal with the consequences. Given the limited resources at an institution, it is wiser to do a careful review during the admissions process than to have to manage problems created by fraudsters once they are on campus.

Good Practice is the Key

To safeguard the authenticity of institutions, as well as to continue to attract quality international students who contribute to the vitality, diversity, and quality of U.S. higher education, it is imperative to follow best practices in the admission of international students. This means that international admissions professionals should have the training and resources they need to make sound professional judgments about the documents that applicants submit, receive the encouragement and support of enrollment managers to research and seek verification of questionable documents, and share the results of the verification process with their colleagues. There is too much at stake to disregard or fall short on responsibilities in this area.

DOCUMENT REVIEW AND VERIFICATION

The best protection against fraud is a solid knowledge base among foreign credential analysts and a strong network of information sharing about document fraud and verification successes. Best practices in international admissions and foreign academic record review call for:

＊ training and continuing professional development for foreign transcript evaluators, so that they are knowledgeable and up-to-date about country educational systems, documentation practices, and events that impact international education;

＊ clear communication to applicants about the documentation required for admission;

＊ careful review and research of the documents that are submitted;

＊ requests for verification of suspicious documents;

✳ appropriate follow-up when verification is received from the issuing institution or educational authority; and

✳ the sharing of success stories in the verification process.

THE INTERNATIONAL EVALUATOR'S PROFILE

Too often the job of reviewing foreign transcripts is given to an inexperienced front-line person. Perhaps nobody in the office is familiar with documents from other countries. Sometimes there is a "fear factor" associated with documents in strange envelopes written in foreign languages. International credential analysts need to be experienced, engaged, detail-oriented individuals who are given the resources required to develop their expertise. They are the first line of protection in the battle against fraud.

TAKING A METHODICAL APPROACH TO DOCUMENT REVIEW

The following outline presents a step-by-step approach to best practices in assembling, reviewing, researching, and seeking verification of documents. Following these practical guidelines will help safeguard your institution against fraud.

Step 1: Assemble the documentation in the application file and assess its completeness.

✳ Learn where to find accurate information on country educational systems, names of credentials awarded, and the documentation practices in the countries which draw the most applicants, i.e., how are documents issued—in what format and what language, and what is the procedure for students to obtain official documentation, etc.

✳ Establish guidelines for the documentation required for a complete application file, including English translations and the use of translations in the evaluation process. Evaluations should never be based on English translations alone. (See "Use of English Translations," on page 189, for more on this topic.)

✳ Develop a procedure for cases in which the required documentation is not available.

✳ Inform prospective applicants of documentation requirements and procedures as early in the process as possible. Be proactive and include this information on websites and all printed information.

✳ Inform prospective applicants of the method(s) for submitting application materials and timelines or deadlines in the process.

✳ Develop a procedure to follow when an applicant submits incomplete or unacceptable documentation. How and when is the applicant informed of this procedure?

✳ Are any of the above points negotiable? Under what circumstances?

✳ In applicant information, clearly define the consequences if incomplete, untrue, or falsified information or documentation is submitted.

✳ Communicate all of the requirements, procedures, and timelines clearly. The keys to receiving complete application files that include all the necessary documentation are to *know what is needed* and then *communicate to applicants what is required* in a precise, clear manner. Using indigenous terminology for the foreign academic documentation is very helpful.

Step 2: Obtain reliable resources to help you review the documentation.

✳ Determine what to research about the documents in the file, and assemble the research tools.

✳ Resources include publications and information on educational systems, maps, foreign language dictionaries, periodical articles, documents, and information provided by previous applicants, etc. Information about the availability of such materials can be obtained from professional associations like AACRAO, conference and workshop materials, and online tools, etc. Also, experienced colleagues are also an excellent resource.

✳ Update and expand the institution's resource collection as new resources become available, educational systems change, technology expands, and research needs change and grow.

Step 3: Review and analyze the documents received.

* Arrange the documents in chronological order.

* Confirm the origin of every document. Is it an original, a copy, or a duplicate? How did the documentation get to the institution and into the applicant/student's file? Is this pathway appropriate for the country involved and the type of document?

* Review the biographical data provided by the applicant and compare with the "story" told by the documents. Pay attention to detail (location, age, level of education, quality of performance, test results, military service, employment history, etc.).

* Locate and confirm key information on the documents using your resources: name and type of document; biographical information about student; name, location, recognition status, type and level of the institution; level, type, and length of program or courses shown on the documents; dates of attendance, and graduation or completion dates.

* If there is a course or subject listing, do the courses correspond to the field of study in which the student was enrolled, and were they completed? Compare assessment or grade results with information about the country's/institution's grading scale. Does the document show credits, units, or other relative weighting of courses? Are they appropriate for that country/institution?

* If the document is presented with an English translation, check the accuracy of the translation by comparing it to other documents from the same country or institution. (*See* "Use of English Translations," on page 189, for more on this topic.)

* Pay attention to the format of the document as well as the contents: does the layout of the document match confirmed sample documents shown in resources or in your files, including type and size of paper, typeface fonts, placement of text, signatures, stamps/seals, date, photograph, etc.? Are the lines of text aligned correctly? Are borders consistent with those seen on verified sample documents? Does the document appear to be unaltered? Are there any noticeable changes to the document, such as erasures, handwritten alterations, deletions, or covering of text? Is there any information missing from the document that should be there? Is information on the document that should not be there? Are words spelled correctly in the native language?

Step 4: Handling discrepancies, problems, omissions, inconsistencies, etc.

* Have another person review the document and resource materials. Ask colleagues who are knowledgeable about the particular country, institution, or field of study to review the document with you.

* If the problem cannot be resolved by checking resources and with input from colleagues, request verification of the documents.

Verifying Irregular Documents

The following section provides step-by-step guidance in seeking verification of irregular documents, using an example that illustrates the importance of the verification process. In 2014, an individual submitted a document to AACRAO International Education Services (IES) with a request for a foreign credential evaluation. Purportedly the document was issued by the former Irish technical board Further Education and Training Council (FETAC), now part of Quality and Qualifications Ireland (QQI), as a "Record of Awards" for "Component Certificates" awarded in 2006, 2007, and 2008. The evaluator began to question the authenticity of the document when research using FETAC and QQI online resources showed that FETAC awards at the time were available only at Levels 1 through 6, with no mention of Level 7. In addition, the document appeared to be issued on plain paper, with no visible security features. The evaluator researched the most effective way to contact QQI to confirm this suspicion, and decided to use the contact form on the QQI website. A QQI representative promptly responded, requesting that a copy of the document in question be emailed to QQI. The QQI representative reviewed the suspicious document and replied as follows:

> *The document you attached for XXX is false and must have been doctored/tempered with. There are no component certificates at Level 7. The Record of Awards paper that we issue has a watermark and security features included on it for future references.*

The AACRAO IES evaluator thanked the QQI representative and completed the evaluation report, noting the verification process that had taken place: Because of irregularities with the document, AACRAO IES had requested a verification review by QQI, which had confirmed that the document was fraudulent. AACRAO IES concluded the evaluation report with a statement that, because the document was confirmed as fraudulent, it has no value as an academic credential.

STEP 1: IDENTIFY THE OFFICIAL SOURCE FOR VERIFICATION OF THE DOCUMENTATION.

✳ Using reliable resources, identify the office or person responsible for verifying documents.

✳ If the issuing institution, organization, examining board, education authority, or ministry has an official online verification database or service, go to that website and review the process for verifying documents. Prepare what is needed in order to use the online system. (*See* "Official Online Verification Databases and Services," on page 190, for more information about online verification services, which are increasing in number.)

✳ If there is no online verification system, locate the appropriate contact information for the verifying office, and consider the most effective way to send the verification request (postal service, courier service, fax, e-mail, telephone, etc.).

✳ Formulate the request for verification. It is helpful to develop a standard form or letter to request verification. Some suggestions:

◆ Determine whether the letter should be written in English or another language, or both, to get a response as soon as possible. If in a language other than English, prepare the request in English first and have it translated by a reliable translator, such as a faculty or staff member. Send the request both in English and the other language.

◆ Clearly state "Request for Verification" in the opening of the request letter.

◆ Include an introduction of both the letter writer and the institution and state the reason for requesting verification (*i.e.*, student has applied for admission at the institution; student has requested transfer credit based on these documents).

◆ Include the student/applicant's name and date of birth or other identifying information for the institution. If the documents include a student identification number from that institution, include that in the letter.

◆ Be clear and specific about what information is needed from the verifier. For example, if the document is not authentic, what further information might be necessary?

◆ Include a copy of the documentation. If there are discrepancies in the document, highlight them.

◆ If the institution has applicants sign a form authorizing release of information from the individual's file(s) at previous institutions, include a copy of that as well. In many countries, student information is the property of the institution, not the student. But in cases in which student information is protected by privacy laws, such an authorization may be required.

◆ Specify a response date if necessary, the format in which a response would be acceptable (for example, in writing), and the language in which the response should be written.

◆ Include contact information for the response.

◆ Request confidentiality. This information is not to be shared with the student or anyone else.

◆ Thank the reader and offer to assist in the future or send informational material from the institution.

STEP 2: KEEP A RECORD OF VERIFICATION REQUESTS.

✳ Once the verification request has been sent, put a copy of it in the applicant's file.

✳ Also start a "Verification Requests" file for copies of request letters with attached copies of the questionable documents. Cross-reference the files so they can be easily retrieved when the response is received.

STEP 3: FOLLOW UP APPROPRIATELY WHEN A REPLY IS RECEIVED.

The receipt of a verification letter is one of the most satisfying experiences in the international admissions office. There are many countries from which it is difficult to get verification, due to factors that the u.s. higher education community may take for granted—limited financial, human, and technological resources; differences in record-keeping systems; corruption; or disruptions in civil life because of natural disasters or warfare. Despite the best intentions of colleagues abroad, cooperation in a procedure that is part of the standard of professional practice in educational administration in the United States cannot always be expected. Thus, receiving a response to a verification request is the first step in the resolution of a difficult situation involving the institution and the student.

✳ Assess the result/response:

◆ Does the information provided adequately answer the evaluator's concerns about the authenticity of the document? Is it conclusive?

◆ If the information provided is not conclusive, what further action needs to be taken? Will another round of correspondence be fruitful? To whom should it be addressed? What other avenues can be pursued if it seems that further contact with the verifying authority would not be productive?

◆ What if a verification fee is requested? Some educational authorities have begun assessing a fee for verification, particularly in areas where resources are limited or a large number of verification requests are received. How does the evaluator handle such a situation?

✳ Take appropriate action. If the documents are verified as being fraudulent, follow-up should be immediate, according to established procedures and guidelines for the consequences to applicants who submit falsified documents. These policies should be defined and communicated to staff and applicants well before this stage of the admissions review process.

Communicating with Applicants about Irregular Documents

Strategies for communicating with students or applicants can range from saying nothing at all to the applicant; to informing the applicant that there are concerns about the documents and asking for explanations and/or assistance in getting verification or "better" documents; to informing the applicant that verification has been requested and that nothing further will be done until verification has been received. Each case involving suspicious documentation needs to be reviewed on an individual basis and handled with sensitivity to its specific circumstances. Working with trusted resources, including experienced colleagues who have successfully navigated cases like these, helps admissions officers and evaluators develop good professional judgment about how to handle cases involving suspicious documents.

Use of English Translations

In order to do an accurate assessment of applicants' previous education, evaluators should insist on receiving official documents in the original language of issue. English translations may be needed, and evaluators need to establish guidelines on how English translations will be used in the evaluation process. An evaluation should always be based on the original credential in the language in which it is officially issued, never on an English translation alone.

Translations should be literal, complete, word-for-word representations of the language in the original documents, prepared in the same format as the original, by a person familiar with both languages. If the evaluator is not familiar with foreign languages, a professional English translation may be required. However, evaluators should keep in mind that the most important feature of a translation is *accuracy* in representing exactly what is written in the foreign language. The issue of *who* does the translation is secondary to the question of *how accurate* it is. In some cases, a student, friend of the applicant, or faculty member may be able to provide an English translation that is as accurate as a translation done by a professional translator.

The accuracy of the translation should be confirmed by the use of reliable resources on the educational system of the country that show the names of institutions and credentials in the indigenous terminology. The evaluator should base the evaluation on the original document, using the English translation only as a tool.

If the translation appears inaccurate or misleading, then the applicant should be required to submit a different, accurate translation. There is no reason why an evaluator should hesitate to request an accurate English translation if necessary. Likewise, evaluators should not jump to conclusions about the authenticity of the original document, or the applicant's intentions, if the English translation is not accurate. The translation is a tool to understanding the official document; any judgments about the authenticity of an official document should be based on the document itself, not on the English translation.

Official Documentation Issued in English

Some countries issue official documentation in English, even though English might not be the main or official language of the country (*see* Figure 19.1, on page 191). In these cases, English translations should not be accepted. Only the official document issued by the institution in English should be considered official for use in the United States.

Official Online Verification Databases and Services

Official electronic databases for storing and retrieving student records can be effective tools in the fight against academic credential fraud. The number of official online credential verification databases and services is growing throughout the world as technological development enables government education authorities, examinations boards, and education and training providers to store and manage student records securely online and make them available to third parties. Since 2012, representatives from Belgium, Canada, China, France, Ireland, Italy, Mexico, the Netherlands, Romania, South Africa, Spain, Sweden, and the United States have signed the Groningen Declaration on Digital Student Data Depositories Worldwide, a statement of commitment to the concept of developing systems of digital student data portability to support the free mobility of students, graduates, skilled workers, and employment seekers on a global scale. AACRAO signed the Groningen Declaration in 2013.[23] Government education authorities and institutions in many additional countries have developed online student record systems which can be accessed by third-party users to authenticate student records and credentials.

Due to differences in laws regarding the ownership of student data, differing approaches to management of student records, and the many kinds of electronic systems in use, there are a myriad of types of online verification systems around the world and ways to access them. Some databases are accessible to the public, requiring only that data from the student's documentation be entered, while other systems include security barriers such as creating a user account, paying a user fee, providing a password or other access credentials that the student must pay for, or a combination of these elements. Colleagues are encouraged to explore the Internet to find these systems when documents call for

---

[23] *See* <www.groningendeclaration.org>.

Countries That Issue Official Academic Documents in English

FIGURE 19.1

- Afghanistan (transcripts in English)
- Australia
- Bahrain
- Bangladesh
- Bhutan
- Botswana
- Brunei Darussalam
- Cameroon (Anglophone)
- Canada (Anglophone)
- Caribbean Region (Anglophone):
  - Antigua and Barbuda
  - Bahamas
  - Barbados
  - Belize
  - Bermuda
  - British Virgin Islands
  - Cayman Islands
  - Dominica
  - Grenada
  - Guyana
  - Jamaica
  - Montserrat
  - St. Kitts & Nevis
  - St. Lucia
  - St. Vincent and the Grenadines
  - Trinidad and Tobago
  - Turks and Caicos Islands
- Cyprus, Republic of (some institutions)
- Egypt
- Eritrea (transcripts in English)
- Ethiopia (transcripts in English)

- Gambia
- Ghana
- Gibraltar
- Hong Kong
- India
- Ireland
- Israel (some institutions)
- Japan
- Jordan
- Kenya
- Korea, South
- Kuwait
- Lebanon (U.S.-patterned institutions)
- Lesotho
- Liberia
- Macau
- Malawi
- Malaysia (U.S.-patterned institutions)
- Malta
- Mauritius
- Namibia
- Nepal
- New Zealand
- Nigeria
- Oman
- Pakistan
- Papua New Guinea
- Philippines
- Qatar
- Rwanda
- Saudi Arabia

- Sierra Leone
- Singapore
- Somalia
- South Africa
- South Pacific Region (Anglophone):
  - Cook Islands
  - Fiji
  - Kiribati
  - Marshall Islands
  - Nauru
  - Niue
  - Samoa
  - Solomon Islands
  - Tokelau
  - Tonga
  - Tuvalu
  - Vanuatu
- Sri Lanka
- Sudan
- Swaziland
- Taiwan
- Tanzania
- Thailand
- Tonga
- Uganda
- United Arab Emirates
- United Kingdom (England, Scotland, Wales, Northern Ireland)
- Western Samoa
- Zambia
- Zimbabwe

verification and use online translators if they are not in English. However, a few words of caution are in order before embarking on this journey:

✻ "Official online verification system" is *not* synonymous with "unofficial student records accessed online." Unofficial online student records accessed by the student for advising and planning purposes are not official verified records, just as a transcript issued to a student should not be accepted when an official transcript is required.

✻ It is important to confirm that the verification system indeed officially belongs to the institution or examining body that issued the documents. Beware the Internet search that results in links to "results services" that appear to be compilations of links to other pages. The goal is to find the official results as posted by the institution or examining body.

✻ If a student's credential or examination result is not found in an official verification system, it should not be assumed that the documentation is inauthentic. Rather, the evaluator should refer to the step-by-step approach to verification outlined on page 186 and attempt to obtain verification by other means, such as email, fax, or postal correspondence.

Recent AACRAO annual meetings and other professional conferences have included presentations on the use of online verification systems, and past AACRAO presentations stored online can be found by visiting the AACRAO website.[24]

....
[24] *See* <www4.aacrao.org/meetings/>.

Listed below are some examples of official online verification systems available currently. By no means exhaustive, this list is meant to give a sampling of the various types of official verification tools currently available online in different parts of the world.

✻ Ministries of education and other education authorities at the national level:

◆ **People's Republic of China:** China Credentials Verification through the CHSI (China Higher-education Student Information), database run by the China Higher Education Student Information and Career Center (CHESICC).

◆ **Mexico:** Registro Nacional de Emisión, Validación in Inscripción e Documentos Académicos (RODAC) (www.sistemarodac.sep.gob.mx). In Spanish, with many sections bilingual Spanish-English. Voluntary registration of authentic credentials by credential holders and use of verification services are free of charge.

◆ **Mexico:** Secretaría de Educación Pública, Registar Nacional de Profesionistas (www.cedulaprofesional.sep.gob.mx/cedula/indexAvanzada.action). In Spanish. Registry of licensed professionals (holding a *cedula*). Several Latin American countries have similar databases of professional license holders.

◆ **Tanzania:** National Examinations Council of Tanzania (www.necta.go.tz). Results of examinations at many levels of education. Click tab "Results," then click the examination acronym. Use information from the examination certificate to choose the year and examination center. Results are listed by student number.

✻ National qualifications agency verification services:

◆ **South African Qualifications Authority** (SAQA) Verifications Service (verisearch.octoplus.co.za). Verifies all levels of awards and qualifications. Requires the third-party user to sign an agreement.

✻ Secondary school examination results verification systems:

◆ **West African Examinations Council** (WAEC) results verification systems: WAEC is a regional examining organization that conducts West African Secondary School Certificate (WASSC) examinations and other examinations in the Anglophone West African countries of Ghana, Liberia, Nigeria, Sierra Leone, and The Gambia. WAEC has developed an efficient, effective system of making examination results available online (or by other means, in some countries) through a "scratch card" system. The test-taker purchases a plastic card that contains a serial number and a scratch patch that when scratched off reveals a personal identification number (PIN). Data from the examination certificate must be entered into the results checker system along with the card serial number and PIN. To provide access to a third party, such as a university or employer, the test-taker must provide the third party with the examination certificate as well as the serial number and PIN from the scratch card. (It is important to note that the "scratch card" alone is not a substitute for an official examination results document.)

The "scratch card" system has been in existence for several years and works well for the verification of WAEC examination results. Each country's WAEC website includes an FAQ section that gives information about how the system works, what types of examinations are included in the database, where the scratch cards can be purchased, and by what means the official results are available. The scratch cards seem to be easily accessible even if the test-taker is no longer in the country in which the test was taken. *See* Figures 19.2–19.4 (on pages 193–195) for a sample WAEC WASSCE certificate from Nigeria, scratch card, and a corresponding online verification result. In this case, all of the information on the certificate matches the information shown in Nigerian WAEC Direct result checker system and the document is authentic.

The West African Examinations Council

West African Senior School Certificate

JUNE 2009

This is to Certify that:

born on: _____, 1990

sex: MALE

having been in attendance at

_____ SCHOOL, OKPARA WATER SIDE

sat the West African Senior School Certificate Examination and obtained the results shown below.

SUBJECT	GRADE
ECONOMICS	E8
GEOGRAPHY	B3
ENGLISH LANGUAGE	C6
MATHEMATICS	C4
AGRICULTURAL SCIENCE	D7
BIOLOGY	D7
CHEMISTRY	C6
PHYSICS	D7
SUBJECTS RECORDED	EIGHT

CD 12

Chairman of Council

Registrar to Council

Candidate No. _____

Certificate No. _____

NGWASSCS _____

Any alteration, erasure or absence of photograph renders this Certificate invalid.

- ⊚ *Ghana:* ghana.waecdirect.org/indexverify.htm
- ⊚ *Liberia:* results.liberiawaec.org
- ⊚ *Nigeria:* www.waecdirect.org
- ⊚ *Sierra Leone:* www.waecsierra-leone.org
- ⊚ *The Gambia:* www.waecgambia.org/resultchecker/
- ◆ India: Council for the Indian School Certificate Examinations (CISCE) (www.cisce.org)
- ◆ India: Central Board of Secondary Education (cbseresults.nic.in)
- ◆ India: Many of the Indian states and some of the Union Territories have official online results databases.
- ✳ Ministries of Education (secondary education results):
  - ◆ Bangladesh: Ministry of Education, Intermediate and Secondary Boards (www.educationboardresults.gov.bd/regular/index.php)
  - ◆ Bulgaria: (www2.mon.bg/AdminRD/mon/). In Bulgarian.

FIGURE 19.3

Sample Scratch Card

- **Democratic Republic of Congo:** (www.eduquepsp. cd). In French. See fields "Résultats par Code Elève" and "Résultats par Noms Elève"; select the year from the drop-down menu (back to 2009).
- **Dominican Republic:** (www.minerd.gob.do/site-see.net/consulta_prueba_nac/Consulta.aspx)
- **Namibia:** (www.moe.gov.na/st_my_results.php)
- **Yemen:** 2009 Secondary examination results (www. yemenindex.net/result-2009-elmi-442708.html)
✳ Universities/higher education institutions:
- **Australia:** Queensland University of Technology, Verification of Qualifications (www.qut.edu.au/about/services-and-facilities/all-services/verification-of-qualifications)
- **Australia:** Monash University (www.monash.edu. au/connect/graduate-search.html)

- **Canada:** York University (www.registrar.yorku.ca/graduation/yuverify/)
- **Nigeria:** Ladoke Akintola University of Technology (lautech. edu.ng/verify/)
- **Philippines:** Angeles University Foundation, Online Verification of Records (www.auf. edu.ph/modules.php?name= gradcheck)
- **Rwanda:** University of Rwanda (UR), Graduation 2015, List of graduates by College saved in pdf (www.ur.ac.rw/?q=node/ 343). The University of Rwanda was formed in 2013 from the merger of the National University of Rwanda (NUR) and other public higher education institutions in Rwanda. The Class of 2015 is UR's second graduating cohort. The NUR also published graduation lists online.
- **Singapore:** National University of Singapore, Registrar's Office, Online Degree Verification Portal (www.nus.edu.sg/registrar/ adminpolicy/degver ify.html)
- **Switzerland:** Universität St. Gallen (HSG) (servi ceportal.unisg.ch/base.aspx?tabid=114). Verification of bachelor's and master's degrees only, awarded since 2001.
- **United Kingdom:** Higher Education Degree Datacheck (HEDD) (www.hedd.ac.uk). Government-funded system for verifying the status of universities and university credentials. Universities must opt in. If a university has not opted in, the entry for that institution shows contact information for the university office responsible for verifying documents.

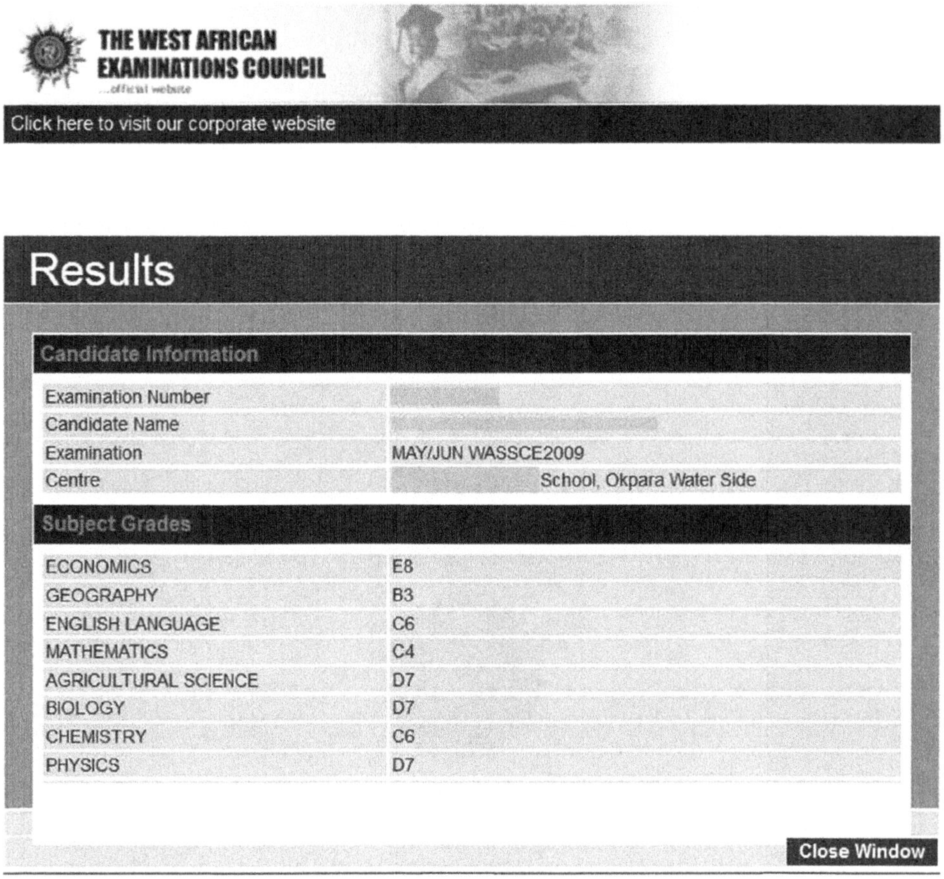

FIGURE 19.4

THE WEST AFRICAN EXAMINATIONS COUNCIL
...official website

Click here to visit our corporate website

Results

Candidate Information

Examination Number	
Candidate Name	
Examination	MAY/JUN WASSCE2009
Centre	School, Okpara Water Side

Subject Grades

ECONOMICS	E8
GEOGRAPHY	B3
ENGLISH LANGUAGE	C6
MATHEMATICS	C4
AGRICULTURAL SCIENCE	D7
BIOLOGY	D7
CHEMISTRY	C6
PHYSICS	D7

Close Window

Sample Online Verification Result

Counterfeit Transcripts and Diplomas

Counterfeit academic documents are produced and sold for the same reasons that counterfeit money exists. Education, or at least an educational credential, is "currency." A counterfeit document can be manufactured by an individual for his or her own use or produced for sale to others. In his book *Counterfeit Diplomas and Transcripts* (AACRAO 2008), fraud expert Allen Ezell presents information on dozens of online vendors that sell counterfeit transcripts from real educational institutions in the United States and around the world. The book also includes a list of at least 80 websites selling counterfeit Russian and Ukrainian educational credentials and describes the large-scale counterfeit document industry in the People's Republic of China. A table in the book shows a comparison of the characteristics of a genuine University of Florida transcript with the features of counterfeit University of Florida transcripts produced by three vendors of fake transcripts.

Vendors of counterfeit credentials may advertise the documents as "replacements," "replicas," or "novelty" items, and issue disclaimers that they are not responsible for the consequences of attempts by customers to present the documents as "real." Some use the wording "fake transcript" and "fake diploma" throughout the text of their websites. Often the websites include samples of the documents available, testimonials about the quality and usefulness of the documents, and "special offers." Some indicate which institutions' transcripts are *not* available; often they are schools who have taken some level of legal action against the supplier, such as a "cease and desist" warning.

THE REGENTS OF

Sherwood University

UPON THE NOMINATION OF THE COUNCIL OF THE UNDERGRADUATE DIVISION
HEREBY CONFER UPON

Alangir

HAVING DEMONSTRATED ABILITY BY GENERAL SCHOLARSHIP
CUM LAUDE · WITH DISTINCTION
THE DEGREE

Bachelor of Science
Physics

WITH ALL THE RIGHTS AND PRIVILEGES THERETO PERTAINING
GIVEN THIS TENTH DAY OF JUNE IN THE YEAR
TWO THOUSAND AND THREE

Carol Anderson
PRESIDENT OF THE REGENTS

William Franklyn
DEAN OF THE UNDERGRADUATE DIVISION

John McCullogh
PRESIDENT OF THE UNIVERSITY

Ronald R. Bowvert
CHANCELLOR

How can an institution protect itself from becoming a victim of this type of fraud? A proactive posture is paramount. Awareness of the problem is crucial, as well as vigilance in following a methodical approach to document review that includes a spectrum of verification procedures—from the use of standard resources to confirm information on transcripts, to written requests for authentication if necessary.

How does one determine the authenticity of a document from a real educational institution in an environment where potentially any institution's transcripts are for sale? Sometimes it is very difficult to tell whether a document is legitimate, especially when the fraudsters have stolen authentic templates, or even bought them from unscrupulous employees of the issuing institution or authority.

To clear up any suspicions about a document, a request for verification of the documentation should be addressed to the issuing institution. For guidance on seeking verification of documents from an institution outside of the United States, see the section on document review and verification above.

To request verification of documentation purportedly issued by a U.S. institution, contact the office of the registrar of the institution. The Family Educational Rights and Privacy Act (FERPA), a set of federal laws protecting the privacy of students in the U.S., includes a provision that student data called "directory information" can be disclosed to the public without specific authorization from the student/former student, unless the individual has requested otherwise. This directory information includes data such as the dates of enrollment, level and mode of enrollment (undergraduate or

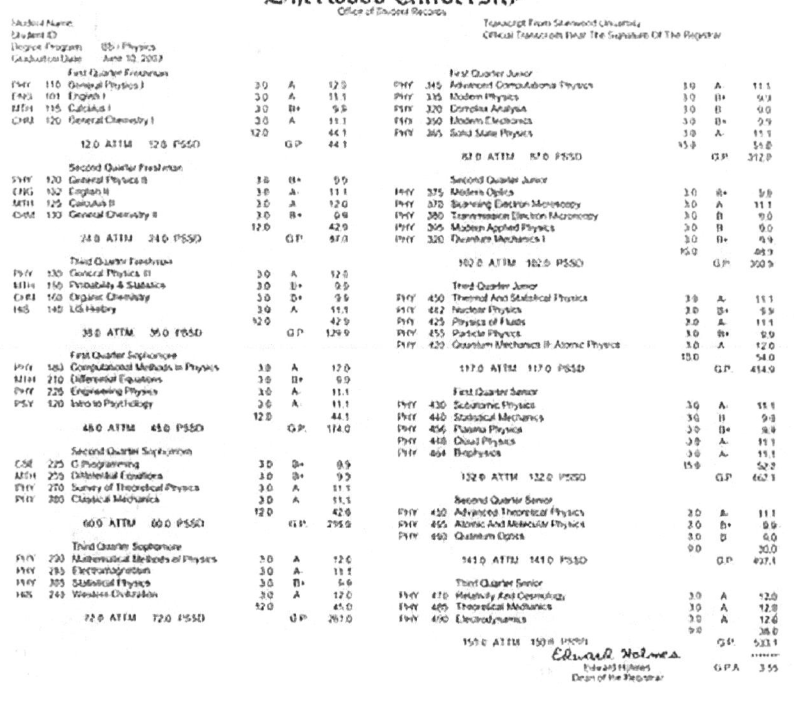

FIGURE 19.6

Diploma Mill Transcript, Sample 1

graduate, full-time or part-time), major, and degree awarded and date of degree, if awarded. For details on FERPA, see *U.S. Department of Education, Family Educational Rights and Privacy Act*[25], as well AACRAO's FERPA-related resources.[26]

Degree Mills, Accreditation Mills, and Bogus Foreign Credential Evaluation Services

A diploma mill or degree mill is an entity that produces and sells documents that appear to be academic credentials (diplomas, degrees, transcripts) from what appear to be universities or colleges, but in reality are academically worthless documents from fictitious educational institutions that represent inappropriately little academic work or none at all. These documents are meant to give the impression of academic achievement, but in reality they are purchased papers that have no academic value.

Awareness of diploma mill fraud is especially important for reviewers of international student records because many of these entities purport to be foreign universities. Typically such an entity will claim to be a university in a country outside of the United States, while the operators themselves may be located in the U.S., located in another country, or have different parts of the process located in different countries. For example, Bear and Ezell (2012) describe a well-known diploma mill ring called the "University Degree Program," an operation masterminded by a rabbi from New York, with telemarketing for "British degrees" done in Bucharest, Romania, mail-forwarding services in Ireland, diplomas printed in Israel, and banking in Cyprus. The book lists three-dozen known fictitious

25 See <www.ed.gov/policy/gen/guid/fpco/ferpa/>.

26 See <http://aacrao.org/resources/ferpa>.

FIGURE 19.7

Diploma Mill Degree, Sample 2

THE REGENTS OF

Shepperton University

UPON THE NOMINATION OF THE COUNCIL OF THE GRADUATE DIVISION
HEREBY CONFER UPON

HAVING DEMONSTRATED ABILITY BY GENERAL SCHOLARSHIP
CUM LAUDE · WITH DISTINCTION
THE DEGREE

Master of Business Administration

WITH ALL THE RIGHTS AND PRIVILEGES THERETO PERTAINING
GIVEN THIS TENTH DAY OF JUNE IN THE YEAR
TWO THOUSAND AND THREE

PRESIDENT OF THE REGENTS

DEAN OF THE GRADUATE DIVISION

PRESIDENT OF THE UNIVERSITY

CHANCELLOR

"university" names used by the University Degree Program. A comparative look at the documents from these "universities" shows that they have the same format, and essentially the same content, except for differences in the purchaser's name, the name and date of the "degree," and course titles on the transcript, depending on the field of "study." (*See* Figures 19.5–19.8 on pages 196–199.) Many spin-offs of this operation exist as former employees have started their own diploma mill businesses.

Accreditation mills represent a related area of fraud. Some diploma mills use claims of accreditation to sell their "degrees." It used to be more common for diploma mills to speak disparagingly of "accreditation" and state in their descriptive materials that they did not need accreditation, did not agree with the philosophy of accreditors, or otherwise were somehow exempt from or above the notion of accreditation. However, in recent times, diploma mills have found that embracing

the concept of accreditation can pay off. Not only do some create their own bogus accreditors to add to the appearance of legitimacy of the "university;" they also sell this bogus accreditation to other bogus entities. Instead of decrying accreditation, they have created ways to make it financially lucrative.

Some diploma mill operations are large fraud rings that also produce other types of fraudulent documents, such as driver's licenses, Social Security cards, and other identification documents. Many offer associated student services, including transcript verification, foreign credential evaluation, and even alumni associations. By calling a toll-free telephone number, the bogus documents can be verified, the accreditation of the university confirmed, and an evaluation of the foreign transcript produced showing that the degree received by the graduate is equivalent to a u.s. degree. These "services" are offered by the same people who set up the fraudulent diploma operation.

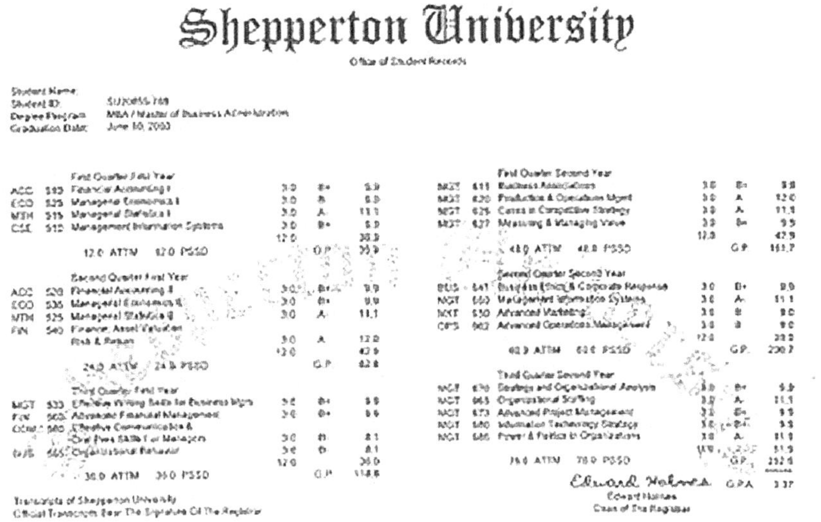
Shepperton University

Office of Student Records

Student Name:
Student ID:
Degree Program: MBA / Master of Business Administration
Graduation Date:

First Quarter First Year

ACC Financial Accounting I
ECO Managerial Economics I
MTH Managerial Statistics I
CSE Management Information Systems

Second Quarter First Year

ACC Financial Accounting II
ECO Managerial Economics II
MTH Managerial Statistics II
FIN Finance, Asset Valuation Risk & Return

Third Quarter First Year

MGT Effective Writing Skills for Business Mgrs
FIN Advanced Financial Management
Effective Communication & Oral Pres Skills For Managers
Organizational Behavior

Transcripts of Shepperton University
Official Transcripts Bear The Signature Of The Registrar

First Quarter Second Year

Production & Operations Mgmt
Cases in Competitive Strategy
Measuring & Managing Value

Second Quarter Second Year

Business Ethics & Corporate Response
Management Information Systems
Advanced Marketing
Advanced Operations Management

Third Quarter Second Year

Strategy and Organizational Analysis
Organizational Staffing
Advanced Project Management
Information Technology Strategy
Power & Politics in Organizations

Dean of The Registrar

FIGURE 19.8 Diploma Mill Transcript, Sample 2

This was the case with the St. Regis University diploma mill operation. The masterminds and agents behind this organization, who operated in Washington State, Idaho, and Arizona, created virtual "universities" and even "high schools" claiming to offer online distance education from Liberia and recognition by the Liberian Ministry of Education. They created a bogus Liberian embassy website that showed that these schools were recognized and accredited by an equally fictitious National Board of Education. (*See* Figures 19.9 and 19.10 on pages 200–201 for an example of a St. Regis diploma and accreditation certificate.) This was accomplished by bribing a Liberian embassy official in Washington DC. In addition, they offered many "student services" and had a foreign credential evaluation service on board to give the degrees U.S. degree equivalencies. It was the tenacity of researchers such as Professor George Gollin of the University of Illinois and federal law enforcement agencies, combined with the hubris of the operators, that brought this outfit down.

How can the international transcript evaluator determine whether an institution is a real, recognized, legitimately-accredited educational institution that actually teaches and awards recognized educational credentials? Understanding the way in which diploma mills work helps in recognizing the nature of these entities. Diploma mills operate in many of the same ways that other fraud operations work—by imitating legitimate activity. Their goal is to look like a real university. Here are some things to watch out for:

- Name: The institution has a distinguished or traditional sounding name or a name similar to a well-known or legitimate institution. (Is your institution's name being used? Check the Internet regularly to see how your school's name, or variations on it, appears.)

FIGURE 19.9

Bogus Degree

St. Regis University

The Regents of the Board of Directors and the
President & Chief Provost by virtue of their Authority have conferred upon

The Degree and Academic Status of

Bachelor of Science

in

Nursing

and granted all the privileges and rights accorded thereto.
Be It Known that knowledge and proficiency has been demonstrated by
completing and satisfying all requirements of the
Regents of the Board of Directors in token whereof the
President & Chief Provost has authorized this status.
In witness thereof, this Diploma is granted by the Board of Directors, and presented on the
Twenty Ninth day of August, Nineteen Hundred and Ninety Eight.

Dean of Studies   Chief Proctor

* Location: The university has a website but no physical address, or there is conflicting information about a physical location.

* Foreign: It gives the impression of being a foreign university, but may be operating from a completely different location. See comments above.

* Internet address: It may use "edu," "ac," or "uk" in the URL, giving the impression of being a U.S. or British educational institution.

* Contact: No contact information is given on the website. The only way to contact the university is by emailing your contact information or providing it via the website.

* Accreditation or recognition: The website includes false, misleading, or meaningless claims of accreditation, recognition, affiliation, membership, or other types of status that are meant to give the impression of legitimacy, but really mean nothing in the legitimate higher education community.

* Speedy degrees: The amount of time required to get the degree is suspiciously fast. A large number of credits, or the whole degree, might be given based on life experience only.

* Costs: The website shows a price list or lump sum prices for the various degrees and transcripts. Different rates might be charged for including specific courses, grades, majors, etc. on the transcript. Payment may be acceptable by credit card or PayPal with the possibility of special deals or discounts for buying immediately.

* Sample documents: The website shows samples of diplomas and transcripts.

* Network of diploma mills: Several university websites may operate from the same computer or network. Researching IP addresses behind domain names, domain registry information, and other

FIGURE 19.10

"behind the scenes" computer information can yield valuable results in investigating a university's true identity.

❋ Support services: Diploma mills set up their own verification services available through a toll-free telephone number; the people answering the phone to verify are the same ones selling the degree. The entity might offer foreign credential evaluation and Apostille services if the institution purports to be foreign.

❋ Advertising: Print advertisements appear in well-respected publications, as well as in popular tabloids and comic books. Electronic media have made worldwide distribution easy and cheap and difficult to pin down just where such activity originates.

Using a methodical approach to document review, as outlined above, is essential to identifying whether the documents presented are from a real, legitimate, and appropriately recognized institution. Research using official and reliable resources is crucial. Mindful of the ways in which diploma mills operate, the evaluator first needs to identify what country the institution purports to be operating in, then determine the legal body in that country that supervises higher education. Is it a national ministry of education, a commission or council for higher education, or a provincial or state authority? Does this legal body publish a list of recognized institutions? Does the suspected diploma mill appear on the list of officially recognized institutions? Once the appropriate authority has been identified, the evaluator should contact that office to ask about the status of the institution in that jurisdiction.

Legal Issues in Degree Fraud

"Aren't diploma mills illegal?" is a commonly asked question. The response is, "it depends." Diploma mills exploit legal loopholes. Where laws are weak, vague, complex, or not enforced, diploma mills thrive. Some diploma mill operations move around the United States and the world to avoid legal trouble and/or set up various parts of their operations in different states/countries so as to make legal prosecution difficult.

In the United States, the establishment of educational institutions is regulated at the state level. Regulations vary from state to state. Some states have no laws or lax or poorly worded laws, while others have clear laws, but little enforcement. The number of states that regulate the use of degrees is growing. On the federal level diploma mill operations have been prosecuted successfully on the basis of federal offenses such as aiding and abetting, conspiracy, false identification, mail fraud, fraud by wire, obstruction of justice, money laundering, criminal forfeiture, trademark violation, and tax evasion.

In other countries education is regulated by law either at the national level or at a sub-national level. Governments oversee the establishment, funding, operation, and administration of educational institutions. Public institutions established by law, or private institutions that have the same legal standing as public institutions, are officially-recognized institutions. Government entities bestow the authorization to offer academic programs and awards.

Complex legal systems and cultures of corruption invite diploma mill fraud around the world. Some countries or regions are noted for problems with diploma mill activity. Many examples of diploma mills exist with operations in areas outside of the United States that have no higher education institutions or where higher education is not regulated, such as some Caribbean Islands, some Pacific Islands, and some cantons of Switzerland. Two well-known examples of diploma mills hail from internationally unrecognized "self-declared autonomous" entities within sovereign countries, the Hutt River Province in Australia and The Principality of Seborga in Italy.

The case of "Ecole Supérieur Robert de Sorbon," a diploma mill run by a man named Christian Prade (also known as Jean Noel Prade and John Thomas) out of a farmhouse in France, illustrates how a diploma mill might distort information about laws related to education to give the impression that it is operating legally within the education law framework of the country in which it is located.

The name "Ecole Supérieur Robert de Sorbon" sounds much like that of the real "Sorbonne," the *Université Paris-Sorbonne (Paris IV)*. Prade's "Sorbon" operation claimed to be giving Ph.D. degrees based on a French law called *Validation des Acquis de l'Expérience (VAE)*.[27] *VAE* or "validation of acquired experience" is a French legal process through which an individual with at least three years of professional experience can request recognition of that experience toward a national qualification listed in the *Répertoire national des certifications professionnelles (RNCP)*, the National Directory of Professional Certifications. In contrast to Prade's claim, the *VAE* process did not enter into any aspect of the Ph.D. degree that he was providing—firstly because the *VAE* process results only in national qualifications, not documents issued by private providers; secondly because the highest level of qualification in which the *VAE* process can result is what would be considered undergraduate-level work in the United States; and thirdly because there is no such degree in the French national educational system as the Ph.D. that Prade's operation was issuing.

In 2011 Prade, who ran the "Sorbon" diploma mill under the name John Thomas, was convicted of fraud by a court in Poitiers, France, for operating what purported to be a university out of a farm in the village of La Trimouille, France. He also headed a credential evaluation scheme in Florida under the name of the American Universities Admissions Program (AUAP), which was sued by AACRAO in 2006 for infringing on the Association's trademark and other deceptive practices.

----

27 *See* Ministère de Education Nationale, l'Enseignement Supérieur et de la Recherche, la validation des acquis de l'Expérience (VAE): <www.education.gouv.fr/cid1106/la-validation-des-acquis-de-l-experience-vae.html>.

Considerations for Policies on Fraud

Proactive policies and clear, viable procedures can be effective tools in fighting fraud. If no policies exist or if existing policies are not effective, not extensive enough, not current enough, or not backed up by effective procedures, the institution should consider the following in establishing or adjusting policies on handling cases involving fraud.

* Define "fraud." Identify the types of fraud to which the institution is vulnerable and the various scenarios in which fraud can play a part. Examine cases of fraud already encountered or seen or heard about from others. What could/should have been done to prevent the problem? What was learned as a result?

* Identify the "market value" of the institution, particularly to international students. What is attractive about the institution? Why would fraudsters want to capitalize on it? What is its reputation? Is it prestigious or an easy target?

* Review the policies of the institution on student and faculty/administrator behavior (academic dishonesty, honor code, code of conduct, code of ethics). Are any of these relevant to the type of fraud it might see?

* Identify the various offices or departments of the institution that should be involved in discussions about policies on handling fraud cases.

* Work with the institution's legal counsel to become informed about federal, state, county, and city laws and ordinances that would be appropriate for the cases encountered.

* A procedure or protocol to follow in fraud cases should be clearly spelled out and communicated to all those who might deal with such cases. Who does what? What is the procedure, step-by-step? Should it be the same in every case? Is there an appeal process if the applicant disputes the findings? What is the procedure for that?

* In addition to policies and procedures, another effective tool in identifying and preventing fraud is a team to coordinate anti-fraud efforts across the campus or organization: keep an eye on the big picture, continuously educate and inform, train others, proactively function as watchdogs and monitor the Internet for usage of the institution's name, assist with questions, prepare cases for review and judgment, track results, and review and critique policy, etc.

* Publish your institution's policies and procedures and consequences for breaking the rules in clear, concise, unambiguous language and in easily accessible locations (in application packets, in publications, on the Web, etc.).

* Incorporate a section in your application materials that must be signed by the applicant, attesting to the truthfulness, completeness, and accuracy of information provided; the understanding that institutions issuing the documents submitted may be contacted for authentication of the documents or further information relevant to the student's education; agreeing to abide by relevant policies and regulations, etc.; and accepting consequences if rules are broken.

* Act quickly when a case of questionable documentation is uncovered. Address the situation immediately, to squelch the flames that can quickly escalate into a raging inferno. Be a confident and assertive first responder, with appropriate policies and procedures to support the findings.

* Seek the advice of experienced, expert neutral third parties if help is needed, in accordance with the guidance of legal counsel. Only use trusted, informed resources, keeping in mind that parties that produce or use fraudulent degrees and transcripts may also operate or use fraudulent verification, accreditation, and foreign credential evaluation services, thus possibly having duped other reputable institutions and services into recognizing their degrees.

* Keep a log or record of cases involving fraud. Cross-reference information and notes between various files so that data is easily retrievable. Note general information in generic files and information specific to a particular student or applicant in the individual's file. This recordkeeping is useful should the person ever apply again.

✳ Incorporate what you learn from each case into the institution's response to such cases. Each scenario presents a different set of circumstances, with new twists and perspectives. Review institutional policy regularly, adjusting it as appropriate.

Resources on Fraud

AACRAO RESOURCES

AACRAO Publications related to Fraudulent Academic Credentials: <www4.aacrao.org/publications/catalog.php?category=4>

AACRAO *College and University Journal* policy and research journal: <www.aacrao.org/resources/publications/college-university-journal-(c-u)>

AACRAO FERPA Guides: <www.aacrao.org/resources/compliance/ferpa>

Ezell, A. 2002. Degree Diploma Mills–Past, Present, and Future. *College and University*. Winter.

———. 2005. Transcript Fraud and Handling Fraudulent Documents. *College and University*. Winter.

———. 2007. *Accreditation Mills*. Washington, D.C.: American Association of Collegiate Registrars and Admissions Officers.

———. 2008. *Counterfeit Diplomas and Transcripts*. Washington D.C.: American Association of Collegiate Registrars and Admissions Officers.

Koenig, Ann M., J. Montgomery, and L. Stedman. 2006. *Guide to Bogus Institutions and Documents*. Washington, D.C.: American Association of Collegiate Registrars and Admissions Officers.

OTHER RESOURCES

Bartlett, T., and S. Smallwood. 2004. Degrees of Suspicion: Psst. Wanna Buy a Ph.D.? *Chronicle of Higher Education.* 50(42): A9. Available at: <http://chronicle.com/article/Psst-Wanna-Buy-a-PhD-/24239>.

Bear, J., and A. Ezell. 2005. *Degree Mills: The Billion-Dollar Industry That Has Sold Over a Million Fake Diplomas.* New York: Prometheus Books. Available at: www.degreemills.com. Book review by Thomas D. Bazley in AACRAO *College and University*, Spring 2005.

———. 2012. *Degree Mills: The Billion-Dollar Industry That Has Sold Over a Million Fake Diplomas, Updated Edition.* New York: Prometheus Books.

Bear, M., and T. Nixon. 2006. *Bears' Guide to Earning Degrees by Distance Learning*. Ten Speed Press.

Carnevale, D. 2004. Don't Judge a College by Its Internet Address. *Chronicle of Higher Education.* November 26. Available at: <http://chronicle.com/article/Dont-Judge-a-College-by-Its/8748/>.

Contreras, A. 2001. International Diploma Mills Grow with the Internet. *International Higher Education.* 24: Summer. Available at: <www.bc.edu/content/dam/files/research_sites/cihe/pdf/IHEpdfs/ihe24.pdf>.

———. 2002. How Reliable is National Approval of University Degrees? *International Higher Education.* 29: Fall. Available at: <www.bc.edu/content/dam/files/research_sites/cihe/pdf/IHEpdfs/ihe29.pdf>.

———. 2003. More Shenanigans: Fake Accrediting in the International Marketplace. A Case Study in Foreign Degree (Dis)approval. *International Higher Education.* 32: 7–9. Available at: <www.bc.edu/content/dam/files/research_sites/cihe/pdf/IHEpdfs/ihe32.pdf>.

Council for Higher Education Accreditation (CHEA). *Important Questions About Accreditation, Degree Mills and Accreditation Mills.* Available at: <www.chea.org/degreemills/>.

Gollin, G. 2003. *Unconventional University Diplomas from Online Vendors or Fraud, Corruption and Scandal: Buying a Ph.D. From a University that Doesn't Exist.* Overview of how diploma mills operate. Available at: <www.hep.uiuc.edu/home/g-gollin/diploma_mills.pdf>.

Hallak, J., and M. Poisson. 2007. *Corrupt Schools, Corrupt Universities: What Can Be Done?* Paris, France: UNESCO International Institute for Educational Planning. See especially Chapter 7, "Exams, credentials and accreditation." Available at: <unesdoc.unesco.org/images/0015/001502/150259e.pdf>.

Noah, H., and M. Eckstein. 2001. *Fraud and Education: The Worm in the Apple*. Lanham, MD: Rowman & Littlefield Publisher, Inc.

Oregon Office of Student Access and Completion, Office of Degree Authorization. 2010. *Diploma Mills*. www.oregonstudentaid.gov/oog-diploma-mills.aspx

Transparency International, The Global Coalition Against Corruption. *Corruption Perceptions Index 2009.* Available at: <www.transparency.org/research/cpi/overview>.

U.S. Federal Trade Commission. 2005. *Avoid Fake Degree Burns by Researching Academic Credentials*. February. Available at: <www.business.ftc.gov/documents/bus65-avoid-fake-degree-burns-researching-academic-credentials>.

———. 2006. *Diploma Mills: Degree of Deception*. October. Available at: www.consumer.ftc.gov/articles/0206-diploma-mills.

U.S. Department of Education. 2010. *Diploma Mills and Accreditation*. Available at: <www2.ed.gov/students/prep/college/diplomamills/diploma-mills.html>.

———. 2010. *Family Educational Rights and Privacy Act.* Available at: <www2.ed.gov/policy/gen/guid/fpco/ferpa/>.

University of Illinois at Urbana-Champaign. 2010. *Information Resources Concerning Unaccredited Degree-Granting Institutions.* A compilation of various resources, including news items and public legal documents by Prof. George Gollin. Available at: <www.hep.uiuc.edu/home/g-gollin/pigeons/>.

TWENTY

HBCU International Graduate Admissions:

Enhancing Institutional Mission for Global Competitiveness

ALEXANDER JUN

Professor of Higher Education
Azusa Pacific University

C. DEAN CAMPBELL

Assistant Dean for Academic Services
Graduate School
North Carolina A&T State University

HBCU International Graduate Admissions:
Enhancing Institutional Mission for Global Competitiveness

In a pre-21st century comparison of higher education across the world in countries both wealthy and developing, one comparative higher education scholar noted that "the university is an international institution with strong national roots" (Altbach 1998, xii). The pursuit of knowledge and academic credentials needed for upward mobility are aspects of the international enterprise of higher education. This enterprise is a competitive one, and institutional leaders seek new approaches to expand their brand in the global marketplace. International graduate students make up 43 percent of more than 886,000 non-resident students studying in the u.s. (IIE 2014c). The most recent report on graduate admissions from the Council of Graduate Schools (CGS) shows that international graduate student admission accounted for two-thirds of the enrollment growth in graduate education between 2004 and 2014 (CGS 2015). In Fall 2014, 66 percent of all international graduate students were enrolled in science, technology, engineering, and math (STEM) fields, but only 27 percent of u.s. citizen/permanent residents were enrolled in those fields. International graduate students remain an important part of sustaining the revenue portfolio and creating financial stability for graduate institutions.

Historically Black Colleges and Universities (HBCUs) have not been immune to these economic realities and are in the midst of a shift from a domestic to an international focus. However, the "dual missions" for HBCUs present unique challenges in providing college access for the "best and brightest" as well as those who are "underprepared as a result of their circumstances—not their abilities" (Taylor 2014, 224–225).

Globalization and Higher Education

Globalization, or "the intensified movement of goods, money, technology, information, people, ideas and cultural practices across political and cultural boundaries," (Nerad, 2000, 2) characterizes the context of international higher education. In this context of commoditized higher education, the u.s. continues to host more international students than any other country, but its share of the population of globally mobile students continues to fall. In 2012, the u.s. attracted 16 percent of all students studying outside of their native country, compared to 23 percent in 2000 (WES 2015). U.S. institutions face increasing competition when attempting to enroll international students who have other choices among high quality postsecondary institutions around the world.

The Changing Demographics of HBCUs

HBCUs were founded to provide access to higher education when state legislation outlawed African American enrollment at Predominately White Institutions (PWIs). Today there are 105 HBCUs which make up three percent of all u.s. higher education institutions and ten percent of Carnegie Classified Research Universities. Twenty-one HBCUs are part of the American land-grant university system. Of all HBCUs, approximately 60 percent offer graduate or professional degrees and 28 percent offer doctoral or professional degrees (Lee 2015). Despite enrolling only 9 percent of all African American undergraduates, HBCUs confer 17 percent of all bachelor's degrees received by African Americans.

Ingram and colleagues predict that African American enrollments in higher education will decrease in HBCUs while the percent of the overall population of African Americans, Latinos, and Asian Americans will be over

50 percent at non-HBCU institutions by the year 2050 (2015). Increases in African and Caribbean international student enrollments at HBCUs have helped to diversify the HBCU student body. In addition, demographics are affected by a shifting public sentiment. At the outset of the 20th century, public sentiment supported federal desegregation policies, but has since shifted to dismantling HBCUs by merging fiscally-constrained HBCUs with PWIs (Ingram *et al.* 2015).

The Social Justice Mission of HBCUs

HBCUs share a common mission of social justice and prioritize serving the African American community, yet also struggle to balance those priorities with adapting to external demands for global relevancy. In fact, the "essential struggle to remain both locally and globally relevant appears to be endemic to the very enterprise of higher education in the 21st century" (Bagley and Portnoi 2014, 9). Nerad (2010) echoes this tension with respect to doctoral education:

> *Institutions responsible for graduate education today must fulfill a dual mission: building a country's infrastructure by preparing the next generation of professionals and scholars for the local and national economy, both inside and outside academia, and educating their domestic and international graduate students to participate in a global economy and an international scholarly community. This dual mission is often experienced as a tension, because universities in many ways operate under a sole national lens.* (2)

Nerad captures the drawback institutions face when choosing to focus solely on institutional mission. Accordingly, the HBCU social justice mission now operates in a competitive marketplace, a context which places demands on institutional financial solvency and competition for resources within and outside the United States. Considering their focus on the needs of local communities, the question remains as to how HBCUs will continue their mission of access to higher education and service to the African American community in the face of demographic changes, general public opinion changes, and globalization in American society and the world beyond.

HBCU Internationalization: Renewal and Competitiveness

Comprehensive internationalization relates to all institutional members becoming involved in the internationalization process, including an exchange of faculty, students, and administrative facilities beyond just field offices (Schoorman 2000). Integrated facets of internationalization involve recognition of its importance to "institutional missions and administrative efforts to engage in strategic planning for internationalization" (9). Such efforts are integrated when they become routine administrative imperatives that do not require justification. The counter-hegemonic perspective of internationalization maintains that higher education exists to advance international social justice and democracy. The content and instruction of the educational process works to "facilitate among students a sense of caring, as citizens of a globally interdependent society, whose goals would be to make the world a better place for all" (Schoorman 2000, 7).

As noted, HBCUs face declining enrollments from African Americans students, in part due to the desegregation efforts in the post-*Brown v. Board of Education* era which opened doors to PWIs previously unavailable. Enrollments and their related revenue streams for African American students at HBCUs are no longer guaranteed in a competitive domestic marketplace. As a result, many administrators have embraced the notion that enrolling and educating students outside of the African American population is critical for the long-term stability, relevance, and competitiveness. Organizing HBCU institutional resources to this end draws on comprehensive and integrated efforts to support international students. HBCUs already have a proven legacy of producing globally competitive graduates—and do so in many cases while under-resourced, but further institutional re-organization and diversification of student enrollments are necessary to better position HBCUs to compete globally.

Oftentimes PWIs adopt strategies which perpetuate the image that students of color are a monolithic group that includes international students as well as domestic students of color (Iverson 2007). The challenges remain for PWIs to diversify their student population for inclusion and excellence (Campbell, Tierney, and Sanchez 2004). However, as explained in the following section, their unique campus context and institutional mission better allows HBCUs to focus more on the international aspect of diversity. As diversity is already embedded into the ethos of HBCUs, this focus might include, but is not limited to, consideration of international recruitment of students from nations in Africa and the African Diaspora (Caribbean/Latin America), the Pacific Rim, countries in the Association of South East Asian countries (ASEAN), and other East Asian regions.

Graduate Enrollment Management: HBCUs Staffing for High Performance

An increasingly popular reorganization strategy graduate institutions undertake is staffing for high performance through graduate enrollment management (GEM). Williams (2008) defines GEM professionals as those who "work proactively to build and maintain relationships across administrative silos...assigning responsibilities based on cost efficiencies, customer service, and expertise" (57). As discussed extensively in other chapters of this volume, graduate international admissions is a product of coordinating staff and other resources to administer credential evaluations, language academies, overseas recruitment, and so on. Consequently, GEM complements the goals and priorities internationalization fosters.

HBCUs are unique among postsecondary institutions in terms of the number of Black administrators on staff who serve students. The majority of public 4-year HBCUs hire full-time Black executives, administrators, and managers at a rate equal to or above racial diversity

metrics in comparison to predominately white 4-year public institutions (Perna, Gerald, Baum, and Milem 2007). Consequently, critical mass hiring rates of Black administrators (registrars, graduate enrollment managers, international student services directors, etc.) make the HBCU workplace a diverse, welcoming climate. Although research on learning in racially-diverse work environments shows mixed results, Black administrators consistently cite isolation and "miasma" (Whites assume African Americans are culturally similar) as workplace inhibitors to high-performance—particularly in predominately white postsecondary institutions and less diverse work settings (Gardner, Barnett, and Pearson 2014; Livers and Caver 2003). Evidence also suggests that the racial composition of the HBCU administration and close relationships staff form with students create an "environment that is less socially and academically isolating, marginalizing, and threatening" (McGaskey 2012, 88). Campbell, Bishop, and Sarin (2016) documented the GEM reorganization process at one HBCU using cultural and workplace learning perspectives. Elements of that work and the GEM internationalization process appear in the case study that follows.

A Case Study: North Carolina A&T State University

North Carolina A&T State University (NCAT) is located in the Piedmont Triad region of the state. Founded as an HBCU in 1891 as a land-grant institution, the university maintains a strong civil rights legacy characterized by the Greensboro Four who staged lunch counter sit-ins in 1960 to protest Jim Crow racial segregation in the south. NCAT is active in research with a Carnegie "doctoral/research university" classification and state university system ranking of third in sponsored research funding. The University's mission prioritizes "preeminence in STEM" including six goals, two of which are of import to internationalization and re-organization. They are:

✴ Foster a more diverse and inclusive campus community by promoting cultural awareness and collegiality, and by cultivating respect for diverse people and cultures; and

* Achieve excellence in academic and operational effectiveness and efficiency (NCAT 2015).

NCAT consistently ranks among the top two institutions nationwide in enrollment among all HBCUs (+10,800 undergraduate/+1500 graduate), with 87 percent of the student enrollment being African American. The University consistently ranks above all other US institutions in conferring the largest number of masters and doctoral degrees to African Americans. Graduate programs in online information technology regularly rank in the top 25 programs nationwide. Table 20.1 shows the makeup of the non-U.S. citizen enrollments. Almost 70 percent of the international student enrollment is graduate students. In the last several years the international graduate student enrollments have remained steady in the 13–16 percent range, making diversity in the graduate programs well above that found in undergraduate enrollments. Table 20.1 shows that international student enrollments have been growing steadily over the last three years and that NCAT remains one of the largest HBCU doctoral institutions and HBCU enroller of international students. The institution's strategic plan calls for a targeted increase in

non-African American student enrollment of 25 percent over the next five years, a near-doubling on currently enrolled students.

GRADUATE FACULTY

Faculty diversity at NCAT is similar to that of the HBCUs' overall composition. Asian, Hispanic, Native American, and international HBCU faculty represents 15 percent of all faculty as of 2001 and White faculty have remained steady around 26 to 29 percent of staff since 1981 (Johnson, Hoskins, and Johnson 2015). Typical faculty participation in international graduate admission is department-focused. Faculty frequently travel to foreign countries to collaborate with other faculty at partner universities, and while on those trips have formed relationships that have led to recruiting international students from overseas. In numerous other cases, faculty are naturalized U.S. citizens who have obtained higher education degrees in other countries or who have worked as faculty or industry professionals in other countries prior to arriving at the University. The Graduate School has sought to capitalize on this faculty experience and background by inviting them to serve on the Internal Evaluation of International Transcripts (IEIT) committee which provides peer-review guidance in the review of foreign credentials in graduate admissions. The

TABLE 20.1: HBCU International (Nonresident Alien) Student Enrollment, 2010–2013

	Total 2013		Total 2012		Total 2011		Total 2010	
	Non-Resident Alien	All Students	Non-Resident Alien	All Students	Non-Resident Alien	All Students	Non-Resident Alien	All Students
Howard University	534	10297	441	10002	514	10583	477	10379
Morgan State University	420	7546	400	7952	366	8018	372	7805
Texas Southern University	399	8703	371	9646	326	9730	289	9557
North Carolina A & T State University	396	10561	329	10636	257	10881	234	10795
Coppin State University	322	3383	264	3612	260	3813	104	3800
Tennessee State University	294	8883	103	8740	80	9165	83	8930
Delaware State University	257	4336	143	4324	110	4154	84	3757
Grambling State University	239	5071	305	5277	384	5207	424	4994
Prairie View A & M University	184	8283	159	8336	150	8425	181	8781
Bowie State University	162	5561	88	5421	81	5608	84	5578

SOURCE: Integrated Postsecondary Education Data System Data Center

Graduate School coordinates professional development opportunities for committee members to attend association workshops, obtain credential evaluation resources, and facilitate networking experiences for faculty members to learn from other full-time admission officers and credential evaluators through the association.

The IEIT served international graduate admissions well in its early years, but as the number of applications have increased, challenges to faculty participation in admissions (Pollack 2008) have been evident in the functioning of the IEIT. There has been a lack of motivation for institutional international admissions, in part because faculty are not made aware of how their recruiting efforts contribute to overall goals, and admission officers also do not clearly account for faculty reward systems. For example, the Graduate School requires that internal evaluators produce a course-by-course evaluation report. This means each faculty member transcribes the transcript to a U.S.-based grading system and includes a U.S.-equivalent grade point average using a conversion scale the evaluator presents in the evaluation. In many cases there has been wild variation in the speed and accuracy with which evaluators complete evaluations. Some interpret the variation as bias internal evaluators hold for applicants for programs in their field rather than providing equal attention to those not in their department. Other managers point to unclear Graduate School expectations communicated to the faculty reviewers.

OFFICE OF INTERNATIONAL AFFAIRS

The Office of International Affairs (OIA) was recently created when the Office of International Students and Scholars (ISSO) merged with the Office of International Programs. Provost and Vice Chancellor Dr. Joseph Whitehead announced a new OIA to "ensure cohesiveness and direction in successfully addressing the international affairs of our students and faculty," (personal communication, July 14, 2015). Staff in OIA retain the same coordinating responsibilities in the issuance of I-20s for newly admitted graduate students as when

they were in ISSO. International applicants admitted to graduate studies submit financial records to ISSO in order to apply for the I-20. The ISSO in turn communicates regularly with Graduate School administrators concerning timing of application review for receipt of the I-20. In some cases international students "transfer" to NCAT from other U.S. postsecondary institutions.

THE GRADUATE SCHOOL

In 2010, the University undertook development of a strategic plan designed to reflect the University's land-grant mission, STEM and interdisciplinary focus, and intellectual climate (*See* Table 20.2).

Included in the plan is an ambitious goal of doubling the graduate enrollment over a ten-year period. The University's seven academic units offer 29 master's degree programs, nine doctoral degree programs, and several graduate certificates—all under the auspices of the Graduate School. All graduate education policy and governance matters are centrally overseen by the Graduate School, including admission and enrollment functions coordinated by the office's ten full-time professional staff, per the GEM philosophies and strategies described above.

TABLE 20.2: NCAT Strategic Plan

Goal 1	Create an intellectual climate that encourages the creative exchange of ideas and increases the quality of the professional environment.
Goal 2	Commit to excellence in teaching, research, public service, and engagement.
Goal 3	Position the university to be a national, premier, research-intensive, doctoral, science, and technology-focused learning institution.
Goal 4	Embrace an entrepreneurial spirit that intentionally engages university and community partners to expand economic development and civic engagement.
Goal 5	Foster a more diverse and inclusive campus community by promoting cultural awareness and collegiality, and by cultivating respect for diverse people and cultures.
Goal 6	Achieve excellence in academic and operational effectiveness and efficiency.

SOURCE: North Carolina A&T State University, www.ncat.edu/about/strategic-plan-Initiatives.html

The Graduate School obtained an agreement with a second language academy in its metropolitan area to increase the pool of prospective international applicants for admission. The memorandum of understanding (MOU) allows for conditional admission for individuals who meet admission requirements for graduate study, but do not meet the University's English language proficiency requirement. Because the requirements of the MOU necessitate several internal adjustments in processing specialized applications of this type, the Graduate School has revised one of its staff positions to centralize the coordinating of language academy conditional admissions processing, international credential review, communications with international applicants, and liaising with OIA. The new Graduate International Admission (GIA) and Credential Evaluation Associate also attends numerous conferences and training meetings with national associations to learn best practices on the review of international credentials.

HBCU International Graduate Admissions: Strategies for Competitiveness

ALIGNMENT OF MISSION WITH SOCIAL JUSTICE AND INTERNATIONALIZATION

International graduate admissions in HBCU internationalization looks to provide access to those historically served by the institutional mission and to those students from overseas seeking the HBCU education experience in graduate education. HBCUs prepare African American, international, and other students to compete globally in the workforce, and to contribute to global democracy. Goal 5 of NCAT's strategic plan (*see* Table 20.2, on page 211) makes explicit the importance of cultivating respect for diverse peoples and cultures. The mission statement of the University indicates that the University "fosters a climate of economic competitiveness that prepares students for the global society" (NCAT 2015). Arguably, in the contemporary landscape of higher education in the United States it is unusual to find a college or university that does not reference the importance of educating students to be better global

citizens. However, the HBCU research university with high concentrations of STEM graduate programs plays a significant role in providing access to fields critical to developing a workforce important to U.S. global competitiveness. In addition, STEM research areas attract international students seeking programs in content areas of high importance in global competitiveness, therein increasing the quality and profile of the institution. Domestically, access for African American students to fields of study important to national security and global competitiveness promotes social mobility for historically disenfranchised communities and encourages success, economic viability, and positions of respect.

EXPANSION OF FACULTY PARTICIPATION IN GRADUATE ADMISSION

Often faculty recruit prospective students while conducting collaborative research abroad. In other cases, prospective students approach the individual professor through email in search of a lab or teaching assistantship in the faculty member's department. These and other acts of service in recruitment reflect how faculty support NCAT, often as ambassadors to those in the external community who wish to enter the NCAT community.

At NCAT, faculty members of the Internal Evaluation of International Transcripts (IEIT) were either not serving full-time or had other competing demands which resulted in limited time to devote to transcript review. Preparation of course-by-course evaluations, a standard practice among professional credential evaluators, was deemed cumbersome or unnecessary. This view drew on past experiences of reviewing individual foreign transcripts for applicants the faculty member had themselves recruited, and in many cases for an applicant to the same graduate program/department of the faculty IEIT committee member. This practice may have worked well when the number of international applicants was small, but became less effective as the number of applications increased.

The Graduate School revised the way faculty participates in the credential review process. Instead of relying on faculty to continuously generate reports reflecting their expertise, the Graduate School developed a database with information that was vetted by faculty experts. By creating a position dedicated to coordinating the transcript review process in graduate admissions, the Graduate School gained more trust from faculty who were participating in international admission. This database is updated annually based on faculty evaluative feedback, but is used by administrative staff following standard criteria established by the faculty. The database includes lists of universities from countries around the world that have been sending international students. The time required to review the transcripts for course-by-course evaluations is now well-documented in the database. The GIA Associate can perform many of the credential review functions that were formerly distributed across a number of faculty reviewers, and in addition maintain the same quality standards in the credential review. Moreover, faculty committee members feel they are contributing to the institution's effort to be responsive to international applicants. These faculty members also believe they can trust the admission process the Graduate School has taken over because of the transparency of the database information and the review process that accompanies it.

INTEGRATION OF ADMINISTRATIVE PARTNERS COMMITTED TO INTERNATIONAL CITIZENSHIP

The adoption of a language academy provides an additional pathway for prospective international students to gain entry to the institution. There are some within the institution — particularly faculty — who question whether the "front door" of graduate admission is opened too wide for international students. But involving more partners who are external to the institution proves useful in helping to socialize administrative staff to new cultural paradigms that benefit both underrepresented students of color as well as international students in higher education (Campbell, Bishop, and Sarin 2016).

Collectively, the three strategies presented above have facilitated ongoing organizational change at NCAT. Faculty participation in international graduate admis-

sion has transformed: faculty are now knowledge generators providing an advisory role to administrators responsible for coordinating transcript reviews. They help identify new recruiting venues for international students through research collaborations with overseas colleagues. In many cases, these research collaborations are in developing nations, making NCAT faculty "knowledge carriers" from the industrialized to the developing world in the international knowledge system. Such opportunities also open doors to research for HBCU graduate students and scholars abroad.

The Graduate School's progress with developing international admissions policies and administrative practices has better enabled it to foster richer on-campus discussions and be a resource to academic departments interested in new curriculum for international studies. Many NCAT international student graduates ultimately return to their home countries and refer family, friends, and professional colleagues to NCAT. These kinds of developments involving those in the graduate community on and off the campus inform discussions for services and curricula, including expansion of master's degrees delivered overseas at partner universities with shared student residency in the U.S. and abroad.

Conclusion

As globalization continues to increase in importance in academe, policymakers and higher education leaders are compelled to compete to recruit and retain the best students while also maintaining crucial streams of revenue to remain financially viable. It is important to underscore that internationalization via upping the enrollment of foreign graduate students should not be motivated primarily by revenue generation, but be rooted in the institution's mission of justice through access and cultural inclusion.

The above discussion of the higher education landscape and one institution's response to that evolving landscape suggest that there is no "one size fits all" solution for institutional competitiveness. Graduate administrators responsible for stewarding enrollments find themselves increasingly mindful of the interplay among institutional mission, internal and external partners, faculty, prospective students, and global context in achieving relevance and excellence for graduate education. In the case of one HBCU, its historical legacy for access to higher education for African Americans serves as a competitive advantage in the higher education arena where institutional players vie to educate global citizens for a more just, equitable, and democratic world.

TWENTY-ONE

International Transfer Credit Evaluation and Methodology

2016 AACRAO INTERNATIONAL GUIDE

CHRISTY M. FRY

Associate Director of Admissions
International and Transfer Recruitment
Colby-Sawyer College

International Transfer Credit Evaluation and Methodology

This chapter discusses the theory and practice of international transfer credit, including evaluation methodology. It is often referred to as an "art and science" because of the need to determine the common denominator (science) of diversified education systems (art).

U.S. postsecondary institutions are increasingly recognizing the value that international transfer students can add to their institutions. Understanding the variables involved in the international transfer credit evaluation process is imperative to ensuring that transfer credit is awarded consistently across a vast number of differing education systems. The essence of the evaluation process is in identifying the "art" of an education system, or what makes it unique, and then using the "science" to formulaically calculate the number of hours in a course and the typical number of credits in a semester or academic year. How to consistently apply these results to one's institutional profile is the culmination of this process. The process begins with defining the evaluation methodology.

Reacquaintance with the U.S. Education System

At the core of evaluation methodology is the comparison of international education systems to the U.S. system. Therefore, one must begin with an understanding of the U.S. education structure and its unique aspects. U.S. postsecondary education begins after 12 years of primary and secondary education, and follows either the semester or quarter calendar. Typically, a postsecondary institution's academic year consists of two semesters, fall and spring, with an optional summer semester. These semesters are 15 weeks in length with a shorter summer semester of 12 weeks; sometimes the summer semester is broken into two or three shorter periods, ranging in length, but commonly six weeks if running two summer semesters. The two 15 week periods amount to 30 weeks of instruction.

The quarter-based system is divided into four quarters and defines three quarters as an academic year (whereby the fourth quarter is optional). The average length of the quarter is ten weeks, making the total number of instructional weeks 30. Quarters are identified as fall, winter, spring, and the optional summer. When comparing the instructional weeks between the two calendar approaches, it is clear that three quarters equals two semesters. As a result, three quarter hours equal two semester hours (or a quarter hour is 2/3 or 0.67 less than a semester hour). This will prove useful to recall later in the chapter when the concept of credit conversion is discussed in detail.

The U.S. unit of learning time or credit originates from the Carnegie Foundation for the Advancement of Teaching.[28] Here the Carnegie Unit, more commonly referred to as the credit hour, was developed and adopted across the country at the K–12 (primary and secondary) and postsecondary levels of education. The application of the credit hour consists of a defined number of hours of seat time equal to a credit, and a defined number of credits to equal a credential (i.e., bachelor's degree). Over the past few years, an industry conversation has emerged regarding this concept of seat time as the only accurate and equitable means of measurement. For now, the seat time definition remains the

---

[28] See <www.carnegiefoundation.org>.

majority measurement tool, as instructed by the International Affairs Office of the U.S. Department of Education.[29]

Seat time must be defined across the various types of courses to provide a clear understanding of the credit hour. For a lecture course, approximately one hour per week in class for 15 weeks equals one credit hour, so the traditional three-credit-hour course would be equivalent to 45 hours of coursework over a semester. The U.S. postsecondary system also distinguishes lab, practice, and independent study courses. These different course types have varying credit hour expectations. One lab hour a week in class for 15 weeks equals one credit hour, so the three-credit-hour course would be equivalent to 45 hours of coursework and between 45 to 90 laboratory hours over a semester. It is similar in value to the lecture course; however, the practice and independent study hour equals three to four hours per week. This totals between 135 to 180 hours for three credit hours during the course of a semester.

Within the U.S. system, 15 credit hours is considered a full-time semester course load. This would be the same for the quarter credit hour. One academic year consists of 30 semester credit hours and 45 quarter credit hours. It will be important to recall these definitions of credit hours within specific lengths of study later in the chapter. By applying the logical reasoning that the human capacity to learn does not differ greatly from one educational system to another, it can be assumed that students absorb similar amounts of content within similar lengths of study.

Institutional Profile

Considering these key features of the U.S. postsecondary education system is a first step in assessing one's institutional profile and determining how a foreign credential translates to the institution. Additional questions can also help to further assess one's institutional profile, such as:

- Does the institution place value on vocational track education?
- Is community service, a language component, internships, or study abroad required?
- Is the institution's transfer credit policy more conservative or more liberal?
- What are the minimum seat hours required compared to your various institutional course types (lab, practice, independent study)?
- Is the institution highly selective, with stringent admissions criteria?
- What type of academic calendar is employed, and what is the definition of full-time credit?

Each of these attributes of the institutional profile must be thoroughly understood when evaluating international credentials for comparability and best fit to the institution.

Evaluation Methodology

Some commonly accepted international transfer of credit practices include:

- Use professionally accepted resources and reference materials;
- Verify accreditation/recognition status of institution prior to conducting evaluation;
- Consider admissions requirements, length of program, program type, and credential/qualification requirements;
- Recognize there are no credential equivalencies, only comparable credentials; and
- Maintain evaluation policies and practices to encompass for inclusion the vast variety of education systems, including periodic reviews.

Some guiding questions for new or unknown credentials include:

- What do you know about the foreign educational framework?
- Does this credential fit in the educational framework? If so, where?

[29] See <www2.ed.gov/about/offices/list/oU.S./international/U.S.nei/U.S./credits.doc>.

- What is the language of instruction? What is the official national language?
- What is the level and type of program?
- What are the entrance requirements to the program?

There are two rudimentary methodological approaches to degree or credential assessment. The first method, year counting, requires the evaluator to compare the number of years to complete the foreign degree to the number of years to complete the U.S. degree. Typically, benchmark credentials are used; for example, high school diploma, first university degree, postgraduate degree, and terminal degree. The ultimate admissions decision results from this comparison. A popular example regarding year counting is the foreign three-year first university degree following the standard 12-year secondary education system. Using the year counting method, this first university degree does not meet graduate admissions requirements when compared to the U.S. system, which shares a similar 12-year secondary education system.

The second method used in comparing foreign degrees to the U.S. system is benchmarking academic credentials. In this method, a high school diploma that leads to a bachelor's or first university degree would be comparable to the U.S. high school diploma regardless of years. This method would also recognize the foreign three-year diploma since the three-year degree is the foreign country's benchmarked credential for a bachelor's or first university degree and leads to graduate studies. This method bases the comparability upon the acceptance of a perception. It is the perception that completion of a credential in a foreign country provides a similar knowledge achievement as would be expected with the comparable U.S. credential.

Of the two methods highlighted, neither takes into consideration the actual accumulation of knowledge compared to the similar U.S. credential, which often creates a dilemma for admissions officers. As a result, many institutions (and private evaluation companies) apply a combination of the two methods in an attempt to balance the questions of equity. When a three-year bachelor's or first university degree is awarded, U.S. institutions do not equally accept it as comparable, though an 11-year secondary credential from the British system is typically accepted. This combination of methods usually begins by applying the year counting method. Sometimes, though, admissions officers discover logical questions or information discrepancies about the credential; in these cases, the benchmarking method is applied since it is likely unclear the number of years actually required for the undefined foreign credential.

For example, a foreign credential that indicates two years of study but does not clearly indicate the credential name will require logical questioning to assist in determining the actual value of the credential. Applying the concept of logical questioning to a foreign credential begins by identifying what is the preceding credential in the education system and then identifying the credential following the foreign credential in question. Is this following credential a first university degree? Are entrance requirements defined? Is the curriculum from an external awarding body? These inquiries help define the foreign credential in question. Once it is clear where it resides within the education system, one may apply the evaluation methodology as outlined previously in this chapter. It is always a best practice to follow inquiries about a credential as far as deemed necessary. The more one learns about a credential, and the more this acquired knowledge is compared to other resources available, the more informed the admissions placement will be.

Admissions Placement

While central government bodies provide admissions placement recommendations in most countries, the U.S. government does not provide this service. The absence of this central body in the U.S. means the responsibility rests squarely on the admissions officer of each institution. That being said, institutions tend to follow common standards and practices when it comes to foreign credentials, but defining common standards remains one of the more basic challenges of foreign credential evaluation. This is exemplified in the theoretical situation of Alaska State University Alpha and Alaska State University Bravo below:

Alaska State University Alpha offers vocational and technical degree programs. Alaska State University Bravo offers teacher education degree programs. If a student with a German Apprenticeship credential applies to both universities, the common standard for Alpha may very well differ from Bravo. Alpha may define an apprenticeship program as a good fit, but Bravo may not, along with the majority of U.S. institutions that do not accept the German Apprenticeship credential.

In the past, professional bodies within the U.S. such as AACRAO, NAFSA, International Qualifications Assessment Service (IQAS), and American Council on Education (ACE) have made attempts to provide common standard recommendations. More recently, some of these same bodies are moving away from defining common standards, allowing for the individual institution to draw its own evaluation conclusions that best match the institutional profile. Evaluation conclusions are judgments of the evaluator and therefore any definition of a foreign credential is an individual conclusion or recommendation, as emphasized by the National Association of Credential Evaluation Services (NACES) and the Association of International Credential Evaluators (AICE). Instead, they are focusing on providing the best resources to assist the admissions officers in evaluating credentials consistently, thus placing the responsibility back upon the autonomous institutions.

Institutions, therefore, collect experiences, collegial discourse, and examples over time and create their own definition of common standards. In doing so, it is important to utilize a few basic guiding inquiries: what is the type of credential, what credential precedes and follows the credential in question, and what are the admissions requirements for the credential? If possible, it may help to include data analysis of how students with this credential have fared academically in the U.S. system. Collecting and assessing this information leads to the establishment of sufficiently researched and supported institution-specific standards.

Accreditation

ACCREDITATION IN THE UNITED STATES

A critical component of due diligence is institutional accreditation or government recognition. U.S. tertiary institutions may obtain four types of accreditation through accrediting bodies recognized by either the U.S. Department of Education (USDE) or the Council for Higher Education Accreditation (CHEA). The types of accreditation available are regional, faith-based, private career, and programmatic. Though international institutions may seek U.S. accreditation, they do not receive oversight from any federal or state body.

CHEA and USDE recognize many of the same accrediting organizations, but not all. Accreditors seek CHEA or USDE recognition for different reasons. CHEA recognition confers an academic legitimacy on accrediting organizations, helping to solidify the place of these organizations and their institutions and programs in the national higher education community. USDE recognition is required for accreditors whose institutions or programs seek eligibility for U.S. federal student aid funds.

Accreditation is an important indicator of quality for receiving institutions, especially in enabling transfer of credit. Other important attributes of accreditation include assuring quality, access to federal and state funds, and creating private sector confidence. International institutions require similar assurances of quality when receiving institutions consider credit transfer. They determine their recognition similarly to the U.S. process.

ACCREDITATION ABROAD

Determining institutional recognition outside the United States may occur in three primary ways: a government agency (*e.g.*, Ministry of Education, Ministry of Higher Education, University Grants Commission), an external authorizing body of the curriculum (*e.g.,* Scottish Qualification Authority, Credit Bank System Korea), or U.S. accreditation.

Government recognition is most easily determined by visiting the official government website. Many websites maintain a directory of recognized institutions, and some also maintain a list of fraudulent institutions. These can be listed via different categories: federal, state, polytechnic, private, or public institutions. Some further distinguish by type of college: independent, branch, or junior college.

The government recognition differs slightly in that the recognition is based upon the curriculum, not the institution. Institutions, conversely, are required to be identified as authorized centers to deliver the curriculum. The final assessment of grade results is conducted by the authorizing body. Typically the authorizing body provides a directory of approved centers on their website.

U.S. accreditation of a foreign institution is possible; however, only CHEA includes these institutions within their directory. USDE does not maintain a directory since it has no governance over these institutions. If a U.S. accreditation agency is identified as the accrediting body, it is important to ensure the accreditation is current. In addition, simply obtaining U.S. accreditation does not automatically indicate that an institution teaches exclusively in English, warranting any English language requirement exemptions. Each institution must carefully assess the official government language and language of instruction separately from accreditation.

IDENTIFYING UNRECOGNIZED PROGRAMS

Without this official recognition to confer degrees, students become at risk for the same challenges as those of a non-accredited U.S. institution. Of further consequence for any student carrying the U.S. degree achieved in combination with transfer credit awarded from non-accredited or unrecognized coursework is the greater risk of the degree not passing an audit by the receiving government. If transfer credit is awarded by

your institution from a non-recognized institution, the receiving government is not required to recognize your institution's degree, even if your institution is fully accredited. For this reason it is vital to learn how to identify programs that do not carry any acceptable form of recognition or accreditation.

Programs without recognition of credential or qualification tend to have some common indicators, including:
- Lack of standard admissions criteria;
- Program completion does not grant eligibility for higher education;
- Do not identify education level;
- Large number of English courses included within the curriculum for non-English majors (*i.e.,* IELTS or TOEFL prep course, Business English, multiple reading, speaking, and writing courses);
- Do not show degree or graduation completion; may only be one semester to one year of coursework listed on a transcript; may offer a certificate instead of a diploma.

Without full disclosure of any of these standards, additional steps should be taken for verification.

Another vital aspect of any international admissions office involves establishing an institutional practice for verification of institutions or curricula beyond the scope of your institutional resources. The most effective manner of verification is to submit the transcript and degree credentials to the identified government body (*e.g.,* the Ministry of Education (MOE), Ministry of Higher Education, or Ministry of Research and Training). To determine the appropriate verification body, utilize country-specific government contacts, UNESCO IBE Country Education Profiles, or the U.S. State Department's EducationUSA. Official directories of recognized institutions are found within the MOE website, and the U.S. State Department's EducationUSA contacts are also an effective means of determining a good point of contact within the government for verifying credentials and/or programs. Other resources, such as AACRAO EDGE, include lists of institutions. Using more than one resource is advisable in the event of non-exhaustive and/or out-of-date lists.

Examples of recognized institutions include:

- An institute or college of a university found on either the MOE directory of independent colleges or the university's official directory of affiliated colleges/institutes; or
- An institution found on the approved center list of any recognized authorizing body or qualification; the approved curriculum is also listed within each approved center.

Examples of unrecognized institutions include:

- A college or institute that is not listed on the official MOE directory; or
- An affiliated college or institute that is identified as owner of curriculum, yet is not listed on the affiliate's official website.

Institutional Type

After gaining a better understanding of accredited/recognized versus unaccredited/unrecognized institutions, and how to verify institutions, it is essential to consider transfer credit implications. The ideal educational bodies to work with are accredited or government recognized institutions. Unaccredited or unrecognized institutions may still provide opportunity for transfer credit (or articulation partnership) through external qualifications such as an industry standard or government vocational curriculum.

Institutions still in the candidacy stage of seeking accreditation constitute a gray area when evaluating transfer credit. This is an important scenario to have defined within institutional policy. Another gray area is loss of accreditation, which requires the evaluator to verify when the accreditation was lost and compare it to the student's attendance period. Options for credit include awarding credit for only those years of valid accreditation, or awarding the entire body of coursework regardless of the timing of lost accreditation as long as the student was continuously enrolled. The

institution should also work with the accrediting body to better define its practice.

Evaluating Grades

The mechanism used to assess knowledge represents another critical aspect of the evaluation methodology process and how it relates to awarding transfer credit. Grades, as they are commonly referred to within the U.S. system, are as varied as educational systems. Grades display the level of proficiency in a subject or overall program by employing letters (A–F or H), numbers (0 to 4, and up), percentage (0–100%), or word descriptors (Excellent to Fail or Distinction to Pass Class). How to interpret these various grades is at the crux of credential evaluation. To establish a foundation of consistency, certain questions can be asked by an institution:

- Are foreign grades converted to the system of the receiving institution?
- Are grades weighted based upon coursework rigor or ranking of institution?
- Are individual institutional grade scales accepted or is only the government's approved grade model accepted?

Every country and institution chooses to handle the topic of grades differently. It is often stated that there is no incorrect way to handle grades as long as the method is consistent and meets one's institutional profile. However, certain known factors regarding grades should function as guidelines regardless of method chosen. Some countries have very forthright and specific grading scales, while the lack of oversight exercised by other countries, despite the existence of Ministry of Education-approved grading scales, sometimes results in the modification of grading scales by individual institutions. Grading systems may also be based upon institution or degree program, while others vary according to education level. Ultimately, though, the comparison is made to the U.S. four-point (4.0) scale.

The U.S. four-point scale equates a pass with a grade of C or above; as a result, foreign grading systems using the concept of pass must not be automatically equated to the U.S. grade of D. A condoned pass within the U.S. four-point scale equates to a grade of C minus or below. The condoned pass indicates a passing grade but a grade not high enough to qualify for graduation. The concept of a D grade is very rare in foreign grading systems. The French 20-point system (where ten is the pass grade, and eight or nine constitute a condoned pass as long as the overall semester average is ten or above) and the Indian system (where a predetermined percentage, usually less than 1 percent below the passable percentage, is a condoned pass) are two such rare examples. When converting to the U.S. four-point system, however, it is possible for a satisfactory pass within a foreign grading scale to equate to a condoned pass grade. For example, a 2.0 out of a 5.0 scale is a pass; however, if you compare it to the U.S. four-point scale, it does not equate to a 2.0 out of a 4.0 scale. It is worth repeating that pass is not automatically comparable to the U.S. grade of D.

Some systems require a higher passing percentage (e.g., 70%) and others, a lower (e.g., 50%). Seventy percent would be satisfactory within the U.S. four-point system because satisfactory signifies a grade eligible for graduation. Fifty would not be considered a condoned pass (ineligible for graduation) within the U.S. four-point system since this grade is comparable to below a 2.0 out of a four-point scale system. This, as a result, is not considered a satisfactory pass. If a system uses a three-tier level of grading, it easily fits within the U.S. system using the A, B, C model. Employing the U.S. system as a consistent guide along the way keeps the interpretation of foreign grading systems from proving too difficult or daunting.

Transfer Credit Evaluation

Armed with an understanding of the U.S. education system and the respective institution's profile, policies, and practices, awarding transfer credit can begin. The three avenues transfer credit may derive from—foreign institutions, study abroad, and advanced standing—share four basic components of consideration: content

and level of course, credit or course value, length of study, and credential type. Questions to ask when considering a credential for possible transfer credit include:

- How is the coursework reported?
- How are the subjects reported, as theory, practice, or both?
- What is the average course load in an academic year?
- What is the typical fulltime duration of the program?
- How many hours/units/subjects are required to complete the program?

Applicability Versus Transferability

The application of transfer credit involves a question of applicability versus transferability. Transferability is understood as meeting the minimum hour requirement (and any other transfer requirements set by the institution) for the course to be awarded in transfer. Applicability involves these same minimum requirements, in addition to course content matching that of another course required within the degree of study at the institution.

Some institutions confirm coursework as transferable but not applicable, meaning that the minimum requirements are met but the course (and content) just does not match any course requirement within the major. Some institutions will award elective credit for transferable courses but it does not apply to the degree requirements. The coursework is reported on the transcript as transfer credit but remains unused.

Credential Type

Next, it is necessary to understand whether the credential is for a three-year diploma program, gap year, or exam-based coursework. This will help determine the length of study to deduce a comparable value to the U.S. system. Specifics such as how the coursework is reported (hours or units; semester or quarter credits) or not reported must be identified. It is crucial to recognize the various units of course measurement before proceeding with the conversion process to U.S. equivalency.

CONVERTING QUARTER AND SEMESTER CREDITS

Many foreign countries use credit systems of a higher value than the U.S., while others do not employ credits at all. The semester credit is the most common with 15 semester credits equaling the average number of credits carried in one U.S. semester, thus totaling 30 semester credits per academic year and 120 credits per U.S. four-year undergraduate program. To convert semester credits to quarter credits, multiply the number of semester credits by 1.5. Conversely, to convert from quarter credits to semester credits, divide the quarter credits by 1.5.

THE EUROPEAN CREDIT TRANSFER SYSTEM

Another popular form of credit reporting is the European Credit Transfer System (ECTS). This system arose upon establishment of the European Union and writing of the Bologna Process. The Bologna Process intends to create a common framework for all European Union countries, thus enabling ease of accessibility and mobility across borders. Having a common credit hour is of particular importance; however, it still requires conversion to U.S. credit. To do so, ECTS credits must be divided by 2 to provide the semester credit equivalent or multiplied by 0.75 to determine the quarter credit equivalency. Generally speaking, one ECTS credit is equal to 25–30 hours of work, and a U.S. semester credit is equal to 15 hours. As a result, it is valid to count the concept of the ECTS credit value as twice that of U.S. credit value. For example, 3 ECTS credits are equivalent to 1.5 semester credits or 2.25 quarter credits; 6 ECTS credits are equivalent to 3 semester credits or 4.5 quarter credits; and 180 ECTS credits are equal to 90 U.S. credits.

Course Content and Level

The course content and level constitutes another very important element in determining transfer credit. Whereas U.S. course descriptions may be easily accessible online and entirely in English, foreign institutions do not always provide course descriptions or syllabi. Even fewer offer the course descriptions in English.

Requesting official course descriptions from the student as soon as possible is critical. Institutions are rarely unable to provide course descriptions, and in those cases an institutional policy must be established. Of specific consequence is determining if the receiving institution will allow the student to self-report content.

Course content is not only important in determining comparability of content, but it also may provide clues to defining another unique trait of the U.S. higher education system: course level, a descriptor not widely utilized in foreign education systems. Undergraduate U.S. courses are generally identified as lower or upper level, which typically applies to first- and second-year courses versus third- and fourth-year courses. It may also refer to the introductory courses in the program sequence leading to the capstone courses at the end of the program sequence.

Attempting to identify course level within foreign education systems may prove difficult; foreign systems do not always place emphasis on strict sequencing, making determining a level almost impossible. If, however, the institution requires some indication of level, a possible solution is ascertaining the length of the program and identifying any coursework from the first half of the program as lower level and the second half of the program as upper level. Institutions must be aware that this practice may not prove as accurate as it is simple and should use their best judgment. For a more fool-proof practice, course descriptions or syllabi should be requested for faculty to assess competency queues and provide comparability to competencies required throughout the institution's program.

In addition to reporting course level, foreign institutions do not always assign course codes, so identifying a course based upon a course code number sequence may not be an option. Requesting a curriculum plan serves as another alternative to determining level in the absence of course codes; many times this will indicate Level One, Level Two, etc., for the length of the program.

Defining the expectation of course content and level within the institutional transfer policy guide will provide the foundation with which to work confidently in these unique cases.

Reporting Formats and U.S. Conversion

The final aspect of the transfer credit evaluation process involves determining the credential reporting type and then converting it to its U.S. institutional equivalent. Academic credentials come in various forms: transcripts, mark sheets, grade notes, exam results, or statement of results. Each one reports the proficiency of subjects attempted within a course of study. How this proficiency is demonstrated varies but the following forms are the most common: credit-based, hour-based, marks/grade-based, and subject/course-based. Below is a step-by-step approach to each of these forms to ensure the most accurate conversion technique.

It is of significance to the conversion process to remember a simple guideline: never award more transfer credit from a foreign institution within an equivalent length of study to the receiving institution. For example, if a foreign transcript reports 50 semester credits for one academic year of study and a typical U.S. institution does not require more than 30 semester credits, then the 50 semester credits must be converted accordingly so as not to award more than a matriculated student at the receiving institution would earn in an academic year. Ultimately, the goal of awarding transfer credit is to provide students an opportunity to progress in their studies, while also ensuring they are meeting the learning outcomes identified within the degree program. Table 21.1 illustrates the U.S. credit hour equivalencies and serves as a useful tool in the conversion process.

CREDIT-BASED CONVERSION

Converting foreign credits to the U.S. credit system requires dividing the equivalent study period of U.S.

TABLE 21.1: U.S. Credit Hour Table

Length of Study	Semester Credit Value	Quarter Credit Value
Bachelor's Degree	120	180.0
One Year	30	45.0
One Semester	15	22.5
One Quarter	10	15.0
15 Lecture/Theory Hours	1	1.5
45–90 Lab Hours	1 semester	1.5 quarters
135–180 Practice/Independent Study Hours	1 semester	1.5 quarters

TABLE 21.2: Converting One Semester of Credits

Course	Credits	Conversion Factor	U.S. Credits
Math	6	0.63	3.78
Science	6	0.63	3.78
English	12	0.63	7.56
Total	**24**		**15**

credits by the total foreign credits in the study period. This is the conversion factor, which is then multiplied with each individual foreign credit to equal the U.S. credit. For example, if the study period is defined as one semester, the equivalent U.S. credits are 15. The conversion factor is determined by dividing 15 by the total number of foreign credits. For example, if the total number of foreign credits is 24 it will result in a conversion factor of 0.63. Each individual foreign subject credit must then be multiplied by the conversion factor of 0.63, as demonstrated in Table 21.2.

HOUR-BASED CONVERSION

To convert foreign hours to U.S. credits, first add the total number of foreign hours per study period and then divide this into the equivalent total number of hours per study period at the receiving institution. This is the conversion rate. To determine the U.S. credits per course, multiply each foreign subject's course hours by the conversion rate. For the example in Table 21.3 (on page 226), the total foreign course hours are 115. Because the study period is determined in one semester, we know the U.S. equivalent study period is 15 credits. The 15 credits is divided by 115 to equal the conversion fac-

TABLE 21.3: Converting One Semester of Hours

Course	Hours	Conversion Factor	U.S. Credits
Math	55	0.13	7.15
Science	60	0.13	7.80
Total	**115**	—	**15**

TABLE 21.4: Converting One Year of Grades

Course	Maximum	Conversion Factor	U.S. Credits
Math	100	0.043	4.30
Science	150	0.043	6.45
Hindi	200	0.043	8.60
English	100	0.043	4.30
History	150	0.043	6.45
Total	**700**	—	**30**

TABLE 21.5: Converting One Semester of Subjects

Course	Grade	Credits
Math	65	5
Science	70	5
History	84	5
Total	—	**15**

tor of 0.13, and then this conversion factor of 0.13 is multiplied by each individual foreign subject.

MARKS-BASED CONVERSION

To convert grade or marks-based credentials to U.S. credits, the conversion factor is determined by dividing the equivalent study period of U.S. credits by the total marks earned. Each individual subject's mark is then multiplied by the conversion factor to equal the U.S. credits. In Table 21.4 the study period is identified as one year; since 30 credits are the U.S. equivalent in this study period, they are divided by the total marks earned, in this case 700. The resulting conversion factor of 0.043 is then multiplied with each subject grade to determine the U.S. credits.

Subject-Based Conversion

Converting subject-based credentials to U.S. credit requires determining the conversion factor. This is completed by dividing the equivalent study period of

U.S. credits by the total number of subjects in the study period. The conversion factor determines the U.S. credits for each subject. In Table 21.5, the study period indicates one semester, so 15 U.S. credits are the equivalent. The total number of subjects in the same study period of one semester is three. The 15 U.S. credits are then divided by the three total subjects completed in the semester. The resulting conversion factor is five, and this indicates the number of U.S. credits for each subject.

In some cases, determining the study period is nearly impossible. Sometimes searching the institution's website will reveal the total program credits, units, and/or subjects. Other times, the study period should be defined as one subject and the conversion method applied subject by subject.

Understanding the conversion process for the various academic credential forms is a vital component of the transfer credit evaluation process. Once greater familiarity with these conversion techniques is obtained and used with foreign institutions, it will be easier to apply them with more confidence to study abroad, advanced standing, and English language coursework.

Study Abroad

For those study abroad experiences approved through an individual's own institution, the coursework is not considered transfer credit in nature. Some institutions choose to only offer experiences approved institutionally, therefore cutting out the need to take into account study abroad transfer credit. Others, though, allow students the opportunity to consider additional experiences beyond their home institutional offerings. It is in these cases that transfer credit would be evaluated using the same practice as that used for transfer credit coming from a foreign institution.

The study abroad provider may utilize a Home of Record (HOR), a common practice within the study abroad industry to facilitate unique programs outside of tertiary institutions to gain recognition and allow matriculated students the opportunity to obtain transfer credit for the experience. Often the HOR is a U.S. accredited institution providing faculty oversight of curriculum, teaching, or actual coursework. If this is the case, the transfer evaluation process immediately becomes more familiar and easier; however, for those study abroad programs where the HOR identified is not within the U.S. accreditation system, the evaluation methodology guidelines in determining institution and/or curriculum recognition as instructed earlier in this chapter should be followed.

Advanced Standing

Secondary curriculum varies among institutions and country educational frameworks. Traditional benchmarking credentials begin with the secondary diploma and move onward to the bachelor's degree. As students complete secondary curriculum and begin to look to university study, there is the potential to identify another level of education—Advanced Standing. The name itself helps define that it is slightly more advanced curriculum. It may be easier to envision the definition as that curricular area transitioning between secondary coursework and first year university studies. It identifies curriculum beyond the required secondary school diploma requirements.

Advanced Standing coursework may differ in delivery—typically taught at the secondary or upper secondary institution, not a university or college. In some instances, it is offered at special curriculum-specific institutions and described as pre-university studies, for example an A-Level College. In these institutions, the Advanced Standing curriculum is usually the only coursework offered. Just as any secondary curriculum, verifying the institution is not the important step; rather, verifying the curriculum and authorizing body is necessary. In the

case of Advanced Standing, the authorizing body is precisely how to complete the verification process.

Course content covered in Advanced Standing curriculum is more robust; in many cases, students are expected to study more in and out of class. Because the course content and study time is increased, it provides an opportunity to consider awarding transfer credit. A general assessment of transfer credit for Advanced Standing is up to one year of university/college study. As a result, The same transfer policy guidelines and methodology used for college or university level transfer evaluation apply to evaluating Advanced Standing for possible transfer credit. The largest variation in application is verifying the level of education and determining the length of study beyond secondary or high school completion requirements. Institutions must include these two additional considerations in any transfer policy. A consistent application of standards is of paramount importance when working with international credentials.

Determining Advanced Standing requires asking critical questions:

* What is the country's minimum required secondary/high school credential?
* Does the minimum resonate with individual, already-established institutional policy?
  * If so, to what extent has the curriculum carried the student beyond the minimum curriculum requirements to complete secondary/high school?
* In comparison to the first university degree, where does this curriculum fall?

It is important to collect as much information about the credential and curriculum as possible. This requires identifying both the preceding credential and the next sequential credential on the individual's educational path. After these inquiries have been conducted, the transfer evaluation may begin using the guiding questions above to evaluate for possible transfer credit.

TABLE 21.6: Advanced Standing Credentials

Country	Secondary Benchmark Credential	Number of Years to Complete	Advanced Standing Credential	Number of Years to Complete
Internationally Recognized	Various[1]	Various	IB	2
Caribbean Countries	CSEC-CXC, GCSE, BGCSE	2 (+ 3 years of lower secondary)	CAPE-CXC	1–2
Germany	Certificate of Maturity	6	Abitur[2]	1
India	SSC	2–3	Diploma in Engineering	3
Internationally Recognized	GCSE or previously GCE O Level	5	GCE A/AS Level	1–2

[1] Often, IB curriculum satisfies secondary school completion requirements in conjunction with one to two previous years of coursework
[2] Must verify when German States changed to 12 year credential, from 13 year, to consider transfer credit

Table 21.6 provides a list of common Advanced Standing credentials; however, this is not an exhaustive list and institutions must define their individual guidelines for determining acceptable minimum secondary/high school completion. This will result in varying lists of common and accepted Advanced Standing credentials.

Using the IB as an example, there are two subject types offered: the Higher Level (HL) and Standard Level (SL). As the name implies, the HL coursework requires more hours and additional content than the SL. A value ratio of 2:1 is commonly applied where HL credit is applied at twice the value of SL. Some institutional practices require a higher subject grade for SL coursework to be eligible for transfer. For example, a HL Math subject grade comparable to a "C" or 2.0/4.0 may require a SL Math subject grade of "B" or 3.0/4.0. This determination often is to address the advanced curricular requirements in HL versus SL content. Ultimately, institutions must determine how the transfer policy will be applied to each unique credential.

The evaluation of content and individual grade is applied in a similar manner compared with a traditional domestic transfer evaluation. When evaluating international credentials, institutions are encouraged to determine their own policies, taking into account numerous variables such as minimum grade requirements and the number of hours (and whether these hours include study hours or only seat hours). Typically, in U.S. institutions, the seat hours are counted rather than study hours. This is an important distinction when evaluating international credentials, as some credentials include a total hour based upon combination of seat and study hours. Remaining consistent when determining hours to credit value is vital, as is applying a standard conversion method. (*See* "Reporting Formats and U.S. Conversion," on page 225.)

GCE A/AS Level curriculum is very similar to the IB credential, in that the AS Level and A Level carry varying values of content and seat time. Again, it is important to adhere to institutional policy to remain consistent.

It is worth mentioning again that a critical aspect of evaluating Advanced Standing is determining where secondary school credentials end and the additional curriculum begins. For those institutions that do not accept the GCSE (or GCE O level) as high school completion, then the GCE AS Level may not be considered Advanced Standing. Typically the AS Level is year one and A Level is year 2; therefore, a GCSE credential considered 11th grade comparable (in U.S. system) would require the AS Level to satisfy high school completion. Only the A Level coursework, in this case, would be eligible for transfer. Because an A Level subject implies two years' worth of content, but one of those years is considered high school completion in this example, institutions must determine how to award course value. Will an institution award the full value or only half the value of the A Level? The answer to this question relies on institutional policy and is yet another example of the importance for the development of such policies.

Credential evaluation for transfer credit consideration requires research of the credential and level of education completed. Understanding Advanced Standing, and how it fits within the continuum of secondary and university curriculum, will provide further clarity for the evaluator when determining what is transfer eligible or not. Remembering that consistency, institutional policy and application of the international credential evaluation methodology when conducting an evaluation are all equally important to ensure the most accurate outcome regardless of curriculum.

English as a Second Language (ESL) Courses

ESL courses are defined as developmental in nature, since often these courses are not taught at a level of comprehension required of curricular expectations within a u. s. English composition course. Various ways exist to handle ESL coursework in terms of potential transfer credit. Some institutions do not award any transfer credit, while others will award a limited number based upon level of course content. Still others will award any ESL coursework as either free or arts and science electives or to fulfill language requirements. Again, a rule of thumb when considering awarding ESL coursework as comparable to a language requirement is to make sure it meets a similar level of content as any other language course offered at the receiving institution. English courses offered at foreign institutions located within countries where English is the official governmental language, as well as language of instruction, would not be considered ESL in nature. Every institution, however, must research and arrive at their conclusions regarding this topic.

Though industry standards do exist regarding each of these transfer credit possibilities, institutions reserve the right to set their individual standards.

Articulation Agreements

Once institutional standards in the form of transfer policy and practice have been established, it will be easier to approach articulation agreements. It is necessary to ensure that these standards are applicable to both domestic and international articulation agreements. Increasingly the articulation agreement is becoming a more popular method to facilitate transfer credit. This method relies heavily upon the cultivation of relationships, thus demonstrating a correlation between strong relationships and successful agreements.

A first step in the creation of articulation agreements is recognizing each of the necessary components. It will become evident during the agreement process with a potential partner just how important it is to have a clear understanding of the make-up of an agreement. Requesting information and documentation correctly from the start not only saves time but also presents the institution in a favorable light; it demonstrates organization and motivation to find a quality partner. This will attract other well-positioned institutions. Conversely, if potential partner institutions are slow or unwilling to provide necessary documentation, they are likely unprepared or unqualified for partnership.

The goal of requesting information and documentation is to acquire enough information to address the main components of an articulation agreement. The Statement of Agreement between institutions and degree programs identifies the potential programs for partnership. A clear degree pathway between the programs should be visible.

The program entrance requirements must include the English language requirements. Depending on the institution and the institutional English language policy, English language exemptions can function as a powerful marketing tool. It is also important to identify whether the partner institution's admissions requirements are similar to those of the receiving institution. If their admissions requirements are less stringent, it is advisable to address any concerns immediately to avoid surprises later. It will also be critical for the partner institution to communicate this effectively with any prospective students.

A clear statement of transfer policy requirements is a crucial component of any agreement. This includes the use of any external curriculum by the partner institution. It is not always clear to prospective students that coursework outside of the approved external curriculum may not be applicable for transfer credit. When conducting the initial evaluation of the partner institution and their curriculum, pay particular attention to the ownership of the curriculum. If the institution uses an external authorizing body's curriculum, then it must be stated within the agreement. The institution must also be verified as an authorized center to administer the curriculum. This verification may be completed online in some cases or by contacting the authorizing body directly.

The essence of the agreement is the actual course-for-course equivalencies (or block statement of transfer). This should be presented in clean and clear tables demonstrating the correspondences between the coursework from each institution. If an institution will utilize block transfer, then the transfer credit will vary slightly in presentation. A table will be necessary to list the coursework of the partner institution the receiving institution is willing to accept towards a finite amount of study time (*i.e.*, one year or two years). Block transfer is seen as a cleaner approach to articulation agreements as it lacks the tedious work of matching individual courses; however, it requires that the receiving institution conduct thorough research of the partner institution's curriculum to ensure the coursework and objectives meet the compulsory learning outcomes of your institution. Accreditation requirements must always be at the forefront in terms of learning outcome deliverables.

A table listing the remaining coursework towards the degree to be completed at the receiving institution is useful. Often, the partner institution will request a general estimation of amount of time to complete the program. Be sure to state this estimation in such a manner that allows flexibility of student performance and

course offerings, as well as indicating whether the estimation includes or excludes any English language requirements. This separate table is also necessary to include if using the block transfer credit model.

Even though the curriculum evaluation is the body of the agreement, a statement of degree completion and inclusion of the academic good standing policy is invaluable because of the different requirements and expectations of degree completion and academic good standing in each educational system. An online link may be provided or the policy spelled out within the body of the agreement to ensure it is read and understood. When choosing to simply provide a link to the online catalog or location of the policy, it should be specifically discussed with the partner institution to highlight any significant differences. This will decrease the chance of any surprises or difficult situations with prospective students.

How does an institution both seek out and attract quality partners? Many institutions debate which model is more effective: signing many agreements in an effort to create many avenues of approach or being more selective to theoretically be more active and productive. This discussion will need to be had within your institution, and it ideally would happen before committing to any major scale articulation initiative. Some things to consider when determining quality articulation partners include:

- Targeted geographical area for recruiting purposes;
- Seek a specific curriculum (*e.g.*, Edexcel/sqa);
- Seek specific degree programs (*i.e.*, to match your institutional offerings);
- History of strong faculty collaboration (*e.g.*, research, faculty exchange);
- Similar institutional scope, brand, and size.

Having identified the model, the next step is to begin creating an ideal institutional profile. Three possible profiles follow; ultimately, there is no right or wrong method.

Placing emphasis on degree areas (*e.g.*, STEM) to increase enrollment in key areas or supplement declining areas

Focusing on diversity within the institutions' international population by targeting partner institutions in specific geographical areas or countries

Increasing institutional brand by seeking partnerships with institutions recognized in key areas

Each of the above models is self-explanatory in nature; however, key variables within these models require greater attention. Even when deciding to emphasize a specific degree area, the quality of institution for collaboration or the nature of the institution (*e.g.*, a research or teaching institution) must be determined. Whether the size and scope of institution is important, or if these are negotiable is another important aspect to consider. Though not always possible, finding a partner institution which speaks to all or as many of the key components of these three models is the best solution.

It is essential to identify a clear degree pathway with the partner institution. An associate degree or a comparable diploma program that would lead into the receiving institution's bachelor's degree, or another bachelor's degree program that shares a common curriculum are examples of how to ensure a degree pathway. Partner institutions wish to see their curriculum valued, while simultaneously assisting their students to progress reasonably in the degree at the transfer institution.

Occasionally, after completing the curriculum evaluation and partner institution review, it becomes clear that the institution is not the best fit for the needs of the receiving institution; however, maintaining the partnership in some degree remains valuable. In this case, a less binding agreement, such as the standard and universally recognized Memorandum of Understanding (MOU) may be something to consider. This option

allows for mutual support and dialogue between institutions over a period of time. The look of a MOU may vary; for example, students being accepted to the transfer institution with the application fee waived or the partner institution inviting the receiving institution's faculty to their campus for a workshop or co-teaching opportunity. The MOU exists as a vehicle to cultivate new relationships and potentially lead to articulation agreements (*See* Table 21.7).

These variables and options take time to research and prioritize, and they may look different from one depart-

TABLE 21.7: When to Use an Articulation Agreement vs. an MOU

Articulation	MOU
Handshake agreement that has grown over time	Handshake agreement, on paper
Focused statement of collaboration, with specifics	General statement of collaboration, no specifics
Course-for-course equivalencies, block transfer	General statement of program interests and admission preferences

ment or college to another within an institution. Formulating articulation agreements is time-consuming, but this time is critical to the effectiveness of any agreement. It is important to minimize unnecessary delays or misdirection.

Conclusion

International transfer credit evaluation and methodology is an exciting and ever-evolving field within international education. Success will be found by remembering throughout the entire process that transfer credit evaluation and methodology is a fluid, subjective art and science. In applying the theories, techniques and models shared within this chapter, trends in methodology will emerge which may be applied to similar credentials. For those new to the field, it is advisable to create a system to save unique and challenging credential examples. This will establish a working resource within the institution. Consistency and due diligence are the constants in a field of constant change.

TABLE 21.8: Professional Resources for the International Transfer Credit Evaluator

Resource	Website
AACRAO EDGE	http://edge.aacrao.org/info.php
Association of International Credential Evaluators, Inc (AICE)	www.aice-eval.org
Council for Higher Education Accreditation	www.chea.org
The College Board Advanced Placement	http://apcentral.collegeboard.com
International Qualifications Assessment Service (IQAS)	http://work.alberta.ca/Immigration/international-education-guides.html
National Association of Credential Evaluation Services (NACES)	http://naces.org/faq.htm
NAFSA : Association of International Educators *(Search Online Guide to Educational Systems Around the World)*	www.nafsa.org
National Center for Education Statistics	http://nces.ed.gov
UK NARIC	www.ecctis.co.uk/NARIC/
UNESCO IBE Country Education Profile	www.ibe.unesco.org/en/worldwide/unesco-regions.html
U.S. Department of Education, International Affairs Office	www2.ed.gov/about/offices/list/ous/international/usnei/us/credits.doc
U.S.NEI, International Affairs Office-UDE	www2.ed.gov/about/offices/list/ous/international/usnei/edlite-index.html
U.S. State Department, EducationUSA Advising	www.educationusa.info/help/research.php

The importance of a robust resource collection cannot be understated. Many professional associations offer some sort of resource center; some are free to access, but the majority have a fee. *See* Table 21.8 for examples. The AACRAO Electronic Database for Global Education (EDGE) is a comprehensive fee-based online database, though there are others as well. More than one resource should be utilized for an industry perspective. It is also useful to gauge the industry continuum for any given credential. This will allow determination of an institution-specific definition with confidence.

TWENTY-TWO

The Art of Credential Evaluation

ELLEN SILVERMAN

Coordinator of International Training and Development
City University of New York

MARGARET WENGER

Senior Director of Evaluation
Educational Credential Evaluators, Inc.

JEANNINE BELL

Senior Assistant Director of International Admissions
University of Colorado Boulder

JENNIFER MINKE

Associate Director of Admission, Texas A&M
University-Kingsville

The Art of Credential Evaluation

It is sometimes said that credential evaluation is an art, not a science. The art of the credential evaluation process comes not only from determining the equivalency of a foreign credential, but also from applying the policies and requirements of an institution in making an admission decision. In the conference session that led to this article, four credential evaluators from four different types of institutions reviewed the same credentials and discussed how those credentials would be evaluated at their respective institutions.

The panelists included evaluators from a private credential evaluation agency (Evaluator A), a mid-sized, rural public research university (Evaluator B), a large, public urban university (Evaluator C), and a mid-sized, public research university (Evaluator D). The focus was primarily on the level of education represented by the credential; the panelists did not determine grade point averages or make other detailed analyses that would normally be part of the process.

Basic Tenets of Credential Evaluation

The documents were reviewed utilizing the framework of the following "basic tenets" of credential evaluation:

✳ *In every geographical area, the range of human intellectual ability can be represented by the standard bell-shaped curve of normal distribution.* This first basic principle is the basis for acceptance of educational credentials between two geographic areas, whether they are as similar as Boston and New York or as different as Turkey and China.

✳ *One educational program can be considered equivalent to another educational program, even if the two are not identical.* Rarely do two students in the same degree program at the same university take identical courses. Yet they both earn the same degree and those degrees are considered to be equivalent. This principle must be extended when comparing degrees from different countries. If a degree program meets the criteria and intent of a credential in another country, they can be equivalent without being identical.

✳ *Completion of one year of full-time academic work in one country is the equivalent of one year of full-time academic work in another country.* This serves as an objective basis for quantitatively comparing educational achievement, whether the two institutions are located in the same country or in different countries.

✳ *There are significant differences between basic and secondary education, and between secondary and tertiary education.* These differences must be taken into account when evaluating credentials. For example, the study of a particular subject—physics, history, etc.—differs significantly from one level of education to another. However, differences in the educational and experiential background of the students result in differences in the depth and breadth of the information that is covered.

✳ *Different levels and types of education have a specific intent (i.e. completing a specific level of education, or serving as a building block which allows access to the next higher level.)* Once a certain level of education is completed, the intent within the country where the study was done may be that the credential awarded is a qualification for the next higher level. Alternatively, it may be a terminal certificate, diploma, or degree meant to lead to employment rather than further academic study. Once the intent within the home country is established, it becomes easier to determine

235

how it might be viewed within the context of the U.S. educational system.

✳ *Experienced, reasonable people can reach different conclusions concerning the equivalence, or lack thereof, between two educational programs.* There is often more than one right answer.

Best Practices of Credential Evaluation

The following best practices were also taken into account:

✳ *Be consistent in the application of policy from one country to another.* When establishing a policy about a credential from a particular country, it is important to consider more than one country in determining the equivalency. For example, if the institution has a policy that a three-year bachelor's degree after twelve years of primary and secondary education is not equivalent to a U.S. four-year bachelor's degree because it lacks significant components of the U.S. degree, the institution can justify this by noting its non-acceptance of Indian or Swiss three-year bachelor degrees. Thus, the institution's policy would be to require a minimum of 16 years of progressive higher education.

✳ *Assess the credential in accordance with the mission, guidelines, and needs of your institution.* Credentials may be assessed differently by receiving institutions based on the needs of the institution, including its mission, degrees offered, state guidelines, and other factors. Various types of U.S. schools will assess an individual's academic credentials differently and place the student accordingly. In general, U.S. schools are looking for a good match between the individual's academic background and their own mission. If a U.S. school has an open acceptance mandate, a student with the minimum credential to complete secondary school may be accepted, and grades are not an issue. On the other hand, a more competitive U.S. college or university may require a minimum number and level of academic subjects to be admissible. This could include minimum grades as well. Therefore, a student may be admitted to one U.S. school and not to another.

Laurea Degree (Italy)

The first credential reviewed was a *laurea* degree awarded by the Università degli Studi di Verona. This is a three-year first university degree. Prior to entering the *laurea* program, the student completes thirteen years of primary and secondary education. The three university representatives considered the *laurea* to be comparable to a U.S. bachelor's degree, considering three years of university study in combination with the thirteenth year of the university-preparatory secondary comparable to a four-year U.S. degree. The representative of the credential evaluation agency indicated that they would consider the *laurea* to represent completion of three years of undergraduate study but *not* the equivalent of a U.S. bachelor's degree. The reasoning for not considering it equivalent to a U.S. degree is that it only represents completion of three years of undergraduate study and that secondary-level study should not be applied toward the requirements of a four-year undergraduate degree.

Bachelor of Science (Germany)

The evaluators reviewed the Bachelor of Science from a University of Applied Sciences (*Hochschule*). This is a three-and-a-half-year first university degree. The minimum entrance requirement is completion of twelve years of primary and secondary education. One university representative [Evaluator C] did not consider this to be equivalent to a U.S. bachelor's degree, but indicated they considered this to be eligible for up to three-and-a half years of undergraduate transfer credit. The credential evaluation representative also did not consider this to be equivalent to a U.S. bachelor's degree because it represents completion of three years of undergraduate study with the half-year often being a semester of practical training. The second university representative [Evaluator D] considered this equivalent to a U.S. bachelor's degree, while the third university representative [Evaluator B] stated that the determination of equivalency would be made by the graduate school.

Diploma in Mechanical Engineering (India)

The evaluators reviewed the Diploma in Mechanical Engineering granted by the State Board of Technical Education and Training in Andhra Pradesh, India. This Board is an official part of the Andhra Pradesh State Government and awards technical diplomas in fields including engineering, medical laboratory technology, pharmacy, and textiles. The Diploma in Mechanical Engineering represents a three-year program that requires completion of Standard Ten (lower secondary) for entry. In India, universities typically exempt technical board diploma holders from the first-year bachelor's degree examinations in a related field. All four evaluators consider this credential as equivalent to completion of a high school diploma from a vocational high school program, plus completion of one year of undergraduate work at the freshman level.

Baccalauréat de l'Enseignement Secondaire and General Certificate of Education Ordinary and Advanced Levels (Cameroon)

Two sets of credentials from Cameroon were reviewed. The first credential was the *Baccalauréat de l'enseignement secondaire* (Baccalaureate of secondary education), the credential confirming completion of secondary education in the French-based system. The other credentials were the General Certificate of Education (GCE), Ordinary and Advanced Levels (O- and A-Levels), awarded upon completion of secondary education in the British-based system. Because Cameroon became a League of Nations mandate after World War I, split into French and British sectors, the country continues to have two distinct educational systems. Both the French credential and the British set of credentials are awarded after seven years of secondary education and are treated as equivalent in Cameroon for purposes of admission to universities and other postsecondary education. However, primary education in the British sector is one year longer than in the French sector. The three university-based evaluators treated the French *Baccalauréat de l'enseignement secon-*

daire (BES) and the British GCE O-Levels as each equivalent to a high school diploma and the British GCE A-Levels as up to one year of undergraduate credit. The credential evaluation agency representative indicated that they consider the BES and the combination of the GCE O- and A-Levels each to be the equivalent of a U.S. high school diploma from a university-preparatory high school program, because they are the benchmark credentials in their systems confirming completion of secondary school.

Voorbereidend Wetenschappelijk Onderwijs Diploma (Netherlands)

The Netherlands has a binary educational system, with both research-oriented education and advanced professional education. The former is done at research universities and the latter at universities of applied sciences. Though each have programs leading to bachelor's and master's degrees, these institutions have different admission requirements. Admission to a research university requires either the *Voorbereidend Wetenschappelijk Onderwijs* (VWO, or Diploma of Preparatory Science Education) or completion of the first-year diploma of a university of applied sciences (*Propaedeuse*). Admission to the first year of a university of applied sciences requires the *Hoger Algemeen Voortgezet Onderwijs* (HAVO, or Diploma of Senior General Education).

The Dutch education system consists of seven to eight years of primary education, four, five, or six years of secondary education (depending on the type of school), and two to six years of higher education (depending on the type of education and the specialization). The HAVO is awarded after completion of twelve or thirteen years of primary and secondary education, with the examination based on the final two years.

Since 1986, the VWO represents completion of thirteen or fourteen total years of primary and secondary education. The student is typically examined externally in seven subjects. When a student enters a university of applied science with a VWO, the program is three years long; when he or she enters with a HAVO, the program is four years long. The three university representatives considered the VWO to be the equivalent of a high school diploma in the United States, and the credential evaluation agency representative indicated that her organization would equate it to a high school diploma and completion of one year of undergraduate work.

BCS Level 4 Certificate, BCS Diploma, and BCS PGD (U.K.)

The evaluators reviewed three credentials from the United Kingdom (U.K.). The first of the U.K. credentials reviewed was a BCS Level 4 Certificate, which is granted through a professional examination given by BCS, The Chartered Institute for IT, a recognized professional organization. The Office of Qualifications and Examinations Regulation (Ofqual) in the U.K. recognizes this certificate as being equivalent to one year of university study at the undergraduate level. All four evaluators consider this credential as equivalent to one year of university study and recommended granting up to one year of undergraduate credit.

The second U.K. credential reviewed was a BCS Diploma Examination, also granted by BCS, The Chartered Institute for IT. To study for this Diploma, achievement of or exemption from the Level 4 Certificate is required. The Diploma in IT is recognized by Ofqual as a level 5 qualification and is the academic equivalent of one year of university study. All four evaluators consider this credential as equivalent to one year of university study and recommended granting up to one year of credit.

The third U.K. credential reviewed was a BCS PGD (Professional Graduate Diploma) Examination, also granted by BCS, The Chartered Institute for IT. To study for the PGD, achievement of or exemption from both the Level 4 Certificate and the Diploma is required. The PGD is recognized by Ofqual as a level 6 qualification and is the academic equivalent to one year of university study. Level 6 qualifications are considered equivalent to bachelor degrees in the U.K. All four

evaluators consider this credential as equivalent to one year of university study. Three of the evaluators also consider this PGD to be equivalent to a U.S. bachelor's degree. The fourth evaluator (Evaluator B), a university representative, stated that the determination of degree equivalency would be made by the Graduate School.

Diploma-in-Engineering Examination (Bangladesh)

The evaluators reviewed the Diploma-in-Engineering Examination. This examination reflects four years of coursework and training after Standard Ten (tenth grade). The three university representatives considered this as the equivalent of a high school diploma from a vocational high school program and, upon review, would possibly grant up to two years of credit. The credential evaluation representative considered this to be the equivalent of a U.S. high school diploma with no undergraduate credit, due to the fact that no exemptions are given for this examination in Bangladeshi universities.

One Size Does Not Fit All

As this article illustrates, one size does not necessarily fit all. There is a standard methodology to arriving at a final determination, but, in the end, each receiving institution or organization must make a determination of how the credential itself will fit within its stated mission, while maintaining the integrity of comparative education. When working with foreign credentials, it is important that the evaluator first understand the purpose of the document within the home country. Once that is determined, it is possible to compare it to a similar credential in the U.S. The evaluator then needs to determine how the U.S. document is generally received within their institution or organization. At that point, the evaluator can determine how best to accept (or deny acceptance of) the international credential. As was mentioned at the start, experienced, reasonable people can reach different conclusions concerning the equivalence, or lack thereof, between two educational programs.

TWENTY-THREE

Outsourcing Foreign Credential Evaluations:

History and Implementation

2016 AACRAO INTERNATIONAL GUIDE

JASMIN SAIDI-KUEHNERT
President and CEO
Academic Credentials Evaluation Institute, Inc.

BETH COTTER
President
Foreign Credential Evaluations, Inc.

Outsourcing Foreign Credential Evaluations:
History and Implementation

The Mutual Educational and Cultural Exchange Program is to enable the Government of the United States to increase mutual understanding between the people of the United States and the people of other countries by means of educational and cultural exchange; to strengthen the ties which unite us with other nations by demonstrating the educational and cultural interests, developments, and achievements of the people of the United States and other nations, and the contributions being made toward a peaceful and more fruitful life for people throughout the world; to promote international cooperation for educational and cultural advancement; and thus to assist in the development of friendly, sympathetic, and peaceful relations between the United States and the other countries of the world. (Fulbright-Hays Act 1961)

A Brief History of U.S. International Education

Prior to World War II, the U.S. was not a primary destination for international students to further their education and to earn a degree. Most came to the U.S. to improve their English, to learn about American culture and history, and to take a course or two as a visiting student at a university before returning home. The devastation brought on by World War II on countries in Europe and Asia not only destroyed much of their infrastructure but also impacted their universities, which were no longer able to meet their citizens' demands for higher education. In the early 1950s, the U.S. found itself extending higher education to people mostly from Europe and Japan whose countries had suffered greatly during the war and helping to fund their

studies. This gesture was later extended to other countries through the introduction of a bill authored by the freshman senator from Arkansas, J. William Fulbright, calling for the use of proceeds from the sales of surplus war property to fund the "promotion of international good will through the exchange of students in the fields of education, culture and science." The legislation—best known as the Fulbright Act—was passed by Congress and signed into law by President Harry S. Truman on August 1, 1946. The final legislative underpinnings of academic exchange came with the Mutual Educational and Cultural Exchange Act of 1961, also known as the Fulbright-Hays Act (Senator Fulbright introduced it in the Senate, and Representative Wayne Hays of Ohio, in the House). This law remains the basic charter for all U.S. government-sponsored educational and cultural exchanges, consolidating all previous laws and adding new features that strengthened the program's authorization for supporting American studies abroad and promoting modern foreign language and area studies schools and colleges in the United States.

According to IIE's 2014 Open Doors Report on International Education Exchanges, in the 2013/14 academic year the number of international students at colleges and universities in the United States increased by eight percent from the previous year, to a record high of 886,052 students, confirming once again that the United States remains the destination of choice for higher education. The United States hosts more of the world's 4.5 million globally mobile college and university students than any other country in the world, with almost double the number hosted by the United Kingdom, the second leading host country. The report also found that more American students—a total of

289,408—studied abroad for academic credit, although the two percent increase represents a slightly slower rate of growth than the previous year (IIE 2014).

Decentralized Education System

Unlike many countries in the world, the United States does not have a Ministry of Education, a centralized government body that oversees the country's education system from preschool to doctoral level and professional education. The U.S. federal government does not have authority over education at any level. The federal government's only official role concerning education is setting conditions for the allocation of federal funding for student financial aid, research, and education-related activities. The U.S. Department of Education—a Cabinet-level agency created by legislation signed by President Andrew Johnson in 1867—was created to collect and disseminate information on the nation's schools for statistical analysis. Within a year of its formation, the Department was demoted to an Office of Education in 1868 to alleviate concerns that it would have too much control over local schools. The Office of Education continued to operate under different titles and under other agencies such as the U.S. Department of the Interior and the former U.S. Department of Health Education and Welfare (HEW) (now Health and Human Services). On October 17, 1979 a law was signed by President Jimmy Carter that converted the Education division of HEW into the U.S. Department of Education (DoE). The U.S. DoE, as we know it today, began operating on May 16, 1980 (U.S. Department of Education 2008).

From its inception in 1867, the Office of Education published information on the educational systems of countries from around the world. As early as 1919, the Office's Comparative Education Section received a request to evaluate the educational credentials of a person who had been educated outside the U.S. This single request motivated the establishment of the Foreign Credential Evaluation Services (FECS), also known as the Foreign Credential Advisory Interpretation Service

(FCAIS), which began evaluating international educational credentials for anyone interested in knowing the U.S. educational equivalent. The service provided by the FECS was free and provided to U.S. secondary schools, universities and colleges, private organizations, professional associations, employers and agencies of the state and federal government, as well as individuals who submitted their non-U.S. educational credentials for evaluation. The evaluation reports generated by FCES included a one-page superficial checklist confirming whether the studies evaluated were equivalent to either a completion of school grade, a high school diploma, completion of a select number of years of postsecondary work, an associate degree, a bachelor's degree, completion of a select number of years of undergraduate study, completion of a select number of years of graduate study, a master's degree, a doctorate degree, or another level of education. The reports provided no further details on the course content, units of credit and grade equivalences, levels of courses, or overall grade point average.

Following the post-WWII influx of international students, U.S. educational institutions not only relied on the services of FCES, but also saw the need to acquire an understanding of educational systems of other countries in order to accurately assess and evaluate their candidates' previous education achievements. This gave rise to "credential evaluation" as an administrative specialty. Typically, the task of evaluating an international student's academic credentials was absorbed by the registrar's office. Over time the responsibility was assigned to the admissions office for undergraduate applicants and to the dean of graduate studies' office for graduate applicants. Some institutions absorbed both undergraduate and graduate applications for admission into one centralized office under the title of international admissions or other similar titles.

FCES continued in its capacity until the Commissioner on Education announced its elimination at a conference on *Foreign Credential Interpretation and Educational Studies* hosted by the Office of

Education in Washington DC on April 6–7, 1966. The announcement spawned a movement by the Office of Education and conference participants who represented several U.S. colleges and universities to work together and find an alternative service to FCES. The Commissioner on Education turned to the National Liaison Committee on Foreign Student Admissions (NLC) to explore this further. On completing its study, the NLC concluded that international credential evaluation was a necessary service, which could be provided by the private sector. The NLC study also demonstrated that institutions and government agencies were interested in receiving more in-depth information than the evaluation reports provided by the FCES and were willing to pay a fee for this type of service. The FCES was terminated completely on June 30, 1970, thus making it possible for private non-governmental agencies to begin offering international educational credential evaluations to the public.

The continued flow of internationals seeking higher education or career and economic advancement in the U.S. based on their previous academic achievements has made it necessary for the individuals processing these documents, whether at academic institutions, state regulatory boards and government agencies, or human resource departments, to rely on the expertise of trained and experienced credential evaluators.

What is International Credential Evaluation?

International credential evaluation is the field related to comparative education in which educational documents or benchmarks from one country are compared with those of another. In the U.S., international credential evaluators seek to compare the educational accomplishments of people from other countries with those of U.S. citizens for both educational and employment purposes. High schools, vocational schools, technical and community colleges, and universities utilize international credential evaluations to place both students and teachers correctly in educational institutions. Employers, immigration attorneys, state regulatory boards and govern-

ment agencies, and the U.S. military all use evaluations in order to determine the appropriate fit or placement of the individual in the work force or the military.

The evaluator must possess a clear understanding of the U.S. system of education as well as the system of education of the country under comparison. A thorough knowledge of both the vocational/technical and the academic educational systems is required. Persons may present documentation of educational attainment at any level from primary/elementary school through postdoctoral study. The ability to correctly analyze and compare international educational credentials is critical to a proper assessment of the individual's appropriate placement in either a school environment or the work-place. International credential evaluations include both the broader, general evaluation known as a document-by-document evaluation, as well as the more specific, detailed evaluation referred to as a course-by-course evaluation.

A document-by-document evaluation describes the educational level attained on each of an individual's educational documents in the country of origin and explains the corresponding U.S. equivalent to that education. This general evaluation includes the name of the institution that issued the credential, the country in which the institution was/is located, the title of the credential as designated by the issuing institution, and the date of the award. This evaluation also includes the requirements for admission to the program of study and the duration or length of the course of study. The corresponding U.S. equivalency to the credential is noted, and, finally, the recognition/accreditation status of the issuing institution in the country of origin is described. This type of evaluation is most often required for admission to non-selective educational institutions and for employment purposes.

A course-by-course evaluation includes all of the information contained in the document- by-document evaluation. In addition, it also lists each of the individual courses included on the student's transcript, calculates the corresponding U.S. semester hours for each course, converts the grades to the U.S. 4.0 grading scale, and includes an overall grade point average (GPA) for all of the courses taken together. This evaluation can also include the number of credit hours taken in the major field(s) of study and indicate whether the courses taken are at the lower or upper division level or the graduate level. The language of instruction and the issuing institution's grading scale are included. This detailed evaluation is most often required for academic purposes, including the granting of transfer credit, admission to undergraduate or graduate school, and preparation for licensure or teaching.

An evaluation of international education is only as reliable as the documentation on which it is based. Thus, determining the authenticity of the documents plays a major role in credential evaluation, and the evaluator must have the necessary resources and skills. Producing reliable, accurate international credential evaluations is an acquired skill that requires education and instruction, access to numerous resources, mentoring by an experienced evaluator, and much practice.

Private International Credential Evaluation Agencies

The U.S. Department of Education does not have the authority to evaluate and assess academic studies completed at institutions in the U.S. or outside of it. With the closure of the U.S. Office of Education's Foreign Credential Evaluation Service (FCES) in July 1969, private agencies stepped in to fill the void. The responsibility to assess and accept or reject courses and degrees from any educational institution in the U.S. or abroad rests with the educational institution, state regulatory board, professional association, employer, governmental agency, or independent credential evaluation service to which a candidate has applied for admission, licensure, employment, or evaluation.

In the absence of a centralized body with uniform standards on international education credential evaluation, there is great diversity in evaluation methodology and reporting of educational equivalences amongst U.S. educational institutions and private independent cre-

dential evaluation services. There are two nonprofit professional associations—each with its own unique set of criteria—to determine the eligibility of providers of international credential evaluation services to membership: the Association of International Credential Evaluators (AICE), incorporated in 1998, and the National Association of International Credential Evaluation Services (NACES), incorporated in 1987. The two associations differ in that AICE has published evaluation standards to which its members subscribe and conform to promote consistency and transparency in the evaluation industry. In addition, AICE offers two membership categories. Endorsed membership is open only to private independent credential evaluation services and requires a rigorous screening including site visits; and Affiliate membership is open to accredited U.S. academic institutions, regulatory boards and professional associations, and ESL schools, ATA-approved translators, recruiters, and lawyers.

Benefits of Outsourcing

In the words of one admissions officer, "Outsourcing allows us to focus on what we do best: advising students on their academic options and helping them through the admissions and enrollment process." As the world's leading host country of international students and scholars, institutions within the U.S. can either fund evaluation services internally or outsource them to an evaluation agency. Some educational institutions—typically with a large international population—have a tradition of providing international credential evaluations as part of the admissions process and are fully equipped to do so. Others, however, do not have an evaluation process in place and yet face increasing numbers of students who have studied outside the U.S. For the latter, outsourcing foreign credential evaluations can be an excellent and helpful option.

Many of the deterrents to preparing credential evaluations in-house are financial. Perhaps no one in the admissions office has the knowledge and skills to evaluate international credentials, or there has been only limited exposure to this field. Many institutions face a lack of resources to fund a full-time position dedicated to international credential evaluation. In some cases, the population of students educated outside the U.S. is too small to justify hiring a full-time evaluator. In addition to the expense of funding such a position, the institution may also lack funds for regular ongoing training. Educational systems all over the world are dynamic and ever-changing, which necessitates continuing education.

In addition, an institution may lack the resources to purchase and maintain an adequate resource library. There have been numerous publications over the years regarding the educational systems of countries and regions all over the world. Many are available for purchase, but others were printed only once, or publication was discontinued because of the small audience for these kinds of materials. Acquiring a good print resource library requires not only monetary resources, but also time to accumulate the appropriate volumes. Searching out helpful resources requires knowledge of what resources are needed and also where to locate them. Numerous resources are available online at no cost to the user. Learning what these resources are and where to look for them requires training and mentorship.

One critical aspect of international credential evaluation is the ability to distinguish original and official documents from inauthentic documents. A good evaluation agency typically compiles a database of sample legitimate documents (as well as inauthentic documents), in order to judge the authenticity of various received credentials. The evaluator also has to become familiar with the world of diploma mills and possess the ability to spot not only altered documentation, but forgeries as well. Resources are needed to invest in the training, the databases, and the collection of materials needed to identify both legitimate and illegitimate documents.

In addition, the credentials evaluator must provide evaluations that are consistent and fair over time and from one country to another. The evaluator needs the resources to track changes in educational systems and degree programs of various countries. For example, sig-

nificant changes have occurred in the higher educational systems of European countries who have subscribed to the Bologna Declaration. The restructuring process continues in many countries today, obliging the evaluator to be familiar with both the pre- and the post-Bologna educational systems. Keeping abreast of changes in various educational systems requires on-going education.

The evaluator also must have access to information regarding grading scales from countries around the world and the ability to convert the grading scales to the U.S. grading system. This requires both training and experience. Again, both written materials and online tools can assist in this area, but the evaluator must know how to access and use them.

Finally, since 9/11, admissions offices have become subject to assuming responsibility for compliance with numerous federal regulations. These responsibilities have taken away time that could have been devoted to international credential evaluation and training. At annual conferences regarding international education, numerous sessions that once studied various country systems are now devoted to understanding U.S. immigration law as it relates to educational institutions.

Outsourcing international credential evaluations provides many benefits. It frees up the admissions office to focus on other critical admissions tasks. If the student obtains and pays for an evaluation provided by an evaluation service, it costs the institution nothing. The resources that would have gone into hiring personnel, training, funding continuing education, building a resource library, tracking changes in educational systems, verifying the authenticity of documentation, and building a database of documentation and evaluations, are available for recruiting, selecting, admitting, and advising students.

What to Look For in Outsourcing Credential Evaluations

With the need for increasing content and authenticity in the evaluation process comes the need for more education, training and experience on the part of the credential evaluator. Institutions seeking to outsource their international credential evaluations are advised to select a service or multiple services that have a proven record of experience in the field. A credential evaluation service needs to demonstrate a history of its evaluation standards and procedures, provide a profile of its executive and evaluating staff's expertise and outline methods it employs for its evaluators to receive continuous professional development. In addition, it is important to determine the different types of evaluation reports provided by the credential evaluation service, the criteria used in accepting academic credentials (*e.g.*, official transcripts directly from the source institutions or original documents versus copies supplied by the student), the standards it employs in evaluating and determining U.S. educational equivalences, and the steps it takes in maintaining a dynamic in-house library of historic and current publications and references. Other criteria to consider are pricing, actual turnaround/processing time with terms of service, and a user-friendly and informative website. Membership with recognized professional associations (*e.g.*, AICE, NACES) is also

important. As the two nonprofit professional organizations that admit eligible credential evaluation services to membership based on objective criteria, AICE or NACES are especially pertinent.

By selecting a reputable evaluation service, the admissions office ensures the most up-to-date evaluation standards and practices. Also, knowing that an evaluation service has a successful track record of producing evaluations recognized by the U.S. immigration service is reassuring when hiring scholars educated outside the U.S. Indirectly, outsourcing also gives the educational institution access to the evaluation service's resources: its library, databases, knowledge and experience, online tools, and training. Finally, building a relationship with a credential evaluation agency creates an understanding between the parties that allows the agency to incorporate any special institutional needs into the evaluation. An ongoing relationship with an evaluation service leads to consistency in the placement of students over time and across educational systems. It also provides the institution with an expert resource to consult when questions arise about credentials and placement.

TWENTY-FOUR

Outsourcing Foreign Credential Evaluations:

Does It Make Sense for Your Institution?

LESLEE M. CLAUSON EICHER

Assistant Director
AACRAO International Education Services

Outsourcing Foreign Credential Evaluations: Does It Make Sense for Your Institution?

In the early days of student exchange, higher education institutions in North America either had significant a international student population or they had few to no international students. Those with the higher population of international students also had a trained staff and did their own foreign credential evaluations in-house, while those with fewer international students were more likely to outsource their foreign credential evaluations when necessary.

The institutions who performed their own evaluations valued their ability to assess their international students' educational backgrounds. It also made for a student-friendly admissions process and helped to ensure a good fit between student and institution. The colleges and universities who outsourced their evaluations valued the simple fact that they did not need to devote time, energy, budget, and resources to understanding foreign educational systems. Both sets of institutions understood—or quickly came to understand—that assessing foreign students' academic backgrounds takes more time, research, and resources than is spent on admitting and placing domestic students.

In spite of increasing political tensions around the world, foreign students continue to flock to the United States. Both two- and four-year institutions are seeing ever-increasing numbers of students with foreign educational records. These may be "traditional" foreign students—F-, J-, or M-visa holders. Or they may be immigrants or refugees who were educated outside of the United States.

The reasons that institutions may or may not evaluate their foreign students' transcripts are varied and include shrinking budgets, growing numbers of international students, competition in and between countries for those prized international student tuition fees, the constant pressure to do more with less, the desire to "internationalize" our campuses, and the increased ease of travel.

Some institutions use a foreign credential evaluation agency on an as-needed basis. Some examples of times when this might be the best option include:

* During the busy part of the admissions cycle;
* When the country of origin is unfamiliar;
* If the admissions or placement judgment is questioned;
* If new staff is being trained.

If the institution does its own international credential evaluations, chances are good that a student-friendly admissions process is in place: one that upholds the institution's admissions standards and helps ensure a good match between student and institution.

But if the institution outsources this important piece of the admissions puzzle, or if it is considering doing so, it is important to undertake thorough research. When a relationship is established with a credential evaluation agency, it should work for both the institution and the students. As is done with other contractors to the institution, judgments should be made about the quality of the final product—the foreign credential evaluation—and how well it fits with the institution's processes and goals.

The History of Foreign Credential Evaluation and Placement Recommendations

In the 1950s, the Cold War had the unanticipated consequence of boosting cultural exchange among countries, especially between the U.S. and the Soviet Union.

Students, scholars, artists, writers, musicians, and politicians moved between countries and helped to defuse tensions that were ever-present at that time. The U.S. Department of Education handled evaluation issues when they were necessary. Because of the increased need for such knowledge, AACRAO began publishing volumes on foreign educational systems, a series titled the World Education Series. These booklets were funded by the United States Information Agency (USIA), and were provided free-of-charge to AACRAO member institutions.

The early 1960s saw the formation of the Council on Evaluation of Foreign Student Credentials (later known as the National Council on the Evaluation of Foreign Educational Credentials). The Council was composed of members from AACRAO, NAFSA: Association of International Educators, the Institute of International Education (IIE), the Council of Graduate Schools (CGS), the College Board, the American Council on Education (ACE), and the American Association of Community Colleges (AACC). Observers on the Council came from the New York State Department of Health and from AACRAO-USAID. The Council's task was to approve placement recommendations in the volumes researched and written by professionals in the field of international education. These volumes originated from the U.S. Department of Education and later from AACRAO's World Education Series. These first publications were later followed with books from JCOW (the Joint Committee on Workshops). In the 1980s, AACRAO's World Education Series and JCOW merged to become PIER (Projects in International Education Research). Placement recommendations appeared in all of these publications, with the intent to guide North American international educational professionals in admitting and placing their foreign student applicants.

Moving further into the 1960s, exchange became more common and numbers grew. It was at that time that the United States Agency for International Development (USAID) and AACRAO formed a cooperative agreement to support and foster the exchange process. AACRAO provided evaluations of USAID scholarship recipients, most of whom were from developing nations. In the 1970s foreign credential evaluation agencies came into existence. These organizations ranged from one-person owner/operator shops, to nonprofit public service organizations, to large, multi-office corporations. The number of foreign credential evaluation agencies continues to grow, but to date there is no comprehensive resource that lists all of the agencies in the country, and there is little guidance on which agencies are reputable.

While there are several membership organizations for foreign credential evaluation agencies (NACES, AICE), these organizations do not oversee or coordinate a standard for U.S. educational equivalencies. Membership in organizations for foreign credential evaluation agencies typically requires an application and screening process, qualified senior-staff on hand, ongoing contributions to the field of international credential evaluation (whether through research, or by presenting sessions or workshops and conference or other training venues), a robust and up-to-date library of credential evaluation resources, and sharing of information with other colleagues in the field. Membership organizations do not, however, set standards or placement recommendations. As such, it is possible that two agencies of a membership organization may evaluate the same credential differently.

Because of an ever-increasing need for knowledge, AACRAO continued to recruit authors to write volumes on international education. Yet by the late 1980s, funding for the PIER series had all but disappeared. Consequently, the Council had lost its reason for existence. It limped along, but was finally dissolved by 2006. It was replaced by AACRAO's International Education Standards Council (IESC) to fill the same role and function of the Council by representing the depth and breadth of U.S. higher education.

What is a Foreign Credential Evaluation?

In the U.S., a foreign credential evaluation does several things. Generally, it analyzes an individual's academic documents to determine:

❋ Who the documents belong to;

❋ Which institution was attended;

❋ What the level and type of study was (*i.e.* secondary, postsecondary, vocational, teacher-training);

❋ Whether the institution has the proper legal status in the legal jurisdiction in which it is located and/or operating. The terminology and process governing the legal status of higher education institutions is not the same around the world.

◆ Recognition: In countries other than the U.S., one generally speaks of "recognition" of higher education institutions. Recognition is a legal process and is regulated at the federal or national level. There are laws governing "recognition" of institutions by the appropriate government bodies (Ministry of Higher Education, Ministry of Health, military, etc.) as well as the operating status of private institutions.

◆ Accreditation: In the U.S., accreditation is both a legal and a quality-assurance mechanism. However, in other countries, accreditation is a relatively new phenomenon that may be administered by government agencies or by private (non-governmental) bodies. It is often a voluntary process. In many countries, academic programs—rather than institutions—are accredited.

❋ What final credential, if any, was earned; and

❋ If the documents are authentic.

The evaluation aims to:

❋ Make recommendations for placement into the U.S. system, based on generally-accepted standards of good practice;

❋ Convert a grade average from the indigenous system into the U.S. grading system; and

❋ Give background information, when appropriate, on the specific way in which the study was completed (*i.e.,* part-time/interrupted/in a program that has since become obsolete/distance education/other).

What Foreign Credential Evaluation Is Not

There are also some things that a foreign credential evaluation does *not* do. These include:

❋ "Giving" credit, degrees, or diplomas. *Foreign credential evaluations are always only advisory.* The receiving institution has the authority to make the final decision whether to accept or grant credit.

❋ Recognizing or accrediting institutions or degrees. A foreign credential evaluation agency is not an accrediting body. As above, the receiving institution has the authority to make the final decision whether to accept or grant credit.

❋ Translating from one language into another. An evaluation is applied comparative education: it compares study done in one system with that in another system, and makes non-binding recommendation as to how the foreign study compares with study in the target country.

The Regulation of Evaluation Agencies

Foreign credential evaluations in the United States are not regulated by law or government agency. Thus, no "official" foreign credential agency or evaluation exists. Correspondingly, there is no licensure or oversight of foreign credential evaluation agencies, nor is there certification for the evaluators who evaluate the credentials. So choosing the "right" agency for the institution will be a very individual decision. There is not a one-size-fits-all solution.

With due diligence, research, communication with colleagues, and sticking to established agencies, it is possible to have a good experience and a long, successful relationship with the evaluation agency that is chosen. There are many good agencies that employ knowledgeable staff with extensive experience. There will also be some bad ones. Some red flags of less-than-legitimate agencies include:

❋ The agency's name sounds nearly identical to the name of an established agency.

❋ The agency clones a legitimate agency's website appearance.

✳ It falsely presents professional membership association.

✳ It may be a "foreign credential evaluation agency" created by a diploma mill to verify the diploma mill's own degrees.

With thorough research, it is possible to find a good evaluation agency. An informed consumer is the best defense against scam artists.

Choosing an Agency

It might seem that the internet would be a good place to begin to gather information about outsourcing credential evaluations, but a Google search of "foreign credential evaluation" yields no fewer than 14 pages of search results. And with no national policy or regulation in the u.s. for foreign diploma equivalencies, it is important to take the proper steps to find the right credential evaluation agency. Following are a few tips to get started:

✳ Ask other higher education colleagues in your area. Find out which agency they use, what they like and dislike about that service or those services, and which one or ones they recommend. Keep in mind that colleges and universities in North America vary widely, so be sure to place the comments you receive from other institutions in the context of their particular type of institution. Your best recommendations will likely come from like institutions: similar size, type, rigor, governance (public or private), accreditation status, use of the internet as a mode of delivery of instruction, single- or multiple-campus, service to specific populations, and other distinguishing characteristics.

✳ Contact evaluation agencies directly.
   ◆ Try a cold call. How is their customer service?
   ◆ Ask for references or testimonials.
   ◆ Ask to see staff bios to determine what the backgrounds of the evaluators are. Have they ever worked at postsecondary institutions? Are they skilled at educational analysis and applied comparative education?

✳ A reputable foreign credential evaluation agency will:
   ◆ Employ principles of good practice. This means that they use standard resources, seek official, primary information whenever available, make consistent judgments, and treat applicants fairly and impartially;
   ◆ Provide clear, published (print or web) information about the services they offer;
   ◆ Charge reasonable fees. If in doubt, the internet can help with a simple survey of prices at some of the better-known agencies;
   ◆ Communicate clearly with applicants at all stages of the evaluation process;
   ◆ Employ experienced evaluators, and invest in ongoing training for these evaluators;
   ◆ Evaluate from documents (as opposed to translations, or from another agency's evaluation);
   ◆ Evaluate only reliable documents that can be verified;
   ◆ Take responsibility for evaluation decisions;
   ◆ Protect client privacy.

✳ Look for the answers to these questions:
   ◆ How long has the agency been in existence?
   ◆ What published information (print or web) is available about their services?
   ◆ What minimum hiring qualifications do they have for their evaluators (how long have the evaluators worked in the field of applied comparative education—foreign credential evaluation?)
   ◆ Do evaluators keep their skills current by attending training classes, workshops, and conferences?
   ◆ Are evaluators and the agency involved in professional associations? Associations sponsor and publish research, they articulate guidelines for best practice; they provide training and leadership. Some examples of professional associations include: AACRAO, AIEA (Association of International Education Administrators), AMIDEAST (America-Mideast Educational and

Training Services, Inc.), EAIE (European Association of International Education), NAFSA: Association of International Educators, International ACAC (formerly known as OACAC, TAICEP (The Association for International Credential Evaluation Professionals);

- Does the agency keep a library of both print and electronic or web resources on which their evaluations are based?

- What evaluation methodology does the agency use? Because applied comparative education is not an exact science, and because the process is not regulated, you may encounter a variety of ways that colleagues or agencies evaluate international credentials.

  - One simple quantitative method is known commonly as *year-counting*. An example of this is:

    A U.S. bachelor's degree usually consists of four years of postsecondary study. The bachelor's degree is studied after completing a twelve-year elementary-secondary sequence. If a foreign-educated student applied to your institution with a three-year bachelor's degree done after a twelve-year elementary-secondary sequence, you might say that the foreign bachelor's degree is not comparable to the U.S. bachelor's degree. 12+3 (foreign system) ≠ 12+4 (U.S. system).

  - Another evaluation method is referred to as *benchmarking*. An example of benchmarking is:

    A U.S. high school diploma requires twelve years of study. It is the credential that allows one to advance to the next level of study (post-secondary), and is hence known as a "benchmark." If a foreign-educated applicant applied for admission with a secondary school diploma earned after eleven years of study, you might say that, in spite of the fact that the eleven-year foreign curriculum is a year short of the twelve-year U.S. curriculum, it is still the benchmark credential in that student's country. It enables

him to advance to the next level of education. So you may consider the foreign secondary school diploma to be comparable to a U.S. high school diploma.

  - The fact is that U.S. foreign credential evaluation agencies, along with U.S. colleges and universities, employ both year-counting and benchmarking. Understanding the difference between the two can help you discern whether an agency produces evaluation reports that are a good match for your students and your institution.

- What documents are required to initiate an evaluation (*i.e.,* official, original, scanned, faxed)? How long and how are documents retained?

- What is their price, and what does that fee include (*i.e.,* a flat fee, or per school; course-by-course, grade average, catalog match)?

- What is their standard turnaround time? Do they offer expedited service, and if so, how much does it cost?

- How is document authenticity verified?

- Are translations required? What is the agency's policy on the acceptability of translations?

- How is the complete evaluation delivered—print or electronic, faxed, mailed, couriered, emailed, other method?

- Customer service: If you have questions or concerns, is there someone at the agency readily available to communicate with you?

Because there is no government oversight for the field of foreign credential evaluation, there is also no body that ensures consistency. Due to the wide breadth of U.S. higher education, and due to varied philosophies in applied comparative education, it is to be expected that two agencies may evaluate the same credential differently. For this reason it is important to pick a single agency that is a good fit with the institution and the admissions processes and stick with it. This will limit the possible conflicts that can arise if an institution gives their students a list of agencies to choose from. An institutional policy can be established as to how to handle students who have applied to your institution and have already had an evaluation done with a different agency. In that case, it should be considered whether the evaluation could be accepted, or whether the student would have to procure a second evaluation from an agency that is appropriate for the institution to which he or she is applying. This will depend in part on the institution's admission policies.

After doing research and tentatively choosing the evaluation agency that is the best match for the institution, it is important to recognize that this will be a two-way transaction. The agency may also make requests of the institution, such as:

✻ Designating one person as the liaison and recipient of completed evaluation reports;

✻ Providing information about the institution's file-processing procedures;

✻ Giving references or testimonials.

There are many advantages to outsourcing an institution's international credential evaluation, but it is imperative to do the proper research to choose an agency that fits well with the institution, to understand the product, and to assess it on an ongoing basis. Ultimately, one agency may be selected to do all of the foreign credential evaluations, some of the foreign credential evaluations, or simply on an as-needed basis. The ultimate goal is to assess and place students fairly and accurately, to ensure a successful experience for the students, the administrators and the faculty. Choosing an agency that works well and effectively, that is experienced, that can meet the institution's needs, and that does thorough, primary research and uses accepted resources will help to make the admissions process and the students successful.

TWENTY-FIVE

The Systematic Approach To Credential Evaluation and Its Challenges

2016 AACRAO INTERNATIONAL GUIDE

GEORGE F. KACENGA

Director of International Enrollment Management
University of Colorado Denver

The Systematic Approach To Credential Evaluation and Its Challenges

The value of accurate credential evaluation in international postsecondary student enrollment—a $30.5 billion global enterprise (NAFSA 2016)—cannot be overstated. On the whole, the U.S. federal government does not impose credential evaluation standards on institutions of higher learning (although encroachments on this front, like the College Scorecard recently announced by the White House, are not unheard of). Therefore, a foreign credential evaluator has autonomy to interpret a wide variety of educational systems from around the world. Because very few educational systems are structured similarly to the U.S. system, it is the credential evaluator's responsibility to consistently understand and translate foreign systems into familiar terms that allow faculty and staff across campus to act in the best interests of both student and institution.

Deep roots form the basis of the education system in the United States. These roots have resulted in a diversity and independence of institutions that constitute both the education system's greatest strength and weakness. Its strength is in allowing academic freedom, research, and diversity of thought and mission. Its weakness is in the U.S. Department of Education's inability to speak where a unified voice or U.S. support would be warranted or beneficial.

The liberal arts component common to most general education or core curricula at U.S. institutions is a remnant of the classical curriculum of England. The applied science tradition of Germany was grafted onto the curriculum in U.S. higher education in the 1800s as the US shifted from an agrarian to an industrial society. The English college tradition took root in the United States. The German university was accepted as a model to address growing needs on the frontier. Thus, in many ways the American university developed as a combination of the English college and German university traditions.

Overview of the U.S. Education System

ACCREDITATION

When one is part of an educational system, it is easy not to recognize the idiosyncrasies of that system; consequently, beginning credential evaluators do not always understand that the U.S. system of education is as complex as any other system they may come across. Other countries may have governmental ministries of education to determine the legitimacy of educational institutions, but in the U.S., institutional legitimacy is conferred by non-governmental accrediting bodies. Although external recognition of quality is not the intention of accreditation, it is often interpreted in this way. The U.S. accreditation process has self-regulation, self-study, and outside consultation to review consistency with the institution's stated mission at its core (Young, Chambers, and Kells 1983).

PRIMARY AND SECONDARY EDUCATION

Primary and secondary education take myriad forms in the U.S. Public education can include governance within local municipalities, charter schools, vocational training, online platforms, and overseas military schools. Private education includes elite options, day schools, and boarding schools with co-ed, single gender, and military prep options. Fee-paying parochial schools have similar structures to the elite schools, and there are a number of overseas independent and American schools. Homeschooling,

Christian, Jewish, and Islamic academies, and other religious schools may follow different patterns.

The typical patterns for primary and secondary school in the U.S. are 1 or 2 years of kindergarten, 6 years of primary school, 3 years of middle school, and 3 years of secondary schooling ((1–2)+6+3+3); or 1 or 2 years of kindergarten, 6 years of primary school, 2 years of middle school, and 4 years of secondary schooling ((1–2)+6+2+4). Other sequences exist depending on state and district regulations.

TERTIARY EDUCATION

In 1908, the Carnegie Foundation established the Carnegie Unit of credit still used by most U.S. institutions (Hollis 1938). Intended to create standardization in education, the Carnegie Unit became a loose scaffolding upon which the structure of quality instruction formed. This included aspects of contact hours, study hours, and lab hours per week and per semester for a typical course of study.

Quality in tertiary education has commonly been defined through the rigor of an institution's admissions process (secondary curriculum, grade point average, SAT/ACT results [entrance examinations], essay quality, letters of recommendation, etc.). This front-loaded determination of a tertiary educational institution's quality is beginning to shift to a back-loaded one, as more attention is focused on outcomes-based measures such as graduation rates, time for program completion, advancement to further study, career placement, experiential learning, and starting salaries.

The Systematic Approach to Credential Evaluation

EVOLUTION OF THE SYSTEMATIC APPROACH

The absence of a unitary governmental body that monitors and guides international credential evaluation has led professional organizations to create a systematic approach that can be employed by all institutions. A milestone event in this effort was the 1996 Milwaukee Symposium. Facilitated by the National Council on the

Evaluation of Foreign Educational Credentials, the Symposium honed the methodology for comparing U.S. and foreign education credentials, which was adopted by several professional organizations, each of which customized it in their own way. The participants and supporters of the Symposium were the American Association of Collegiate Registrars and Admissions Officers (AACRAO), Education Evaluators International, Education International, Educational Credential Evaluators, Inc. (ECE), Graduate Management Admissions Council (GMAC), Graduate Record Examination (GRE), International Education Research Foundation, Inc. (IERF), Josef Silny and Associates, Test of English as a Foreign Language (TOEFL), NAFSA: Association of International Educators, and World Education Services (WES).

Milwaukee Symposium recommendations formed the cornerstone of credential evaluation for many institutions and equipped institutional staff to make reasonable, informed placements of international applicants. Symposium recommendations also equipped academic institutions with the means to provide in-house evaluations when the cost (or need to pass an additional charge onto international applicants for an independent third-party evaluation) was acknowledged as a likely barrier to application completion and enrollment.

ELEMENTS OF THE SYSTEMATIC APPROACH

Student achievement is the driving consideration of the systematic approach to evaluating international student applications. A credential evaluator needs published information about the country or education system under review (in print or online), useful institutional contacts (e.g., Latin American Center, Asian Studies Center, etc.), colleagues in the field, professional conferences, and individual country files to capture miscellaneous information, case studies, and decisions. Maintenance of these contacts and resources yields a consistent interpretation of similar credentials over time. Establishing a consistent position for the academic institution—across colleges and departments—

is imperative for the admissions office and foreign credential evaluator to maintain integrity and to treat students fairly.

APPLICATION REQUIREMENTS

An international student's application should include: age, birthplace, citizenship status, an 'academic library' that includes the names of institutions attended/dates of enrollment/locations of institutions, and all diplomas received or in progress. The documentation supporting the student's academic background must be official and in the original language with a certified English translation.

Lists of all courses and grades for each year are required, sometimes referred to as a "grade report" or "statement of marks"; use of the term "transcript" alone can, in India for example, refer to a list of courses with prescribed contact hours but no evidence of performance in the courses.

If letters of recommendation are required in the application process, it is important to specify the source and the nature of the content desired in the letter. It is also important to understand that, for international students, access to an instructor or employer with English language proficiency may be extremely limited or unavailable, so methods to acquire a certified English language translation may be needed. Test scores required for admission need to be clearly articulated (*e.g.*, TOEFL, GRE, SAT, GMAT), with possible alternatives in the event of limited or unavailable testing. Many countries have national tests used for placement into higher education, which may allow insight into a student's aptitude and potential for success in the U.S. academic setting.

ESTABLISHING EDUCATIONAL CHRONOLOGY

The credential evaluator must review the educational systems of the countries in which applicants have obtained credentials. This can be both time-consuming and difficult if published information is scarce, which often is the case for credentials older than a decade.

Fortunately, the vast majority of credentials come from familiar systems.

The evaluator must then establish primary, secondary, and tertiary benchmarks and typical ages at entry and departure for each level. The age of an applicant should be identified at each level of schooling and then compared with the standard age of students at each academic level and when diplomas should have been awarded (Fletcher and Aldrich-Langen 1998).

One year in another education system is generally viewed as comparable to one year in the U.S. This guiding principle is particularly useful when foreign transcripts capture academic performance in terms of hours, outcomes, or a system of credits that varies from the U.S. Carnegie Unit system. Education maps (see Figure 25.1, on page 260) are a convenient way for evaluators to visualize educational chronology (Snyder and Hoffman 2000, 7).

Gaps, detours, parallel programs, or failures must be accounted for in the educational chronology. At times, failures may not appear on consolidated transcripts and may not be factored into the final grade point average (GPA). Each institution should determine how to handle this to ensure consistency. Some may accept the highest possible GPA as reported, while others may factor in past failures to better assess a student's likelihood of success. Further, what may appear as a suspiciously extraordinary accomplishment may have been duly achieved through summer school, above-average course enrollment, or a special program; these modalities of finishing a degree should not be discounted (Fletcher and Aldrich-Langen 1998).

Poor translations can mistakenly convey a wildly different interpretation than what a credential records in the original language, so knowing the educational nomenclature of the home country is important for recognizing such errors. For example, it is not unheard of in the credential evaluation mythos for new credential evaluators to inaccurately translate the French secondary diploma, the *baccalauréat*, as a bachelor's degree and place a student well past her/his current academic

FIGURE 25.1

Education Map

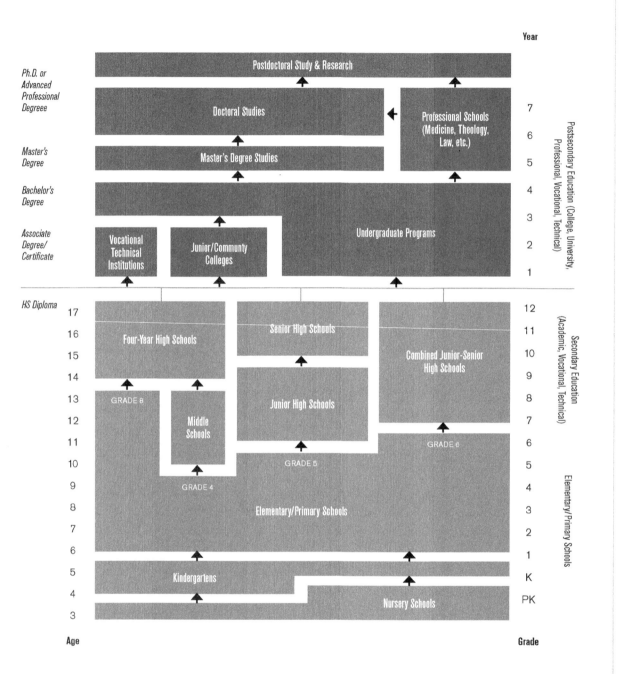

achievement (Assefa 1988). A survey of age, an education map, and original language documents helps evaluators avoid such mishaps.

OFFICIAL ACADEMIC RECORDS

Official academic records are least likely to have been tampered with by the student or third party, but in many countries a student will receive only one official transcript and diploma, so there is justifiable concern about mailing it overseas at the request of an admission officer. Certified copies can be accepted. They will bear an original seal and signature of the institution or examining body. Notary verifications are not reliable. The institution evaluator may also choose to review unofficial records but require that original records be presented at orientation or during the first semester (this remains a controversial approach). In these instances, a hold is usually applied to the student's account to prevent further registration until official records have been provided. In some instances, the applicant may claim that records are unavailable, but this is rarely the case—more likely, it simply is inconvenient for the applicant to acquire certified copies or official documents, especially when outside the home country and relying on friends or family to assist. If documents genuinely are unavailable, such as may be the case for refugees, after an academic institution is closed, or where there is current geopolitical unrest, an evaluator should pursue documentation of the reason from the student, a Ministry of Education official, or an EducationUSA representative and convene a special committee to determine next steps on a case-by-case basis.

ESTABLISHING TYPES OF EDUCATION PROGRAMS AND GRADING SCALES

Once an official record is submitted, the type of education program (*e.g.*, academic, vocational) must be noted. In addition, the evaluator must determine (a) if the program was actually completed or (b) if not completed, how far from completion it was. At this point, the evaluator should consider what academic program the student would qualify for in the home country and establish the quality of that program. Therefore, the evaluator must possess knowledge of the home country's educational system and its selectivity at the secondary and postsecondary levels.

Knowing the grading scale that is being used is important. For example, the typical grading scale for French documents is 1 to 20, with 20 serving as the high mark. The French grading system is severe and a grade of 19 or 20 is rarely awarded. Marks of 14 to 16 are typical for high achievers (Assefa 1988). Obtaining a school profile issued by the school with the credential that shows grade distribution and marks of the highest ranked student lends additional perspective. Keeping internal records and consulting colleagues familiar with the education system under review (*e.g.*, EducationUSA offices) helps to identify variations among schools in the country.

MAKING A PLACEMENT RECOMMENDATION

Armed with a full understanding of the academic history of the applicant, based on an official academic record in the original language together with a certified English translation, the evaluator needs to assess the quantity and quality of the student's achievement and make a placement recommendation. Decisions should maximize the student's chances of success at a U.S. institution while being consistent with both the treatment of U.S. students and other students from the same country and/or type of educational system.

Challenges Associated with the Systematic Approach to Credential Evaluation

FRAUDULENT DOCUMENTS[30]

Authenticity is paramount in the credential evaluation process. The most authentic document is an official transcript validated by the signature of the official academic records officer with the seal of the institution mailed directly in a sealed institutional envelope. Other letters of certification issued directly by the records officer (and validated) are also relatively secure. Most records that may have been in students' hands, such as copies of transcripts or letters, grade reports, diplomas, or graduation lists, are not official (World Education Services 2004). A growing trend is for registrars to employ third-parties such as Naviance or Parchment to

---

[30] For more on this topic, *see* Chapter 19: Fighting Fraud in the Admissions and Registrar's Offices.

distribute official records electronically. These, too, are acceptable.

When suspicious about the authenticity of a document, the evaluator can take several measures: a call or email to the issuing institution to verify dates of attendance, degrees granted, and/or honors received; and/or writing for more details or returning the actual document (or a copy) to the issuing institution for verification. The response rate may be low. Many evaluators will interview an applicant and, when a document other than an official transcript is submitted, ask the applicant to request that an official grade report be sent directly to the admissions office.

Pressure to compromise established policies often accompanies approaching deadlines. For example, when enrollment is low and there is a need to fill seats. The credential evaluator should proactively adopt official positions on these matters well in advance to forestall compromising the institution's integrity.

There are a number of questions to ask when assessing a grade report for authenticity:

* Did the grade report arrive directly from the records officer? Was it in a sealed envelope with institutional postage?
* Is the postage from the correct country of origin?
* Does the grade report contain the signature of the registrar and the institutional seal?
* Is the date of issue recent?
* Does the grade report have format consistency with grade reports previously received from the issuing institution?
* Do the official application documents align with the timeline and accomplishments as outlined on the applicant's résumé?

Several professional organizations monitor trends in foreign credential evaluation. Some governments, including China, have developed clearinghouses like the *China Academic Degrees and Graduate Education Development Center* (CDGDC) to address the concern

within the global academic community concerning instances of applicant fraud.

If a fraudulent document has been received, the institution inferred should be notified and the original or copy of the document returned. It is important to report the case to the primary credential evaluator on campus and possibly the university legal counsel, depending upon the circumstances.

As part of the evaluation process, the issuing institution must also be authenticated. The proliferation of diploma mills makes it important to verify institutions with local ministries of education. This can be done easily in many cases through online resources. Some sites try to aggregate this information, such as the *International Association of Universities' Worldwide Database of Higher Education Institutions, Systems and Credentials*, but finding the primary source for each country is preferred as these aggregate sites can be outdated.

DETERMINING ENGLISH LANGUAGE PROFICIENCY POLICY

Developing an English language proficiency (ELP) policy is not an essential part of in-house foreign credential evaluation, but enforcement of the campus policy often is. Waivers of the ELP policy are sometimes based upon an applicant's citizenship, native languages, or the language used by the institutions in which the applicant was educated.

Satisfying the ELP policy is commonly achieved by requiring a third-party administered examination of academic English or by using the institution's own intensive English program (IEP) to establish a local quality assurance measure. The minimum scores are usually commensurate with the level of English instruction available to support the international students.

There is no one-size-fits-all ELP policy. Most successful policies have established benchmarks, with the opportunity for a case-by-case review for exceptions. Voluminous exception requests can warrant revision of the base policy.

DEALING WITH PERCEPTIONS OF ARBITRARINESS

Two independent, experienced foreign credential evaluators can reach different conclusions when evaluating a foreign educational credential. From the 1950s through the 1980s, leaders in the profession worked to establish placement recommendations. During the past thirty years, the trend has been to equip academic institutions with the information necessary to make their own informed decisions. This trend benefits both institutions and students, but it may produce a perception of arbitrariness when all someone wants is "the answer." One-person offices, new or untrained credential evaluators, and uninformed leaders may find themselves in a real quandary when a quick answer is required. For this reason, every campus must develop competent in-house credential evaluation resources. Professional conferences, webinars, newsletters, web forums, and networking are good places to start for any in-house credential evaluator.

Resources include but are not limited to:

* *AACRAO Transcript* eNewsletter
* Education Credential Evaluators: *The Connection*
* EducationUSA
* *ICEF Monitor*
* IERF 'Index' Publications
* NAFSA IEM KC ACE Subcommittee newsletter
* *NAFSA Newsletter*
* Private provider newsletters
* *The Chronicle: Weekly Briefing*
* *The PIE Weekly*
* World Education Services: *World Education News & Reviews*

Conclusion

The U.S. educational system today is a global enterprise broader than its founders could ever have envisioned. Whether the impetus for students to seek an overseas education is an aspiration for education for the sake of self-realization, the pragmatic pursuit of money or employment, or a combination of these, the influx of applications for admission from foreign educated applicants in recent decades necessitated a systematic approach to foreign academic credential evaluation. This approach yields consistent interpretation of international credentials, fair and timely access to programs, eligibility for financial aid and scholarship, and promotion of the reputation of U.S. higher education.

The U.S. higher education system increasingly enjoys the benefits of growing international student enrollment which leads to student diversity, new ideas in the classroom and laboratory, filling vacancies caused by fluctuating domestic enrollment, and increased tuition revenue because international students sometimes pay more than double the rate of in-state students. To remain attractive to students around the world, and to treat them fairly throughout the application process, it is incumbent on today's postsecondary institutions throughout the U.S. to gain the competency necessary to execute fair, consistent evaluations that best serve their institutions and international students.

TWENTY-SIX

Vocational Education in Foreign Education Systems:

An Overview of Selected Pathways

2016 AACRAO INTERNATIONAL GUIDE

ANATOLY TEMKIN | Chairman, Department of Computer Science
Boston University Metropolitan College

ALEXANDER CHUCKLIN | Evaluator/Translator, General Manager
North American Educational Group

Vocational Education in Foreign Education Systems: An Overview of Selected Pathways

This compilation will examine some learning programs within further education, adult education, and professional education sectors. These are non-standard study programs compared to established and widely-implemented higher education systems (bachelor's, master's, and Ph.D. schedule). This selection has an explicit emphasis on professional associations, memberships, and qualifications related to acquisition of a dedicated set of skills for a job-specific area.

Compared to traditional higher education study there may be noticeable differences in program content, delivery methods, and practical components; however, the long-existing differentiation between vocational (professional in nature) and strictly academic education is fading considerably. Employers have realized some of the intrinsic benefits of incorporating vocational training within a traditional academic program syllabus. As a result, universities have integrated vocational and general education elements more than ever before and used apprenticeships to provide valuable on-the-job experience (Kogan Page Ltd. 2014).

The following discussion begins by defining the key characteristics of credentials in question, the same mechanism for establishing comparability of any foreign academic credential. These include admission requirements, program content, qualification awarded, and access to the next level. To implement proper placement of students who are transferring to U.S. institutions, two major questions must be answered: Where does the credential fit in its country of origin's educational system? And, where does the credential fit in the U.S. academic credential ladder?

A Basic Evaluation Methodology

The following list shows the basic steps of the credential evaluation process. The method begins with a review of the program(s) of study in question, to referencing to an existing benchmark(s), and establishing a comparability/equivalence.

* Education completed
* Institutions attended
* Study (program) content
* Components to be measured with benchmark credential using key credential profiles
* Council placement recommendations, application rationale
* Comparability/equivalence

Selected credentials from various areas of the world will be reviewed in order to provide a broad sample of vocational credentials and their placement in the U.S. academic credential ladder.

Selected Credentials from the United Kingdom, Jamaica, Sierra Leone, and India

"Today, certain types of external qualification cross the boundaries between further and higher education. Several higher education institutions (HEIs)—particularly those that gained university status in the 1990s and in 2005—deliver advanced professional qualifications and higher national diplomas or certificates from awarding bodies. At the same time there has been a significant shift towards further education (FE's) involvement in delivery of these types of qualification, and a greater input from private sector colleges" (Kogan Page Ltd. 2014, 3).

267

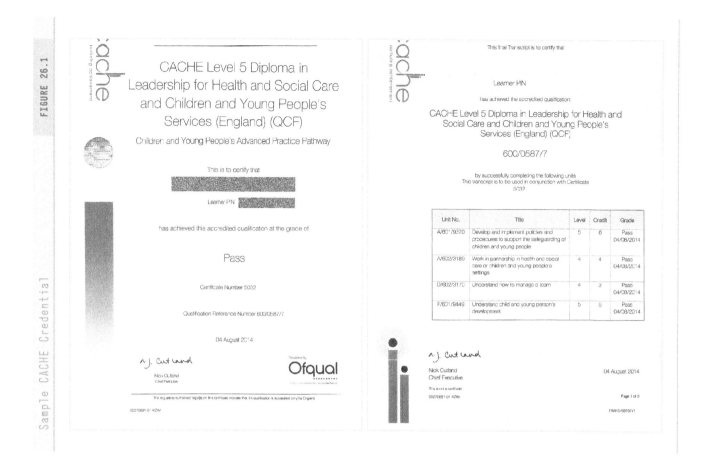

Note: Jamaica, Sierra Leone and India all have Anglophone education systems that were established during the time of colonization. These are still being linked to the UK education system and its development.

United Kingdom

EXAMPLES OF VOCATIONAL CREDENTIALS

✳ Level 5 Diploma in Leadership for Health and Social Care and Children and Young People's Services, issued by the Council for Awards in Care, Health, and Education (CACHE). Study is attended at Blackburn College, UK on a part-time basis (adult education) and consists of mandatory and optional units at Level 4 and 5 that have their own credit value. (*See* Figure 26.1.)

✳ National Vocational Qualification (NVQ) Level 3, issued by the Qualification and Curriculum Authority (QCA), Northern Ireland Council for the Curriculum, Examinations and Assessment (CCEA), CACHE. Study is attended at Blackburn College, UK. All qualifications are set at a level, from Entry to Degree. This study precedes Level 5 Diploma program and covers the first part (Level 1, 2, and 3) in order to progress to a Diploma study program. (*See* Figure 26.2.)

✳ Diploma in Brewing, formerly known as Associate Membership of the Institute of Brewing and Distilling, is issued by the Institute of Brewing, with Certificates in Modules 1, 2, and 3. This credential is a measure of the candidates' theoretical knowledge of brewing science and technology. There is neither educational qualification nor work experience specified for sitting the Associate Membership examinations. Modularization of the syllabus and examinations is designed to allow for a wide range of candidates' scientific background. (*See* Figure 26.3.)

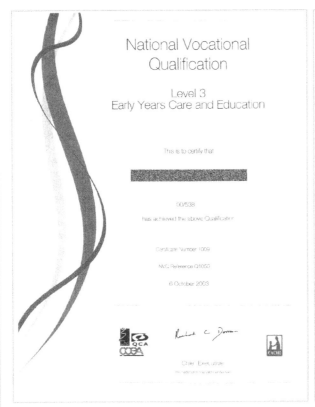

National Vocational Qualification in Early Years Care and Education

Unit Code	Title	Number
97/C2	Provide for children's physical needs	U1028666
97/C3	Promote the physical development of children	U1028669
97/C5	Promote children's social and emotional development	U1028670
97/C7	Provide a framework for the management of behaviour	U1028671
97/C10	Promote children's sensory and intellectual development	U1028672
97/C11	Promote children's language and communication development	U1028673
97/C15	Contribute to the protection of children from abuse	U1028674
97/C16	Observe and assess the development and behaviour of children	U1028675
97/E3	Plan and equip environments for children	U1028676
97/M7	Plan, implement and evaluate learning activities and experiences	U1028677
97/P2	Establish and maintain relationships with parents	U1028678
97/C14	Care for and promote the development of babies	U1028679
97/M2	Manage admissions, finance and operating systems in care and educational settings	U1028684
97/P8	Establish and maintain a child care and education service	U1028689

NVQ Reference:
The code is allocated by QCA once an NVQ has officially been accredited. It provides a unique and unchanging reference. QCA references are allocated to all qualifications and units on the National Database. This qualification was accredited by QCA for use from February 1998.

GN793/1/12353

FIGURE 26.2   Sample NVQ Credential

AWARDING BODIES

The following awarding bodies provide qualifications for continuing, secondary, and vocational education.

The Council for Awards in Care, Health, and Education (CACHE) is an awarding organization for the Care and Education Sector established in 1945 by the Ministry of Health as the National Nursery Examination Board. Its qualifications are used by over 1,000 colleges and training providers in the U.K. and abroad (Margolis 1991). They are awarded at several levels from pre-vocational level on up (Kogan Page Ltd. 2014).

The Qualifications and Credit Framework (QCF)/ National Vocational Qualification (NVQ) reflect the skills, knowledge, and understanding a student possesses in relation to a specific area of work. Certificates are awarded for successful performance demonstrated through a variety of academic and practical assessment procedures. As of 2011 the QCF replaced the National Qualifications Framework (NQF); it is now the national credit transfer system for education qualification.

STUDY

CACHE offers QCF qualifications and units from entry level to Level 4. Each unit and qualification has its own credit value which indicates how long it could take on average for a learner to complete. One credit represents approximately ten hours of learning time. Students can build up their units at their own pace and put them towards a full qualification.

Associate Membership at the Institute of Brewing and Distilling (IBD), London, (now called "Diploma in Brewing") represents a job-specific vocational qualification. It is awarded after completion of IBD Module III examinations and recognized as being equivalent to a NVQ Level III vocational qualification awarded by professional bodies in the U.K.

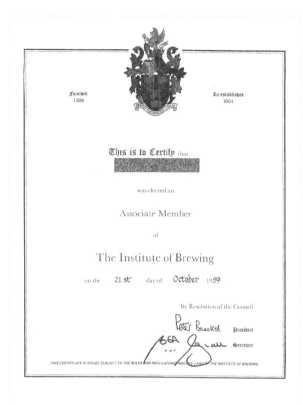

STRUCTURE

As of October 2015, the types of qualifications awarded by education institutions at sub-degree, undergraduate (first cycle), and postgraduate level (second and third cycles) are described in the Regulated Qualifications Framework (RQF). It is important to note that the RQF uses the same levels that were used previously with Entry 1–3 and Levels 1–8. The RQF includes the Framework for Higher Education Qualifications (FHEQ) for England, Wales and Northern Ireland and the European Qualifications Framework (EQF—not covered in this publication).

Table 26.1 represents a list of newly accredited qualification levels in relation to the previous qualification.

GRADING

The grading system used in some qualifications is *distinction credit/merit* or simply *pass*. However, certificates are increasingly issued on the basis of acquisition of skills or knowledge for particular competencies (Margolis 1991; Kogan Page Ltd. 2014).

In the QCF framework every unit and qualification has a credit value, where one credit represents 10 hours of learning time.

COMPARABILITY/EQUIVALENCE

Level 5 Diploma from CACHE represent no less than four years of postsecondary professional education. In accordance with the British QCF/NVQ qualification

TABLE 26.1: U.K. Accredited Qualification Levels

Level	Regulated Qualifications Framework (RQF) examples	Framework for Higher Education Qualifications (FHEQ) Examples
Entry	▸ Entry level certificate ▸ Entry level Skills for Life ▸ Entry level award, certificate and diploma ▸ Entry level Functional Skills ▸ Entry level Foundation Learning	—
1	▸ GCSE (grades D-G) ▸ Key Skills level 1 ▸ NVQ level 1 ▸ Skills for Life level 1 ▸ Foundation diploma ▸ BTEC award, certificate and diploma level 1 ▸ Foundation Learning level 1 ▸ Functional Skills level 1 ▸ Cambridge National level 1	—
2	▸ GCSE (grades A*-C) ▸ Key Skills level 2 ▸ NVQ level 2 ▸ Skills for Life level 2 ▸ Higher diploma ▸ BTEC award, certificate and diploma level 2 ▸ Functional Skills level 2 ▸ Cambridge National level 2 ▸ Cambridge Technical level 2	—
3	▸ AS and A level ▸ Advanced Extension Award ▸ Cambridge International award ▸ International Baccalaureate ▸ Key Skills level 3 ▸ NVQ level 3 ▸ Advanced diploma ▸ Progression diploma ▸ BTEC award, certificate and diploma level 3 ▸ BTEC National ▸ Cambridge Technical level 3	—
4	▸ Certificate of higher education ▸ Key Skills level 4 ▸ NVQ level 4 ▸ BTEC Professional award, certificate and diploma level 4	▸ Certificate of higher education ▸ HNC
5	▸ HND ▸ NVQ level 4 ▸ Higher diploma ▸ BTEC Professional award, certificate and diploma level 5 ▸ HNC ▸ Higher National Diploma	▸ Diploma of higher education ▸ Diploma of further education ▸ Foundation degree ▸ Higher National Diploma
6	▸ NVQ level 4 ▸ BTEC Advanced Professional award, certificate and diploma level 6	▸ Bachelor's degree ▸ Graduate certificate ▸ Graduate diploma
7	▸ BTEC Advanced Professional award, certificate and diploma level 7 ▸ Fellowship and fellowship diploma ▸ Postgraduate certificate ▸ Postgraduate diploma ▸ NVQ level 5 ▸ BTEC Advanced Professional award, certificate and diploma level 7	▸ Master's degree ▸ Postgraduate certificate ▸ Postgraduate diploma
8	▸ NVQs level 5 ▸ Vocational qualifications level 8	

award system this level of study is equivalent with a bachelor's degree, or a Higher National Diploma level award in FHEQ system. This credential may be regarded as comparable with U.S. Bachelor of Science level degree.

Diploma in Brewing is a measure of the candidates' theoretical knowledge of brewing science and technology, which may be regarded as comparable with a vocational postsecondary qualification offered at a U.S. community college or vocational/technical institution.

Jamaica and Sierra Leone

EXAMPLES OF VOCATIONAL CREDENTIALS

✳ Certificate of Association Membership issued by the Association of Chartered Certified Accountants (ACCA). Individuals prepare for the qualifying examinations in various ways. Level 1 and Level 2 Examinations may be internally or externally examined. Full-time coursework for all three of the association's examinations normally take three years. Part-time, evening, or correspondence courses usually take a minimum of five years.

✳ Transcript issued by the Association of Accounting Technicians, London, United Kingdom

✳ Certificate of Membership issued by the Institute of Chartered Accountants, Sierra Leone. All studies/examinations are attended locally at The Institute of Chartered Accountants Sierra Leone (ICASL).

✳ Certificate Stage Examinations Result confirming successful completion of Level 1 Preliminary and Level 2 Professional ACCA Examinations issued by the Association of Chartered Certified Accountants (ACCA), Completion of Levels 1 and 2 allows for the award of a BSc (Hons) in Applied Accountancy from Oxford Brookes University.

(*See* Figure 26.4, on page 273, and Figure 26.5, on page 274, for sample credentials and certificates.)

AWARDING BODIES

The Association of Chartered Certified Accountants (ACCA), Glasgow, United Kingdom, was founded in

1904. As one of the professional accounting bodies in the U.K., the ACCA has contributed to the training and development of services in the field of accounting, providing a route to qualification as a certified accountant. It consists of 320,000 members and students in 170 countries. It is one of the six member bodies of the Consultative Committee of Accountancy Bodies (CCAB) and a member of the International Federation of Accountants (IFAC) in the United Kingdom.

The Association of Accounting Technicians (ATT), London, United Kingdom, was founded in 1980 in the U.K. ATT is one of the largest dedicated bodies for qualified accounting technicians, located in London and with branches all over the world. ATT provides professional recognition for support staff working in accounting and finance with qualified accountants (PNAs, CPAs, and CAs). These accounting qualifications are at a technician rather than professional level. Their enrollment is approximately 100,000 worldwide.

The Institute of Chartered Accountants of Sierra Leone (ICASL) is a professional accountancy body.

STUDY

The three levels of examinations offered by ACCA are Level 1 Preliminary Examination, Level 2 Professional Examination, and Level 3 Final Examination. The lower level examination must be completed before the next level is attempted. Exemptions may be granted in Level 1 and Level 2, based on degrees in accounting or equivalent qualifications. No exemptions are given to the Level 3 Final Examinations. All papers for Level 3 must be attempted at one sitting.

Level 1 Preliminary contains five sections: accounting, cost and management accounting I, economics, law, and business mathematics.

Level 2 Professional includes nine sections: auditing, company law, taxation, cost and management accounting II, quantitative analysis, information systems in development and operation, the regulatory framework of accounting, advanced accounting practice (a two-part paper), and one from the following: executorships

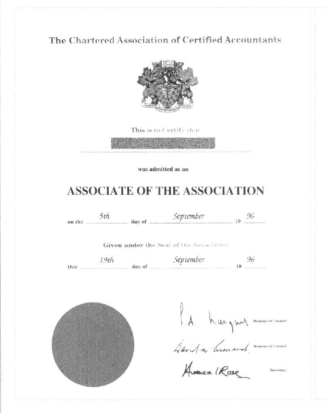

and trust law and accounts; organization and management managerial economics; U.K. public sector financial management; and insolvency.

Level 3 Final has four sections: advanced financial accounting, financial management, advanced taxation, and auditing and investigations.

Individuals may prepare for the ACCA qualifying examinations in various ways. Full-time courses are offered at colleges and polytechnics for the Level 1 and Level 2 Examinations, and these may be internally or externally examined. Full-time courses for all three of the Association's examinations normally take three years (Margolis 1991; UCAS 2004; Kogan Page Ltd. 2014; Wang and Dupigy 2004).

General note: The accounting profession is not regulated. Membership in a professional accounting body is not a license to practice, but an indicator that the standards of education and training have been met.

GRADING

Merit = A; Distinction = B+; Credit Pass = B; Pass = C; Fail = F

COMPARABILITY/EQUIVALENCE

Academic records represent three years (full-time basis) of progress in a professional qualification study program. Graduation from this program gives access to certification and professional employment. The completed academic coursework may be identified as equivalent to the completion of an undergraduate program in Accounting (three years).

Professional Membership with the Association of Chartered Certified Accountants represents three years of professional study (upper and graduate levels). In the U.K. this qualification level is considered to be equivalent to a master's degree. This is a professional qualification which provides access to professional employment in Sierra Leone. Completion of this study program

FIGURE 26.5

Member

This is to certify that

was admitted a Member of the Association
on 30 April 2010

Given under the Seal of the Association
on 12 June 2010

President   Deputy President   Secretary

Association of Chartered Certified Accountants

0753696   00802713

Examination History Details		Relevant Dates:
Name:		Registration Date: 25th April 2001
Registration Number: 0753696		Passes Date: 8th August 2008
Date: 15th August 2013		Associate Date: 30th April 2010

Syllabus December 2001 - June 2007

Paper		Result	Mark	Exam Session
1.1GBR	Preparing Financial Statements	Pass	58	December 2001
1.2	Financial Information for Management	Pass	51	December 2001
1.3	Managing People	Pass	56	December 2001
2.1	Information Systems	Pass	55	June 2002
2.2ENG	Corporate and Business Law	Pass	62	June 2002
2.3GBR	Business Taxation	Pass	50	June 2002
2.4	Financial Management and Control	Pass	50	December 2002
2.5GBR	Financial Reporting	Pass	59	December 2002
2.6GBR	Audit and Internal Review	Pass	53	December 2002
3.3	Performance Management	Pass	56	June 2003
3.4	Business Information Management	Pass	50	December 2005

Syllabus December 2007

Paper		Result	Mark	Exam Session
F1	Accountant in Business	Conv. Pass		June 2007
F2	Management Accounting	Conv. Pass		June 2007
F3UK	Financial Accounting	Conv. Pass		June 2007
F4ENG	Corporate and Business Law	Conv. Pass		June 2007
F5	Performance Management	Conv. Pass		June 2007
F6UK	Taxation	Conv. Pass		June 2007
F7UK	Financial Reporting	Conv. Pass		June 2007
F8UK	Audit and Assurance	Conv. Pass		June 2007
F9	Financial Management	Conv. Pass		June 2007
P1	Governance, Risk and Ethics	Pass	54	June 2008
P2INT	Corporate Reporting	Pass	57	June 2008
P3	Business Analysis	Pass	51	June 2008
P5	Advanced Performance Management	Conv. Pass		June 2007
OPTENG	Business Information Management Option	Conv. Pass		June 2007

The Association of Chartered Certified Accountants
2 Central Quay 89 Hydepark Street Glasgow G3 8BW UK
Tel +44 (0)141 582 2000 Fax +44 (0)141 582 2222
www.accaglobal.com

The Institute of Chartered Accountants of Sierra Leone
Private Mail Bag 832, Freetown, Sierra Leone
86 Siaka Stevens Street 3rd Floor Sierra Leone
Tel +232 22 228116 Fax +232 22 228146

Professional Part 1

This is to certify that

completed Professional Part 1 of the
ACCA examinations in December 2001

The subjects covered were:

1.1	Preparing Financial Statements	Pass
1.2	Financial Information for Management	Pass
1.3	Managing People	Pass

0753696

**THE ASSOCIATION OF CHARTERED CERTIFIED ACCOUNTANTS
THE INSTITUTE OF CHARTERED ACCOUNTANTS OF SIERRA LEONE**

Professional Part 2

This is to certify that

completed Professional Part 2 of the
ACCA examinations in December 2003

The subjects covered were:

2.1	Information Systems	Pass
2.2	Corporate and Business Law	Pass
2.3	Business Taxation	Pass
2.4	Financial Management and Control	Pass
2.5	Financial Reporting	Pass
2.6	Audit and Internal Review	Pass

0753696   1203621/2963/1482

**THE ASSOCIATION OF CHARTERED CERTIFIED ACCOUNTANTS
THE INSTITUTE OF CHARTERED ACCOUNTANTS OF SIERRA LEONE**

Sample ACCA/ICASL Credential

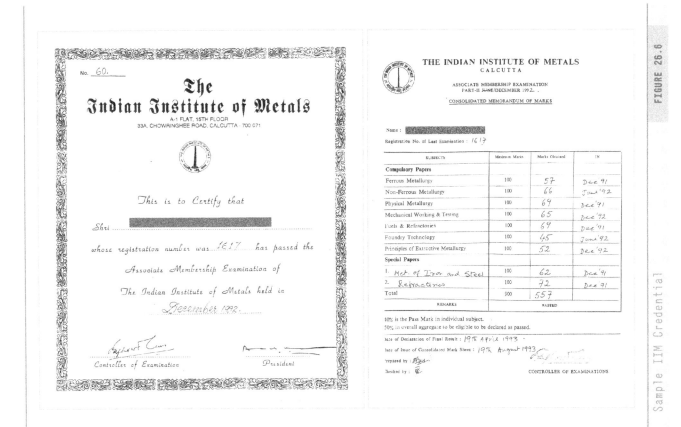

FIGURE 26.6

Sample IIM Credential

may be regarded as comparable with completion of Bachelor and Master of Science degree programs (specializing in accounting).

India

EXAMPLES OF VOCATIONAL CREDENTIALS

❋ Associate Membership Examination (Certificate of Completion) issued by The Indian Institute of Metals (IIM), Calcutta, India. Courses are taken at participating institutions. (*See* Figure 26.6.)

❋ Associate Membership issued by the Institution of Electronics and Telecommunication Engineers (IETE), India. (*See* Figure 26.7.)

❋ Intermediate Examination Certificate and Final Examination Certificate issued by the Institute of Chartered Accountants of India (ICAI). For Intermediate Examination: six papers are required including courses in Advanced Accounting, Business Law,

Data Management. For Final Examination: eight papers are required including various courses in Advanced Accounting, Business Law, Data Management, Taxation. Each paper includes a 3 hour exam. (*See* Figure 26.8, on page 277.)

AWARDING BODIES

The Indian Institute of Metals, Kolkata was founded in 1946. It is the professional society of metallurgical engineers.

The Institution of Electronics and Telecommunication Engineers (IETE) was founded in 1953. IETE publishes nearly 50 percent of India's technical papers in related areas and facilitates the acquiring of engineering degree/diploma equivalent qualifications. The institution is under the supervision of the DOEACC (Department of Electronics Accreditation of Computer Courses) and approved by the All India Council for

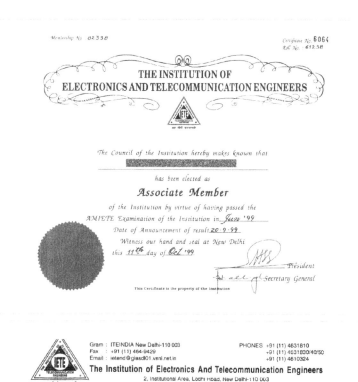

Technical Education (AICTE) responsible for the development and standards of technical education system in India (Sweeney 1997).

The Institute of Chartered Accountants of India (ICAI) was founded in 1949. ICAI conducts a pre-professional foundation course and the professional course of Chartered Accountancy, coordinates the required practical training, and holds qualifying examinations (Sweeney 1997).

STUDY

Graduates/associate members of the Indian Institute of Metals are recognized by the Union Public Service Commission as having the same academic qualification as the Bachelor of Engineering in Metallurgical Engineering (Sweeney 1997).

The Associate Membership Examination (formerly called Graduateship Examination) issued by the IETE includes two Sections (A and B) each of which has two parts (Part I and Part II); all subjects in Section A and all subjects in Part I of Section B are compulsory (Sweeney 1997).

Part II of Section B is divided into Group I, II, and III (choice of one Group required and three elective subjects within that Group required) (Sweeney 1997).

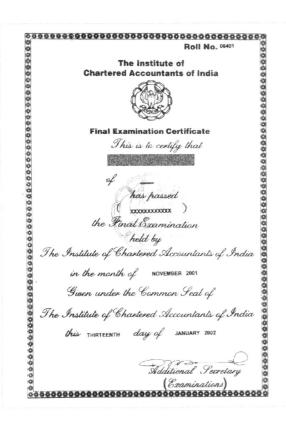

FIGURE 26.8 Sample ICAI Credential

Chartered Accountant Designation in the ICAI is awarded to members (either Associate or Fellow) of the Institute who wish to practice as Chartered Accountants. Associate Member/A.C.A. is awarded to a person who has served under a practicing chartered accountant for the prescribed period and has passed the Institute's Final Examination. Fellow Member/F.C.A. is awarded to a person who has been an associate member and has been in continuous practice for at least five years (Sweeney 1997).

RECOGNITION IN INDIA
Final Examination recognized by the Association of Indian Universities (AIU) as the equivalent of an Indian master's degree for higher studies if a bachelor's degree has been obtained first. At least 39 universities and the Indian Institutes of Management (Ahmedabad and Calcutta) recognize the associate membership for admission to the Ph.D. degree program (Fellow Program at the LIMs) for which a M.Com. or M.B.A. degree is the usual prerequisite (Sweeney 1997).

GRADING
Grading is on the basis of a maximum of 100 marks for each subject on the examination. For a pass the candidate is required to obtain a minimum of 35% (varies up to 50%) of marks in each course.

COMPARABILITY/EQUIVALENCE
Associate membership from The Indian Institute of Metals represents the equivalent of a four-year university-level technical education. It requires completion of undergraduate level academic courses as well as relevant practical experience and provides access to graduate training in India and professional employment. The coursework completed may be considered comparable

with a U.S. Bachelor of Science degree program (Metallurgical Engineering concentration).

Associate membership from the Institution of Electronics and Telecommunication Engineers (IETE) represents the equivalent of a four-year university-level technical education. The cumulative coursework completed in this program may be considered comparable with completion of a U.S. Bachelor of Science degree program (Electronic and Telecommunication Technology concentration).

Intermediate and Final Examination Certificates from Institute of Chartered Accountants of India (ICAI) represent additional upper-level undergraduate education and provide access to further tertiary training in India. The completed coursework may be compared with completion of undergraduate study program (concentration in Economics/Accounting).

TWENTY-SEVEN

AACRAO EDGE:

History, Development, and Future

JOHNNY JOHNSON
Director of International Programs and Professor Emeritus
Monterey Peninsula College

ROBERT WATKINS
Assistant Director of Admissions
The University of Texas at Austin

GLORIA NATHANSON
Associate Director, Undergraduate Admissions
University of California Los Angeles (retired)

WILLIAM J. PAVER
Assistant Dean of Graduate Studies
The University of Texas at Austin (retired)

AACRAO EDGE: History, Development, and Future

The AACRAO Electronic Database for Global Education (AACRAO EDGE) is a project designed to provide contemporary and ongoing information and standards for the evaluation of foreign credentials. It serves applicants seeking to be admitted to educational institutions in the United States, as well as individuals presenting foreign credentials for employment, professional licensure, and immigration.

History and Development of EDGE

In 2002, the joint agreement between NAFSA and AACRAO regarding research and development of international publications was dissolved. The inter-associational committee, known as PIER (Projects for International Education Research) was accordingly disbanded. The inter-associational committee which reviewed placement recommendations for PIER publications, the National Council on the Evaluation of Foreign Educational Credentials (The Council) continued to function.

In response to the recognized needs for international publications by AACRAO members, the 2001 Board of Directors established a new committee, the International Publications Advisory Committee (IPAC). At the same time, there were questions regarding the viability of the continuation of the inter-associational Council. In response to this concern, the AACRAO Board also established the International Evaluation Standards Council (IESC). Members were not appointed to the IESC at that time with the understanding that it would be available in case of the demise of The Council. The Council was disbanded in 2006.

The EDGE project began in 2004 and was completed in 2009. The software development for EDGE was overseen by Bill Paver, University of Texas at Austin (retired) with funding from the Paver Family Foundation. Initial EDGE team members met frequently and developed the initial guidelines for authors, created early country profiles, reviewed and approved the earliest placement recommendations, and developed the EDGE user's manual. The developing team consisted of:

* Mary Baxton, California State University, Northridge
* Dale Gough, Director, AACRAO International Education Services
* Johnny Johnson, Monterey Peninsula College
* Gloria Nathanson, University of California Los Angeles
* Bill Paver, University of Texas-Austin (retired)
* Robert Watkins, University of Texas-Austin

Authors of the country profiles were recruited among the many experts in international evaluation throughout the U.S. The developers of EDGE proposed a team of experts be appointed to review and validate the placement recommendations. In 2009, an EDGE review team was selected based on knowledge of the field, commitment to international educational exchange, proven leadership and participation at all levels of activity in the field, and seniority. The review team consisted of:

* Karlene Dickey, Stanford University (retired)
* David Horner, Michigan State University (retired) and former NAFSA President
* Cliff Sjogren, University of Michigan and the University of Southern California (retired) and former Interim AACRAO Executive Director

✳ Leo Sweeney, University of Missouri, Kansas City (retired) and former AACRAO President and NAFSA President

The team met for two days in Austin in December of 2009. Also in attendance were Dale Gough and Jeff Petrucci of AACRAO; Johnny Johnson, Monterey Peninsula College (retired); Gloria Nathanson, UCLA (retired); Bill Paver, UT Austin (retired); and Robert Watkins and Deana Williams of UT Austin. The review team produced a written report which included the following recommendations and summary:

REVIEW TEAM OBSERVATIONS AND RECOMMENDATIONS

The EDGE project builds on the work of those who produced the AACRAO World Education Series, PIER, the Handbook on the Placement of Foreign Graduate Students (The Graduate Handbook) and The Country Index. Electronic and updated regularly, EDGE is more comprehensive than previous efforts and covers every major educational system in the world. The program is organized in a logical and easy-to-use format, particularly for those with some experience in the field. The program covers 237 educational systems and offers up-to-date profiles of the educational system, their credentials, grading scales, educational ladders and placement recommendations.

REVIEW TEAM SUMMARY

The EDGE project was created to enable AACRAO to publish up-to-date information for use by foreign educational credential evaluators and to provide a referential standard for the field of applied comparative education. In both cases it has succeeded admirably. Many of the largest and most prestigious universities and university systems in the country use EDGE and the U.S. government routinely consults EDGE when making decisions on visa and immigration matters. The project is well-organized and comprehensive. Many areas of the world that have never been thoroughly researched, and

where information was very hard to attain, are now covered in EDGE.

University-based admissions professionals now have access to a resource that is easy-to-use, comprehensive, and contains guidelines for all the countries and territories in the world. These guidelines have been vetted by seasoned professionals and are based upon best practices in the field. For the 675,000 students who come from foreign countries and enroll at U.S. institutions annually, and for the university-based professionals who must evaluate and place these students, EDGE provides a clear and balanced reference point with information that is far more current than materials admissions personnel have had to rely on in the past. In addition to this, there are many other organizations, including the U.S. government, state boards and credentials agencies for which EDGE is a valued resource in the placement of hundreds of thousands of additional persons presenting foreign academic credentials. EDGE will continue to be a valuable resource for any AACRAO institutional member that enrolls foreign students.

THE AACRAO INTERNATIONAL TASK FORCE ON INTERNATIONAL ADMISSIONS AND CREDENTIAL EVALUATION

In 2013, the AACRAO Board appointed a 28-member task force on International Admissions and Credential Evaluation. The taskforce was chaired by former AACRAO Vice President for International Education, Gloria Nathanson. Members of the task force represented all sectors of U.S. higher education. Prominent among the taskforce recommendations, which were contained in the report released in July 2014, were the following concerning the future of EDGE:

✳ *Management of EDGE*: That plans for the transition of EDGE to a new generation be made and that a viable oversight structure be established. In this regard, it was specifically recommended that an internal management group be established with members coming from both the AACRAO membership and AACRAO International Education Services.

* *Professional Development*: That EDGE form the basis for new professional development training opportunities for AACRAO members and international education research in general.
* *Study Abroad*: That EDGE be used for professional development training of faculty and staff in academic departments, admissions offices, and study abroad offices to better evaluate the quality and effectiveness of study abroad programs.

The IESC meets bimonthly to consider suggested updates to EDGE that come from structural changes in educational systems, the evolution and development of new credentials, inquiries and suggestions from the field, as well as requests from the U.S. and other national governments, organizations, and professional boards. Frequent updates are made to EDGE as part of this process. In addition, IESC meets twice yearly to review the program and to chart direction.

Using EDGE

AACRAO EDGE is the only standard that is reviewed and approved by a membership-based, non-profit higher education organization which is voluntary and broadly representative of U.S. higher education. The database was developed by a group of experienced professionals and contains 237 educational system profiles that include credential advice for thousands of foreign educational credentials.

Each country profile includes:
* An overview of the country's educational system
* An educational ladder
* Credentials offered by that country
* Degrees or credentials required for access to each level
* What profession or further studies each credential leads to
* Secondary and postsecondary grading scales
* Tips on how to evaluate coursework for transfer credit to U.S. institutions
* A listing of the resources utilized for the profile

* A placement recommendation for each credential based on a review by five senior credentials analysts appointed by AACRAO
* A listing of the accredited institutions in each country, or a link to them
* A glossary containing educational terminology for that country

The country profiles can be accessed by geographical regions—Oceania, Europe, Asia, Africa, North America, and South America—or alphabetically. After the country is selected, information contained in that country profile will appear under eight tabs: Overview, Educational Ladder, Grading Systems, Credentials, Institutions, Resources, Author, and Glossary. Each country profile begins with a map and relative geographic location information, followed by a brief history of the country and overview of the educational system.

The educational ladder is a graphical representation of the education system. This building block format includes benchmarks which represent completion of the following levels of education: primary/elementary school, middle school, secondary school, vocational programs, undergraduate education, postgraduate education, professional programs, doctoral programs, and postdoctoral studies. When a substantial reorganization of the education system of a country has occurred, more than one educational ladder will be provided, with corresponding dates listed applicable to each education system.

Grading systems for both secondary and tertiary education are provided. In the Credentials tab, a chronological list of credentials is provided, along with a brief description for each credential, academic placement recommendations, and sample credentials.

The Institutions tab provides a comprehensive list of educational institutions at all levels, often via a link to that country's Ministry of Education. Under Resources, both print and online bibliographic resources are provided. Finally, a short biographical sketch of the author(s) responsible for each profile is provided, as well

TABLE 27.1: AACRAO EDGE Placement Recommendation Template

Less than High School Graduation	The [qualification] represents attainment of a level of education comparable to less than completion of senior high school in the United States. May be placed in Grade (x).
High School Graduation	
Vocational/technical diploma	The [qualification] represents attainment of a level of education comparable to completion of a vocational or other specialized high school curriculum in the United States.
Academic	The [qualification] represents attainment of a level of education comparable to completion of senior high school in the United States.
With advanced standing credit for academic education	The [qualification] represents attainment of a level of education comparable to completion of senior high school in the United States with the possibility of awarding up to one year of advanced credit.
With advanced standing credit for vocational/technical education	The [qualification] represents attainment of a level of education comparable to completion of senior high school in a vocational or other specialized high school curriculum in the U.S. with the possibility of awarding up to one year of advanced standing credit if the technical/vocational subject matter is deemed acceptable.
Postsecondary	The [qualification] represents attainment of a level of education comparable to x year/s of university study in the United States. Credit may be awarded on a course-by-course basis.
University Preparatory, e.g., India, Middle East	The [qualification] represents completion of a university preparatory program with no advanced standing or transfer credit.
Diploma supplement, e.g., Bologna, Russia, NIS Título, e.g., Mexico, Latin America	Regardless of the number of years of study, this document is insufficient to determine degree completion. Always require the submission of the [qualification] or degree certificate which shows that the degree was awarded. If the student cannot provide such documentation, credit may be awarded on a course-by-course basis.
Bachelor's Degree	The [qualification] represents attainment of a level of education comparable to a bachelor's degree in the United States.
Graduate Level Coursework	The [qualification] represents attainment of a level of education comparable to x years of graduate study in the United States.
Master's Degree	The [qualification] represents attainment of a level of education comparable to a master's degree in the United States.
Doctoral Degree/Doctorate	The [qualification] represents attainment of a level of education comparable to an earned doctoral degree in the United States.
Professional Qualification	The [qualification] represents attainment of a level of education comparable to a first professional degree in [field] in the United States.
Teacher Certification	The [qualification] is comparable to completion of teacher certification in the United States.
A-Levels, As-Levels, ECTS	Each A-level subject passed represents completion of the introductory sequence of that subject in the United States. Credit may be awarded for academic subjects on a course-by-course basis. Two AS-levels = one A level 60 ECTS credits = 30 semester credits
Post-Doctoral Study	The [qualification] represents attainment of a level of education comparable to post-doctoral study in the United States.
Vocational/Non-Academic Qualification (no academic credit/advanced placement)	The [qualification] represents attainment of a vocational/non-academic qualification. Admission and placement should not be based on this credential alone.
Professional vocational qualification (secondary)	The [qualification] represents attainment of a professional vocational qualification obtained at the secondary level of education and is comparable to a similar secondary level qualification in the United States.
Professional vocational qualification (postsecondary)	The [qualification] represents attainment of a professional vocational qualification obtained at the postsecondary level of education and is comparable to a similar postsecondary qualification in the United States.
Advanced professional specialization	The [qualification] represents advanced, highly-specialized education in a professional field, following the first professional degree in that field.
Graduate Admissions with Deficiencies	Depending upon the breadth and depth of courses completed, and depending upon institutional policy, may be accepted for graduate study contingent upon completion of undergraduate courses determined by academic department review.

as the date on which the profile was last updated. Where appropriate, a glossary of educational terms is included.

An added feature of EDGE is the inclusion of out-of-print AACRAO publications. These resources are invaluable in determining proper placement for those presenting credentials from earlier iterations of the educational system at hand. A sample of an EDGE profile can be found at edge-preview.aacrao.org.

EDGE Placement Recommendations

In order to standardize the placement advice offered in AACRAO EDGE, the committee developed a placement recommendation template. Table 27.1 (on page 284) shows the most recent version of the placement recommendation template.

The Future of EDGE

Research on foreign educational systems is ongoing and is vetted at regularly scheduled meetings of the International Education Standards Council (IESC). The EDGE admin team is responsible for the functioning of the AACRAO EDGE database. In this volunteer enterprise, we look to subscribers to assist us in keeping EDGE an up-to-date, valuable and user-friendly resource. Questions and suggestions for improvement are always welcome at edge@aacrao.org and opportunities to author or contribute to an EDGE profile can also be directed to this address.

In-House Credential Evaluation Services:

Lessons Learned at the University of Phoenix

2016 AACRAO INTERNATIONAL GUIDE

MARC BOOKER

Associate Provost
University of Phoenix

NATHAN CICCHILLO

Director
Admissions and Evaluation
University of Phoenix

BETH SIMPSON

International Evaluation
Operations Manager
University of Phoenix

In-House Credential Evaluation Services:
Lessons Learned at the University of Phoenix

dmitting students with international academic credentials constitutes a daunting venture for any institution. With so many variables surrounding the admissions process, the risk and uncertainty surrounding the admission of these students can be quite intimidating. However, implementing an international admissions and evaluation department can prove rewarding as these students typically enter postsecondary or graduate level education with a determination to succeed and an eagerness to learn. They bring multiple measures of diversity to the institutional academic community, which broadens the collegiate experience for the student population as a whole.

For over 15 years, University of Phoenix has had a designated International Admissions and Evaluation Department whose mission is to assist students with international academic credentials gain admission into the University. The department has evolved over the years to keep pace with the ever-changing higher education landscape. The evolution required a foundation of data and research to determine the best approach for servicing the University's population of students with international credentials. This chapter will explore how University of Phoenix's International Admissions and Evaluation Department has evolved, what lessons the institution has learned from its experience, and what other institutions can glean from this experience as they pursue creating an internal credential evaluation department at their own institution.

Department Evolution

The International Admissions and Evaluation Department at University of Phoenix has undergone a substantial evolution over the past 15 years to meet the changing conditions for international credential evaluation, stemming from an increased focus on international student mobility. Prior to 2002, most international student applicants were referred to professional evaluation agencies to obtain credential evaluations, as the department did not have the resources or knowledge to adequately perform most internal evaluations of international academic credentials. Two exceptions to this practice existed for students with credentials from institutions in Canada and Mexico. The University had a high number of students attending from both Canadian and Mexican institutions, thus the department was familiar with these educational systems.

In 2002, the University began to experience a considerable increase in international student enrollment. As a result, the International Admissions and Evaluation Department took this opportunity to expand the services offered to international students. After an analysis was conducted to determine the countries from which the highest numbers of students were enrolling, the department broadened its knowledge base in order to appropriately evaluate applications from high enrollment countries. The list of countries evaluated internally increased commensurately over the years. This process of continuous growth continued through 2006. To help support the expansion of evaluation services, policies governing recruitment of new employees were amended in order to find candidates with multilingual skills or international academic system competencies to become international evaluators.

In 2007, the International Admissions and Evaluation Department conducted another analysis of its international student enrollment trends and an inventory of its available resources. This was in response to changes made within the industry, such as the pending Bologna implementation, as well as interest in implementing similar educational structures outside of Europe. The findings of the assessment prompted the University to develop and implement plans for growing staff, resources, and countries evaluated. The decision was made to broaden internal international evaluation services to include all countries (except for Somalia, Turkmenistan, and Afghanistan, due to extreme obstacles in obtaining documentation and verifying document authenticity), as this would allow the University to provide a better level of service for its relatively large population of students with international academic credentials. As part of the assessment, the University focused on the British, French, Spanish, Soviet/Russian, American, and Indian educational systems, as these key educational structures provided the foundation for assessing and evaluating most systems of education.

Industry publications were purchased to reinforce the consistency of evaluations. Additionally, more evaluators were added to the department to support growth efforts. Hiring centered on employees with foreign language skills and experience stemming from cultural and educational exposure to foreign educational systems.

Today, the International Admissions and Evaluation Department consists of a Director of Admissions, an International Operations Manager, and 14 international evaluators. The team has over 110 years of collective international evaluation experience, is proficient in 16 languages, and many staff have attended postsecondary institutions outside the U.S., adding to their breadth of experience. The size of the department has allowed the University to provide many different services and create robust internal resources for support. The scope

of credentials reviewed by the University is notable. Within the past five years, the University has reviewed documentation from over 175 distinct countries. Table 28.1 shows the most common countries evaluated during that timeframe.

TABLE 28.1: Most Frequently Evaluated Countries from 2010 to 2014

Country	Number of Student Applicants
Philippines	2,431
Canada	1,703
India	1,408
Nigeria	817
Mexico	494
United Kingdom	473
Jamaica	357
Ghana	294
Colombia	293
Cuba	269

The bulk of the expansion stemmed from the increase of international students attending the University's online campus. This student base was more diverse than in years past and required a higher level of expertise for support. Additionally, the University wanted to be better positioned to adapt to the rapidly changing landscape of higher education. Analysis has shown that the goals of this expansion have been met through greater student support and institutional adaptability.

Internal Resources

A critical component to properly working with students with international academic credentials is creating a repository of internal resources to guide the philosophy and practices for the evaluation of international credentials. Internal resources help build a solid foundation for working with and servicing an institution's international population of students. It is important to link admissions policies and procedures with concrete evaluation methods to maintain a consistent process with little-to-no defect rates. This is best accomplished by the creation of documents that detail both student policies and processes.

The Policies and Procedures Manual houses international admission and transfer policies for all students at the University. Policies pertaining to English language proficiency requirements, foreign nursing licensure needs, managing students with visas or other immigration statuses, and document verification protocols are all detailed in this Manual, which International Evaluators consult when making admission decisions for international students. When creating internal policies and procedures, institutional leaders should first identify what criteria is required to meet institutional requirements. Once these policies are established, leaders should turn their attention to how evaluators determine if institutional standards and requirements are met by student submissions.

To provide additional consistency when conducting file evaluations for students with international academic credentials, the University has created a repository of information to support these evaluations. The University's internal intranet site, called the International Handbook, houses information on every country's educational system—recognized institutions, non-recognized institutions, native language, credential types, and transfer procedures. The International Handbook lists over 25,000 institutions recognized by their respective country's authorized regulatory body. The information for these institutions includes institution websites, known admissions requirements, credentials offered, and contact information. These resources serve as a guide to assist the University's international evaluators when determining how to apply transfer credit from an international institution in relation to the University's policies. They are one of the evaluator's primary sources of information when conducting an international evaluation. Because the International Handbook has been calibrated to the University's policies and procedures, it does not replace the need for external resources or databases, but helps to triangulate the student's submission with the University's policies

and information found from the international academic credential evaluation community.

External Resources

Although the creation of internal resources and policies is a critical component for the evaluation of students with international credentials, it is of almost equal importance to stay current on information and trends found in the international academic credential evaluation community. As the International Admissions and Evaluation Department has grown at University of Phoenix, the set of resources used has also increased commensurately. The Department currently maintains a substantial library of printed references that have been collected over the past 15 years. The foundational resource on which many of the department's practices, policies, and methodology are based is the *AACRAO International Guide*. The library also contains the AACRAO Project for International Education Research (PIER) series and Country Guides, country-specific volumes published by Education Credentials Evaluators (ECE), the International Education Research Foundation's (IERF) *New Country Index* volumes I and II, and the National Association of Foreign Student Advisors' (NAFSA) *A Guide to Educational Systems Around the World*. Other resources in the library are volumes published by organizations and entities from other countries, such as the *Handbook of Indian Universities* and *The Commonwealth Universities Handbook*. It is recommended that each institution that serves students with international academic credentials invest in some print resources to provide a reference point for appropriate admission and registrar personnel working with students.

To keep pace with developments in education systems around the world, University of Phoenix does not rely exclusively on print resources. The International Admissions and Evaluation Department maintains contacts with many external evaluation agencies, ministries of education, embassies and consulates, and Education USA. The department subscribes to AACRAO's Electronic Database for Global Education and the World Higher Education Database (WHED) maintained by United Nations Educational, Scientific, and Cultural Organization (UNESCO) to gain exposure to education systems around the world and changing conditions. Additionally, numerous websites are regularly consulted and reviewed. These include institution and ministry sites such as European Network of Information Centers—National Academic Recognition Information Centers (ENIC-NARIC), Netherlands Universities Foundation for International Cooperation (NUFFIC), the Education Audiovisual and Culture Executive Agency (EACEA) of the European Union, and NAFSA. Membership in NAFSA, AACRAO, and Pacific Association of Collegiate Registrars and Admissions Officers (PACRAO), as well as conference participation serve as other key resources.

Professional evaluation agencies also play a key role in serving the University's population of students with international credentials. National Association of Credential Evaluation Services (NACES) member agencies are a significant resource used in conducting research within the University. The International Admissions and Evaluation Department regularly conducts internal reviews to ensure that best practices are followed, and agencies may be consulted to confirm the University is operating within acceptable industry practices. While the department relies heavily upon publications such as the *AACRAO International Guide,* agency contacts are often able to provide extremely detailed clarification at a country- or institution-level for a specific student's evaluation. Agency information may also be more current, given the swift nature of change in the educational system for many countries. Occasionally, some sets of credentials may raise questions that warrant an outside consultation. Moreover, state regulations may require agency evaluations, as is the case for degree programs leading to teacher and sometimes nursing licensure. For example, evaluations by Commission on Graduates of Foreign Nursing Schools (CGFNS) are required to validate foreign nursing credentials in certain scenarios. For document verification purposes, the University will honor evaluations completed by professional evaluation agencies requiring that official and original records be submitted prior to completing the evaluation. Even when creating internal practices to assist with the evaluation of international academic credentials, leveraging outside resources and agencies in the international academic credential evaluation community is vital to ensuring thorough and accurate evaluations.

Methodology and Approach

As each institution is unique and has a different institutional mission, the methodology an institution uses to evaluate international credentials may differ from another institution. Identifying a methodology that aligns with an institution's mission and student population is a critical step in building a comprehensive strategy to support students with international academic credentials. University of Phoenix supports an open access philosophy and therefore, the International Admissions and Evaluation Department's goal is to provide a credential evaluation that accurately places a student in the proper program level and meets the institutional requirements for admission. International admissions decisions adhere to the best standards and practices of the industry, as are outlined in the *AACRAO International Guide* and World Education Services' (WES) World Education News and Reviews (WENR) newsletter. To make sure that the University does not place any unwarranted burdens on the population of students with international academic credentials during the admissions process, it endeavors to provide clear information on the necessary credentials for admission as well as available services which can be used to evaluate a student's academic credentials for placement prior to enrollment. Institutions with selective admissions processes or that have competitive admissions requirements may approach their methodology differently and view the comparability of academic credentials differently to support their institutional needs. The following contains University of Phoenix's methodology and may provide a framework for other institutions developing their methodology.

The International Admissions and Evaluation Department evaluates both undergraduate and graduate admission files. Recognition of the student's prior institution by the appropriate government authority, completeness of documentation, and the level of the international study completed are the first items considered when evaluating a student submission. At both the undergraduate and graduate level, several common requirements are also present such as meeting English language proficiency requirements and verifying legitimacy of academic credentials. Both of these steps are completed after a comparability assessment of the academic credentials. Students that do not meet the minimum academic requirements would be unable to proceed with the admissions process. Breaking down student submissions into a step-by-step process with a sequence of events is efficient and avoids unnecessary work.

When evaluating transfer credit, evaluators look at course weight and the grade or mark earned. Grades are converted using grade equivalencies found in publications, such as the PIER guides, AACRAO EDGE, WES, and other agencies, or based on institution-specific information. Course weight is converted into comparable semester credits by term, most often by using a coefficient based on the attempted weight value of the courses for the given term of study as documented on the academic record. Evaluators consider how the sending institution assigns course weight, such as maximum marks, credits, or the coefficient value (Frey 2003). Once grades and credits are converted, evaluators determine how the activity will be articulated at the University. Content is reviewed for general education credit eligibility and appropriateness of transfer. Additionally, content is reviewed to determine academic level, such as lower-division, upper-division, and graduate level.

As part of the official file evaluation process, potential course waivers are reviewed and applied. However, students seeking to have courses waived with foreign coursework need to supply a course description or syllabus for the foreign course seeking to be applied as a waiver course. This helps ensure the course content is similar enough to warrant waiving the course. Finally, special attention is paid to changes in academic systems over the years in which academic credentials were completed, as the use of different methods and criteria for the same country may be required depending on when the student attended their prior institutions.

For graduate admission file purposes, upon confirmation by the appropriate educational authority from the country which issued the academic credentials (typically the Ministry of Education), the evaluator will review for credential comparability to the United States bachelor's degree or appropriate preparedness for graduate level studies. Evaluators verify admission requirements for the international credential, as well as where that credential fits into the country's educational benchmarks. Resources used include institution websites, educational ladders published in print resources, AACRAO EDGE, and placement recommendations in those resources.

In 2007, following a two-year study and pilot program, the University determined that applicants with specific three-year baccalaureate degrees from certain countries could be admitted to certain graduate level programs. This was done after allowing students into certain programs on an exception basis, and then monitoring these students' academic progression and results. While three-year degrees do not directly equal a U.S. bachelor's degree, the data indicated that students with specific three-year degrees from certain countries are comparably well-prepared to succeed in some graduate programs, a finding in alignment with the University's mission for accessibility. It is worth noting that variation exists among NACES members regarding comparability of three-year postsecondary degrees. Specific limitations are placed on the three-year degrees considered for graduate admission, and not all programs are eligible for the admission of students holding three-year degrees internationally (after consideration of student progression, discipline alignment, and external requirements). The three-year bachelor's degrees must lead to graduate-level study in their own country. The majority of three-year degrees accepted under this provision have come from India, and additional countries represented under this process include Pakistan and Bologna participant countries. Piloting a program to accept international degrees in the manner above is not a statement on how other institutions should treat these degrees for admissions purposes, but is provided to give insight into how the international admissions and evaluation department can inform policy and help an institution make decisions that fulfill its stated mission.

Although the methods and approach described above are common to the majority of file evaluations completed by the International Admissions and Evaluation Department, there are occasional exceptions. Outliers may result from student specific conditions, such as an inability to obtain complete and acceptable academic records due to war or natural disaster. A student appeals process exists for such instances. The University also reserves the right to refer these students to an independent evaluation agency for assistance if an internal decision cannot be reached. In other cases, something unique to a country or institution must be factored into the evaluation process. As an example, the department does not evaluate educational documents from Afghanistan, Turkmenistan, or Somalia in-house, due to extreme obstacles in obtaining documentation and verifying document authenticity. Students with academic records from these countries are referred to external evaluation agencies for support. As an institution determines its methodology and approach for evaluating credentials, it becomes important to identify the guidelines and borders in which its services will accommodate students or where additional support may be necessary.

Processes and Services

The documentation needed to assess admissibility and credential comparability can add to the cost and time needed for the enrollment of students with interna-

tional academic credentials entering U.S. institutions. Identifying the processes and services that an institution will provide to a student with international credentials can ease this process and help with providing a clear path for a student to enter an institution. To help international students minimize the administrative burden of enrolling in a degree program, University of Phoenix offers free translation, pre-evaluation, document verification, and official file evaluation services when possible. International students enrolling at University of Phoenix can elect to use an external professional evaluation and translation service. The results of those professional services are still subject to the University's admission standards and do not guarantee admission to the University—there may be differences of opinion on credential comparability. However, students still need to meet all other admission requirements of their chosen program at the University.

The services offered at University of Phoenix have expanded over the years as the International Admissions and Evaluation Department has grown in skill and experience. To date, the University provides free translations for documents received in Spanish, French, and Russian. These translations are completed in-house by certified employees. Although it may not be feasible for institutions to offer their own internal translation services, having employees with foreign language experience can assist with the understanding and evaluation of international academic records from countries that may be high feeders to an institution.

The University has also implemented a pre-evaluation service that allows students to submit unofficial copies of their academic record to the University to determine if the student possesses the necessary and appropriate documentation required to progress and gain admission. Upon completion of the pre-evaluation, the University will provide the student with a preliminary placement and transfer credit recommendation based on the unofficial documentation submitted. Pre-evaluation results are unofficial as the University makes the decision using photocopies of official academic records provided by the student. Students deemed inadmissible based on the pre-evaluation results because of insufficient documentation submitted have the option to provide additional documentation, such as a diploma or other academic credential documentation to validate their coursework or credentials obtained from the previously attended institution. Students who have credentials appropriate for admission based on the pre-evaluation results are then required to send their original academic record documents to University of Phoenix to proceed with the admission process. Students receive the results of the pre-evaluation prior to submitting official academic records for the verification process because the sensitive nature of original academic records can make it difficult to obtain multiple sets of documents given the limited mobility of academic records around the world. The pre-evaluation process helps students to choose the most appropriate program, given their interests and qualifications, and presents a clearer picture of what needs to happen to meet degree requirements. If an institution has direct expertise concerning the academic credentials from a specific country, the creation of a pre-evaluation process may assist in helping students determine institutional fit before investing time and money.

Unfortunately, document fraud is a significant issue within the international admissions community, therefore, institutions creating their own international academic credential process must create procedures for the verification of international academic records. University of Phoenix uses document verification protocols as the primary method to combat fraud when determining the authenticity of international academic records. Therefore, the University requires that all international documents be verified either through an in-house process, through official documentation issued directly by the prior institution attended, or through a professional evaluation agency that conducts document verification. Students are required to submit their original academic record issued directly by the prior institution attended to the University in order for

the documents to be assessed for authenticity. This process requires examination to determine if any alterations have been made to the source document; verification of whether the documents are original and not photocopies, and whether they match the student's demographic information provided; and in some cases, following up with the issuing institution to determine validity of the credentials. Some professional evaluation agencies like WES, IERF, and Josef Silny & Associates (JS&A) perform credential verification on original academic credentials with varying processes. Institutions unable to verify international academic credentials internally can hire professional evaluation agencies to conduct verifications. If a student has been issued an evaluation report from one of these agencies, University of Phoenix will typically honor its verification decisions. From time to time, after exhausting all resources, University of Phoenix may not be able to render a verification decision on documents. In these cases, the University will reach out to the issuing institution, appropriate governmental authorities, or industry experts such as Education USA for assistance. Upon completion of the verification process, in most cases students may request return of their academic credentials from the University. Limited document mobility for academic credentials around the world makes this an important option for students.

It is important to note that the University considers the verification process separate from the evaluation process. During the verification process, documents are authenticated as original academic records—that is, unaltered documents issued appropriately by the international institution. The documents are typically reviewed for comparability during the pre-evaluation or official file evaluation of the student. This allows the student to keep their original international academic records in their possession until they need to be sent to the University. Regardless if an institution uses internal or external processes to assess international academic records, it is critical that both an evaluation process (to determine comparability) and a verification process (to determine authenticity) occur to properly assess international academic credentials

To reach an official evaluation decision, a student's admission file undergoes a standard process where the admission application and academic credentials are reviewed to ensure they meet all admission requirements for the University and the program. During this process a student's English language proficiency is assessed, a student's visa status is reviewed, courses are transferred and applied towards degree requirements, and course waivers may be evaluated on a student record to satisfy a student's major course of study. If a student does not meet the English language proficiency requirement, he or she will be instructed to complete an English language proficiency exam. Commonly accepted English language proficiency exams are TOEFL, Berlitz, TOEIC, and Pearson Test of English. These require that the student must at least score in the B2 band of the Common European Framework, as is the widely accepted practice within the industry.

The admission file process and other associated services offered by University of Phoenix to students with international academic credentials are reviewed annually to reduce redundant steps and ensure process efficiency. Because University of Phoenix reviews thousands of international academic credentials annually, implementing process efficiency tools allows the University to remain productive when working with international academic student records. Institutions working with students with international academic records should break down processes in a similar manner to help identify resource constraints and design appropriate services to assist students within their institution.

Training

Training is an essential component of ensuring accurate and compliant international admission operations, whether an institution offers internal services or outsources the majority of its academic credential evaluations. With the amount of countries University of Phoenix evaluates internally, and the volume of stu-

dents the International Admissions and Evaluation Department sees annually, a dedicated training and professional development program is critical. As the International Admissions and Evaluation Department has expanded, several approaches to training have been used. These approaches have been influenced to a certain extent by the number of countries evaluated internally, but experience has proven that the most effective approach for training is to focus on methodology and practice. Additionally, an emphasis on research skills and deductive decision making has been implemented as part of the training program because the review of international academic credentials often requires that the evaluator confirm their findings using multiple sources. International evaluators at University of Phoenix are first trained on reviewing University and programmatic admissions requirements to understand the institution's philosophy and guidelines for the review of admission files. This is primarily achieved through in-person instruction with trainers and the review of domestic student files to reinforce learning through practical application. Once evaluators demonstrate a consistent level of proficiency processing domestic student files, the evaluators begin training for international academic records.

The introductory phase of international academic credential evaluation training addresses resources, best practices, how to look at the structure and benchmarks of a system of education, and the overarching concepts and definitions of comparability and equivalence in the international academic credential community. In the next phase of the training, focus shifts to the systems of education around the world. These are broken out initially by areas of influence, such as British, French, Spanish, Soviet/Russian, American, and Indian systems. Training continues to move through systems, focusing last on those systems that do not fit a particular pattern, such as that of Vietnam. The training approach is designed to layer on new content once an evaluator demonstrates competence in the prior area reviewed. This approach has the benefit of allowing the

International Admissions and Evaluation Department to identify gaps in knowledge for the evaluator in training, as well as improve training materials.

The International Admissions and Evaluation Department has found that training for international credential evaluators cannot always be bound to a pre-defined time frame. On average, it takes three to six months for evaluators to complete all training modules. However, it may take a full 18 months of practical international evaluation experience before an evaluator demonstrates the knowledge and confidence required to be independently proficient in the role. The University's experience also shows the importance of refresher trainings to address deficiencies within an evaluator's competencies. These constitute a vital part of an evaluator's ongoing professional development, addressing the changing conditions of educational systems around the world.

The training program is supported through quality control measures established by the department. All evaluations completed within the training period are reviewed for accuracy, and feedback is provided to the evaluator so that they can learn and improve. Once the evaluator begins to demonstrate proficiency with their completed evaluations, the International Admissions and Evaluation Department considers the initial training complete, and the evaluator is then subject to the same quality standards and metrics as an established international evaluator. Once the introductory three- to six-month training timeframe is complete, all evaluations are checked for accuracy by more tenured evaluators in the department, until the new evaluator consistently demonstrates proficiency. Creating a dedicated training program to help new evaluators, combined with a peer mentoring program, is a crucial step towards scalable and sustainable internal credential evaluation operations.

Quality Control

Because of the complicated nature of educational systems around the world, international evaluation processes carry an inherent risk as each individual student submis-sion can present unique and unforeseen challenges. Therefore, institutions that work with international students should implement quality control procedures to ensure accurate and compliant evaluations. Quality control is essential to ensure that evaluations remain fair and consistent, to preserve the student experience, to mitigate fraud, and to maintain compliance. A dedicated quality control process can help provide immediate feedback to improve evaluation results and evaluator skills, while quickly identifying issues or red flags for potential fraudulent or incomplete student submissions.

As indicated previously, the International Admissions and Evaluation Department at University of Phoenix reviews 100 percent of all international evaluations while an evaluator is in training. This is recommended for any institution with new evaluators to provide feedback to the evaluator while also ensuring that errors are not made on student submissions. Once an evaluator finishes the initial training period, the proportion of files reviewed by the quality control auditor is reduced to 15 to 25 percent. Evaluators are also teamed up with a peer mentor during this time to provide additional audit support on files outside of the standard quality control process. All work by the department, such as document verifications, pre-evaluations, and official file evaluations are subject to the quality control process. This ensures that:

✳ Department processes were followed;

✳ Institutional policies were upheld;

✳ Credential comparability decisions were accurate;

✳ Students met English language proficiency requirements;

✳ International credits were converted correctly;

✳ General Education designations were reviewed and applied correctly towards degree requirements; and

✳ Students were admitted correctly based on institutional requirements for admission.

After files are reviewed for quality, data is collected and reviewed to identify any trends based on the results.

Evaluators receive their quality scores on a weekly basis. If undesirable trends are identified, department training will be created to address those deficiencies. In addition, coaching or individualized training may be conducted for evaluators failing to meet the quality standards established by the International Admissions and Evaluation Department. The continual cycle of conducting quality control reviews and leveraging the results to improve departmental and evaluator competencies has been extremely useful in building up the department's skills and capabilities as international credential evaluators. An ongoing quality control process ensures practice, accuracy, and consistency in mitigating risk and validating a quality result.

Lessons Learned

Five primary lessons have been learned in the approximately 15 years since University of Phoenix began taking steps to conduct in-house international evaluations:

USE ALL AVAILABLE RESOURCES

When determining the admissibility of an international student, arbitrary and snap-judgment decisions can lead to inconsistent evaluations, a poor student experience, and create risk for an institution. It is essential to review and maintain resources regularly. It is equally important to use resources that are widely accepted within the industry to guide admissions decisions. Additionally, internal resources that evaluators can easily access to support the international processes for the institution are vital. Departments should re-assess and review external resources on a regular basis as web resources are updated and changed often and new volumes are published. As these resources are updated, internal resources should also be updated accordingly.

REGULAR EXAMINATION OF POLICIES AND PROCEDURES

Policies and procedures should be periodically reviewed and assessed to ensure that they are valid and appropriate, and changes should be recorded for historical reference purposes. Reviews help maintain sound practices

and methodologies and ensure university policies are not deviating from widely accepted industry standards. As policy or processes are updated, it is helpful to catalog these updates for future reference. It is important to know and understand the rationale behind these updates.

BE READY TO ADAPT

Education as an industry is fluid, and reform is constant. Some countries, such as India, plan significant changes on a regular basis, as often as every five years. Sweeping reforms like the Bologna Agreement can dramatically change systems of education. Or, as the dissolution of the Soviet Union demonstrated, politics can play a significant role. Departments of international admissions and evaluation must be aware of and ready to plan for and adapt to those changes.

KNOW YOUR LIMITATIONS

There are limitations to what any evaluation entity can accomplish based on the knowledge and resources available. Not every institution has the capability to hire evaluators to support an in-house process. It is important to know the limitations of both staff and the institution. Be cautious not to overextend resources as this can lead to a decline in student satisfaction, quality, and employee morale. Therefore scalable, carefully planned expansion is necessary to implementing a successful process in-house.

BECOME PART OF THE INTERNATIONAL ADMISSIONS COMMUNITY

Community is essential to the long-term success of an International Admissions and Evaluation Department. By attending and participating in industry conferences and other industry forums, relationships and connections are established. This allows institutions to share information, best practices, and industry trends related to international admissions. Assisting the international student population can be an overwhelming experience, which can be made much easier with support from other entities within the international academic credential community.

In conclusion, the creation of internal services for the evaluation of international credentials should not result in isolationism. In fact, as University of Phoenix's experience has indicated, successful international academic credential operations require collaboration and support from both external and internal resources and partners. Protocols to continuously review processes and external information are paramount in keeping up with trends in the international academic credential community.

Dedicated investment in international admission operations is essential to accomplish this and create a functional department that can accommodate the breadth and scale of evaluating credentials from countries around the world. Although requiring effort to implement, with the right tools and resources the international credential evaluation process can be a rewarding experience for both students and the institution.

TWENTY-NINE

Articulation
Agreements
at the American
University of Beirut

2016 AACRAO INTERNATIONAL GUIDE

HALA ABOU ARRAJ | Associate Registrar
American University of Beirut

Articulation Agreements at the American University of Beirut

This chapter provides a synopsis of how articulation agreements serve higher education institutions, an overview on the types of agreements at the American University of Beirut, and a discussion of the internal university factors affecting the development and the implementation of these agreements. The following basic questions will be answered: As higher education institutions become complex, what are the reasons for the development of articulation agreements? What types of agreements have been developed? And, what factors affect the implementation and development of transfer agreements?

An articulation agreement is a pathway between two or more colleges or universities and their academic programs involving the transfer of courses between the institutions. Other names given to articulation agreements include transfer agreements, transfer guides, and transfer pathways. Transfer agreements can be analyzed and assessed from three different perspectives: the sender's perspective, the receiving institution's perspective, and the student/learner's perspective. Articulation agreements attempt to simplify the transition from one school to another by facilitating a continued and smooth pathway for the transfer of courses. The sending institution benefits by marketing the acceptability and validity of their program and courses in the eyes of outside universities. The receiving institution benefits by covering the lost costs of attrition by filling the seats with a diverse selection of students from other colleges/universities. Finally, when following a set of pre-approved course plans, the student benefits from the transfer agreement by having an expanded educational experience while avoiding courses that are not applicable towards his/her desired academic credential. Having a clearly-articulated transfer agreement reduces the loss of course credits which are often the result of ad hoc enrollment.

Establishing Transfer Agreements

Multiple factors have led to the growth in the number and type of articulation agreements and transfer arrangements between local, regional, and international higher education institutions. With the expansion in the population of students, both majors and programs have become ever more diversified as a result of knowledge streaming. Additionally, the volume and scope of international activities in the educational sector has expanded during the past two decades. Globalization and technological advancements have led to increased student mobility between universities, through the blurring of borders and national systems associated with transnational education (Techler 2004, 7). As a consequence, transfer agreements—whether horizontal or vertical—between higher education institutions have expanded and increased. Horizontal agreements involve communication between partners with the same level of knowledge or the same type of credentials/degree awarded, while vertical agreements comprise communication between partners with different levels of knowledge or different credentials. In most cases, transfer agreements occur horizontally. Horizontal mobility normally creates a "win-win" situation for the two institutions in reaching a higher level of reflection (Techler 2004, 14).

The modernization of educational systems has helped universities adapt to the evolving expectations of modern societies in numerous ways, including standardizing curricula, with the goal to promote mobility between regional and international universities. Standardization of courses and curricula has become the norm in order to promote efficiency through continuous curriculum evaluation. Moreover, it promotes quality and comparability amongst universities. The move to standardize curricula is the natural outcome of modern influences such as accreditation boards and regional councils. As a result, a major goal of the modern university is to make courses that are unified, universal, and objective, in an attempt to facilitate mobility and transfer credits between institutions (Elwell 1999, 2).

The globalization of the educational sector has spawned articulation and transfer agreements between American and European universities resulting in student enrollment in different and disparate educational systems. Most European universities follow the European Credit Transfer System (ECTS) established by the European Union for the purpose of recognizing studies completed abroad and reaching standardization between the different educational systems of the European Union. The main goal of ECTS is to promote the exchange of academic information among European institutions of higher education in order to facilitate student mobility. Such agreements increase the chance for future research and academic cooperation between universities, contributing to the globalization of education.

Internationalization and globalization have dictated increased mobility between students, the implementation of modern and flexible curricula, and openness to new higher education systems such as the European ECTS credit system, all of which have led to the growth in the number and type of articulation agreements and transfer arrangements.

Agreements at the American University of Beirut (AUB)

AUB is a private, independent institution of higher learning founded in 1866. It is the oldest university in the Middle East and is located in Beirut, Lebanon. The university functions under a charter from the state of New York and is governed by a private, autonomous Board of Trustees. The university became co-educational in 1922 and English is the language of instruction. At present, AUB has seven faculties: Agricultural and Food Sciences, Arts and Sciences, Engineering and Architecture, Medicine, Health Sciences, School of Nursing and Olayan School of Business. AUB offers programs leading to bachelor's, master's, and PhD degrees in a liberal arts setting. It is a globally connected university which welcomes international students from over 75 countries around the world.

The university encourages all students to take advantage of opportunities to study abroad in order to gain a global perspective and enjoy an enriching academic experience. AUB promotes partnerships and collaborates with a number of high quality universities and institutions throughout the world. These partnerships have been developed as a key feature of the university's internationalization strategy to enhance AUB's position as a globally connected university. In addition, AUB aims to develop international links that promote student and staff mobility and support the advancement of knowledge and innovative research through Erasmus Mundus partnerships such as Dunia Beam, Element, Medastar, Dunia Beam and Tempus, and more recently through Eramus+ bilateral agreements.

Before 2000 AUB faced a major problem related to transfer arrangements. These arrangements were usually informal, often developed as a courtesy between institutions or as a cooperative endeavor between administrators. As a consequence, students attempting to transfer credits lacked explicit guidance on the transfer procedures and career path selection. Noting the increase in the number of students seeking transfer credits from universities abroad—mainly in the U.S. and in Europe—there was a need for the establishment of formal arrangements. The Office of International Programs (OIP) at the university provides support to all international students through services including but not limited to pre-arrival information and advice; on-site orientation, mentoring and intercultural activities;

demystification of processes and procedures at the university; and support in obtaining visas and residence permits. Through its Study Abroad Program, OIP also promotes exchange opportunities and advises AUB students wishing to pursue international academic experiences that are academically challenging, professionally relevant and personally engaging.

This section will describe the types of transfer agreements which exist between AUB and various universities and will attempt to assess the validity of those agreements. The Memorandum of Understanding (MOU), Affiliation or Direct-Enrollment Agreement, Consortium Agreement, and Student Exchange Agreement are the most commonly used transfer agreements at AUB. These are in addition to the Erasmus+ agreements, which promote student exchange, faculty mobility, and staff training.

MEMORANDUM OF UNDERSTANDING (MOU)

In many universities, a Memorandum of Understanding (MOU) is a necessary first document before a specific contract or exchange agreement can be drawn up or signed. The MOU officially documents the fact that two or more institutions have agreed, at the most senior levels, to having common educational purposes which can be met by joining forces; thus it needs to be signed by the provost or president of each participating university. The MOU is usually a simple, short, legal document, sketching out (often in bullet point fashion) the areas of endeavor in which two institutions plan to discuss specific collaborations. It does not bind the institutions to a specific project, nor does it authorize such activity without a further signed agreement.

Memoranda of Understanding are normally used as "no strings attached" agreements between two higher education institutions to test the viability and favorability of establishing future formal agreements based on curricula, programs, and course similarities. Another advantage of the MOU is that it permits a smooth transition and lays the groundwork for a transfer of course credits between both institutions. A third advantage is

related to the personality growth of students experiencing a new culture and a new academic setting. Most testimonials have stressed the favorability of the cultural diversity dimension.

At the American University of Beirut, Memoranda of Understanding can be grouped according to their performances and productivities into three categories:

* Active memoranda, which refers to valid and operating memoranda;
* Recently signed memoranda, which are identified by the signing of the agreements (normally less than two years), and which are in the process of initiating or launching new activities; and
* Activity declining memoranda—includes memoranda that used to be active but have witnessed a reduction of activity after a certain period of time.

AFFILIATION OR DIRECT-ENROLLMENT AGREEMENT

An affiliation agreement is a signed understanding between two offices of international programs establishing that University A will review study abroad applications from University B and provide certain services to accepted study abroad or visiting students from that university. It does not require University A to commit to sending an equal number of students to the partner university, and it also does not require approval of the dean or provost, nor does it require a pre-existing MOU. Two types of affiliations can be characterized: (1) institutional affiliations where the agreement is affiliated with the institution as a whole, and (2) program affiliations where affiliation is related to a specific program in the institution. This type of agreement is popular among technical and professional programs/institutions.

At the American University of Beirut, a major advantage of the direct-enrollment agreement is that it encourages vertical transfers for promoting and exchanging different technical or professional information especially in the field of engineering. An additional advantage is that it promotes competence of professionals by providing intellectual characteristics within various educational environments. AUB students are exposed to different work methods, and different problem solving technicalities, which enhance and sculpt their professional thinking methods and results in increasing coordinated educational programs to achieve the best service.

CONSORTIUM AGREEMENT

Consortia are different forms of joint collaborative relationships between two institutions. Consortia aim at saving funds through coordination between the different institutions to increase visibility and through achieving a shared knowledge. Consortium agreements were originally designed to foster inter-institutional cooperation among a group of colleges and universities for the purpose of enhancing services within a geographic region. More recently, as information and communication technologies have increased the availability of resources for research and developmental purposes, universities have joined with corporations and government agencies to branch out and form national and international consortia. The parameters of academic cooperation can vary in scope by level of control (public-private), discipline (computer science, engineering, medicine), and service provider (libraries, universities, science laboratories).

At the American University of Beirut, consortium agreements are made between two or more universities that recognize registration at each location for financial aid purposes. It also certifies that only one of the two institutions can administer Title IV and state financial aid to ensure that the student does not receive U.S. federal funding from two sources. This is typical for students coming from the U.S. The purpose of the consortium agreements is to specify and describe the policies and procedures for the provision of courses under the terms and conditions, rights, and obligations defined between the two institutions.

The American University of Beirut was successfully engaged in a consortium with two other universities from the region for the implementation of a Pro-Green Diploma in the Middle East. Main strengths of the agreement include assisting professionals in acquiring the diverse and critical problem solving skills needed to advance in their green technology careers, developing expertise in green technologies related to applications in energy, water, and building in Lebanon and the region, and fostering problem solving competencies among professionals pursuing careers in green industries.

However, there have been continuous efforts to promote student mobility in program development and this necessitated the use of additional human resources. Moreover, the challenge of creating more flexible and open higher education programs to cater the learners' needs is a major concern at the university.

STUDENT EXCHANGE AGREEMENT

A student exchange agreement is typically signed after an MOU between two universities is already in force and commits each university to sending a specific number of students—often two to four per semester or year for a specified and finite number of years—with each student paying the normal tuition fees at their home university in order to cover the tuition costs of the visiting student from the partner university. Because of the tuition-reciprocity requirement of such a partnership, most universities choose to enter into an exchange agreement only when there is a strong likelihood that their students will have a high level of interest in going to the partner university's location and when courses relevant to their students' degree requirements are offered by the partner university in a language which students can comprehend well. Bilateral Exchange agreements are the most common partnerships implemented at AUB; many AUB students engage in one or two semesters as exchange students in a European, American, or regional university.

At the American University of Beirut, there are transfer agreements written with around 40 universities. Transfer credit is assessed on a course-by-course basis and the total transfer credits generally do not exceed 30 credit hours. All AUB transfer agreements include general information stipulating the purpose of the agreement and the number of students to be exchanged and signatures of approval from the institutional representative of the cooperating institutions. These agreements also include financial, academic, and administrative responsibilities of the institutions towards each other as well as the duration of the agreement, and other general provisions for transfer credits. Legal considerations are also covered.

Erasmus Mundus Exchange for Scholars

The American University of Beirut participated in four Erasmus Mundus partnerships encompassing 32 European university partners, as well as individually signed agreements with partner universities around the world. Today, AUB has 12 Erasmus+ agreements in place shown in Table 29.1 (on page 308). These provided AUB students, professors, and academic staff with funded mobility to European universities. For professional research, faculty members engaged in a one month period of travel which includes paid transportation and a stipend for living expenses. The European Union generally required that funded scholars be Lebanese nationals (or long-term Palestinian residents of Lebanon) who have not lived or worked in Europe for more than 12 out of the last 60 months. Moreover, the DUNIA BEAM partnership was open to nationals of Jordan, Syria, and Palestine. Funded scholars needed to have a permanent faculty or staff position at AUB.

Normally, scholars had to submit a workplan to the sponsoring university. Similarly, faculty from other universities were eligible to apply to AUB for a "teaching visit." European countries and universities that fell under this category are listed under Table 29.1. The transfer partnerships encompassed various programs and fields of study that demonstrated their respective research strengths. The diversity and variety of the Erasmus Mundus partnership—covering humanities to social sciences to professional medical sciences to engineering—was a sign of its efficiency in promoting research cooperation and the exchange of research capabilities.

Transfer agreements are crucial for professional growth and development of students, faculty members and administrators. Those agreements available at the American University are essential to the establishment of networking between universities, which is the biggest step towards globalization and internalization.

UNIVERSITY NETWORKING

Transfer agreements contribute greatly to international networking especially through the Memoranda of Understanding and the exchange agreements. The American University of Beirut has been involved in a series of partnerships covering Europe, North America, Middle East, North Africa and Asia as apparent in List 1. Among those partnerships is Erasmus Mundus which includes four main partnerships: ELEMENT, WELCOME, MEDASTAR, and DUNIA BEAM. The geographical presentation of these four programs is restricted to Europe. AUB has benefited greatly from these transfer agreements in both education and research through acquisition of new knowledge and introducing project-organized problem-based learning. Many of these partnerships have continued as bilateral Erasmus+ agreements. This gives an important intercultural aspect to both disciplinary and interdisciplinary studies at the university. The impacts of these agreements have been apparent in three categories: curricula and course development, joint development courses, and human resources development.

Studying abroad for one or two semesters is useful for broadening a student's coursework. The number of students from AUB taking advantage of this opportunity has been increasing over the past five years. Among the benefits of those agreements are the opportunities to learn unfamiliar technology (especially for students majoring in engineering), intercultural experiences, working with foreign mentors, and improved career opportunities after graduation. Most students have mentioned the personality building they experienced in addition to their exposure to new educational settings and environments as positive attributes of study-

TABLE 29.1: International Partners of the American University of Beirut

Europe

- Aarhus University (Denmark)
- Danish School of Media & Journalism (Denmark)
- Ecole d'Ingénieurs de Purpan (France)
- Ecole Superieure de Chimie Organique et Minérale (France)
- Freie Universität Berlin (Germany)
- Institut d'Etudes Politiques de Paris (Sciences Po, France)
- Lund University (Sweden)
- Politecnico Di Torino (Italy)

- RWTH Aachen University (Germany)
- School of Advanced Social Studies (SASS), Slovenia
- Södertörn University (Sweden)
- Technische Universität München (Technical University of Munich, Germany)
- Universidad Carlos III de Madrid (Spain)
- Università degli Studi Mediterranea di Reggio Calabria (Italy)
- Università Iuav di Venezia (Iuav), Italy
- Université de Genève (Switzerland)

- University of Bologna (Italy)
- University of Granada (Spain)
- University of Limerick (Ireland)
- University College Dublin (Ireland)
- University College London (U.K.)
- University of Zurich–Institute of Political Science (Switzerland)
- Uppsala Universitet (Sweden)
- Zeppelin University (Germany)

Middle East & North Africa

- American University of Iraq–Suleimaniya (Iraq)
- Al Akhawayn University (Morocco)
- Chung Ang University (Korea)
- The American University in Cairo (Egypt)
- Bogazici University (Turkey)

- Bilkent University (Turkey)
- Frederick University (Cyprus)
- Koç University (Turkey)

- Middle East Technical University–Orta Doğu Teknik (Turkey)
- Üniversitesi Turkey
- Yeditepe University (Turkey)

North America

- American University
- Amherst College
- Augsburg College
- Boston University

- Escuela de Agricultura de la Region Tropical Humeda (Earth University, Costa Rica)
- George Washington University
- University of Montreal (Canada)

- University of New Mexico
- University of Pennsylvania

CREDIT: Hala Dimachkieh, Director, Office of International Programs

ing abroad. These factors contributed greatly to their chances of finding better jobs, since they were amenable and open to new settings and experiences.

Joint courses were offered between the American University of Beirut and the Salzburg Academy for students majoring in Media Studies. Two joint courses were developed and offered for a three-week period in Salzburg, Austria and have been offered on a yearly basis for the past four years. The topics of the courses were "Global Change, Cooperation & News" and "Global Media Literacy." The main benefits of the joint courses have been providing students with a unique learning environment, gaining a global aspect to the perception of the university in the local setting, and the development of a close relationship between faculty members from the different universities involved, which has laid the foundation towards nurturing new ideas for education, research, and cooperation.

Human resource development is another important outcome of those agreements where faculty and staff members go for a certain period of time for professional growth. The visitors acquire new skills and knowledge and learn to apply those skills when they return to their home universities. Staff members at AUB went to a university in Spain for one month where they were introduced to the processes and procedures involving transfer students and equivalencies of courses at the host university. Staff members were exposed to new problem solving methods that they applied to their work at AUB.

In conclusion, experiences and partnerships such as Erasmus Mundus and Erasmus+ prove their usefulness in living up to the demands of the university, in terms of meeting the challenges of globalization, fostering innovation in teaching methods, increasing professional growth, and keeping up-to-date educational information.

Factors Affecting Transfer

Serban, Kozeracki and colleagues, among others, discuss the influence of the "transfer culture" in the university, the role of higher-level administration, and the university programs and strategies on the efficiency and overall impact of transfer agreements.

First, the creation of a "transfer culture" within the university is important for advancing and progressing transfer agreements. Transfer culture includes the following items (Serban, Koseracki, *et al.* 2008, 3):

* The perception of transfer as a high institutional priority by the university;
* The establishment of rigorous curriculum which includes writing, critical thinking, mathematics, and the sciences;
* Introduction of innovative, flexible, and research-based pedagogies;
* Environment of belonging where the student is stimulated to achieve high results; and
* Intensive academic support programs such as academic counseling, peer tutoring, and reciprocal learning techniques.

Second, the roles of the president and the higher administration of the university are crucial to establishing such a transfer culture. By setting the agenda for their universities, they can direct and control the development of the transfer culture, thus increasing the expectations and goals for transfer. This culture also needs to be taken back and applied to the advising and admissions processes as well as extending to the faculty roles (Ibid 2008, 3). This can be done by building and supporting programs that increase transfer, continuously reviewing institutional policies and practices, building and strengthening partnerships with other universities by supporting faculty relationships, and providing incentives for both faculty and students to work together by encouraging research based courses.

The third factor affecting transfer agreements are the university's programs and strategies. University programs include (Ibid 2008, 4):

* Improved student awareness about transfer requirements
* Good advising
* Effective university counseling which tackles efforts to support transfer students hinge upon knowledge of transfer policies and programs, student characteristics and needs, and effective evaluation of interventions
* Effective communication between the different channels of the university
* Establishment of transfer centers to support transfer students' needs and institutional capacity and successful implementation and effectiveness. Major questions that need to be answered are related to the needs and goals of the transfer students, courses that they are taking, availability of classes and services to meet their needs, and continuous evaluation of transfer programs between universities.

Finally, transfer agreements are heavily centered on academics and how courses can be transferred as part of the degree requirements curriculum. All agreements should be defined keeping the endpoint in mind—that is, graduation requirements and how the courses will be articulated at the degree-awarding institution.

To sum up, transfer agreements prosper under a "transfer culture" established at the university and backed up by a clear perception of the president's role in the transfer process. This is coupled by the establishment of university programs and strategies that fortify transfers between students and strengthen networking connections between faculty members of the different universities.

Conclusion

Networking between academic institutions through transfer agreements is a growing need in a modern society where innovation and flexibility are clear indications of success in a complex environment. Networking is promoted further because of the globalization and internationalization in higher education institutions, standardization of courses, and increased student mobility between universities. In order to keep up with current social challenges, the American University of Beirut has been networking with regional and international higher education institutions through a series of partnerships including: Memoranda of Understanding, Consortia, Affiliation Agreements, and Exchange Agreements. Professional development partnerships are mainly signed with European universities including representatives from across Europe such as France, Sweden, Denmark, Austria, and Germany. At AUB, these partnerships have contributed to curricula and course development and have enhanced communication between faculty members and departments within the university through the establishment of joint development courses. Finally, professional development for both staff and faculty members is an additional positive outcome of these partnerships.

It should be noted that there are certain factors that affect transfer agreements in the university. The diffusion of a "transfer culture" through the university helps create sustainable transfer agreements, especially when coupled with backup and support from the higher administration, typically originating from the strategic plans and actions established by the university. This is not to say that transfer agreements are without problems, however, they are minor when compared to the benefits derived by students, administrators, faculty members, the institution, and ultimately national education achievement. Finally, the role of transfer agreements is growing worldwide, and many educators believe that they will have a growing role in the landscape of higher education in the future.

THIRTY

Study Abroad:
Elon University's Framework for Complete Accessibility

ROBIN STRAKA

Associate Registrar
Elon University

Study Abroad:
Elon University's Framework for Complete Accessibility

Elon University set a goal in its 2009 strategic plan, The Elon Commitment, to provide 100 percent study abroad access. The Commitment states that "study abroad will be enhanced to include stronger curricular roots and rich international experiences in service, leadership, internships, and language study" (Elon University 2015a). Evidence of the Commitment abounds in the steady growth in the number of students studying globally under institutional, affiliate, and non-affiliated programs. Participation in study abroad has grown from 131 students selecting from more than 40 programs in Fall 2006 to more than 500 students abroad in Fall 2015 selecting from nearly 90 semester programs (*see* Figure 30.1, on page 314).

Many factors affect Elon students' decisions to study abroad, such as cost, curriculum considerations, academic eligibility, health, and the diversity of programs offered. Therefore, the university provides as much academic information as possible at the beginning in order for students to select the program which best serves their needs. Each student and each study program bring unique academic needs and requirements to the table. At the same time the university must balance giving students opportunities not offered on the home campus while maintaining the integrity of the university's degree. This means two constituencies—students and faculty—must be able to navigate the variety of educational opportunities they encounter.

The first key to making a study abroad opportunity work for Elon students is ensuring that the university makes information readily available to faculty. Just as our students are educated to live in a global society in which they will encounter differences and similarities, so should the faculty approach the assessment of educational opportunities from study abroad host institutions. Before discussion of a specific program can begin, stakeholders must understand the framework within which the program operates. Department chairs and faculty need to understand differences in credit values (what do you mean the students at that university carry 60 credits in a semester?), grade scales (is 1 the high or low grade on that four-point grade scale?), terminology (is it a module, a unit, a subject, a course?), and approaches to academic content (are prerequisites expressed or implied?) which may exist. At Elon, the staff of the Global Education Center (GEC) and the University Registrar's office work together to research these questions. The registrar's office designates a point person who receives critical training on international tertiary education systems through resources such as AACRAO International Education Services.

Once the framework for the conversation has been provided, discussion of specific program details can follow. Departments or programs may request options that address an interest or need to study in a particular country or region. Others address the academic needs of a specific major such as management or education. Elon University's collaborative process is a partnership among the GEC, the registrar, and the faculty. The staff of the GEC identifies and vets new programs. They then provide the registrar's office with links to course offering and academic structure information. The registrar in turn provides the GEC with feedback on the academic model and credentials and requests clarification or additional information as needed. The GEC solicits

FIGURE 30.1

Elon University Study Abroad

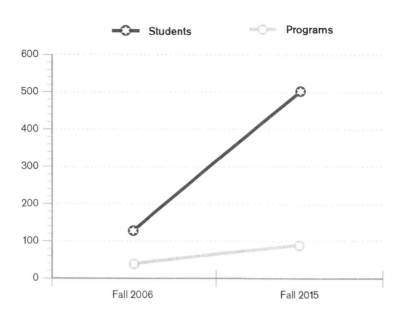

the additional information requested from the potential host program.

Recently, the GEC was asked to find a program which would serve the academic needs of students in a particular major. The program was identified and staff from the GEC conducted a site visit. Based on the information compiled, the GEC determined that the proposed program met the needs specified. They forwarded provider information to the registrar and the department chair. The registrar had the following questions and observations:

✱ The following information was identified from the provider's website: XXX is a branch campus of YYY University in the U.S. Transcripts will be issued by YYY University. Please confirm this detail.

✱ Will the courses be listed on the YYY University transcript under the subjects listed on the XXX website? If so, what course numbers will YYY use? If not, how does YYY list them on the official transcript?

✱ If transcripts are issued by YYY University, semester hours for each course will transfer as awarded by YYY.

As a result of the registrar's questions, the GEC solicited the required additional information from the provider. While this part of the process was underway, the registrar and the academic department chair conferred on the transfer equivalents of individual courses.

Once the program details are delineated, information is then provided to academic advisors and/or faculty who serve as academic advisors. When advisors understand study abroad offerings, they can enthusiastically help their advisees review study abroad opportunities and weigh the pros and cons of the available options. Supporting the advising process by providing program-specific details is a second key to study abroad success.

For example, one of Elon University's affiliate programs offers courses for students in the third year of a particular major and therefore best serves students who have already completed certain foundation or core courses in that discipline. These conditions are not stated outright in the provider's materials. They are inherently understood by people in that country's educational system, but not overtly stipulated as pre-conditions or specific prerequisites. The staff of the GEC and the registrar's office had to investigate how the courses offered fit into the degree structure at the host institution, assess how it compared to the structure of the equivalent Elon major, and provide this background or explanatory information to academic advisors and faculty in the relevant department. Conducting the necessary research is a time- and labor-intensive effort requiring extensive collaboration and cooperation between the registrar's office and the GEC, but one that pays significant dividends to the student.

Planning for a semester-long study abroad experience is a complex undertaking for students. There is no magic button a university can give students that will answer all of their questions, submit all the forms, and make all the travel arrangements. They have to navigate a complex system of home institution application, host program application, visa application, housing selection, additional costs, and travel information, to list just a few concerns. Add to the mix the academic planning process (it is *study* abroad, after all) and the process can seem daunting. A university cannot complete the process for the student. But it can make the process more approachable by anticipating academic planning questions and providing the students with as much information as possible in the research and application stages. The third key to study abroad success is making sure students understand the difference in the academic opportunities afforded by the range of study abroad options available. The process starts with the student's goals. For those students who need help clarifying their plans, Elon's Global Education Center (GEC) provides numerous resources, including a series of questions to help them identify their interests or needs. These include:

✳ "Do I want to study in a specific country or region?"

✳ "Do I want to live in a large city?

✳ "Do I want to be on a program with a high level of support services, or a more independent program?" (Elon University 2015b)

Knowing the answers to questions like these can help students choose between a faculty-led, short-term program and a semester-long study abroad opportunity offered through an affiliate provider. Once they have identified their specific needs, they can turn to the academic planning component.

When selecting a study abroad program, it is imperative that students completely understand their progress toward degree completion and how a semester abroad fits into their plans. Some majors such as those in the STEM disciplines may have more structured course sequences, while majors in the humanities may be more flexible in sequence. The student may have recently changed or added a major. Major requirements such as student teaching can limit the semesters a student can study abroad.

Successful planning for a semester abroad requires that students fully comprehend what adjustments they can make to their planned course selection or requirement completion and whether or not they have room for free electives. Many students at Elon have this well in hand before they even start reviewing study abroad opportunities. Others need assistance with the planning process. To help them, the registrar developed a set of questions to serve as a guide. (*See* "Study Abroad Course Selection Considerations," on page 316.) While a student may have an affinity for a particular study abroad location, the answers to the academic planning questions can sometimes lead them to select another program which may better support both personal and educational goals.

Once they have developed an academic plan with Elon and have selected a study abroad program, students can start the application and course selection/transfer of credit process. Students require the same information as the faculty—course/credit structure (how many courses or modules constitute a full load?), grade scale, prerequisites, etc. This becomes especially critical because the class registration process at universities in other countries is often far different than in the U.S. Among the registration scenarios students may encounter:

✳ In many locations, students do not register for classes until the start of the semester. Consequently, the timing of the release of semester schedules is often close to the start of the term involved.

✳ For some study abroad programs, students are given a list of typical offerings when they are in the application process at the home institution, but do not receive the schedule of offerings until they arrive in the host country.

✳ The list of courses to be offered may be published in advance, but not the meeting schedule. There may be day and time conflicts between students' first choices.

✳ Students may encounter other issues such as full courses, cancellations, etc.

Consequently, they often have to secure additional approvals on short turnaround. The more completely students have fleshed out possibilities and options beforehand, the more easily they can handle the academic decisions they may face at the start of a semester abroad.

One of the many facets of study abroad success is the ability of faculty and students to understand and to simultaneously navigate two educational systems—that of the home institution and that of the host program. There can be differences in terminology, timing, etc., but there are also similarities. Students register for courses, earn grades, attend classes, and so on. Open communication and the ready supply of detailed information are the starting blocks of what can be a life-changing journey. They change the planning process from a challenge to a collaboration that celebrates the potential for student growth which study abroad can foster.

Study Abroad Course Selection Considerations

✳ What requirements do I need to complete during the semester I'm studying abroad in order to graduate on time? How much flexibility do I have with my course selection?

◆ In my major(s)?

◆ In my minor(s)?

◆ In Core Curriculum requirements?

◆ Is there any specific Elon course(s) or requirement(s) that only fits in my schedule the semester I hope to study abroad?

◆ Do I have room to take any free electives during the semester I'm abroad?

✳ How many semester hours do I have to complete during the semester I'm studying abroad in order to graduate on time?

✳ What courses are being offered at the host institution? Which ones seem, based on the course descriptions, to be a good fit for the course(s) I need to take?

✳ Select courses from offerings based on your answers to questions 1 and 2.

✳ Think through some alternate scenarios and develop second and third choices accordingly. In other words, "if I don't get my first choice of courses or if I can't satisfy the Elon requirements I was hoping while I'm abroad, what else can I take and still graduate on time?"

THIRTY-ONE

Axact:
A Diploma Mill Case Study

ALLEN EZELL | FBI Agent (Ret.), Education Fraud Consultant

Axact: A Diploma Mill Case Study

Diploma mills and accreditation mills devalue earned degrees, confuse the public, and defraud students. This chapter will focus on the largest alleged diploma mill in the world today, Axact (Pvt.) Limited. It will bring to light its operational methods, advise college administrators on how to identify its fraudulent degrees, and describe the current investigation into the company.

The investigation into Axact is ongoing by Pakistan's Federal Investigation Agency (FIA), British Home Office, Interpol, and the Federal Bureau of Investigation (FBI). Numerous Axact top executives and others have been jailed and five others are currently fugitives. No trials have yet taken place, thus there have been no final judicial rulings.

The Axact Empire

Since its founding in 1997, Axact (Pvt.) Ltd., based in Karachi, Pakistan has sold over 220,000 high school and college diplomas to buyers in 17 countries. According to one Axact official, the company entered the "online education business" around 2000 (Kamal 2016). Some buyers paid $399 for a fake diploma, while others paid up to as much as $200,000-$400,000. The company's total revenues from this business may approach one billion dollars, flowing through 35 bank accounts in 19 countries. Axact had call centers in Karachi, Rawalpindi, and in Pakistan's capital, Islamabad, using 900 sales agents ('registrars'), with 110 'quality assurance auditors' monitoring the calls day and night. Their main targets were residents of nearby Gulf Region countries, resulting in

124,000 shipments of documents (56 percent of sales), and the United States with 65,000 shipments of documents (29 percent of sales). Axact had 1,100 websites; 370 fictional high schools, colleges, and universities; 150 accreditation mills; and 400 term paper/research mill sites. In recorded calls, sales personnel used impersonation, threats, extortion, and blackmail to extract more money from previous diploma buyers. Counterfeit documents, including U.S. State Department Apostille attestations, were used.

As a result of an exposé on May 17, 2015 in the *New York Times* (NYT), the FIA seized over 2.2 million diplomas and counterfeit State Dept. Apostille attestation documents during raids in an Axact printing facility. The FIA also seized servers, computers, and business and accounting records, during multiple raids on Axact offices in all three cities. Later, the FIA closed and sealed the Axact offices, froze their bank accounts, arrested its top officers, and petitioned the Court to add seizure of all Axact hard assets along with the 1,100 motor vehicles registered in Axact's name, which it did.

Legal Status of Diploma Fraud

Neither the United States nor Pakistan have federal criminal statutes outlawing the advertising, sale, issuance, possession, or use of diplomas issued by diploma mills nor the issuing of false accreditation documents by accreditation mills. The United States has federal criminal statutes dealing with wire fraud (interstate wire communications), mail fraud, and several computer frauds, which have been used to successfully prosecute diploma and accreditation mills. Pakistan does not have any cybercrime statutes as of yet.

Hiding in Clear Sight

Most diploma mills hide on the Internet amongst legitimate online educational institutions. They may also use fake high schools, personnel agencies, job offers, and scholarship sites to lure the potential victims. However, Axact operated somewhat openly, under the umbrella of an IT company. At Axact's 'Team Meet' in 2013–14, Chairman Shoaib Shaikh unveiled their plans and picture for 'GalAxact,' the futuristic massive office complex for Axact, which would include a building complex of 3.5 million square feet, five 16-storied office towers, a helipad covering an area of 80 ft., a monorail, and would enable 20,000 Axact employees to work in a single shift (Axact 2016b).

Axact also made public its vision of "a prosperous and a thriving Pakistan" in its "Plan 2019" to make available, at reasonable prices, food, shelter, healthcare, education, and judicial assistance to every Pakistani by 2019 (Shaikh 2013). This was to be paid for by Axact donating 65 percent of their IT export revenues to charity (Shaikh 2013).

Axact's Products

Axact is a highly-diversified diploma mill. According to former employee, their main income streams are from:

* **Prior Learning Assessment** (PLA) as used with new customers in their sale of degrees. New customers were advised that they qualified for a scholarship. When contacting them as a prospective student, the author was awarded the "90 percent Presidential Scholarship," with only 10 percent remaining to be paid in order for the degree to be awarded based on life, academic, and work experience.
* **Research and Sponsored Programs** (RSP). These term and research paper sites offer customized research to buyers. During a federal civil law suit against one of its fake institutions—Belford High School—it was discovered that Axact had obtained the login credentials for hundreds U.S. colleges and university library website pages, which it used to steal content from publications.

* **Sale of degrees** and purported legalization/attestations through embassies and ministries of higher education which were used ostensibly to add support and validation to the diplomas already sold (Jamshaid 2015).

Axact profited from the sale of diplomas from multiple fictional schools, sold by up to 900 salesmen with weekly goals of up to $10 million. In 2015, Axact's "flagship" U.S. schools were Must University (using a mail drop on Market Street, San Francisco, CA) and Paramount California University (using an address in Irvine, CA). Axact sales techniques included key phrases such as "advance your career with a global degree," "executive education program," and a $5,000 "exclusive referral discount." Axact also created a "search engine optimization" department to ensure that internet searches on Axact schools and other products resulted in their product appearing at the top of the search results. In addition, Axact had a group of employees working on "Proxy Student Services," whereby students in legitimate U.S. schools were offered the opportunity to send all their academic assignments to Axact, which would then conduct the necessary research, prepare the assignment, and forward them electronically to the professor at the school as if they were being sent directly from the student, for a fee of $40,000.

Identifying Axact Websites

Axact's "school" websites have a professional look and feel, stock photos, student models, and fantastic graphics.[31] Most Axact school sites have the following traits in common:

* School has a .com extension, not .edu, (only two Axact schools had .edu extensions)
* No physical address is given
* Only a toll free number is given
* School 'over sells' its legitimacy

---

[31] See <en.wikipedia.org/wiki/Axact>.

* Numerous logos of supposed 'accrediting entities' are displayed, with links
* Student pictures are stock photos
* 70–90 percent 'scholarships' are available, including "Presidential Scholarships"
* 'Exclusive scholarships' are offered to those students in the United States (up to 75 percent)
* A price chart reflecting tuition at competitor schools is displayed
* A 'dancing green box' appears offering 24/7 'live chat' with school officials
* Same 'faculty' can be found at other schools
* No cost per credit hour given; only a flat price for entire degree program
* Lifetime 'verification' is touted, as well as Embassy certification and U.S. State Department Apostille.
* Numerous awards given to the school are listed
* A disproportionately large number of alumni are listed for relatively new school
* An excessive number of departments and majors are listed
* Domain registration is hidden under a third-party registration

Some of the comments made about the school, faculty, and graduates/students, include:
* 70 percent of faculty hold PhDs in their fields
* Offering 70 different majors, in 16 diverse schools
* 80 percent of alumni work for Fortune 500 companies
* "Employability" to 100 percent

Innova University (2016) touts its Presidential Scholarship with eligibility criteria "so minimum that 90 percent of the applicants qualified for it." It also provides a "substantial fee waiver" of 20 percent if tuition is paid in one single payment or a "9 percent discount if paid in two installments." Innova University is one of the very few "schools" with a physical address listed: 2711 Centerville Road, Wilmington, Delaware 19808. This is the address for Corporate Service Company,

which appears to be a third-party company that prevents direct access to identification of its clients.

Political Climate Giving Rise to Axact

Several incidents took place in Pakistan and neighboring countries which may have played a role in the growth and success of Axact. In 2002, President Pervez Musharraf issued an executive order establishing a new minimum education requirement of a bachelor degree for any Member of the National Assembly (MNA) (the lower house of Parliament in Pakistan). This new order effectively disqualified about 29 percent (about 60) of the 207 MNAs elected in 1997 (Afzal 2013). As a result, many MNAs obtained fictitious academic credentials. This issue plagued Pakistan politics through 2010 and garnered considerable press.

In 2012, Syed Ahsan Shah, Provincial Minister for Industries in Balochistan, was disqualified by the Balochistan High Court for possession and use of a fake degree. When questioned by reporters about his supposed educational credentials being used in Pakistan politics, he commented "A degree is a degree! Whether fake or genuine, it's a degree! It makes no difference" (Khan and Toosi 2010).

In surrounding areas, investigations were also launched into diploma mills. In 2013, the Education Ministry in Saudi Arabia began a campaign against fake credentials, identifying nearly 620 employees in government offices using fake bachelor's, master's, and doctoral degrees (Geo TV 2013). The Central Bureau of Investigation (CBI) in India, after conducting an investigation regarding forged university degrees, advised the court that "51,156 fake degrees have been issued in the state," many of these used to obtain jobs in higher education (Vyas 2010). Estimates run as high as 25,000 of India's 350,000 primary school teachers may be using fake credentials. After the disclosure of the scandal, at least 1,400 Indian primary school teachers resigned during an amnesty period in 2015.

From 2010 to 2015, authorities in China also conducted sting operations regarding fraudulent academic credentials. One such sting resulted in the arrests of at least 67 ESL and TEFL expat teachers and recruiters involving fake diplomas and TEFL certificates (ESL 2016). Reports in 2013 indicated that China has over 100 universities which do not have proper accreditation nor permits, and lists of these diploma mills have been posted by ShangDaxue.com, a university web resource company (Florcruz 2013). These and other types of fraudulent documents are sold openly on the streets in China.

Media Attention and Court Cases

In November 2009, the United States District Court in Detroit, Michigan, heard a civil suit for fraud, wherein Elizabeth Lauber *et al*. sued Belford High School. This later became a class action suit representing 30,000 victims who had purchased Belford High School diplomas and GEDs. Additionally, Belford High School was charged with violating the Racketeer Influenced Corrupt Organization (RICO) statute. Salem Kureshi testified that he personally owned Belford High School and Belford University and managed their operations from his apartment. Kureshi stated that he was in no way affiliated with Axact. On August 11, 2012, the court awarded a default judgment of $22,783,500 to the plaintiffs. No money was ever collected. Kureshi, who remained in Karachi, has been identified as a low level employee at Axact, and has cooperated with the FIA and is now considered an 'approver' in the current Axact case.[32]

For the last nine years, Axact has been the subject of various stories by reporters in the United Kingdom (*The Daily Mail*), in Saudi Arabia (*Saudi Gazette* and *Compunet Arab News*), and in the United States (www. GetEducated.com). None of the stories attracted as much worldwide attention as did the May 17, 2015 Declan Walsh story, "Fake Diplomas, Real Cash; Pakistani Company Axact Reaps Millions," which appeared on the front page of the *New York Times*. It was followed by several other articles and an editorial.

In November 2014, Axact whistleblower Sayyad Yasir Jamshaid, a former employee in Karachi, made contact with Dr. John Bear and Ezell and requested assistance on how best to expose Axact for the massive fraud that it was. He had been employed at Axact as a Quality Control Auditor and was assigned to one of the sales teams which sold diplomas in the Gulf Region. He had quit his job after photographing certain company records. He then fled Pakistan for Dubai, UAE. Declan Walsh interviewed Jamshaid in Dubai for three days, and Jamshaid agreed to be named as a source of information in the upcoming NYT article. As a result, after the story was published, a number of other former employees surfaced, also giving their stories and documents to the press.

Aftermath of NYT Exposé

Shoaib Shaikh, founder and CEO of Axact, took several positions after the NYT story was published. He claimed the company was innocent and threatened to sue the NYT (no lawsuit ever materialized). He later admitted that Axact had issued 147 Ph.D. degrees to customers in the United Arab Emirates. After about 17 hours of questioning over several days by the FIA, he told the FIA the location of the Axact printing facility adjacent to their main office building and accompanied them there. After seizing about 2,200,000 blank diplomas, school identification cards, accreditation documents, and counterfeit U.S. State Department Attestations, the FIA arrested both Shaikh and his co-founder, Viqas Atiq.

In an article on May 20, 2015, Altaf Hussain, founder and leader of the Muttahida Qaumi Movement (a secular political party in Pakistan), expressed his shock and grief over the allegations. He called for an investigation, and said that if the allegations were found to be true, "exemplary punishment should be given to the people involved in it so that no one could even think about committing such a monstrous fraud in the future" (Hussain 2015). Hussain demanded that Axact senior

---

[32] An "approver" is deemed to be a cooperating witness who is granted immunity, with their statements having been recorded before a judicial magistrate.

management be added to the Exit Control List (No Fly) and warned that the fact that intelligence agencies in Pakistan were unaware of the alleged fraud should be a wake-up call for the nation (Hussain 2015).

The NYT exposé also alarmed government officials. Parliament officials tasked the Interior Minister with forming a special committee to investigate all allegations. The length and breadth of the Axact scandal humiliated Pakistan and resulted in a local and regional media frenzy.

The investigation resulted in FIA raids on Axact offices in three cities, the removal of at least 75 employees in broad daylight in police vehicles, as well as the seizure of Axact computers and servers, business records, and closing of offices. During this time, the FIA froze associated bank accounts, reclaimed 1,100 vehicles registered to Axact, and took all of its hard assets using anti-money laundering statutes. They then conducted interviews with hundreds of Axact employees, with over 15 becoming 'approvers' and agreeing to testify on behalf of the government. These 'approvers' ranged from low-level employees—call center personnel, printing shop manager—to several 'regional directors' whose stories were recorded before a judicial magistrate. At least one of these 'approvers' is a high ranking official at Axact headquarters in Karachi.

Tools for Protecting Institutions

This chapter provides only a short summary of the workings of Axact, described as the world's largest diploma mill. While diploma mills continue to exist both domestically and internationally, it is hoped that a criminal enterprise of this size, length of operation, diversified fraudulent practices, and sales successes will not surface again.

The Dominican Republic and El Salvador

2016 AACRAO INTERNATIONAL GUIDE

MICHELLE A. BIRCH | President
Global Education Group, Inc.

The Dominican Republic and El Salvador

Dominican Republic

PRIMARY, MIDDLE, SECONDARY EDUCATION

There are two pre-higher education systems in place in the Dominican Republic: the Traditional System (effective through Ley Orgánica No. 2909 dated June 27, 1951 and modified by Ley No. 3644 dated October 5, 1953) and the Reformed System (effective through Ordenanza 1-86 and Ley Orgánica de Educación No. 66 dated April 9, 1997).

Traditional System

The traditional system consists of 6 years of primary education plus 6 years of lower and upper secondary education (consisting of a 2-year intermediate cycle followed by a 4-year upper secondary cycle). Qualifications are:

* Primary: *Certificado de Suficiencia en Los Estudios Primarios* (Certificate of Proficiency in Primary Studies) upon conclusion of 6 years of primary education
* Middle: *Certificado de Suficiencia en los Estudios Intermedios* (Certificate of Proficiency in Intermediate Studies) upon conclusion of the 2-year intermediate cycle
* High School: *Bachillerato* (Baccalaureate) upon conclusion of the 4-year upper secondary cycle; with options of academic, vocational, and technical streams.
* *Maestro Normal*: secondary-level teaching qualification for primary level teachers consisting of one to two years of upper secondary study after grade 10 (phased out in the 1990s)

Reformed System

The reformed system consists of 8 years of primary and middle education plus 4 years of secondary education. This system has a large number of specialization options available during the 4-year secondary cycle. Qualifications are:

* Primary and Middle: *Educación Básica* (Basic Education) leading to the *Diploma de Terminó de la Educación Básica* (Diploma of Conclusion of Basic Education) upon conclusion of 8 years of primary and middle education (consists of two 4-year cycles—grades 1 to 4 followed by grades 5 to 8)
* High School: *Educación Secundaria* (Secondary Education) leading to the *Bachillerato* (Baccalaureate) in a specific track upon conclusion of 4 years of secondary education; numerous specializations

TECHNICAL EDUCATION

Technical programs may be at the secondary or higher education level and vary in duration. The status of the issuing institution, length and content of program, and entry requirements should be carefully considered. Final qualifications awarded can be listed as *Técnico* (Technician), *Tecnólogo Superior* (Higher Technologist), *Técnico Superior* (Higher Technician), or *Técnico Profesional* (Professional Technician), among others. Programs range in length from 1 to 3 years.

TEACHING EDUCATION

Effective in the 1990s, all teaching programs were moved to university level. Qualifications are:

* *Maestro Normal*: secondary level teaching qualification for primary level teachers consisting of 1 to

TABLE 32.1: Suggested U.S. Equivalents, Dominican Republic

			Suggested U.S. Equivalent
General Grading System			
A	Excelente (Excellent)	90–100	A
B	Muy Bueno (Very Good)	80–89	B
C	Bueno (Good)	70–79	C
D	Deficiente (Deficient/Fail)	0–69	F
Traditional System Qualifications			
Primary: *Certificado de Suficiencia en Los Estudios Primarios* (Certificate of Proficiency in Primary Studies)			Grade 6
Middle: *Certificado de Suficiencia en los Estudios Intermedios* (Certificate of Proficiency in Intermediate Studies)			Grade 8
High School: *Bachillerato* (Baccalaureate)			High School
Maestro Normal (Teacher)			Vocational High School
Reformed System Qualifications			
Primary and Middle: *Educación Básica* (Basic Education) leading to the *Diploma de Terminó de la Educación Básica*			Grade 8
High School: *Educación Secundaria* (Secondary Education) leading to the *Bachillerato* (Baccalaureate) in a specific track upon conclusion of four years of secondary education; numerous specializations			High School
Technical Education			
Técnico (Technician), *Tecnológo Superior* (Higher Technologist), *Técnico Superior* (Higher Technician), *Técnico Profesional* (Professional Technician), among others.			Individual qualifications must be reviewed thoroughly to determine U.S. equivalent. May be secondary or higher education level and vary in duration.
Teaching Education			
Maestro Normal (Teacher)			Vocational High School
Profesor(a) (Teacher), *Certificado de Estudios Superiores* (Certificate of Higher Studies)			2 to 3 Years of College Level Study
Licenciado(a)/Licenciatura (Licentiate) (in Education area)			Bachelor's Degree
University Education			
Licenciado(a)/Licenciatura (Licentiate) (in a specific major)			Bachelor's Degree
Ingeniero(a) (Engineer), *Arquitecto(a)* (Architect), professional *titulo* (degree)			Bachelor's Degree
Certificado de Postgrado (Postgraduate Certificate)			1 year of undergraduate or graduate level study at a U.S. university (course content must be reviewed)
Especialista (Specialist)			Graduate level study at a U.S. university or professional qualification (course content must be reviewed)
Maestría (Master)			Master's Degree
Doctor (Doctor) or *Licenciado(a)/Licenciatura* (Licentiate) in a professional area			First Professional Degree in the Field

2 years of upper secondary study after grade 10 (program phased out in the 1990s).

✳ *Profesor(a)* (Teacher), *Certificado de Estudios Superiores* (Certificate of Higher Studies): post-secondary level teaching qualification for secondary level teachers consisting of 2 to 3 years of postsecondary study after high school.

Licenciado(a)/Licenciatura (in Education area): 4 to 5 years of university level study after high school.

UNIVERSITY EDUCATION

University education takes place after completion of high school level study and follows a first degree followed by postgraduate degree pattern. Qualifications are:

* *Licenciado(a)/Licenciatura* (in a specific major): 4 to 5 years of university level study after high school.
* *Ingeniero(a)* (Engineer), *Arquitecto(a)* (Architect), professional *título* (degree): 4 to 6 years of university level study after high school.
* *Certificado de Postgrado* (Postgraduate Certificate): approximately 1 year of study after a Licenciado/Licenciatura program.
* *Especialista* (Specialist): 1 to 3 years of postgraduate study after a first degree (in medical or legal fields, these are professional in nature).
* *Maestría* (Master): 1 to 3 years of postgraduate study after a first degree (often with thesis).
* *Doctor* (Doctor): first professional degree in areas such as Medicine, Veterinary Medicine, Dentistry, Pharmacy, Law.

ADDITIONAL TIPS

When assessing secondary credentials, it is advisable to request both the final school transcript along with the official final examination results and diploma. Students will often *not* have the diploma and only possess the final examination results. A determination can be made based on the school transcript and final examination results alone if carefully reviewed.

Teaching qualifications must be carefully reviewed for time period, content, entry requirements, and program length in order to ascertain the level of instruction.

El Salvador

Of note, The *Bachiller/Bachillerato General* upper secondary program was revised in 1991 to consist of 2 years of study. The *Bachiller/Bachillerato Técnico/Vocacional*

upper secondary technical or vocational program was not revised and remains at 3 years of study.

PRIMARY, MIDDLE, SECONDARY EDUCATION

The pre-higher education system consists of 9 years of *educación básica* (basic education) followed by 2 to 3 years of *educación media* (upper secondary education), for a total of 11 or 12 years. Qualifications are:

* *Diploma de Educación Básica* (Diploma of Basic Education) upon completion of 9 years of *educación básica* (basic education).
* *Bachiller/Bachillerato* (Baccalaureate), *Bachiller/Bachillerato General* (General Baccalaureate) upon completion of 3 years of *educación media* (upper secondary education) until 1991 and upon completion of 2 years of *educación media* (upper secondary education) after 1991.
* *Bachiller/Bachillerato Técnico/Vocacional* (Technical/Vocational Baccalaureate) upon completion of 3 years of technical/vocational *educación media* (upper secondary education).
* *Bachillerato Pedagógico* (Pedagogical Baccalaureate) upon completion of 3 years of *educación media* (upper secondary education) with a focus on teaching (eliminated after the 1968 Education Reform when all teaching education became university level).

TECHNICAL EDUCATION

Most technical programs are postsecondary level; however, the status of the issuing institution, length and content of program, and entry requirements should be carefully considered. Final qualifications awarded can be listed as *Técnico* (Technician), *Tecnológo* (Technologist), *Técnico Avanzado* (Advanced Technician), among others. Programs range in length from 1 to 4 years.

TEACHING EDUCATION

Effective after the 1968 Education Reform, all teaching programs were moved to university level. Qualifications are:

TABLE 32.2: Suggested U.S. Equivalents, El Salvador

				Suggested U.S. Equivalent
General Grading System				
A	Sobresaliente (Excellent)	9–10		A
B	Bien (Good)	7–8.9		B
C	Aprobado (Pass)	6–6.9		C
D	Suspenso (Fail)	0–5.9		F
Primary and Secondary Education				
Diploma de Educación Básica (Diploma of Basic Education)				Grade 9
Bachiller/Bachillerato (Baccalaureate), *Bachiller/Bachillerato General* (General Baccalaureate)				High School
Bachiller/Bachillerato Técnico/Vocacional (Technical/Vocational Baccalaureate)				Vocational High School
Bachillerato Pedagógico (Pedagogical Baccalaureate)				High School
Technical Education				
Técnico (Technician), *Tecnológo* (Technologist), *Técnico Avanzado* (Advanced Technician), among others				Individual qualifications must be reviewed thoroughly to determine U.S. equivalent. Programs vary in duration.
Teaching Education				
Profesor(a) (Teacher)				Bachelor's Degree
Licenciado(a)/Licenciatura (in Education area)				Bachelor's Degree
University Education				
Licenciado(a)/Licenciatura (in a specific major)				Bachelor's Degree
Ingeniero(a) (Engineer), *Abogado(a)* (Attorney), *Arquitecto(a)* (Architect), professional *titulo* (degree)				Bachelor's Degree
Maestría (Master)				Master's Degree
Doctor (Doctor)				First Professional Degree in the Field
Doctor (Doctor), *Doctorado* (Doctorate)				Ph.D.

* *Bachillerato Pedagógico* (Pedagogical Baccalaureate): upon completion of 3 years of *educación media* (upper secondary education) with a focus on teaching (eliminated after the 1968 Education Reform when all teaching education became university level).
* *Profesor(a)* (Teacher): university level teaching qualification for primary or secondary level teachers consisting of 4 to 5 years of university level study after high school.
* *Licenciado(a)/Licenciatura* (in Education area): 4 to 5 years of university level study after high school.

UNIVERSITY EDUCATION

University education takes place after completion of high school level study and follows a pattern of first degree followed by postgraduate degree. Qualifications are:

* *Licenciado(a)/Licenciatura* (in a specific major): 4 to 6 years of university level study after high school.
* *Ingeniero(a)* (Engineer), *Abogado(a)* (Attorney), *Arquitecto(a)* (Architect), professional *titulo* (degree): 4 to 6 years of university level study after high school.
* *Maestría* (Master): generally 2 years of postgraduate study after a first degree (often with thesis).

✳ *Doctor* (Doctor): first professional degree in areas such as Medicine, Veterinary Medicine, Dentistry, and Pharmacy.

✳ *Doctor* (Doctor), *Doctorado* (Doctorate): research oriented degree with dissertation completed after a minimum of three years of study.

ADDITIONAL TIPS

When assessing secondary education credentials, documentation should be carefully reviewed with regard to time period of study since there have been changes to the system over time.

Many university level programs contain credit hours that mimic u.s. semester credit hours.

When reviewing a *Doctor* (Doctor) degree, careful review of the entry requirements, program details, and content should be undertaken in order to assess the degree accurately.

THIRTY-THREE

Undergraduate Transfer Students from China

2016 AACRAO INTERNATIONAL GUIDE

OLIVIA CHEN

Assistant Director, Undergraduate Admission
University of California, Los Angeles

Undergraduate Transfer Students from Chi..

tarting in the 2009–2010 academic year, China became the leading country of international students studying in the United States, breaking a seven-year lead by India (Institute of International Education 2015). Historically, the number of exchange students from China has fluctuated due largely to changes in political and economic policies. For example, the 1970s saw a substantial increase after a major economic reform initiated by Deng Xiaoping, marking years of upward economic mobility for many families in China.

Since then, the number of Chinese students engaged in undergraduate, graduate, and educational exchanges in the U.S. has only grown. As of 2014, 274,439 students from China are engaged in educational studies, accounting for 31 percent of the entire international student population in the U.S. (IIE 2015a).

While the number of undergraduate students from China trails behind those seeking graduate degrees, the increased interest and rate of growth for undergraduate degrees will likely outpace graduate students in the coming years. With this added interest, the type of undergraduate students from China will likely grow in complexity. The student profile from China will no longer only be one of direct entry from high school, but also include those who are seeking higher education through other ways, namely through the transfer route.

This chapter addresses salient issues related to transfer students from China. First, the types of transfer students from China will be identified, along with some of their motivations for choosing the transfer process rather than direct entry. Then, an overview of the Chinese education system will be provided and credential evaluation discussed. This section will examine credentials seen at the undergraduate transfer level and provide recommendations for credit transfer. Next, Chinese transfer students enrolled at community colleges will be examined, with a closer look at the implications of their presence and growth. Finally, future trends affecting the enrollment and recruitment of international students will be discussed, along with how these issues affect the Chinese transfer student population.

Understanding and Identifying Transfer Students from China

The World Bank's latest China census reports an approximate population of 1.4 billion residents (World Bank 2014). As a growing nation, China has not only seen an increase in its overall economic output, but also the growth of its middle class. The emergence of the middle class has historically led to higher human capital spending, namely in education (Pezzini 2012). This is further corroborated by Tsang (2013) in her qualitative study of Chinese middle class families; she has found that many parents in this group have the financial means, connections, and cultural motivation to encourage their children to study in private transnational institutions in China and at universities abroad (Tsang 2013).

To gain a better understanding of why students from China seek to transfer to universities in the U.S., it is crucial to understand the factors that lead students to seek education abroad in the first place. Academics have studied the variety of "push-pull" factors affecting international students' decisions to study abroad. Push factors are those originating from within the country, which include social, economic, or political forces,

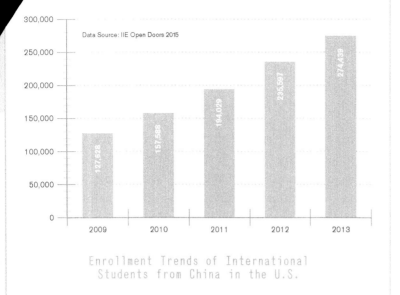

Data Source: IIE Open Doors 2015

Enrollment Trends of International
Students from China in the U.S.

Fudan University. Students and parents do not prefer second-tier Chinese universities because of their perceived lack of academic quality and prestige. Some of these universities have been unable to meet enrollment quotas set by central government authorities due to lack of interest (Xinhua 2015). Transferring, while a plausible option in the U.S., is difficult between institutions in China. Students require the approval from both the current and prospective institutions to initiate the transfer, and often the signatures of the heads of the departments as well (Ringer 2000).

Students and parents will weigh their educational options as early as before taking the *gaokao*. Many students and their parents will rest their decisions on their chances of admission domestically, and if they know their chances of being accepted into a top-tier is low, students will also apply to institutions in the U.S., the United Kingdom, Australia, and other international locations as an alternative plan (White 2011).

A second push factor in the decision-making process of studying in the U.S. is the quality and flexibility of academic programs. Chinese students place a greater emphasis on the higher quality of education and experiences at international institutions when comparing them to their domestic universities (Bodycott 2009). Many of these students perceive the Chinese system as rigid and lacking student focus (Bodycott 2009). The structured nature of China's curriculum, which is overseen by the Ministry of Education, limits the ability of students to choose their own academic courses and to change majors.

A pull factor to consider is the perceived employment opportunities that come with a U.S. degree. Many students and parents believe that international education opportunities will lead to better job prospects and promotions at home (Tsang 2013; White 2011). The

while pull factors are reasons outside of a student's home country that attract or "pull" them to study abroad (Mazzarol and Soutar 2002).

PUSH-PULL FACTORS: MOTIVATIONS FOR STUDYING ABROAD

Chinese students are influenced by both push and pull factors in their decision to seek university education in the U.S. One push factor is rooted in how the competitive education system in China—particularly in the higher education sector—is motivating many students to improve their chances of admission to a university by also applying internationally. To put this into perspective, in 2014, it was reported that over 9 million students in China sat for the national university entrance examination known as the *gaokao* (Knowlton 2014). About 7 million earned a spot in one of over 2,000 national higher institutions, a shortage of 2 million spots for college-age goers (Knowlton 2014). Of this group, some will choose to retake the *gaokao* the following year, but for others, opportunities abroad may be a more immediate option.

Even if many are able to secure a spot at a Chinese national university, not all will be admitted into competitive top-tier choices such as Peking, Tsinghua, and

perceived prestige of a foreign degree "pulls" many students into studying abroad, and the potential return on investment of their international education is a very strong incentive to look outside of China.

TYPES OF TRANSFER STUDENTS

Given the competitiveness of domestic admissions, the rigidity of the educational curriculum, and the perceived higher earning potential of a U.S. degree, many Chinese students are motivated to earn postsecondary degrees in the U.S. While many will apply directly from high schools, a growing number are considering transferring from Chinese institutions

The second type of transfer student from China that is growing in the U.S. is one that enrolls at a community college. International recruitment at the community college is a more recent phenomenon, as colleges find new ways to internationalize their college campuses. There are also added financial benefits, as international students pay three to four times the tuition of a domestic student at a community college (AACRAO 2015). In 2014, there were 87,963 international students studying at community colleges in the U.S. (IIE 2015a). While the number of international students has fluctuated over the years, Chinese students became the largest international population enrolled at community colleges in 2013, and they currently account for close to 17 percent of the total international student enrollment at community colleges (IIE 2015a).

Understanding the motivations of Chinese students in studying abroad can help enrollment management administrators better tailor their recruitment strategies and goals to this student population. While many international students share similar reasons for seeking an education abroad, not all are motivated by the same reasons. The profile of Chinese international students is changing, with many now seeking alternative ways to gain education at four-year institutions through the transfer process.

Education Overview and Implications for Credit Transfer

The previous section identified the motivations for transfer and the two types of transfer students from China studying in the U.S. The following is an overview of the Chinese education system, leading into a discussion and recommendation for evaluation of Chinese credentials at the transfer level.

STRUCTURE OF THE CHINESE EDUCATION SYSTEM

The Chinese education system is highly-structured and governed by the Ministry of Education. The official language of instruction at all levels of education is Chinese (Mandarin or Putonghua). Most schools operate on an academic year running from September until June, consisting of two 20-week semesters.

China's current educational system was shaped in large part during the government of Mao Zedong, who in 1949 declared the country a one-party communist state. Most private institutions were closed down or converted into state-run schools. Over the years, the growing population and the demand for education has allowed for private institutions to also operate in China. Private institutions exist at all levels of academic study, and their curriculum does not entirely subscribe to the national curriculum created by the Ministry of Education.

Primary and Secondary Education

The Chinese primary and secondary educational system is structured similarly to that of the U.S., with 9 years of compulsory education. Primary and secondary education lasts 12 years and is divided into a 6-3-3 structure:

* 6 years of primary education (*xiaoxue*)
* 3 years of lower or junior middle school education (*zhongxue*)
* 3 years of upper or senior middle school education (*gaozhong*)

The educational system emphasizes testing as a measure of a students' proficiency at each level of education.

After completion of a prescribed curriculum at the lower or junior middle school level, students will have completed compulsory education. At this stage, they will also have the choice to continue on to senior middle school by sitting for the senior middle school exam (*zhongkao*). The *zhongkao* is mandatory for entrance into senior middle schools, and it can also be used for entry into junior secondary vocational programs.

Once students enter into an upper or senior middle school program, education will last three years and culminate with a graduation examination known as High School Academic Proficiency Test (*xueye shuiping ceshi* or, in some provinces, *huikao*).

The High School Academic Proficiency Test is administered twice a year. There are three formats to the proficiency exam, with each of the 23 provinces responsible for administering the test (WENR 2011). The only exceptions are in the provinces of Guangdong, Hunan, Hubei, and Shanxi, where the exam is administered by the schools (WENR 2011).

Higher Education

In 2014, there were a total of 2,529 higher education institutions in China (China Ministry of Education 2015), which included universities and research institutions, adult higher education institutions, private and independent colleges, and vocational colleges.

Typical postsecondary degrees in China that admission officers may encounter at the transfer level are:

* *Zhuanke* diploma: short-cycle diploma, awarded upon completion of two years of short-cycle college study. Vocationally-oriented.
* *Xueshi xuewei* degree: Bachelor's degree. Awarded upon completion of a four-year undergraduate program (*benke*) at a higher education institution. Professional programs in medicine, architecture, and some engineering and music programs could last approximately five years. Academically-oriented.
* *Shuoshi xuewei* degree: Master's degree. Awarded upon completion of two to three years of post-

graduate study at a higher education institution or research institution.
* *Boshi* degree: Ph.D. degree. Awarded upon completion of three to five years of doctoral studies after the completion of a master's degree (which is a requirement for admission).

Admission to Universities

Admission into university is dependent on the results of the national university entrance examination commonly known as the *gaokao*. Top-tier and national "key" universities, including those that are under the supervision of the Ministry of Education, require higher *gaokao* scores for admission, and as such, are highly competitive.

The *gaokao* is administered over two to three days during the month of June. In the past, the Ministry of Education would write the exam and administer it at the different provinces. Most provinces and municipalities today have the autonomy to create their own exams. Provinces opting not to write their own must use Ministry-created exams (WENR 2011). Each province or municipality sets their own passing minimums. In addition, there is no age restriction for taking the *gaokao* and students are not barred from taking the test multiple times.

The exam tests students in a variety of subjects. The first component of the exam includes three compulsory subjects in Chinese, math, and a foreign language. The second part requires students to choose one additional subject from either the sciences or humanities stream. The third component of the exam requires either a comprehensive test in the arts or sciences category, or a choice of one test from either of these two areas.

Higher Education Curriculum

In the early 1950s, the Chinese higher education system was patterned after that of the Soviet Union (Ringer 2000). A broad curriculum in arts, social sciences, and natural sciences was offered at a small number of universities, while a larger number of institutions would offer more specialized/technical education in applied sciences, law, medicine, foreign languages, finance and trade, and teacher training (Ringer 2000).

Over the years, higher education changed to align more to a Western-style of education. One of the key elements is in the adoption of the credit system, similar to that of the U.S. Despite wide acceptance, there is still no standardized method for displaying credits, and universities set their own parameters on how they report credits on transcripts.

Some institutions may choose to show hours of contact in lieu of credits. In rare instances, some schools choose not to display credits or hours at all. These institutions will include the coursework a student has attempted and the grades earned, but do not include the number of credits or hours of study. This does not imply that the student did not earn any credits for their courses; it may simply be the institution's way of displaying coursework in their transcripts. Admission officers are encouraged to request additional information regarding the total number of credits attempted in the program.

Degrees at the bachelor's level usually last about four years; however, progression is closely regulated. For example, students must complete the necessary number of credit hours in the four years of their bachelor's program. Although the Academic Degrees Committee of the State Council and the Ministry of Education regulate degrees, there is no unified entity that dictates the number of credits required for graduation from an academic program. The number of credits required for graduation will vary by university and by program.

Although most universities operate on a semester system, Chinese students typically have as many as 60 contact hours in one semester (Ringer 2000), as opposed to 30 to 45 contact hours in the U.S.

Curriculum at the higher education level offers little flexibility. Depending on the university and the program, students will have a set core of classes to complete in usually four years (five or more for some programs in medicine, architecture, engineering, and music). There is a prescribed order of completion, so most students will be in the same classes throughout their educational career. This also allows students to take mostly upper-division courses in their final two years of undergraduate education (Ringer 2000).

Implications for Awarding Transfer Credit

At the undergraduate transfer level, admission officers will typically encounter students with courses from *zhuanke* (short-cycle colleges), and *benke* (four-year college programs). Because of the complexity and size of China's higher education sector, officers will also encounter similar credentials offered through adult higher education and vocational institutions.

The recommendation for awarding transfer credit will depend on the type of institution (*i.e.,* four-year university, junior college, adult higher education institution, etc.) and program (*zhuanke* or *benke*) in which a transfer student was previously enrolled.

It is important to research carefully the institutions from which students transfer by consulting the recognized institution lists published by the Chinese Ministry of Education.[33] The type of institution will be a good indicator to the nature of the courses (academic or vocational) that the student has completed.

Transcripts from Chinese institutions do not have course prefixes or course-level designation, which complicates the awarding of transfer credits during the admission process. Because most undergraduate Chinese students will follow a prescribed curriculum, it is recommended that the first two years of study be designated as lower-division credit, with subsequent courses in the third and fourth year awarded as upper-division.

The undergraduate *benke,* or bachelor's curriculum, consists of approximately 20 percent general education classes, 10 percent foreign language, 50–55 percent major-related courses or upper-division classes, and 15 percent elective courses (Drewitz 2011).

[33] *See* en.moe.gov.cn

A notable component of the undergraduate curriculum in China is the inclusion of political courses and military theory/training, in line with the mission of the Chinese Community Party in promoting its political ideologies. In addition, completion of the undergraduate program (and part of the graduation requirement) is the thesis or graduation project. Transcripts showing a graduation thesis or project usually indicate completion of an undergraduate program and, as such, the attainment of a bachelor's degree.

Although courses and titles will vary by program, there are a number of common undergraduate classes that most students will take. These include:

✳ Accounting
✳ Basics of Marxist Theory
✳ Calculus
✳ Chemistry
✳ Chinese
✳ Deng Xiaoping Studies or Moral Cultivation
✳ English/Foreign Language
✳ Foreign Trade
✳ History of China/History
✳ Linear Algebra
✳ Literature
✳ Macroeconomics
✳ Mao Zedong Thoughts
✳ Mathematics/Advanced Mathematics
✳ Microeconomics
✳ Military Theory/Training
✳ Philosophy
✳ Physical Education
✳ Physics
✳ Political Economics
✳ Practice/Internship
✳ Situation and Policy
✳ Thesis/Graduation Project
  (Source: Drewitz 2011)

Prior to awarding transfer credit, it is important that an institution's admission practices align with its institutional academic policies and regulations for credit transfer. Since policies will vary by campus, there exists no unified method of credit transfer. These recommendations are based on common credential practices, but admission officers are urged to consult with other credential agencies and their own registrar's office.

Transfer Students at the Community College

In the previous section, the layout of the student population transfering from Chinese higher education institutions was provided, along with a discussion of issues in awarding transfer credit from Chinese credentials. In this chapter, the second source of transfer students from China will be considered—those currently enrolled at community colleges. The growth of Chinese students enrolled at community colleges will be examined, and relevant issues in the internationalization of community colleges will be addressed.

MOTIVATIONS FOR STUDYING AT COMMUNITY COLLEGES

Chinese students are increasingly considering community colleges as a more affordable option to earn postsecondary degrees. Although international students pay higher fees at community colleges, the cost of attendance is significantly lower than at many four-year institutions (*ICEF Monitor* 2015a).

Chinese students' enrollment at community colleges has not always been widespread. Name-brand recognition in the international student community is still one of the most important factors driving choice (Tekle, Quintal, and Taylor 2005), and community colleges have not traditionally been known as a model of education outside of the U.S. According to Brown (as quoted in Clark 2012), "students in those countries, parents in particular, tend to be hung up on the name." Brown suggests that students and parents view community colleges as not as prestigious as four-year universities.

The growth in Chinese students enrolling at community colleges, however, is a good indicator in perceptual shift. Many Chinese students are considering other benefits of attending community colleges aside from savings in tuition. English preparation programs are offered at many community colleges, a second "pull" factor in attracting international students. These programs may also be combined with academic college classes to create "pathway programs." For students with little or no English preparation, enrollment in English intensive and pathways programs is a jump-start into college education in the U.S.

Others also consider the less restrictive admission process as a factor in attending community colleges. At many selective four-year institutions in the U.S., standardized tests scores such as the ACT or SAT are required for admissions. Both exams are not administered in China, which limits a large number of students from taking the test. Those who have the financial means choose to pay additional costs to travel to countries outside of China to take the exam, but for many others, cost and access discourages them from applying directly to four-year universities. Community colleges become a viable option for many Chinese students who are seeking to eventually enroll at a four-year university without the added testing costs and preparation.

A fourth motivating factor is time to degree completion. Some community colleges have combined high school programs with associate degrees, where international students enroll during the equivalent of their 11th grade of high school and simultaneously earn credits for both a high school and an associate degree. This type of program is prevalent at some Washington community colleges, and is heavily marketed as a fast-track opportunity to transfer to a four-year university.

Understanding Chinese students' motivations to attend community colleges has ramifications for international recruitment and admissions. On one hand, the recruitment message needs to be tailored to market the opportunities that are uniquely available at community colleges. While universities use rankings, strength of academic programs, location, size, alumni, and/or research/internship opportunities to draw international students to their campuses, such strategies may not always be relevant to community colleges.

Recruitment messages need to be crafted in relation to the strengths of community colleges, such as low costs, pathways programs, less-selective admission requirements, fast and easy access to four-year universities, and transfer rates. Even marketing programs differently by designating them as "2+2" pathways can affect perception and interest.

On the other hand, administrators can also anticipate program needs of the Chinese international market by understanding their motivations for considering community colleges in the first place. Colleges can create or even revamp existing programs that are attractive to the international student population.

INTERNATIONALIZATION AT COMMUNITY COLLEGES

In last five years, community colleges have developed international student recruitment plans through direct recruitment, agent contracts, and armchair recruitment methods. A more collaborative approach has also been developed to educate international students about the benefits of studying at and transferring from a community college. For example, the American Association of Community Colleges (AACC) developed a guide for international students about U.S. community colleges. Further international partnerships have also been developed between AACC and other institutions and government organizations in China, Brazil, Indonesia, India, and Mexico to promote awareness of educational opportunities through community colleges.

Community colleges were originally created to address the needs and demands of their local communities but socioeconomic, political and cultural changes have pushed many to revisit their roles in educating the next wave of global citizens (Treat and Hagedorn 2013). Administrators are increasingly focusing on the benefits of internationalizing their community colleges, not only seeing international students as financial contributors but also as ambassadors that will help domestic students become more globally-versed.

As the educational mission at community colleges changes to address internationalization goals, other supporting departments will also be called to address the challenges of international students on their college campuses. Student services, academic advising, and academic departments will all likely have more diversified responsibilities in helping international and domestic students integrate into college life. The unique needs of the international student population should also be carefully considered, and support for these departments is crucial in growing and maintaining enrollment of international students. Many successful internationalization models at community colleges exist in the U.S. Enrollment administrators are urged to carefully consider these successes when evaluating international goals at their colleges.

International Education Agents

Another area of debate is the use of educational agents in the recruitment of international students (*see* Chapter 8: International Student Recruitment Agents). In a report prepared by the National Association for College Admission Counseling (NACAC), approximately one-fourth of postsecondary institutions of higher education in the U.S. use commissioned agents for international recruitment (2013).

The use of agents is predominant in countries where "experts" or intermediaries are paid to access programs and services. A large number of educational agencies exist in China, where many provide native-language guidance of the U.S. education system for students and parents. On the recruitment side, colleges and universities are able to tap into the country knowledge of many of these agencies, and save on costs from not hiring a full-time staff to recruit internationally.

The controversy, however, lies in the unethical practices of some of these agencies. Scandals regarding application fraud, institutional misrepresentation, exorbitant fees, and false promises have negatively affected the reputation of agents. While some of these exist, there are other independent agencies that follow strict certification processes and national standards of good practice. Institutions should recognize the potential benefits of working with agencies to further their

international recruitment goals, but should also research extensively on their practices, fee structures, accreditation procedures, and communication methods before signing agreements with them.

International efforts at community colleges and in universities should integrate services and foster collaboration among departments. College administrators should consider the level of leadership and support they can avail to all departments involved in the process. Institutions should also be cognizant of how programs are overseen, and what levels of accountability to stakeholders are in place. Recruiting, admitting and retaining international students, thus, is a multifaceted and collaborative process.

Trends

Colleges and universities should anticipate socio-political and economic shifts in the international marketplace, even in the face of growing demand for postsecondary studies. Even subtle changes could affect the recruitment and admission of students. In this final section, the trends affecting future recruitment and enrollment of international students are addressed. Some of these trends apply specifically to the Chinese transfer population, but other trends also have ramifications on the overall international student body.

ACCEPTANCE OF THE *GAOKAO* FOR ADMISSIONS

In May 2015, the University of San Francisco (USF) announced that it was accepting *gaokao* results in lieu of SAT and TOEFL exams (Sharma 2015). Along with one-on-one interviews, a student's score on the *gaokao* would be used as part of the admissions process. USF is not the only institution to use *gaokao* results for admission, but the number of U.S. universities accepting the exam is still low.

The Chinese Ministry of Education has recently embarked on a campaign to convince global universities to recognize the exam as a reliable measure of Chinese students' abilities (Sharma 2015). Several universities in Australia, including the University of Sydney, consider *gaokao* results for admissions (*ICEF Monitor* 2015a; Sharma 2015). Sharma notes that institutions in Italy, France, Germany, and Spain have accepted *gaokao* scores as well, but on an individual basis (2015).

While the immediate replacement of *gaokao* scores over other widely-used standardized exams is unlikely, USF's decision could spark discussions on the merits of the Chinese college entrance exam. The test measures knowledge in a variety of subjects, and officials in China are convinced that because of this, *gaokao* students have the skills and knowledge to perform well even at institutions outside of China.

The potential acceptance of *gaokao* scores at U.S. universities may push more Chinese high school students to apply directly to four-year institutions instead of attempting the transfer route. With little space at some of China's most coveted universities, Chinese students will continue to go abroad if the *gaokao* becomes a more widely-recognized exam.

CHINA'S INCOME INEQUALITY AND POLITICAL INSTABILITY

China has seen unprecedented growth in the last ten years, but more recent forecasts supports a slowdown in economic output (OECD 2015). The government has enacted policies to stabilize its currency but investors abroad and in China worry. Growing number of Chinese upper-class families have invested their assets abroad due to unpredictable political and economic changes (Shambaugh 2014), but for those in the rising middle class, opportunities to move assets abroad may not be easily available. Income inequality between social classes, furthermore, is growing (Shambaugh 2014). This has affected the spending power that families will have on education, particularly one abroad.

Increased political frustrations, especially in autonomous regions like Hong Kong and Xinjiang (Wasserstrom 2014), could also affect the number of students seeking to study in the U.S. Students may look more closely at locations where greater academic autonomy and less educational disruptions exists, a possible trend as political dissent and oppression occur more frequently in China.

RISE OF PRIVATE UNIVERSITIES

The private education sector in China has developed significantly in the last ten to fifteen years (Ringer 2000). The creation of private colleges and universities was a response to China's interest in expanding education to the masses and creating a more specialized workforce. Although the government has been critical and cautious of the practices at private institutions, they have developed legal frameworks to allow them to operate (Ringer 2000).

Private universities account for 6.6 percent of student enrollment in China, educating about 1.34 million students of the 20.2 million enrolled in formal higher education in 2006 (Hayhoe and Lin 2015). Private institutions enroll a large number of students who may not be able to gain admissions at public institutions because of low scores on the *gaokao*. Even though it is still a secondary choice for many because of the perceived lack of prestige, highly-ranked private institutions in China have been able to attract students and meet their enrollment quotas (Butrymowicz 2012).

Higher tuition rates deter some from enrolling in private institutions, but these schools are meeting market demands by creating popular programs in such fields as television and broadcasting, engineering, advertising, and design to make them more competitive (Hayhoe and Lin 2015). While this system of education is by no means free from governmental regulations and is more often marred by academic and financial oversight woes (Lin 2015), its emphasis on majors that are driven by employer demand, coupled with involvement and internship opportunities modeled just like many global institutions (Hayhoe and Line 2015), will nonetheless compete for the same Chinese student market that U.S. universities and colleges rely on.

GLOBAL COMPETITORS

Countries such as Canada, Australia, United Kingdom, and Singapore are becoming more active in the recruitment of international students. While the U.S. still dominates international student enrollments in the global marketplace, competitors are creating national policies and international partnerships that will negatively impact U.S. competitiveness (Altbach 2004b). In addition, many countries also offer scholarships and financial aid incentives to attract international students. In the case of some universities in Australia, for example, scholarships are awarded to Chinese students based on high *gaokao* scores (Ross 2013).

Many undergraduate scholarships for international students are offered directly through U.S. institutions. But at the federal level, undergraduate scholarships are minimal. Funding programs, such as the Fulbright, award scholarships to international students but many are available only at the postgraduate level. The federal government has provided limited funding and cohesive direction to encourage international exchange and cooperation (Altbach 2004b), despite the fact that international students have contributed over 30 billion dollars to the U.S. economy in the 2014–2015 academic year (NAFSA 2016).

DUAL AND JOINT DEGREE PROGRAMS

Transnational dual and joint degree programs have been described as internationalization tools (Redden 2014b). In dual degree programs, students earn two degrees from two separate institutions. Joint programs, on the other hand, are ones that are endorsed by the two different institutions and may involve study abroad exchange but in the end, result in the conferring of one degree.[34]

Many such agreements have existed over the years; one notable program is the University of Michigan–Shanghai Jiaotong University Joint Institute, which has operated since 2006. Students in the Joint Institute study at Shanghai Jiaotong University for two years, apply for transfer to the University of Michigan where they finalize their last two years of coursework, and then return to their home institutions to complete their graduation project and thesis to obtain their second degree.

Joint and dual degree programs are well-established in China (Redden 2014b). They give Chinese students the opportunity to experience a U.S. curriculum without the hefty cost of a four-year degree obtained in the U.S. They are also highly useful in recruiting transfer students through an established memorandum of understanding with a Chinese university.

Questions for Further Research

It is hoped that the discussions in this chapter have been informative, but also lead to additional research. Questions regarding recruitment, student services, and academic successes are all areas of further interest. For example: Are Chinese students transferring directly from universities in China more or less successful than those transferring from U.S. community colleges? How will the acceptance of the *gaokao* indicate college preparedness and readiness in Chinese students? How will the economic and political landscape change Chinese students' motivations to study abroad? These are some topics for further research.

This chapter introduced two subsets of Chinese transfer students currently studying in the U.S., and highlighted the unique challenges that these two populations pose in the context of recruitment, admissions and student services. In an increasingly complex marketplace, understanding the key factors in motivating this population will inform U.S. admissions efforts in crafting campaigns and support services for retention and transfer success. Generalized practices, while convenient to replicate, may not always be beneficial in working with this unique group, and efforts must be implemented in the context of each institution's strength and core mission.

---

[34] For more on this topic, *see* Chapter 13 Dual Degree Programs.

34

External Examination Assessment

in International Secondary Education Systems

2016 AACRAO INTERNATIONAL GUIDE

MARSHALL HOUSERMAN

Senior Evaluator
Educational Perspectives

External Examination Assessment in International Secondary Education Systems

In the United States and Canada, graduation from high school is attained by completing a requisite set of courses or high school units. Assessment is done by individual schools and, in turn, individual teachers, until the student completes the required courses and is eligible for a high school diploma and graduation. This internal assessment system is used by admissions officers at U.S. higher education institutions in determining the admissibility of students to higher education programs. In many educational systems around the world, completion of high school is determined by a set of examinations either prescribed by a governmental organization or by an approved external examining authority. These examinations, graded and assessed by independent external examiners—not courses graded and assessed by the student's individual teachers—are what determine completion of high school and in turn a high school equivalent completion credential.

This chapter outlines external assessment educational systems and discusses the pros and cons of external assessment versus internal assessment. The chapter concludes with a discussion of the challenges and opportunities such examinations present to U.S. higher education representatives and some points admissions officers will want to keep in mind when reviewing these documents for admission.

What is External Examination Assessment?

As stated above, external examination assessment is commonly referred to as standardized testing in the U.S. It is completed by a third party. This external examination and assessment may be set by a governmental organization, such as the Ministry of National Education in France, or by approved third-party, nongovernmental examiners such as Assessment and Qualifications Alliance (AQA) and Pearson in the United Kingdom. Some external examination assessment systems provide a rigid syllabus for the teacher and school to follow, while others allow more autonomy, as long as the student is prepared for the subject matter covered on the examination. In some educational systems, such as the British/Commonwealth model, external examinations are the central focus and measurement of successful secondary school completion and hence graduation. Some educational systems that use external examination assessment may place strong emphasis on a set of examinations for university admission or employment, though they may also offer a diploma or some other completion credential based on the school's own internal assessment. Finally, external examinations in countries such as China and Korea are completed outside the normal secondary school system and do not represent an equivalent secondary school completion credential; however they are often the sole determining factor in admission to higher education. Recently, some U.S. universities have investigated using the Chinese entrance examination, the *gaokao,* as a qualification for admission to U.S. higher education.

Benefits of External Examination Assessment

Proponents of external examination assessment often cite fairness and objectivity, standard measurement of student and school/teacher performance, and the tamping down on cheating and bribery that may influence internal assessment as significant reasons that external assessment is preferable. In other words, external assessment levels the playing field. Imagine this scenario: Secondary School A suffers a severe case of grade inflation, and all students receive at least a grade of 'B' on a U.S. 'A–F' grading scale. Secondary School B grades on a strict curve, so even students prepared to succeed in higher education often receive grades of 'C' in their assessments. An admissions officer for a higher education institution may not know that Secondary School A inflates all grades and Secondary School B does not. They may not have the time or the resources to make that determination. So while many students at Secondary School B are prepared and could succeed quite well in higher education, this particular institution fails to recruit or admit these students. Now when these students are imported into an external assessment educational system, Secondary School A suddenly finds that many of their students are the equivalent of 'C' students if using a national external assessment. Furthermore, many Secondary School B students may rise from 'C' to 'B' students. Proponents of external assessment argue this better reflects students' actual preparedness to succeed in higher education.

External assessment also negates a teacher or school's subjectivity toward individual students. For example, Student A tries hard and studies thoroughly for each assignment and examination, but does not quite grasp all the concepts. The teacher sympathizes with Student A and wants to reward the effort, thereby awarding Student A an overall grade of 'B' for the course. Student B meanwhile does not stand out to the teacher, quietly completes assignments, and does not actively engage. Though Student B performs at the same level or above the level demonstrated by Student A, the teacher only awards Student B a 'B-/C+' for their performance. An external examination assessment would measure these two students more equally and fairly, with teacher bias being eliminated from the equation.

This standard measurement is important to educational researchers and officials looking for ways to assess individual student performance, as well as teacher and school performance. External assessment provides insight into which schools are performing better overall and which schools are underperforming. It provides an easy way to break down student and teacher performance and show opportunities for future improvements. External assessment also assists in educational efforts to target and study high-performing schools and best practices by teachers. Educational researchers in New South Wales, Australia, studied the classrooms and teaching methods of the best performing teachers and classrooms on the Grade 12 Higher School Certificate. They found that classrooms were relaxed, prepared for the curriculum, and still maintained some degree of autonomy from just teaching to the examination. Recommendations were then provided to other teachers and schools looking for best practices in preparing for Higher School Certificate examinations (Ayres, Sawyer, and Dinham 2004).

Stephen Heyneman points out that external assessment limits cheating and bribery (2009). Blind assessment performed by an external examiner limits the opportunities for bribing a teacher or school official for better grades. While we do not think of bribery in education as common practice in the U.S., in some countries this is a stark problem. For example, students in the countries of the former Soviet Union are more likely to accept cheating on assignments or examinations as normal than students in the U.S. (Grimes and Rezek 2005). The term bribery often conjures notions of large payouts or some other significant monetary incentive. Certainly, there are educational systems where school teachers or officials are more 'bribable' than others. However, if bribery is not necessarily a large cash payout or a new car, it could, in subtle ways, exist in an internal assessment system. Might a teacher be influenced by a bouquet of flowers, a new mug, or chocolates? Does that create questionable subjectivity in assessment scores? These are issues that external assessment systems attempt to weed from secondary school and the determination of a student's ability to succeed outside of secondary school.

The Rigidity of External Examinations: Negative Effects

External assessment is strongly argued against by most educators in the U.S., who point to the rigidity of its effects and the limits it places on students and teachers. Furthermore, while meant to level the playing field, external assessment may only highlight the divisions in secondary education between the "haves" and the "have-nots." Detractors of external assessment point out that it severely limits the teacher and school's control over the curriculum. The loss of autonomy puts all the importance on what is taught in the hands of either a group of elected or selected officials that may or may not understand the educational needs of different and distinct educational communities. While perhaps less of an issue in subjects such as mathematics and physical science, such concerns ring loudly in the humanities and social sciences. Currently, such a debate is embroiling educators that teach the Advanced Placement (AP) examinations in their U.S. History courses, as the AP now mandates that the examination focus on the idea of "American Exceptionalism," an idea disagreed upon by historians and political scientists alike.

External examination assessment may also limit who succeeds. External examination favors good test-takers and punishes students that have learning disabilities or quite simply demonstrate their understanding of the curriculum better in ways other than completing a three-hour examination. In the United Kingdom, students with learning disabilities often receive additional time on the General Certificate of Secondary Education (GCSE) examinations, as well as other vocational secondary qualifications (Joint Council for Qualifications 2015). However, even that is hotly debated, and in 2013 many schools lost the ability to provide students additional time, with educational officials noting that the requests likely resulted from schools seeking to give every student more time and boost their results. Furthermore, students in the UK with learning disabilities are often offered an alternative pathway to further education or employment, exacerbating differences

between students rather than promoting inclusion (The Telegraph 2013).

Some educational systems using external examination assessment limit the choices students have in their future education and employment decisions. In the U.S., students often undertake a diverse education ensuring study in a multitude of subjects prior to graduation. In higher education, they are encouraged to explore various educational offerings and choose or design their own major field of study. However, in most external examination assessment systems, students select the examinations that will grant them access to higher education in a narrow or specialized field of study. Often, students sit for examinations in a selected family of studies, for example, a scientific, humanities, or social sciences stream. Admission to a university program is based on scores in those subjects, for specifically related majors. Students are left with less autonomy in their major or future educational pursuits as a result.

Models of External Examination Assessment

External examinations take on varying degrees of importance depending on the country and educational system. In some, such as the UK, they are the sole factor in determining successful completion of secondary education. In some systems based loosely on the Commonwealth model, such as in the Caribbean, external examinations are an important factor in determining successful completion of secondary education, but individual secondary schools may also provide a diploma based on internal assessment. China and Korea employ external examinations as the sole determining factor for admission to higher education, though officially internal assessment determines successful completion of secondary education. Provided below are brief examples of various models of external examination assessment.

THE BRITISH MODEL

Higher education officials in the U.S. may be most familiar with the British model. Students in England,

Wales, and Northern Ireland typically sit for two sets of examinations in their secondary education, most commonly the General Certificate of Secondary Education (GCSE) and the General Certificate of Education, Advanced Level (A-Levels). In Scotland, students sit for their own set of external examinations at Standard or Intermediate Grade and Higher Grade, with all examinations prepared and assessed by the Scottish Qualifications Authority.

In the U.K., examining boards have existed since the mid-19th century as a way to examine and determine a student's successful completion of secondary education and preparedness for higher education. Currently, six approved examining boards offer the GCSE and A-Level examinations. One exmaining board, Cambridge International Examinations (formerly University of Cambridge International Examinations) provides examinations and assessment for students at British-designed secondary schools around the world, including the Cambridge Pre-U Curriculum, sometimes found at high schools in the U.S. Schools may decide which examinations they offer to students and how to deliver the curriculum. Some students may attend a public secondary school offering a typical day of classes, while others may work with individual tutors toward successful completion of particular GCSE or A-Level examinations. The latter is more common in so-called sixth-form colleges where students study for A-Level examinations.

Students typically sit for GCSE examinations upon completion of five years of secondary education preceded by six years of primary education, for a total of eleven years of primary and secondary education. If prepared, students may sit for the examination prior to Grade 11; often particular subjects are completed a year earlier than the rest of the examinations. Students may also retake examinations in the same subject, attempting to achieve a higher grade, without penalty. The examining board issues examination results directly, rather than through the student's secondary school or educational institution. Therefore, if a student com-

pletes exams with five examining boards, they will be issued five official examinations results, one from each examining board. Certificates are also awarded annually, meaning if a student completes an examination with an examining board in 2012 and again in 2014, the student will receive an official GCSE certificate for each year.

Based on the rigor and content examined, completion of GCSEs typically represents the equivalent of successful completion of high school in the United States. The number of examinations a U.S. higher education institution will require for successful completion may vary by the institution's openness or selectivity in their admission enrollment practices. Typically, higher education institutions in the U.K. look for successful completion of at least five GCSEs as part of a student's admission, though students often study for and take examinations in seven to nine subjects. Successful GCSEs are graded on a scale from 'A–G' with a grade of 'U' noting that a student did not achieve a satisfactory or passing result. Students sitting GCSEs in 2017 will encounter a new grading system, based on numerical points where 9 is the highest possible achievement and 1 the lowest. According to information provided by the Office of Qualifications and Examinations (OfQual), this change is meant to provide a clearer assessment than the current system and make it more difficult to achieve a high numerical result as examiners were constantly stretching the limits of the 'A' grade on GCSE examination results (OfQual 2015).

Upon completion of GCSEs, students may study for a further two years in a secondary school or a college preparing for the General Certificate of Education, Advanced Level. Students often narrow their focus in A-Level examinations and complete study in three to four subjects related to their prospective study in higher education. After the first year, students may sit for the General Certificate of Education, Advanced Subsidiary Level (AS Level) examination representing one-half of the Advanced Level. In the U.S., courses and subject matter studied at the AS and A Level usually represent general education covered in the first year of university studies. In the U.K., higher education institutions typically require minimum completion of at least one A Level in combination with other examinations such as AS-Level examinations.

There are other external assessment examinations completed by students in the U.K. as alternatives to the GCSEs and A Levels. Often these are examinations in less traditional academic subjects such as business or information technology. One example of this is the OCR Level 2 National Certificate in ICT, an externally assessed course in Information and Communication Technology that represents the equivalent of completing a GCSE. Other examinations at the same level of assessment may represent completion of a vocational qualification. The City and Guilds of London Institute offers a National Vocational Qualification in Construction at Level 2, the National Qualification Framework level for upper-secondary education. Students may opt for a more concentrated assessment from an external provider than the A-Level examinations provide. For example, students interested in higher education in sports studies may complete Pearson's BTEC Level 3 Diploma in Sport, rather than sitting for A Levels (or in combination with A Levels). Holders of this qualification may use their diploma to apply to U.K. higher education institutions in study related to sport, but are more limited in their major fields of study at university than holders of A Levels.

It should be noted that other Commonwealth countries also employ external examinations as their main assessment method in secondary education. In Anglophone West Africa, these examinations are most commonly administered by the regional West African Examinations Council. Other countries using similar external examinations include Cameroon, Uganda, Zimbabwe, Malaysia, Singapore, and, until recently, Hong Kong, among others. All are patterned on the British model, and many regional or national examining bodies in these countries prepare their examinations in collaboration with examining bodies in the U.K.

THE CARIBBEAN MODEL

The Caribbean Examinations Council (CXC) was established in 1972 in part to provide a standard assessment of academic achievement and secondary education completion to secondary school students in the Commonwealth Caribbean tailored to the educational culture and needs of Caribbean students. Previous to the CXC's establishment (and for some time after) secondary schools in the Commonwealth Caribbean used British external examinations for assessment and admission to the Caribbean's main university, the University of the West Indies. As the flagship institution of the Commonwealth Caribbean, the University of the West Indies relies on external examination assessment to provide an objective measurement of prospective students' educational achievement and suitability for higher education, regardless of their island nation of birth.

Similar to the GCSEs, in most of the Commonwealth Caribbean, students complete examinations toward the Caribbean Secondary Education Certificate (CSEC) during Grade 11, however the only statutory requirement is that the student be age 16 or older. CSEC examinations are offered in varying subjects at both the Basic and General Proficiency levels. There are no minimum or maximum restrictions on how many CSEC examinations a student may sit for at one time. CSEC examinations are assessed using a Roman numeral grading system from I–VI with I representing the highest passing grade and VI representing a failing grade.

CXC also provides external assessment similar to the British A-Level examination. Known as the Caribbean Advanced Proficiency Examinations (CAPE), these are typically completed two years after CSEC examinations. Previously, CAPE examinations resulted in admission to the second year of university study or exemptions toward study programs at the community college level. Recently, CXC has changed the focus of these external examinations, culminating in the award of an associate degree upon successful completion of seven CAPE examinations.

For university and college admission purposes students must typically successfully pass five CSEC examinations at the General Proficiency level; two of these examinations must be in English and mathematics. Community colleges and postsecondary technical programs may require fewer examinations at the General Proficiency level or no CSEC examinations at all.

The Caribbean model differs from the British; while external examination is the preferred assessment method, especially for determining suitability for entrance to higher education, secondary schools in the Commonwealth Caribbean do provide internal assessment and their own benchmark completion credentials. Individual secondary schools in Jamaica, for example, highlight the difference between students merely completing Grade 11 and those graduating from secondary school in the credentials they award. A Leaving Certificate implies no more than that the student completed Grade 11 and left the school. It does not signify successful completion of secondary school or graduation of any sort. However, a Diploma or some other statement of graduation is a recognizable benchmark credential signifying successful completion of secondary education.

THE CHINESE MODEL

Many Asian countries base successful completion of secondary education on internal assessment from a student's secondary school. In China, this internal assessment results in the award of a Senior Middle School Graduation Certificate. The official certificate is regulated by the Ministry of Education, but documentation and results are based on internal assessment from a student's secondary school and issued directly by the secondary school. The Senior Middle School Graduation Certificate represents successful completion of secondary education and is the recognized benchmark credential in China. Grades are typically represented in percentage format on a scale from 0 to 100, with a score of 60 required for successful completion of the course.

Students applying to university must also sit for an external examination, regulated by the Ministry of Education—the *gaokao* examination. These examinations, completed in Grade 12, are the sole factor deciding a student's admissibility to university, as well as which programs of study and which universities he or she may apply to. The *gaokao* is purported to be the toughest examination in the world. Students preparing for and taking the *gaokao* are said to suffer from "gaokao fever," attending school for extended periods and often studying with individual tutors at night. Likened to the SAT and ACT examinations in the U.S., this external achievement examination is the central and deciding factor for students applying to university in China, unlike the U.S. educational system where universities have greater flexibility in determining admissibility than solely relying on the SAT or ACT scores. Poor achievement on the *gaokao* may result in the student being ineligible for university study in any program at any university. The pressure for outstanding achievement on the *gaokao* is enormous.

The central focus of the *gaokao* in Chinese secondary education, combined with the ability to verify official results and lessen the risk of subjective influences, has led some higher education institutions in other countries, including the U.S., to consider accepting the *gaokao* examinations, either in lieu of other standardized achievement tests such as the SAT and ACT or as the academic record of importance (instead of the internal assessment provided by the student's secondary school). At least three universities in the U.S.—New York University, Suffolk University, and the Illinois Institute of Technology—currently review the *gaokao* for admission and another, the University of San Francisco, is currently implementing a pilot program in admissions (He 2015). According to a 2015 *ICEF Monitor* report, the Chinese Ministry of Education is encouraging international higher education institutions to accept the *gaokao* as the standard admission assessment of Chinese students. This one examination determines which, if any, university the student can attend and the subjects he or she can study. A poor score on the *gaokao* can either hamper an individual's chances at pursuing higher education or make it next to impossible.

Tips for Admissions Officers

How to assess external assessment in determining a student's admissibility ultimately depends on the needs and standards of the higher education institution reviewing the documents for admission. These needs may also vary depending on which program of study the student selects.

Higher education institutions with more selective admissions may want to review the standards for admission set by more selective higher education institutions in the student's home country. For example, a student from Jamaica would need to present successful completion of five CSEC examinations at a grade of III or better for admission to the University of the West Indies. Higher education institutions with moderately selective or selective enrollment policies may want to consider the minimum number of examinations required for admission to a postsecondary program at Caribbean higher education institutions when determining admissibility. An open enrollment institution may simply wish to review if the student graduated from their secondary school, in the event the student cannot produce or did not sit for CSEC examinations.

Admissibility may also depend on what expectations are set by an individual state, by a public college or university, or by the constraints of a board of trustees for a private institution. For example, public colleges or universities requiring demonstration of successful completion of units in a varied range of subjects may find students lacking the requisite units if only reviewing external examinations. Additionally, external examinations do not represent the actual time a student spent studying a subject and therefore, should not generally be used in determining the amount of high school units in a particular subject. In this instance, an admissions office may want to review both the external examinations and the internal academic records provided by the secondary school. The documents of the secondary school may not represent the benchmark or completion credential in that system of education, but they will allow for a review of how much time a student spent in class preparing for each subject. Where an external examination is presented for a course, admissions should consider that grade instead of any internal assessment provided by the secondary school, as it represents the final achieved grade in the student's country of study.

Flexibility, understanding the differences in external and internal assessment, and the various roles of importance external assessment plays in a particular country's educational system constitute the most crucial factors in determining admissibility to a U.S. institution. Whether a higher education professional is a firm supporter of external assessment or a vehement opponent, the majority of countries in the world use some form of external assessment to determine a student's achievement in secondary school and admissibility to higher education. Assessing the institution's needs and matching them to the official and available documentation is most important.

THIRTY-FIVE

Ukraine: Education in a War Zone

KRISTINA ZALUCKYJ

Evaluator
Educational Perspectives

Ukraine: Education in a War Zone

Today's Ukraine differs from even two years ago. The Revolution of Dignity started in late November 2013 after then President Viktor Yanukovych announced he would not sign the Association Agreement with the European Union. Citizens came out to Maidan Nezhalezhnosti (Independence Square) in Kyiv to protest the decision and promised to stay until the agreement was signed. The agreement signified a decision to favor strengthening relations with the European Union. Instead of yielding to the public display, Yanukovych signed a partnership agreement with Russia that strengthened Ukrainian–Russian trade relations. For three months citizens stayed at Maidan, exerting constant pressure to make it clear to the political authorities that change was expected of them. Unwilling to relinquish their oligarchic and corrupt ways, Yanukovych and his inner circle fled Ukraine in mid-February 2014. Ukraine's special service troops, the Berkut, were given orders to break up the crowds of people by force, using weapons as well as fire. The protesters refused to disperse and reinforcements in the form of snipers were positioned on the roof of Hotel Ukraina overlooking Maidan and killed nearly 100 demonstrators and injured hundreds more.

Immediately following these events at Maidan, Russian troops forcibly annexed Crimea in March 2014. In April 2014, still reeling from these events, Russian soldiers entered the region of Donetsk Oblast under the guise of needing to provide protection to the Russian-speaking citizens. Russian separatists also invaded Luhansk Oblast and attempted to occupy and annex the region of Donbas. In May 2014, they created the "Donetsk People's Republic" (DNR) and "Luhansk People's Republic" (LNR) after holding an illegitimate election. Earlier in Crimea, a similar election was held.

The separatists' presence continues to wreak havoc on citizens' daily lives, impacting their work, families, residences, and resources for living (*e.g.* food, water, gas, etc.), as well as education. Ukrainian troops and the Anti-Terrorist Organization (ATO) have been trying to keep stability in the volatile areas of Donbas where intense fighting continues, while simultaneously reclaiming and liberating occupied cities from the separatists' control. Crimea is less chaotic due to the complete takeover. This chapter will review what has changed for education within Crimea and Donbas as a result of the war and occupations, how education is recognized and perceived by Ukraine's Ministry of Education and Science, the Ministry's efforts to ensure all school-aged children earn an education, and how schools are operating in Donbas during this time.

Education System in Ukraine

In Ukraine, the total length of primary and secondary education is eleven years, with compulsory studies beginning at age six or seven, totaling nine of the eleven years. The academic year begins on September 1. Primary school is four years and basic secondary is five years. Upon completion of compulsory study, students earn a Certificate of Basic General Education (*Свідотство про базову загальну середню освіту*). To complete basic education, five state examinations must be passed: Ukrainian Language, Mathematics, Biology, Geography, and one elective determined by the school (foreign language, humanities or a minority language: Crimean

Tatar, Hungarian, Moldovan, Polish, Romanian or Russian) (NORRIC 2009).

Upon completion of two additional years of senior secondary education, by age 17 students earn their Certificate of Complete General Secondary Education (*Атестат про повну загальну середню освіту*). Final examinations for completing secondary education entail compulsory subjects of Ukrainian Language and Ukrainian History. Similarly, upon completing Grade 9, three other subjects are determined by the school: foreign language, humanities, and a minority language (NORRIC 2009). These state examinations are administered by External Independent Testing, overseen by the Ministry of Education and Science. The examinations are intended to provide a standard measurement for higher education admission.

Throughout Ukraine, there were 20,249 general primary-secondary educational schools in the 2007–2008 academic year whose language of instruction was Ukrainian (NORRIC 2009). In 2009, about 6 percent of secondary schools (totaling 1,253) in Ukraine used Russian as their language of instruction (NORRIC 2009).

In 2005, Ukraine signed the Bologna Process agreement, with the goal of aligning the education system to the European standards by the 2012–2013 academic year (NORRIC 2009). Although some schools began the transition, the Ukrainian education system as a whole did not complete the transfer. The change in system was to include one additional year of secondary study, making primary and secondary school a combined 12 years long. It also became a goal in higher education to transition from using study hours and grade descriptors to the Bologna system and applying letter grades and ECTS (European Credit Transfer and Accumulation System) credits to university programs. While the European-modeled system is being used inconsistently among a handful of universities, the adjustment to one additional year of secondary study is currently on hold.

Currently, a 12-point grading system is used at the secondary level with corresponding grade descriptors, as shown in Table 35.1.

TABLE 35.1: Secondary Level Grading Scale

Grade	Descriptor	Translation
10, 11, 12	Відмінно	Excellent
7, 8, 9	Добре	Good
4, 5, 6	Задовільно	Satisfactory
1, 2, 3	Незадовільно	Unsatisfactory
—	Зараховано	Pass

The same grade descriptors are used at the post-secondary level. Grading systems for both levels of education include a grade of "Pass." Subjects with an earned grade of "Pass" were successfully completed at the satisfactory level or higher.

The value of the diploma has remained the same during this transitionary period. The document is recognized in Ukraine as both an educational certificate and professional license (Tempus 2012, 3). Postsecondary diplomas offered in Ukraine are as follows:

* *Диплом молодший спеціаліст* (Diploma of Junior Specialist): a professional qualification. Recipients are eligible to enter bachelor's degree programs in the same field of study. Advanced standing may be granted from this credential upon admission into a bachelor's program.

* *Диплом Бакалавр* (Diploma of Bachelor): the first degree and offered in all disciplines, with the exceptions of medicine, dentistry, pharmacy, and veterinary medicine, which are integrated programs. It is four years in length.

* *Диплом Магістр* (Diploma of Master): follows the *Бакалавр* degree; it is one to two years in length.

* *Диплом Спеціаліст* (Diploma of Specialist): a five-year integrated program. The degree's format is derived from the former Soviet education system. Completion of this program allows for eligibility into master's and Candidate of Sciences studies. The Diploma of Master has been gradually replacing this credential since the 2009–2010 academic year.

* *Кандидат Наук* (Candidate of Sciences): a minimum of three years and the highest credential an individual can earn in Ukraine (NORRIC 2009, 24).

Internally Displaced People and Student Statistics

Many citizens of both Crimea and Donbas became internally displaced people (IDPs) after leaving their region during the fighting, whether voluntarily or by force. It is difficult to get an accurate count of the displaced population because, despite encouragement to register with the government, not all IDPs have done so. There are various reasons for not registering; some families plan to continue moving within Ukraine (either within Donbas or further from the conflict zone but still within greater Ukraine) and others intend to return home within a short time. Families who register find it easier to become established in the new community and receive more resources and opportunities to connect with others.

In December 2014, it was estimated that over one million people had been internally displaced. Of this population, approximately 130,000 children were displaced as a result of the war (A World at School 2014). As of July 10, 2015, over 1.3 million IDPs were counted, per a report by UNICEF, and 174,442 children are included in the overall IDP population (UNICEF 2015). Approximately 578,500 additional people have fled Ukraine to neighboring Belarus, Poland, and Russia (ACAPS 2015). Cities throughout Ukraine are welcoming the IDPs and children are encouraged to enroll in local schools. The impact has led to an increase in class size, from 30 students to 38–40 students per class at Kyiv School N° 309, which welcomed 218 Donbas IDP students in 2014–2015 (Removska 2014). Six months after the start of the war, about 50,000 preschoolers, school children, and university students changed their location of study (A World at School 2014). In total, over 30,000 students from Donbas began the 2014–2015 school year in new schools.

Crimea

Despite similarities in the Russian separatists' activities, changes in education have been imposed differently in Crimea than in Donbas. The referendum annexing Crimea has brought Russian influence on all aspects of life, including education. Immediately after the referendum, Ukrainian textbooks were either packed up for storage or sent to Donbas to be replaced by the Russian curriculum and textbooks (Tyshchenko and Smirnov 2015). Russian curriculum was mandatory at the start of the 2014–2015 school year in Crimea. Additionally, a more rigid five-point grading scale was implemented, eradicating Ukraine's twelve-point scale used in secondary schools. Concurrently, the use of the Russian five-point scale negates previous efforts of the Ukrainian Ministry of Education and Science to align education with the Bologna system.

Ukrainian language studies are widely deemphasized and only as valuable as other foreign languages, rather than as a pillar for educational advancement. Pointedly, Taurida National V. I. Vernadsky University closed their Ukrainian Linguistics department as a result of these changes. Crimea has a large Tatar population who returned around the time of the collapse of the Soviet Union after being forced to leave the peninsula following the Second World War. Tatar language for the Tatar population has been minimized in primary and secondary schools, as well as schools where classes were previously taught in the students' native language. Presently, only fifteen schools are teaching in Tatar in Crimea (Tyshchenko and Smirnov 2015). Secondary school teachers who previously taught Ukrainian have been mandated to undergo retraining in other subjects. Failure to adhere to this decree results in unemployment. All of this has been done to ensure conformity to the new education system and the prescribed curriculum.

In addition to retraining, teachers of other subjects outside of Ukrainian linguistics reported during the 2014–2015 school year that schools were required to observe new holidays customarily celebrated in Russia, including Russian Constitution Day, Day of the Heroes of the Fatherland, and the Day of the Russian Elections (Tyshchenko and Smirnov 2015). Students were also required to participate in competitions, such as essay contests detailing the value and importance of a particular aspect of Russian life (law, war, history, and so forth). Through these mechanisms, Crimean authorities have instituted an atmosphere highly intolerant of Ukrainian identity, which includes prohibiting Ukrainian symbols in schools (Tyshchenko and Smirnov 2015). The goal of this approach is to cultivate a new sense of nationalism, moving away from Ukrainian identity and instead shifting loyalty towards Russia.

The curriculum in primary and secondary schools in Crimea is generally taught in Russian only. Four schools in Crimea were still teaching students in the Ukrainian language at the start of the 2014–2015 school year (Tyshchenko and Smirnov 2015). By January 2015, only one school in the city of Yalta maintained the language of instruction as Ukrainian (Tyshchenko and Smirnov 2015). Much of the data and statistics relating to school population, enrollment, and number of open schools have yet to be disclosed, though these known facts paint a clear picture of the developing culture in Crimea.

There are major differences between the Ukrainian and Russian curriculum in the subjects of history and social studies. The Russian history curriculum emphasizes state history from the fifteenth through the eighteenth centuries (Tyshchenko and Smirnov 2015). This poses a concern for students preparing for state final examinations, as the subject matter disseminated in the classroom is preparing the students for neither Russian nor Ukrainian state examinations. The recent curriculum changes have created an information gap within the students' education. Despite this, the Ukrainian Ministry of Education and Science continues to welcome and encourage students to sit for secondary education examinations or continue with university study in Ukraine and has provided guidelines for doing so.

DNR/LNR Separatist-Occupied Territory

Fighting within both Donetsk and Luhansk Oblasts has persisted, though the separatists' primary focus is on Donetsk. The Russian separatist-occupied areas "Donetsk National Republic" and "Luhansk National Republic" are not recognized by the Ukrainian govern-

ment as independent or separate entities from Ukraine. After one full academic year, it is too early to tell what the overall impact is from the changes in the education system in the DNR and LNR. Such changes in education include abolishing Ukrainian language as the compulsory language of study, the disbanding of the Ukrainian history department at Donetsk National Technical University, and the compromised journalism department of the university, which was surrounded by defamatory rumors. Within higher education, the DNR's Ministry of Education is making an effort to preserve the university's competition in the goods and services market. This system parallels the patron-client relationship of the Soviet era.

Ukraine's Ministry of Education and Science, headed by Serhiy Kvit (former Rector of National University of Kyiv-Mohyla Academy), is not recognizing any changes in university heads within the DNR or LNR. This includes Serhiy Baryshnikov, the acting head of Donetsk National University, which is functioning illegitimately according to Ukraine's Ministry of Education and Science. Baryshnikov resigned from the university in 2013 after being accused of bribery by a student (Ministry of Education 2015). The lack of acknowledgement by the Ministry of Education and Science of any changes at universities either in the DNR or LNR is the only allowable form of expressible protest against the separatists' presence and take over. Any shift in recognition of university heads or self-proclaimed Ministries of Education would negate Ukraine's refusal to acknowledge the DNR and LNR as separate from the rest of the country.

The DNR has its own proclaimed Minister of Education, Ihor Kostenko. Previously, he was a professor at Donetsk State Management University's general and administrative management department. Despite the lack of recognition from Ukraine's Ministry of Education and Science, the DNR's Ministry of Education continues under Kostenko's leadership. Upon appointment, Kostenko quickly began visiting higher educational institutions within the DNR after the start of the occupation (Trebor 2014). During his visits, Kostenko met with deans to discuss the new rules for the educational establishment. Armed men joined Kostenko during the visits. He continuously stressed student safety and the impossibility of beginning the academic year while active conflict persists in the war zone.

Ten thousand Ukrainian school children living in terrorist-occupied DNR did not start the 2014-2015 school year on September 1, as over 900 schools within the DNR's territory were damaged (Euromaidan Press 2014a). As for students completing postsecondary study in the DNR, they will not be able to obtain Ukrainian Diploma of Bachelors or Diploma of Specialist degrees, as their study is not recognized by the Ukrainian Ministry of Education and Science. Instead, upon graduation, students will receive a DNR diploma which is being touted as a "dual" degree to be recognized by both local DNR and Russian officials. The DNR is promising a 25 percent increase in student stipends for staying in the area. It is unclear from where the funds have been obtained and unknown if the increase in stipend has been distributed to students.

Universities in Donbas

As fighting intensified and Russian separatists continued to invade, Donetsk National University made the decision on September 30, 2014 to relocate outside of the war zone. After the separatists stormed the University and took over, Donetsk National University's officials felt it was important to preserve the institution. The university formally opened temporarily in Vinnytsia on November 3, 2014 for the academic year. With limited resources, materials, and equipment, the university is functioning in the state-owned Crystal Jewelry Factory. It is reported that 70 percent of academic staff and 60 percent of university students relocated. Students are studying full-time, part-time and via distance education. Donetsk National University is one of 16 higher educational institutions that have moved outside of the separatist-occupied territory around the start of the 2014-2015 school year (Ministry of Education 2015).

University of Luhansk also moved out of the separatist-controlled area of the city. It is interesting to note that consistently, if a university from Donbas has not been taken over by separatists, their website is reflective of their relationship and connection to Ukraine. These institutions' emblems contain yellow and blue, the colors of Ukraine's flag, and/or Ukraine's coat of arms, the trident. If the higher educational institution has been taken over by the separatists, the institution's emblem as well as the dominant colors have been changed to red, blue, and black—the colors of the DNR and LNR. Additional information regarding changes as a result of leaving is sometimes noted on the institution's websites.

Students residing in the separatist-occupied zones who wished to leave and transfer to another university during the 2014–2015 school year had to state their intent formally by December 12, 2014 (Ministry of Education 2015). To do so, university students had to declare their transfer intention in writing and apply for admission as a transfer student to the university of their choice. The Ministry of Education and Science mandated all universities in Ukraine to admit these students for the following semester. This was an effort by the Ministry of Education and Science resulting in a bill that ensured a smooth, streamlined, and accommodating process for students from the Ukrainian side's Anti-Terrorist Organization (ATO) zone. Prior to this most recent school year, some students from the ATO zone felt that the process of applying to transfer to another university was more bureaucratic than that for postsecondary students from Crimea who had more liberty in the transfer request process (Herashchenko 2014). Crimean university students were simply required to write a letter of intent requesting transfer to their desired university.

Crimean secondary students interested in sitting for Ukrainian State examinations were encouraged to apply for refugee status in Ukraine prior to registering for the examinations (Tyshchenko and Smirnov 2015). ATO-residing students experienced difficulties based on the inability of the Ministry of Education and Science to guarantee the preservation of the students' study grant in conjunction with their transfer to a new school. The Ministry of Education and Science is allowing graduates to receive Ukrainian Diplomas and Matriculation Certificates to accommodate the understanding that not everyone is able to move outside of the conflict zone for various reasons (Ministry of Education). According to Ukraine's Ministry of Education and Science, no complaints were registered from students indicating their transfer request was denied.

Student Life in Donbas

Since the war broke out after the separatists entered Donbas, life for the people residing in the area has changed dramatically. The stronghold of the fighting in Donetsk Oblast was centered at the recently built state-of-the-art Donetsk Airport. Today, it is completely destroyed and nearly every house near the airport is also damaged (ACASP 2015). In Donetsk and Luhansk Oblasts, by the end of the summer of 2014, the Ukrainian government estimated that 117 schools were partially or completely destroyed and only 1,735 schools were functioning for over 500,000 students (UNICEF 2014). Nearly 150 schools have closed due to the war, impacting about 50,000 children. A total of 187 educational institutions have been damaged or destroyed; of these institutions, 147 remain closed (A World at School 2014). Just before the start of the 2014–2015 school year in Lysychansk in Luhansk Oblast, which was liberated from the separatists, eight of 22 schools were heavily damaged by the fighting, though seven of these schools had been repaired before the start of the academic year (Ministry of Education).

With the fighting and turmoil, many people, including teachers, left the area and moved within Ukraine. Donetsk's city mayor, Oleksandr Lukyanenko, oversees schools and noted in 2014 that about half of the teachers had left. The mayor estimates about 70,000 students still remained in Donetsk (UNICEF 2014). In Slovyansk, in Donetsk Oblast, over 200 first graders started the 2014–2015 school year (Ministry of Education). This

accomplishment is attributed to the ATO's efforts in repairing three schools and one kindergarten. Many feel that ensuring schools continue to operate is the best option for the children, as it provides a sense of security and structure in an unstable environment.

In January 2015, Deputy Minister of Education and Science, Pavlo Polyanskiy, announced the student populations in Donbas for the 2014–2015 school year. Within Donetsk Oblast, 57,500 kindergarteners enrolled in 553 kindergartens, and 160,000 students enrolled in 601 schools. Of these schools, 510 of the kindergartens are in Ukrainian territory, and 462 of the schools are located in the separatist-controlled area where the Ministry of Education and Science does not have any control. In Luhansk, 15,500 kindergarteners are enrolled in 210 kindergartens, and 58,000 students are enrolled in 315 schools. Within separatist-occupied Luhansk, there are 338 kindergartens and 315 schools (Ministry of Education 2015). Within the separatist-occupied areas of Donbas, 25 schools have moved, including 16 universities.

Grade 11 students residing in the separatist-occupied area are estimated at 4,000 to 5,000 in Donetsk and about 3,000 in Luhansk (Ministry of Education 2015). Of these, about 3,000 Donetsk students and about 2,000 Luhansk students will apply for higher education (Ministry of Education 2015). Ukraine's Ministry of Education and Science anticipated in January 2015 that students in the occupied areas would not be ready for year-end examinations and complete their secondary education on time. Follow up, or any sort of confirmation of this prediction, has yet to be published.

The Ukrainian Ministry of Education and Science has reportedly received a high volume of mail from teachers in the separatist-occupied portion of Donbas posing many questions, expressing concern, and seeking information from the Ministry of Education and Science. The efforts of supporting and caring for the students by these teachers are recognized by the Ukrainian Ministry of Education and Science. Unfortunately, as these teachers have remained in the occupied zone, Ukraine's Ministry of Education and

Science has no authority to assist them as the teaching process, textbooks, syllabi, and curriculum used in the classrooms are not that of Ukraine.

Provisions for Education

Although Ukraine's Ministry of Education and Science does not recognize proof of study completed under either the DNR's Ministry of Education or LNR's Ministry of Education, Ukraine's Ministry of Education and Science has made provisions to allow secondary students to take state examinations and start postsecondary study in Ukraine. The Ministry of Education and Science passed a bill to ensure the right to education for primary, secondary, and postsecondary students for IDPs and those in the ATO zone. These provisions are applicable for both Donbas and Crimean students. The bill regulates the educational transfer process outside of the conflict zone, including the moving of universities and educational institutions, their materials, and technical equipment. Under the current circumstances, this is the extent of the authority possessed by the Ministry of Education and Science.

In spring 2014, secondary education completion examinations through Ukraine's External Independent Testing were held July 1–July 15 for students from Donbas. The overall number of examination takers for potential university admission was expected to be lower than the previous year, despite the fact that the opportunity to take the examination was open to all students. University candidates from Donbas who registered for the 2014–2015 school year totaled 7,000 as opposed to 35,000 registrants from Eastern Ukraine the year before the war broke out (Ministry of Education 2015). Additionally, Crimean students at the end of the 2013–2014 school year totaled 600 examination registrants (Ministry of Education 2015). As the Russian curriculum and examination system was implemented in Crimea the 2014-2015 academic year, the total number of examination registrants from Crimea was also limited.

In January 2015, to help secondary-level students in Donbas continue their studies, the Ministry of Education and Science of Ukraine, encouraged secondary schools to increase the use of technology to promote distance learning. The Ministry of Education and Science anticipated a further decrease in the number of examination registrants from both Donbas and Crimea due to the war. Such accommodations have been made strictly for mobility purposes when deemed necessary; examination content was to be at the same level of rigor as previous years.

The Ukrainian Ministry of Education and Science published a list of schools that are supporting students studying externally and sitting for final examinations. These schools are allowed to issue school leaving certificates for students leaving school in Donbas. All students from these areas had conditions specifically established for them by the Ministry of Education and Science in order to be eligible to sit for the examinations. Prior to sitting for the state final examinations, parents had to write and submit an application addressed to the principal of the chosen school, requesting that their child take the national examination through that particular school as an external studies student (Ministry of Education 2015).

Crossing checkpoints to enter and exit the conflict zone can be tedious and difficult, especially when crossing frequently; as a result, many schools who volunteered to take conflict zone students have also agreed to house the students during their examination dates. Ministry of Education and Science approved boarding schools and health institutions were opened for conflict zone students and their parents for this purpose. Housing facilities at these schools allowed parents and students to stay for two or more months as the student finished the school year, prepared for examinations, and applied to universities. In total, 191 schools voluntarily opened their doors for Donbas and Crimean students (Ministry of Education 2015).

The Ministry of Education and Science confirmed that all students who sat for final examinations administered by the state at the end of the 2014–2015 school year would receive national school certificates upon obtaining successful results, regardless of their residency. Examinations for the 2014–2015 school year were held June 3 through June 26 with Ukrainian Language and Literature on June 9. If for whatever reason occupation-zone students could not sit for the Ukrainian Language and Literature examination on the prescribed date, a makeup date of June 27 was available. Information was disseminated through the Ministry of Education and Science news updates on their website.

Checking Recognition and Education Authenticity

As DNR and LNR diplomas awarded at any level of education are not recognized by Ukraine's Ministry of Education and Science, verification of academic credentials will be more important than ever before within Ukraine. Some universities, such as Donetsk National University, have left the separatist-occupied territory but are still state-recognized institutions. Any diplomas awarded to students from the relocated university will be considered authentic and recognized by Ukraine's Ministry of Education and Science.

Until autumn 2014, secondary and postsecondary level studies up to Diploma of Specialist degrees were verifiable through the Ministry of Education and Science's verification portal, Osvita. By late October 2014, Osvita was replaced with Info Resource. The new verification portal is available only for students who completed postsecondary in 2015. Info Resource (www.inforesurs.gov.ua/) is currently in Ukrainian only and intended to be accessible exclusively by universities in Ukraine. Previously stored information from Osvita is being transferred to Info Resource. An alternative method of verifying academic credentials is through Ukraine's National Information Centre for Academic Mobility (ENIC-NARIC Ukraine) website: http://enic.in.ua/index.php/en. Credentials must be accompanied by an Apostille that has been registered with the Ministry of Education and Science. Examples of Ukrainian state-issued documents can be viewed at

ENIC-NARIC Ukraine: http://enic.in.ua/index.php/en/education-documents-examples. Examples of Russian-state issued documents can be viewed at Russia's National Information Centre for Academic Mobility (ENIC-NARIC Russia): www.russiaenic.ru/rus/diplom.html.

Other Changes

In addition to changes and accommodations within education in the war zone and separatist-occupied areas, Ukraine's Ministry of Education and Science continues to make other reforms. In light of the most recent events, the Ministry of Education and Science is developing a history unit on the Revolution of Dignity and the war with Russia, both of which are to be incorporated into the history curriculum for Grade 11. The new unit is expected to be ready for the 2015–2016 school year and will be included in history textbooks as an addendum. Furthermore, a renewed focus on patriotic and military education is spurring additional curriculum development. The intent is to prepare the youth for life and service in the armed forces. This subject is also expected to be introduced in the upcoming school year. There is also an interest in including spiritual education to the standard secondary-level curriculum. This subject's curriculum is anticipated to be developed with the help of clergy and non-governmental organizations. The ultimate goal of the Ministry of Education and Science is to educate people and prepare them to be capable to think independently, solve problems, and apply practical learning and knowledge in everyday life, as opposed to merely memorizing information.

Prior to the recent events within the state, the Ministry of Education and Science was planning to transition primary and secondary education from being collectively eleven years to twelve years. With the current situation, this transition has been temporarily postponed. A focus on reforming both secondary and postsecondary education is taking priority over extending secondary study to twelve years, including the simplification of the syllabi and curricula in secondary education.

Within higher education, university autonomy and the quality of education are being emphasized. To aid in accomplishing this goal, the Ministry of Education and Science has required each postsecondary institution to present their plans for future development. Upon review of these plans, the Ministry of Education and Science is determining which institutions to close or merge. In 2007, there were 920 accredited higher education institutions (NORRIC 2009). By the 2011–2012 academic year, there were 846 higher education institutions in Ukraine, of which 661 were public and 185 were private (Tempus 2012). In January 2015, there were 802 higher education institutions in Ukraine. Only one month later, the total number of higher education institutions had decreased to 317 (Ministry of Education 2015). By the end of 2015, it is anticipated that 270 higher education institutions will remain open after closures and mergers. The Ministry of Education and Science assures that these changes are to benefit citizens.

Conclusion

After reviewing the educational system in Ukraine and the current situation in Crimea and Donbas, it is evident that the war is impacting every aspect of daily life, including education. As education is run under the guidance of the country's Ministry of Education and Science, the matter of politics can easily cross into the management and administration of education. Efforts are being made to ensure that even with the ongoing war, schoolchildren and university students can continue studying and learning so as to prepare themselves for the future. Ukraine's Ministry of Education and Science's hands-on approach and efforts to keep education at the forefront shows in the reforms already implemented within the Ukrainian government since the Revolution of Dignity and the ousting of the previous government.

As the fighting continues, it is evident that the challenges experienced during the 2014–2015 academic year will continue into the 2015–2016 school year and may persist until the war ends. However, all of this is still uncertain. Ultimately, the 2014–2015 school year was a year marked by efforts to provisionally ensure that the pupils of Ukraine could continue learning during a time of chaos and disruption in their lives.

Regardless, the ongoing war in Eastern Ukraine and the annexation of Crimea is impacting the academic career of a generation of Ukrainian children and young adults preparing to venture into the professional world. The current situation and ongoing events will continue to impact education in Ukraine both currently as well as for the future. Once the war is over, questions of what will happen next within the country and education system specifically–what may change and what reforms may emerge or be deemed necessary–might arise. As the current situation progresses, these questions and possibly others will need to be reviewed and addressed.

THIRTY-SIX

The Korean
Non-Formal
Education System

2016 AACRAO INTERNATIONAL GUIDE

ANTHONY SABO

Evaluator
Educational Perspectives

The Korean Non-Formal Education System

oday more than ever, education is becoming more accessible for people of all social classes. This chapter will examine the non-formal education system that was established in Korea as a means to combat educational inequality, along with how its overall effects have helped Korea transform from a developing country to a country that is now an educational model of quality and structure.

History of the Current Korean Structure

Korea's educational system has been recognized as an emerging power in education and is now considered one of the major and renowned systems in the world. However, before the current educational system, Korea faced many battles that caused the nation to struggle. In 1948, after the division of Korea, South Korea adopted a U.S.-style education system. This new style of education was structured with six years of primary education, three years of lower secondary, and three years of upper secondary education, followed by four years of undergraduate study for completion of a bachelor's degree (Ministry of Education 2001). Along with this new system, the Korean Ministry of Education (MOE) was established. The MOE establishment led to a more centralized system that could ultimately generate growth not only in the education sector, but also help improve the Korean economy (International Qualifications Assessment Service 2009).

As a result of its educational initiatives, Korea experienced large economic and population growth in the early 1970s. Before the 1970s, higher education focused mainly on science and technology. Since then, higher

education in Korea has widened its scope to include more majors outside of the once standard science and technology fields. Naturally, with these new fields and opportunities, graduates from universities were rewarded with new job opportunities that ultimately helped the growth of the Korean economy (Bae 2011).

During education reforms in the 1970s through the 1990s, Korea's schools experienced a large growth in enrollment. Between 1970 and 1990, high school enrollment rates grew from 28 percent to 88 percent. Higher education institutions experienced similar growth. While in 1970 there were a total of 168 universities with 201,436 enrolled students, by 1990, 1,691,681 students were enrolled in 206 universities (Bae 2011).

Current Educational System

As mentioned previously, the current structure of the Korean education system is a twelve-year pattern of primary and secondary education (6-3-3). Education in Korea starts with the completion of six years of primary education. In primary schools, students focus on building the basic abilities and skills for learning and daily life (International 2009). Tuition is free for all, however available space is limited and many schools fill up quickly. Elementary school is followed by six more years of secondary education. Students attend middle school for three years (Grades 7 to 9). Here, students enhance the skills learned in elementary school (Ministry of Education 2001).

Afterwards, students diverge and attend either a general high school track or a vocational trajectory for three years (Grades 10 to 12). The completion of Grade 12 leads to either the General High School Certificate of Graduation or Vocational High School Certificate of

2016 AACRAO INTERNATIONAL GUIDE

369

Graduation. Admission into high schools is fiercely competitive, as it is based not only on test scores, but also a student's extracurricular activities. Once selected, students are placed in a lottery for enrollment into a high school of their choice. For those students who are not able to get into a high school, they must start their life in the workforce (International Qualifications Assessment Service 2009).

The Korean reform focused on many areas to improve the overall quality of education, while also providing equal opportunities for all. New entrance examinations and lotteries in certain schools created more opportunities for students to enroll in the school of their choice (Ministry of Education and Human Resources Development 2001). However, a culture which inflicted overwhelming pressure for children to perform at a high level persisted. The stress of secondary-level students studying to gain admission to a competitive high school affects all members of the family. Students spend long hours at school and even longer hours studying at night. Some wealthier families obtain tutors for their children to push them to do well and obtain admission into a good school by doing well on their College Scholastic Ability Test (CSAT) (International Qualifications Assessment Service 2011). Despite the reforms of Korean education, many students are unable to afford tutoring and thus are left behind. Over time, this has led to an education gap within higher education, as less fortunate students are unable to attend colleges either because of cost or lower scores.

Tertiary education in Korea is similar to U.S. postsecondary education. Institutions range from junior colleges that offer associate degrees to universities that offer diplomas, bachelor's, master's and doctoral degrees (Bae 2011). Although they are comparable to institutions in the United States, tuition tends to be significantly less in Korea. Both national universities—considered equivalent to U.S. public universities—and private universities grant bachelor's, master's, and doctoral degrees. While the average undergraduate university tuition at a national university is approximately

$2,500 per semester, the private universities' tuition averages around $4,000 per semester. Tuition often varies depending on major, as concentrations in the sciences tend to be more costly than the humanities (Korean Government 2016). Both are far less expensive when compared to universities in the U.S. where the average state tuition is around $9,000 per semester (College Data 2015).

As mentioned before, there is often a large amount of pressure on students to perform well. At universities, the pressures and expectations remain. The students that attend these schools are the ones that have received good scores and whose families are able to afford for them to go. They usually continue to perform well, leading to promising careers for graduates (High Performance 2014). However, students that are unable to meet the expectations or may have lacked the resources for educational support, have often been left behind to fall into the educational gap.

Non-Formal Education

In the late 1990s, Korea started a major restructuring of their educational system. In a response to the inequality that existed in the education system, the Korean Ministry of Education created a non-formal educational system that allowed for students to complete higher education work towards degrees in two different ways, known as the Credit Banking System (CBS) and the Bachelor's Degree Self-Study. These programs allow individuals to overcome factors that might not allow them to follow the traditional higher education pathway. Such limitations include financial limitations and lower scores from high school records and/or CSAT that prevent admission to traditional education programs (International Qualifications Assessment Service 2011).

In 2008, the Ministry of Education formed the National Institution of Lifelong Education (NILE) to oversee non-formal education in Korea, including basic adult literacy, extracurricular education, and career training. The NILE sets new educational policies, projects, and curriculum to better Korea's non-formal education (Ushe 2014).

CREDIT BANKING SYSTEM

The Credit Banking System (CBS) monitors the progress of students throughout their education, helping them work towards an associate or bachelor's degree while they study outside the traditional classroom. The CBS allows for many to continue to work during the day and attend classes at night, and is also popular for employees who wish to take courses to advance their career (Grubb 2009). It consists of a four-stage process that allows students to earn college credit in multiple ways. Its curriculum includes courses and set examinations for students to follow in which they earn college credit once a course is completed. When a student enrolls in this program, they are also enrolling at a university as a part-time student. This allows students to follow a specific path and move through the program at their own pace while receiving guidance from a university or college (Ministry of Education and Human Resources Development 2001).

BACHELOR'S DEGREE SELF-STUDY

The Korean non-formal education system offers another option for students who chose the non-traditional path. Since students enrolled in these programs often work during the day or reside in rural areas with limited access, their busy schedules or inability to travel may make it hard to attend night classes. The self-study course is designed for individuals to study from home without attending classes at institutions (NILE 2015a).

As part of the Bachelor's Degree Self-Study program, the Educational Broadcasting System (EBS) provides learning opportunities through televised lectures, radio, and the Internet. Students can take these lectures and courses as long as needed to obtain proficiency. Self-study culminates with an examination on the subject which, if passed, gives students university credit (Ministry of Education and Human Resources Development 2001).

The Self-Study program's four-phase examination process helps students receive credit towards the degree they work for. The first phase is basic knowledge on any liberal arts or general education course taken during the first year of undergraduate studies. The second and third phases are evaluations of overall knowledge of the major skills associated with the subject of academic study. The fourth and final phase is an overall comprehensive examination. Students may be exempted from portions of the program if they have previous study from universities or the credit banking system (NILE 2015a). Once these four phases are completed, a student is then eligible to receive their bachelor's degree.

DEGREES AND TRANSCRIPTS

Students who choose to complete degrees in the non-formal education system are required to fulfill the same credit requirements as those enrolled in the formal education system. For a degree track, students can pursue either an associate degree or bachelor's degree (International Qualifications Assessment Service 2011). In the Credit Banking System, the credit requirements for an associate degree are 80 credits for a two-year degree or 120 credits for a three-year associate degree. The minimum requirement to obtain a bachelor's degree in either formal or non-formal education programs is 140 credits. Students can choose to receive their degree directly from the Ministry of Education or from the specific college where they submitted their examinations (NILE 2014). Usage of the CBS is not limited to obtaining a degree; many students who enroll choose to take courses to help advance their career (National 2015, 13). As mentioned above, students enrolled in a Bachelor's Degree Self-Study program are required to complete four examinations before being conferred a degree. There is no credit issued for these examinations on the official transcript for the Self-Study program; however, some institutions may award credit for the examinations based on their own procedures.

The transcripts for non-formal education students are issued by NILE or from a university in the program.

Impact

Since its inception in the late 1990s, the non-formal education system has seen significant growth within Korea. For starters, the number of institutions participating in the non-formal education system has increased over the years mainly because the program has attracted a large number of students due to the ease and affordability of these programs. A study by the Korean Educational Development Institute showed a total of 379 non-formal institutions at the end of the 2009 calendar year. This was a steady increase from 2007 when there were only 314 active non-formal education institutions (Bae 2011). Adding 65 more centers in this short time period has helped fulfill the Ministry of Education's overall goal to expand education and make it more accessible for students across the country.

From 2009 to 2014, enrollment in adult education, which requires a high school diploma, has increased by 37 percent. Adults between 25 to 34 years old have had the highest participation rate followed closely by the next age group of 35 to 44 year-olds. The older the population, the lower the participation rate (NILE 2015b). Many of the participants in non-formal education programs were employed and came from villages or smaller-to medium-sized cities. They enrolled for various reasons including stabilizing their employment, as well as improving their job-related performance (NILE 2015b).

In 2004, 555,542 bachelor's degrees were awarded in Korea. Of these, 23,547, or 4.3 percent, were awarded from the non-formal education system.

Conclusion

The Korean education system underwent many changes between the 1950s and early 2000s. The government focused on education as a way to usher Korean society into a new successful age. Its overall goal was to provide a quality education accessible to the entire Korean population regardless of social class or geographic location. The reforms not only improved the quality of the Korean education system, but also created opportunities for once neglected individuals to overcome the education gap. The Korean non-formal education system has provided a user-friendly plan for individuals seeking education. Students have been able to study at their own pace without facing the burden of costs and time that come with formal education. This alternative form of education has led to more individuals seeking and obtaining education.

37

Evaluating Credentials from Mexico

2016 AACRAO INTERNATIONAL GUIDE

MANDIE L. BROOKS

Associate Registrar
Alexander College

Evaluating Credentials from Mexico

The basis for Mexico's current educational structure was established with the passing of the 1917 Constitution. The Constitution made education free and compulsory for all citizens, and began the process of transferring educational authority from the Catholic Church to the federal, state, and municipal governments. Enrollment steadily increased in the decades to follow, largely as the result of a growing population that nearly doubled between 1950 and 1990 (Instituto Nacional de Estadistica, Geogradia e Informática [INEGI] 2001). Education, however, remained inaccessible for many families who relied on their children working from a young age to support the family. This reality would persist until the late 1990s when a severe economic crisis (the Peso Crisis) resulted in changing views on the value of education. To combat rising unemployment, the government prioritized community-based educational programs, targeting rural and migrant families. For many Mexicans, the economic crisis spelled out a potentially precarious future for farming and industry; families began to realize that a more secure future for their children could be obtained through education.

Among numerous reforms resulting from the economic crisis of the 1990s, Mexico's federal government implemented a massive socioeconomic recovery program called Progresa in 1998. The aim of the program was to improve access to education and healthcare for the country's poorest families and rural communities by providing bursaries to families who kept their children in school. Selected families or communities now receive a bursary provided that their children are regularly attending school and medical clinic visits. Funding amounts increase with each grade level (to a maximum of 20 percent of a family's monthly income) and are also higher for girls (Wodon *et al.* 2003). The program name was rebranded in 2002 as Oportunidades, and again in 2014 as Prospera (Sooyhung and Shaikh 2014).

Whether the result of a transformed economic climate, urbanization, globalization, new government initiatives in education, or more likely a combination of all of these, it is clear that Mexico's population is increasingly looking to education for a more secure future. This shift came about rapidly, however, and led to unprecedented enrollment growth at all educational levels. Overcrowding at public schools led to a boon in private education in the 2000s, particularly the estab-

TABLE 37.1: Population Summary

Category	Data Year	Result
Population	2014	123.8 million
Gross National Income, per capita	2014	$9,980 U.S.
School Enrolment, Primary	2013	105%
School Enrolment, Secondary	2013	88%
Ratio of boys to girls in primary and secondary education	2013	103%
Poverty Rate	2012	52%

SOURCE: 2014 World Databank

lishment of international schools, distance education, and hundreds of private colleges and universities. Even with the additional capacity added by the private sector over the last 20 years, the educational system remains seriously overtaxed. Teacher to student ratios of one to thirty or more are common across the country, and teachers often work overtime to compensate for modest salaries [Organization for Economic Co-operation and Development (OECD) 2006]. Teacher protests and school closures due to strike action have been regular occurrences in Mexico since the mid-1980s. From 2013 to 2014, a historic two-year long protest involved more than 600,000 teachers and resulted in school closures of up to three months (De la Luz Arriaga Lemus 2014).

Follow-up studies on Progresa have shown improved enrollment and retention rates overall and, most notably, increased retention of girls at the secondary level (Lee and Shaikh 2014). The future of the program is a topic of debate by the current government, however, which reports that the program has had no effect on the country's overall poverty rate in the 17 years since its inception (Nacional de Prospera Programa de Inclusion Social 2014). It is estimated that close to 52 percent of Mexico's population are living in poverty, and the country suffers one of the lowest secondary enrollment rates in the world (The World Bank 2014).

Education and the Indigenous Population

Educational inequity is a serious problem in Mexico, particularly where the indigenous people are concerned. The indigenous population of Mexico is comprised of more than 60 different distinct ethnolinguistic groups, representing approximately 15 percent of the country's total population. The incidence of poverty among the indigenous population is high, and access to education is poor. Most indigenous people live outside of urban centers and at a great distance from the nearest schools. They also speak an indigenous language as a first language and may or may not be able to speak Spanish. It is estimated that 25 percent of indigenous people aged fifteen years and older are illiterate (Navarette 2013).

The Secretariat of Public Education has made some effort to increase access to education for the indigenous peoples, namely through the Prospera program.

Customized indigenous education programs have been implemented in recent years at the preschool and primary levels. These programs aim to educate children and also their families and communities. At the secondary level, skills-based job training programs and distance learning options are targeted at indigenous persons. Private donors and foundations have emerged in recent years to offer postgraduate scholarships for indigenous persons.

Educational Structure

Education in Mexico is free and compulsory to the ninth grade, and follows a 3 + 6 + 3 + 3 model.

* *Educación Inicial* (Early Education)—Infants aged 43 days to 3 years
* *Educación Prescolar* (Preschool Education)— Years 1 to 3, ages 3 to 6 years
* *Educación Basica Primeria* (Primary Education)— Grades 1 to 6, ages 6 to 11 years
* *Educación Secundaria* (Lower Secondary Education/Junior High School) also called Educación Básica (Basic Education)—Grades 1 to 3, ages 12 to 14 years
* *Educación Media Superior* (Upper Secondary Education/Senior High School)—Grades 1 to 3, ages 15 to 17 years
* *Educación Tercieria* (Tertiary Education)

The postsecondary structure follows the U.S. model and is categorized as professional/vocational, undergraduate, graduate, and doctorate.

Early Education

Infants aged 43 days to three years may attend *educación inicial* (early education). The aims of the program are to promote the development of physical, emotional, social, and cognitive skills, and to involve the family in the education process. The program is offered in three forms depending on how many hours the family wants or needs the infant to be in care each day.

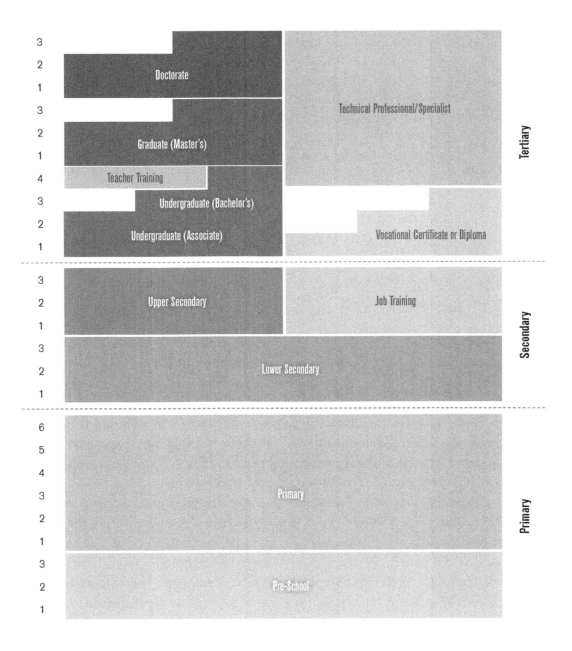

FIGURE 37.1

Mexico Education Structure

ESCOLARIZADA (SCHOOLED) OPTION

Infants enrolled in the 'schooled' option are cared for in *Centros de Desarrollo Infantil* (CENDI) (Child Development Centers) and follow an educationally-focused program. Families can choose for their child to attend full days or to attend mornings or afternoons only. The program also includes regular medical check-ups and meals.

SEMIESCOLARIZADA (SEMI-SCHOOLED) OPTION

Infants enrolled in the 'semi-schooled' option are cared for in *Centros de Educación Inicial* (CEI) (Early Education Centers) by a combination of teaching assistants and community volunteers. The hours of care at these centers are shorter than in the fully schooled option and meals are not provided. The program focuses on educating families in marginalized urban areas.

TABLE 37.2: Grading

Letter Grade	Percentage (%)	U.S./Canada Equivalent
10	100	A+
9	90—99	A
8	80—89	B
6—7	60—79	C
0—5	0—59	F

NOTE: Pass mark = 60 percent

NO ESCOLARIZADO (UNSCHOOLED) OPTION

Infants enrolled in the 'unschooled' option are cared for in *Módulos de Atencion* (Care Units) where they are supervised by community volunteers while their parent(s) attend a series of one-hour parenting workshops.

Preschool and Kindergarten

Attendance at *educación preescolar*, also called *jardin de niños* (kindergarten) became mandatory for all children aged three to six years old with the passing of the Law of Obligatory Pre-Schooling in 2002 (Dirección General de Planeación y Estadística Educativa 2014). The aim of the preschool program is to promote the development of children through educational work, play, and related activities (Secretaría de Educación Pública 2013). Year levels are numbered 1 to 3.

Although enrollment is mandatory, a 2014 report by the SEP indicates that the percentage of children enrolled varies widely by state. Less than 65 percent of preschool-aged children are enrolled in many of the northern states, while an average of 80 to 90 percent are enrolled in the central and southern states. Some of the most populous central and southern states, notably Queretaro, Durango, and Tabasco, report enrollment greater than 100 percent of capacity (Secretaría de Educatión Pública 2014).

Primary Education

Compulsory education begins with six years of *educación primeria* (primary school) from the ages of six through eleven. Grade levels are numbered 1 to 6.

In their 2014 statistics report, the SEP acknowledges that enrollment at primary schools exceeds capacity in all states. Certain central and southern states are experiencing overcrowding at 115 percent of capacity (Secretaría de Educación Pública 2014).

Lower Secondary Education/ Junior High School

Compulsory basic education is completed by three years of *educación secundaria* (lower secondary school/ junior high school) from the ages of 12 through 14.

Students choose one of two tracks: *General* (general/ regular) or *Para Trabajadores* (vocational). Grade levels are numbered 1 to 3.

The secondary system is characterized by variations in capacity and enrollment across the states. The southern states are the best equipped to handle demand and report enrollment of approximately 90 percent of capacity. By contrast, a number of central and northern states are experiencing enrollment of up to 120 percent of capacity (Secretaría de Educación Pública 2014).

GRADING

(*See* Table 37.2.)

CREDENTIALS

* *Certificado de Educación Secundaria* (Certificate of Lower Secondary Education)—Represents completion of three years of general secondary education, equivalent to completion of Grade 9 in the U.S./ Canada

* *Certificado de Estudio Técnico Nivel Medio Basico* (Certificate of Technical Studies, Lower Secondary)— Represents completion of three years of vocational lower secondary education, equivalent to completion of Grade 9 in the U.S./Canada

SCHOOL SUMMARY

As of 2014, there are 6.6 million children enrolled at 37,924 lower secondary schools. The teacher to student ratio is approximately 1 to 27 (Secretaría de Educatión Pública 2014).

Job Training

After completion of the compulsory education system (Grade 9), students who choose the vocational track of lower secondary must choose a further three years of technical senior high school or completion of a short three to five month *capacitación para el trabajo* (job training) program. Job training programs are regulated by the SEP and provide practical basic training for employment in the industrial, agricultural, or service sectors.

Job training programs are classified according to whether the program focuses on general or specific competencies. *Educación competencia ocupacional* (education for job competency) focuses on general readiness for work, while *educación basada en competencias* (competency-based education) provides training in a specific skill area.

CREDENTIALS

Educación Competencia Ocupacional (Education for Job Compency)

* *Reconocimiento Oficial de Competencia Ocupacional* (ROCO)—Official Recognition of Job Competency; no equivalent credential in the U.S./Canada

Educación Basada en Competencias (Competency-Based Education)

* *Cursos Regulares y para el Modelo de Educacion Basada en Competencias* (EBC)—Certification of

Competency-Based Education; no equivalent credential in the U.S./Canada

SCHOOL SUMMARY

As of 2014, there are 1.7 million youth enrolled at 6,029 job training institutes (Secretaría de Educación Pública 2014). The teacher to student ratio is approximately 1 to 26 (Secretaría de Educatión Pública 2014).

Upper Secondary Education/ Senior High School

Though education is compulsory only until the end of ninth grade, students are encouraged to continue to *educación media superior* (upper secondary education/ senior high school) from the ages of 15 through 17. Grade levels are numbered 1 to 3.

At the beginning of this education level, students may choose to follow the general academic track *preparatoria/bachillerato general* (general high school) or one of three technical/vocational streams: *bachillerato tecnologico* (technical high school), *profesional técnico* (technical professional school), or *professional técnico bachiller* (vocational high school).

In their 2014 statistics report, the SEP acknowledges that the country's upper secondary schools are operating at a national average of 105 percent of capacity (Secretaría de Educación Pública 2014).

Open and Distance Education

Online high school completion programs have been offered to adult learners and youth living in rural locations since the late 1970s. Programs offered through distance education are *formación para el trabajo* (job training) and *educación media superior* (upper secondary school).

GRADING

(*See* Table 37.2, on page 378.)

CREDENTIALS

The following certifications are equivalent to completion of regular senior high school (Grade 12) in the U.S./Canada:

* *Certificado de Bachillerato*—Certificate of High School
* *Certificado de Bachillerato General*—Certificate of General High School
* *Certificado de Preparatoria Abierta y Distancia*—Certificate of Preparatory Open and Distance Education

The following certifications are equivalent to completion of vocational senior high school (Grade 12) in the U.S./Canada:

* *Certificado de Bachillerato Tecnológico*—Certificate of Technical High School
* *Certificado de Profesional Técnico Bachiller*—Certificate of Professional Technical High School
* *Titulo de Bachiller*—High School Completion

SCHOOL SUMMARY

As of 2014, there are 4.7 million youth enrolled at 17,245 upper secondary schools. This number is further distributed as 2.8 million enrolled in general high school programs, 1.4 million in technical and professional programs, and 500,000 in vocational programs (Secretaría de Educatión Pública 2014).

Tertiary/Postsecondary Education

Admission to *educación superior* (tertiary/postsecondary education) requires completion of *educación media superior* (Upper Secondary Education/Senior High School). The postsecondary structure follows the u.s. model and is categorized as professional/vocational, undergraduate, graduate, and doctorate.

Technical University

Professional and vocational programs result in a technician's certificate or diploma and are normally two to three years in duration. These programs usually involve certification and issuing of a professional title such as bookkeeper, mechanic, etc.

GRADING

(*See* Table 37.2, on page 378.)

CREDENTIALS

* *Titulo de Técnico Superior Universitario* (Higher Technical University Degree)—Equivalent to two to three years of study in a university technical program in U.S./Canada
* *Certificado de Pasante/Carta de Pasante* (Internship Letter)—A letter issued by the issuing institution to verify completion of a program; equivalent to three to five years of specialized university study in U.S./Canada
* *Titulo de...(profession)* [(name of profession) Degree]—If four or more years in duration, it is equivalent to completion of a specialized/technical bachelor's degree program in U.S./Canada.

SCHOOL SUMMARY

As of 2014, there are 147, 000 youth enrolled in technical undergraduate programs at 292 colleges and universities (Secretaría de Educatión Pública 2014).

Undergraduate Teacher Training Degree

A *Licenciatura en Educación Normal* (Undergraduate Teacher Training Degree) requires four to five years of study and is equivalent to a bachelor's degree and professional teaching license. A successful graduate will earn both their undergraduate degree and a separate *Titulo Profesional* (diploma). Completion of a *Licentiatura* degree permits a student to pursue postgraduate studies.

GRADING

(*See* Table 37.2, on page 378.)

CREDENTIALS

The following degrees represent completion of an undergraduate degree with an additional license or certification to practice in a regulated field, equivalent to the attainment of a bachelor's degree in the U.S./Canada:

* *Licenciatura Educación Inicial*—Bachelor of Early Education
* *Licenciatura Educación Preescolar*—Bachelor of Preschool Education
* *Licenciatura Educación Primaria*—Bachelor of Primary Education
* *Licenciatura Educación Secundaria*—Bachelor of Secondary Education
* *Licenciatura Educación Especial*—Bachelor of Special Education
* *Licenciatura Educación Física*—Bachelor of Physical Education
* *Licenciatura Educación Artística*—Bachelor of Art Education
* *Licenciatura Educación Tecnológica*—Bachelor of Technical Education
* *Licenciatura Educación Bilíngüe*—Bachelor of Bilingual Education

SCHOOL SUMMARY

As of 2014, there are 132,000 students enrolled in undergraduate teacher training programs at 484 colleges and universities (Secretaría de Educatión Pública 2014).

Technical University Undergraduate Degree

A *Licentiatura Universitaria y Tecnológica* (Technical University Undergraduate degree) requires four to five years of study and results in the awarding of a bachelor degree and professional license or other qualification. A graduate will earn their undergraduate degree and a separate *Título profesional* (degree). Completion of a *Licentiatura* degree permits a student to pursue postgraduate studies.

GRADING

(*See* Table 37.2, on page 378.)

CREDENTIALS

* *Licenciatura/Título de Licenciado(a)* (University Degree)—If four or more years in duration, it is equivalent to completion of a bachelor's degree program in the U.S./Canada.
* *Licenciatura/Título de* (field of study or profession)—If four of more years in duration, it is equivalent to completion of a bachelor's degree program in the U.S./Canada.

SCHOOL SUMMARY

As of 2014, there are 2.9 million youth enrolled in undergraduate programs at 12,790 colleges and universities (Secretaría de Educatión Pública 2014).

Postgraduate Education

Students with a *Licenciatura/Título de Licenciado(a)* may continue to postgraduate studies for a further two to three years. Programs are categorized as either research-based or specialty-based. The majority of postgraduate programs are offered at autonomous (private) institutes.

GRADING

(*See* Table 37.2, on page 378.)

CREDENTIALS

* *Diplomado en (field of study or profession)/Diploma de Especialización en (field of study or profession)* Diploma in (field of study or profession)—Equivalent to completion of one to two years of postgraduate study in the U.S./Canada
* *Grado de Maestría* (Master's Degree)/*Maestría en (field of study or profession)* Master of (field of study or profession)—Equivalent to completion of a master's degree in the U.S./Canada

SCHOOL SUMMARY

As of 2014, there are approximately 49,000 students enrolled in postgraduate programs at 2,144 universities and autonomous institutes (Secretaría de Educatión Pública 2014), including more than 200 technological, industrial, and agricultural institutes (Tamez Guerra *et al.* 2006).

Doctoral Studies

Students with a *Grado de Maestro(ía)* (Master's Degree) may continue to doctorate studies for a further four years.

GRADING

(*See* Table 37.2, on page 378.)

CREDENTIALS

✴ *Grado de Doctorado(a)* (Doctoral Degree) or *Doctorado(a) en (field of study or profession)* Doctorate in (field of study or profession)—Equivalent to completion of a doctoral degree in the U.S./Canada

✴ *(Grado de) Doctorado en Veterinaria/Odontología/Cirugía* (Veterinarian/Dentist/Dental/Surgeon Degree)—Equivalent to completion of a professional doctorate degree in the U.S./Canada

Appendix A:
Timeline of Events in Applied Comparative Education

Prepared by George Kacenga, Director of International Enrollment Management, University of Colorado Denver, and based in part on *Evaluating Foreign Educational Credentials in the United States: Perspectives on the History of the Profession* by James Frey (2014).

1867

U.S. Office of Education (OE) is established as a branch of the U.S. Department of the Interior. OE staff members publish information on the educational systems of other countries.

1910

The American Association of Collegiate Registrars and Admissions Officers (AACRAO) is established.

1919

Comparative Education Section (CES) of the U.S. Office of Education receives a request to evaluate the educational credentials of one foreign-educated person. This single request evolved into the Foreign Credential Evaluation Service (FCES) (also known as the Foreign Credential Advisory Interpretation Service [FCAIS]).

1946

The Fulbright Act is passed, providing financial support from government resources to promote educational and cultural exchange between the United States and other nations.

1948

International student enrollment surpasses 25,000 for the first time (*Open Doors* 2015)

1948

The National Association of Foreign Student Advisers (NAFSA) is established.

1952

Educational Systems of the World by Martena Tenney Sasnett is published by the University of Southern California Press (838 pages).

1955

OE's CES publications begin to include the kinds of information needed to evaluate the educational credentials of individual applicants, such as the nature and level of individual educational institutions and programs, the identification of officially recognized tertiary-level degree-granting institutions, the official names of secondary-level and tertiary-level certificates, diplomas, and degrees, and admission requirements, graduation requirements, and grading scales. Foreign credential evaluators use these slim publications to assist in their work through the end of the 1960s.

1955

AACRAO appoints a Committee on Evaluation of Foreign Student Credentials to develop a series of publications on foreign educational systems, which include recommendations for the placement of students from those systems into U.S. educational institutions. The result is AACRAO's World Education Series (WES).

1955

To ensure that the placement recommendations in its WES volumes are accepted by the members of other organizations interested in foreign students, AACRAO helps organize an inter-association group to formally approve the placement recommendations. Known as The Council on Evaluation of Foreign Student Credentials (The Council), in 1977 it is renamed the National Council on the Evaluation of Foreign Educational Credentials (The Council).

1957

Do-It-Yourself Evaluation of Foreign Student Credentials, written by William Strain, is published.

1962

A Guide to the Admission and Placement of Foreign Students, edited by Martena Tenney Sasnett, is published in March 1962 with the assistance of the Institute of International Education (IIE).

1964

NAFSA establishes the Admissions Section [ADSEC], a professional section in the association for persons involved in foreign student admissions. At the same time, NAFSA changes its name to National Association for Foreign Student Affairs, keeping the NAFSA acronym.

1964

The Milwaukee Council for International Education (MCFIE), comprised of regional international educators, meets for the first time. The MCFIE meets several times a year with mixed membership as an open forum for pertinent dialogue regarding trends in international educations.

1964

NAFSA receives the first of a series of grants from the Office of Student Support Services (OSSS) of the Bureau of Educational and Cultural Affairs (CU) of the U.S. Department of State to establish the NAFSA Field Service. The Field Service has two missions: to support the development of publications and other projects that would improve the professional skills of university and college personnel who work with foreign students and to support projects that would improve the experiences of foreign students while they are in the United States. OSSS funding of the Field Service ended in the 1990s, and the Field Service was terminated by NAFSA in 1996.

1965

Between 1965 and 1972, two-day follow-up credential evaluation workshops are held in several regions of the United States to bring to other admissions officers the information produced by a series of two-week workshops produced by ADSEC. This activity is cosponsored by ADSEC, AACRAO, the College Board, IIE, and NAFSA.

1966

The Educational Systems of Africa by Martena Tenny Sasnett and Inez Hopkins Sepmeyer is published by the University of California Press (1,550 pages).

1966

The Comparative Education Section (CES), sometimes referred to as the Comparative Education Branch (CEB), of the OE stops producing relevant publications.

Funding is provided by the OSSS for AACRAO and NAFSA to produce publications and workshops.

1966

OE announces that FCES will be curtailed, beginning July 1, 1966, and that it will be terminated completely by July 1, 1968. A conference on Foreign Credential Interpretation and Educational Studies, held by OE, takes place in Washington DC April 6–7, at which representatives from several universities and colleges and educational organizations are officially informed of the OE decision.

1966

AACRAO reorganizes into five administrative groups to improve coordination of its activities. To encourage those members involved in the admission of foreign students to maintain their membership in AACRAO instead of (or in addition to) joining the newly established Admissions Section (ADSEC) of NAFSA, one of the new AACRAO administrative groups (Group II) was created to focus on international education.

1967

OSSS is instrumental in the establishment of educational advising services for prospective students in other countries, beginning in 1967-68 with offices throughout India in cooperation with the U.S. Educational Foundation in India (USEFI). Now known as EducationUSA, this worldwide network is supported by OSSS-funded Overseas Advising Workshops and U.S.-Based Training (USBT) programs.

1968

The National Liaison Committee on Foreign Student Admissions (NLC) asks OE for financial assistance for developing a proposal for the creation of a central foreign credential evaluation service. James S. Frey, then Director of Foreign Student Services at the University of Wisconsin-Milwaukee, is asked to conduct the study the feasibility of establishing this service under non-governmental auspices. A grant is approved on September 26, 1968. Mr. Frey concludes that a foreign credential evaluation service is needed; that it could operate outside of the government; that it ought to offer more information than is being provided by FCES; and that academic institutions and government agencies are willing to pay for this type of service. The NLC forwards the report of this study to OE. No further action on this topic is reported by OE or the NLC.

1968

AACRAO and NAFSA set up a Joint Committee on Workshops (JCOW) to develop and administer overseas credential evaluation workshops for members of both associations.

1969

NAFSA ADSEC Field Service publications are designed to assist foreign student admissions officers with the credential evaluation and admissions processes, including *A Guide to the Admission of Foreign Students* and *Guideline: Selection and Admission of Foreign Students*.

1969

Ted Sharp and Inez Hopkins establish the International Education Research Foundation, Inc. (IERF) as a non-profit organization created to receive the income generated by the future sales of *The Country Index*, first published in 1971.

1969

Ted Sharp and Inez Sepmeyer established Credential Evaluation Service, a for-profit organization and the first private foreign educational credential evaluation service in the world. A few years later they convert Credential Evaluation Service to non-profit status and merge it with the other services of IERF.

Late 1960s

ADSEC and the NLC develop a series of regional Credential Evaluation Projects to coordinate the volunteer activities of ADSEC members who responded to requests for credential evaluation assistance from U.S. universities and colleges that enrolled fewer than 100 foreign students. The four regional projects

were later combined to form the National Evaluation Project (NEP). The NEP is replaced by an electronic listserv in the 1980s.

1970s

The Office of Student Support Services (OSSS) becomes a division of the U.S. Information Agency (USIA) and then a division of the U.S. International Communication Agency (ICA). Later it is transferred back to the U.S. Department of State.

1970

FCES stops accepting requests pertaining to educational credentials from countries in South Asia, Southeast Asia, Sub-Saharan Africa, and the Western Hemisphere. On 30 June 1970, FCES is terminated completely. A few years later CES is dissolved.

1971

IERF's *The Country Index* is published for the first time by Ten Street Press, a resource for interpreting the educational experiences of students who did not study in the United States.

1974

World Education Services, Inc. (WES) is incorporated in September 1974 with Stephen H. Fisher as its President and Josef Silny as Vice President.

1980

The Education division of the U.S. Department of Health, Education, and Welfare is converted into the U.S. Department of Education by a law signed by President Carter on October 17, 1979.

1980

James Frey files incorporation papers for Educational Credential Evaluators (ECE). Incorporation was approved by the Secretary of State of Wisconsin on November 19, 1980.

1985

OSSS funding for publications and workshops produced by AACRAO and NAFSA is significantly reduced.

1987

National Association of Credential Evaluation Services, Inc. (NACES) is incorporated in Delaware in March 1987. NACES is an association of private and independent foreign educational credentials evaluation services committed to formulating and maintaining ethical standards in the field of foreign educational evaluation.

1987

WES publishes *World Education News & Reviews* (WENR). It provides current information about educational institutions and systems throughout the world.

1989

AACRAO and NAFSA sponsor a symposium in Oregon on Foreign Educational Systems: Future Directions in Research and Information Management. Implementation of the recommendations of the Oregon Symposium results in the merger of JCOW with the AACRAO World Education Series (WES) into a new inter-associational committee: Projects for International Education Research (PIER). Administrative duties related to PIER, predominantly financial administration, rotated between AACRAO and NAFSA.

1990

NAFSA changes its name to NAFSA: Association of International Educators, keeping the same acronym.

1993

AACRAO establishes its Office of International Education Services (OIES), an in-house credential evaluation service. Originally set up to evaluate foreign educational credentials for educational institutions that were members of AACRAO and for government agencies and professional associations, the activities of OIES were expanded in October 1997 to include evaluation reports for all purposes, including requests from individual foreign-educated applicants.

1994

The NACES certificate of incorporation and bylaws are revised and again approved by the state of Delaware.

1994

European Network of Information Centres (ENIC) are established by the Council of Europe and UNESCO. National Academic Recognition Information Centres (NARIC) are established by the European Commission. Each country in Europe has an ENIC, a NARIC, or an ENIC/NARIC.

1994

OSSS funding for publications and workshops produced by AACRAO and NAFSA is eliminated.

1996

United States Network for Education Information (USNEI) is instituted as the United States representative to the ENIC/NARIC network in Europe.

1996

AACRAO replaces its support of PIER publications with its own new series of Country Profiles.

1996

The Milwaukee Symposium, organized by the National Council on the Evaluation of Foreign Educational Credentials, develops a methodology for evaluating foreign educational credentials that is more transparent than the placement recommendations formerly approved by the Council. This methodology is designed to enable foreign educational credential evaluators to examine constituent elements of educational credentials, compare them to U.S. educational benchmarks, and draw their own conclusions.

1998

AACRAO publishes a report entitled *Toward Century II, Report of AACRAO Task Force 2000*. The report supported the case for third-party credential evaluation services given limited staffing resources at most academic institutions.

1998

The Association of International Credential Evaluators, Inc. (AICE), a nonprofit organization, is incorporated in 1998 in Nevada.

1999

NAFSA introduces online country profiles. These profiles do not replace any previous credential evaluation resource publications, which should which remain as valuable resources for credentials issued prior to 1999.

2001

In 2001, in anticipation of the demise of both PIER and the National Council on the Evaluation of Foreign Educational Credentials, AACRAO establishes an International Publication Advisory Committee (IPAC) to replace the research and publication functions of PIER, and an International Evaluation Standards Council (IESC) to replace the placement recommendation processes of the Council. Both IPAC and IESC are staffed solely by AACRAO members.

2002

AACRAO and NAFSA terminate Projects for International Education Research (PIER).

2004

NAFSA replaces its professional sections with knowledge communities (KCs). ADSEC is merged with the Association of Teachers of English as a Second Language (ATESL), the Community Section (COM-SEC), and the Overseas Advisors (OSEAS) to form the Recruitment, Admissions, and Preparation (RAP) Knowledge Community. The RAP KC is renamed the International Enrollment Management (IEM) KC in 2011.

2006

AACRAO and NAFSA withdraw their support for the National Council on the Evaluation of Foreign Educational Credentials. This marks the end of inter-associational cooperation in providing information and assistance to foreign educational credential evaluators.

2006

The Council, which had prepared formal placement recommendations for admission-related publications and workshop reports since 1955, is dissolved in March.

2011

ECE coordinates a free online forum called The Connection.

2015

The first general meeting of The Association of International Credential Evaluation Professionals (TAICEP) is held in Toronto, Canada.

Appendix B:
Helpful Organizations, Agencies, and Institutions

Alliance for International Exchange
1828 L Street, NW, Suite 1150
Washington, DC 20036-1912
Tel: (202) 293-6141
Fax: (202) 293-6144
E-mail: lheyn@alliance-exchange.org
www.alliance-exchange.org

**America-Mideast Educational and
Training Services, Inc. (AMIDEAST)**
2025 M Street, NW, Suite 600
Washington, DC 20036-3363
Tel: (202) 776-9600
Fax: (202) 776-7000
E-mail: inquiries@amideast.org
www.amideast.org

**American Association of
Community Colleges (AACC)**
One Dupont Circle, NW, Suite 410
Washington, DC 20036
Tel: (202) 728-0200
Fax: (202) 833-2467
www.aacc.nche.edu

**American Association of State
Colleges and Universities (AASCU)**
1307 New York Avenue, NW
Washington, D.C. 20005
Tel: (202) 293-7070
Fax: (202) 296-5819
E-mail: info@aascu.org
www.aascu.org

American Council on Education (ACE)
One Dupont Circle, NW
Washington, D.C. 20036-1193
Tel: (202) 939-9300
Fax: (202) 833-4760
www.acenet.edu

American Institute for Foreign Study (AIFS)
1 High Ridge Park
Stamford, CT 06905
Tel: (203) 399-5000
Fax: (203) 399-5590
E-mail: info@aifs.com
www.aifs.org

**The Association for International Credential
Evaluation Professionals (TAICEP)**
www.taicep.org

**Association of American Colleges
and Universities (AAC&U)**
1818 R Street, NW
Washington, DC 20009
Tel: (202) 387-3760
Fax: (202) 265-9532
www.aacu.org

**Association of International
Education Administrators (AIEA)**
AIEA Secretariat
Duke University
Box 90404, 107 Franklin Center, 2204
Erwin Rd.
Durham, NC USA 27708-0402
Tel: (919) 668-1928
Fax: (919) 684-8749
E-mail: aiea@duke.edu
www.aieaworld.org

**Association of International
Credential Evaluators (AICE)**
P.O. Box 6756
Beverly Hills, CA 90212
Tel: (310) 550-3305
Fax: (310) 550-3305
E-mail: info@aice-eval.org
www.aice-eval.org

British Council
Bridgewater House
58 Whitworth Street
Manchester
M1 6BB
United Kingdom
Tel: +44 (0) 161 957 7755
Fax: +44 (0) 161 957 7762
www.britishcouncil.org

**Canadian Bureau for International
Education (CBIE)**
220 Laurier West, Suite 1550
Ottawa, ON K1P 5Z9
Canada
Tel: (613) 237-4820
Fax: (613) 237-1073
E-mail: info@cbie.ca
www.cbie.ca

The College Board
250 Vesey Street
New York, NY 10281
Tel: (212) 713-8000
www.collegeboard.org

Colleges and Institutes Canada (CiCan)
1 Rideau Street, Suite 701
Ottawa, Ontario K1N 8S7
Canada
Tel: (613) 746-2222
Fax: (613) 746-6721
E-mail: info@collegesinstitutes.ca
www.collegesinstitutes.ca

**Commission on Graduates of Foreign
Nursing Schools (CGFNS)**
3600 Market Street, Suite 400
Philadelphia, PA 19104-2651
Tel: (215) 222-8454
Fax: (215) 662-0425
E-mail: info@cgfns.org
www.cgfns.org

**Council for Higher Education
Accreditation (CHEA)**
One Dupont Circle NW, Suite 510
Washington DC 20036-1135
Tel: (202) 955-6126
Fax: (202) 955-6129
E-mail: chea@chea.org
www.chea.org

Council of Graduate Schools (CGS)
One Dupont Circle, NW, Suite 230
Washington, DC 20036
Tel: (202) 223-3791
Fax: (202) 331-7157
E-mail: general_inquiries@cgs.nche.edu
www.cgsnet.org

**Council on International
Educational Exchange (CIEE)**
300 Fore Street
Portland, ME 04101
Tel: (207) 553-4000
Fax: (207) 553-4299
E-mail: contact@ciee.org
www.ciee.org

**Council for International
Exchange of Scholars (CIES)**
1400 K Street, NW, Suite 700
Washington, DC 20005
Tel: (202) 686-4000
Fax: (202) 686-4029
E-mail: Scholars@iie.org
www.cies.org

Educational Credentials Evaluators (ECE)
PO Box 514070
Milwaukee, WI 53203-3470
Tel: (414) 289-3400
E-mail: eval@ece.org
www.ece.org

EducationUSA
U.S. Department of State, Bureau of Educational and Cultural Affairs
www.educationusa.state.gov

EDUCAUSE
1150 18th Street, NW, Suite 900
Washington, DC 20036
Tel: (202) 872-4200
Fax: (202) 872-4318
E-mail: info@educause.edu
www.educause.edu

Educational Testing Service (ETS)
P.O. Box 6000
Princeton, NJ 08541-6000
Tel: (609) 771-7670
Fax: (609) 734-5410 (610) 290-8975
E-mail: etsinfo@ets.org
www.ets.org

ERIC – Institute of Education Sciences
655 15th St. NW, Suite 500
Washington, DC 20036
Tel: (800) 538-3742
www.eric.ed.gov

**European Association for
International Education (EAIE)**
PO Box 11189
1001 BT Amsterdam, The Netherlands
Tel: +31-20-344 5100
Fax: +31-20-344 5119
E-mail: info@eaie.org
www.eaie.org

Foreign Policy Research Institute (FPRI)
1528 Walnut St., Suite 610
Philadelphia, PA 19102
Tel: (215) 732-3774
Fax: (215) 732-4401
E-mail: fpri@fpri.org
www.fpri.org

The Fulbright Program
809 United Nations Plaza
New York, NY 10017-3580
Tel: (212) 984-5327
Email: Scholars@iie.org
www.iie.org/fulbright

**Graduate Management
Admission Council (GMAC)**
PO Box 2969
Reston, VA 20195
Tel: (703) 668-9600
Fax: (703) 668-9601
www.gmac.com

**International Education and
Research Network (iEARN)**
475 Riverside Drive, Suite 450
New York, NY 10115
Tel: 212-870-2693
Fax: 212-870-2672
www.iearn.org

**International Educational
Research Foundation (IERF)**
Post Office Box 3665
Culver City, CA 90231
Phone: (310) 258-9451
Fax: (310) 342-7086
E-mail: info@ierf.org
www.ierf.org

**International English Language
Testing System (IELTS)**
825 Colorado Boulevard, Suite 112
Los Angeles, CA 90041
Tel: (323) 255-2771
Fax: (323) 704-3444
E-mail: ielts@ieltsusa.org
www.ieltsusa.org

**International Research &
Exchanges Board (IREX)**
2121 K Street, NW, Suite 600
Washington, DC 20005
Tel: (202) 628-8188
Fax: (202) 628-8189
E-mail: irex@irex.org
www.irex.org

Institute of International Education (IIE)
809 United Nations Plaza
New York, NY 10017
Tel: (212) 883-8200
Fax: (212) 984-5452
E-mail: info@iie.org
www.iie.org

LASPAU
25 Mount Auburn Street, Suite 203
Cambridge, MA 02138-6095
Tel: (617) 495-5255
Fax: (617) 495-8990
E-mail: laspau-webmaster@
calists.harvard.edu
www.laspau.harvard.edu

Linden Educational Services
1770 Orange Avenue
Costa Mesa, CA 92627
Tel: (949) 612-8131
Fax: (240) 743-4132
E-mail: linden@lindentours.com
www.lindentours.com

NAFSA: Association of International Educators
1307 New York Avenue, NW, Eighth Floor
Washington, DC 20005-4701
Tel: (202) 737-3699
Fax: (202) 737-3657
E-mail: inbox@nafsa.org
www.nafsa.org

National Association of Graduate Admissions Professionals (NAGAP)
PO Box 14605
Lenexa, KS 66285-4605
Tel: (913) 895-4616
Fax: (913) 895-4652
E-mail: info@nagap.org
www.nagap.org

National Association of Credential Evaluators (NACES)
E-mail: info@naces.org
www.naces.org

National Association of Independent Colleges and Universities (NAICU)
1025 Connecticut Ave., NW, Suite 700
Washington, DC 20036
Tel: (202) 785-8866
Fax: (202) 835-0003
www.naicu.edu

National Collegiate Athletic Association (NCAA)
700 W. Washington Street
P.O. Box 6222
Indianapolis, Indiana 46206-6222
Tel: (317) 917-6222
Fax: (317) 917-6888
www.ncaa.org

NASPA: Student Affairs Professionals in Higher Education
111 K Street NE, 10th Floor
Washington, D.C. 20002
Tel: (202) 265-7500
Fax: (202) 797-1157
Email: office@naspa.org
www.naspa.org

Oregon Office of Degree Authorization
1500 Valley River Drive, Suite 100
Eugene, OR 97401
Tel: (800) 452-8807
Fax: (541) 687-7414
www.oregonstudentaid.gov/oda.aspx

Universities Canada
1710-350 Albert Street
Ottawa, Ontario K1R 1B1
Canada
Tel: (613) 563-1236
Fax: (613) 563-9745
E-mail: info@univcan.ca
www.univcan.ca

U.S. Department of Education
400 Maryland Avenue, SW, 7E-247
Washington, DC 20202
Tel: 1-800-USA-LEARN
www.ed.gov

World Education Services (WES)
Bowling Green Station
PO Box 5087
New York, NY 10274-508
Tel: (212) 966-6311
Fax: (212) 739-6100
www.wes.org

References

A World at School. 2014. Ukraine conflict stalls education for 50,000 children. Retrieved from: <www.aworldatschool.org/news/entry/ukraine-conflict-stalls-education-for-50000-children-1463>.

AACRAO. *See* American Association of Collegiate Registrars and Admission Officers.

ACAPS. 2015. *Eastern Ukraine: Conflict.* Retrieved from: <http://acaps.org/img/documents/b-acaps-bn-ukraine-conflict-30-jan-2015.pdf>.

ACE. *See* American Council on Education.

Afzal, M. 2013. Do barriers to candidacy reduce political competition? Evidence from a bachelorís degree requirement for legislators in Pakistan. Paper. *Brookings Brief.* Retrieved April 3, 2016 from: <www.brookings.edu/~/media/research/files/papers/2013/09/barrier%20political%20competition%20afzal/revised_barriers%20to%20candidacy_pc.pdf>.

Albrecht, T.J. 2007. *Challenges and Service Needs of Undocumented Mexican Undergraduate Students: Students' Voices and Administrators' Perspectives* (unpublished doctoral dissertation). The University of Texas at Austin. Retrieved from: <www.lib.utexas.edu/etd/d/2007/albrechtt61669/albrechtt61669.pdf>.

Altbach, P.G. 1998. *Comparative Higher Education: Knowledge, the University, and Development.* Greenwich, CT: Ablex Publishing.

———. 2004a. Globalisation and the university: Myths and realities in an unequal world. *Tertiary Education and Management.* 10(1): 3–25.

———. 2004b. Higher education crosses boarders: Can the United States remain the top destination for foreign students? *Change.* 18–24.

Altbach, P.G., and J. Knight. 2007. The internationalization of higher education: Motivations and realities. *Journal of Studies in International Education.* 11: 290–305.

American Association of Collegiate Registrars and Admission Officers. 1965. Placement recommendations to be used with U.S. Office of Education Bulletins. In *Chile: A Guide to the Academic Placement of Students from Chile in Educational Institutions in the United States.* Washington, D.C.: AACRAO.

———. 1970. Report of AACRAO-AID Conference: University-Government Cooperation in Programs for Students from Abroad.

———. 2009. Conference Presentation: Choosing and Using a Foreign Credential Evaluation Service: Tips for Best Practice.

———. 2015. *Community Colleges Increase Overseas Recruitment.* Retrieved from: <www.aacrao.org/resources/resources-detail-view/community-colleges-increase-overseas-recruitment>.

American Council on Education. 2012. *Mapping Internationalization on U.S. Campuses.* Washington, D.C.: ACE. Retrieved from: <www.acenet.edu/news-room/Documents/Mapping-Internationalizationon-US-Campuses-2012-full.pdf>.

American University of Beirut. *University Catalogue 2015–16.* Office of the Registrar. Retrieved from: <www.aub.edu.lb/registrar/Pages/catalogue15-16.aspx>.

Andrade, M.S. 2006. International students in English-speaking universities: Adjustment factors. *Journal of Research in International Education.* 5(2): 131–154.

———. 2009. The value of a first-year seminar: International students' insights in retrospect. *Journal of College Student Retention.* 10(4): 483–506.

Armour, S. 2003. Diploma mills insert degree of fraud into job market. *U.S. Today.* September 28. Available at: <http://usatoday30.usatoday.com/money/workplace/2003-09-28-fakedegrees_x.htm>.

Assefa, A.M. 1988. *France: A Study of the Educational System of France and a Guide to the Academic Placement of Students in Educational Institutions of the United States.* Washington, D.C.: American Association of Collegiate Registrars and Admissions Officers.

Association of Universities and Colleges of Canada. 2014. *Canada's Universities in the World: AUCC Internationalization Survey.* Ottawa: AUCC.

Australian Education International. 2009. *Using Education Agents.* Retrieved from: <s3.amazonaws.com/pieronline-studentexperience/accounts/1/Site/9/3236_Using_Education_Agents_pdf_original.pdf>.

Axact. 2016a. *Lifestyle: Live Larger than Life with Axact.* Retrieved April 2, 2016 from: <www.axact.com/lifestyle/>.

———. 2016b. *Axact's Grand Expansion, GalAxact.* Retrieved February 19, 2016 from: <www.axact.com/news/infrastructure.asp>.

Ayres, P., W. Sawyer, and S. Dinham. 2004. Effective teaching in the context of a Grade 12 high-stakes external examination in New South Wales, Australia. *British Educational Research Journal.* 30(1): 141–165.

Bae, Sang Hoon Kim, Young-Chul Ban, Sang-Jin Huh, Kyung-Chul Lee, Young-Hyun Son, Byung-Gil Huh, Kyung-Chul Kim, Ee-gyeong Na, Jung Han, SoongHee Kim, and Chang-hwan. 2011. *Brief Understanding of Korean Educational Policy.* Seoul: Korean Educational Development Institute.

Bagley, S.S., and L.M. Portnoi. 2014. Setting the stage: Global competition in higher education. *New Directions for Higher Education.* 2014(168): 5–11.

Bao, L. 2009. Faculty Development and Campus Internationalization: A Case Study. Ph.D. Dissertation.

Barefoot, B.O. 2005. Current institutional practices in the first college year. In *Challenging and Supporting the First-year Students: A Handbook for Improving the First Year of College,* edited by M.L. Upcraft, J.N. Gardner, and B.O. Barefoot. San Francisco: Jossey-Bass.

Barron, P., L.J. Gourlay, and P. Gannon-Leary. 2010. International students in the higher education classroom: Initial findings from staff at two post-92 universities in the UK. *Journal of Further and Higher Education.* 34(4): 475–489.

Beane, B.A. 1985. A Model for Foreign Student Retention and Attrition: A Case Study of SUNY–Buffalo. Ph.D. Dissertation. State University of New York–Buffalo.

Beck, K.V. 2009. Questioning the emperor's

new clothes: Towards ethical practices in internationalization. In *Canada's Universities Go Global*, edited by R. Desai-Trilokekar, G. Jones, and A. Schubert. Toronto: James Lorimer & Company.

Bear, J. 2005. Diploma mills: The $200-million-a-year competitor you didn't know you had. In *Guide to Bogus Institutions and Documents*, edited by A. M. Koenig, J. Montgomery and L. Stedman. Washington, D.C.: American Association of Collegiate Registrars and Admissions Officers.

Bodycott, P. 2009. Choosing a higher education study abroad destination. *Journal of Research in International Education*. 8(3): 349–373.

Boyer, S.P., and W.E. Sedlacek. 1988. Noncognitive predictors of academic success for international students: A longitudinal study. *Journal of College Student Development*. 29(3): 218–223.

British Council. n.d. *Guide to Good Practice for Education Agents*. Retrieved from: <www.britishcouncil.org/sites/britishcouncil.uk2/files/guide-to-good-practice-for-education-agents.pdf>.

Butrymowicz, S. 2012. In China, private colleges, universities multiply to meet higher-education demand. *The Washington Post*. February 12.

Callahan, K.M. 2015. The Internationalization in Student Affairs in the United States from 1951–1996. Ph.D. Dissertation. The Florida State University. ProQuest Dissertations Publishing, 3724194.

Campbell, C., N. Bishop, and S. Sarin. 2016. Case study: Applying communities of practice in graduate enrollment management for a cultural interpretation of workplace learning. *Journal of Research Initiatives*. 2016(1). Retrieved from: <http://digitalcommons.uncfsu.edu/jri/>.

Campbell, C., W. Tierney, and G. Sanchez. 2004. *The Road Ahead: Improving Diversity in Graduate Education*. University of Southern California: Center for Higher Education Policy Analysis.

Canadian Bureau of International Education. 2009. *Canada First: The 2009 Survey of International Students*. Ottawa: CBIE.

———. 2014. *A World of Learning: Canada's Performance and Potential in International Education*. Ottawa: CBIE.

Carter, K., and Y. Xu. 2007. Addressing the hidden dimension in nursing education: Promoting cultural competence. *Nurse Educator*. 32(4): 149–153.

CBIE. *See* Canadian Bureau of International Education.

CGS. *See* Council of Graduate Schools.

Chang, C. 2013. *Recruitment Agents: A Legal and Regulatory Overview*. Retrieved from: <www.britishcouncil.org/sites/default/files/recruitment-agents-a-legal-and-regulatory-overview.pdf>.

CHEA. *See* Council for Higher Education Accreditation.

Cheema, U. 2016. US court freezes bank accounts of Axact-owned shell companies. *The News*. February 24. Retrieved April 3, 2016 from: <www.thenews.com.pk/print/100618-US-court-freezes-bank-accounts-ofAxact-owned-shell-companies>.

Chen, B. 2011. An Emerging Trend of Mandarin-Speaking International Students. Paper presented at the annual meeting of the American Psychological Association, Washington, D.C.

China Ministry of Education. 2015. *Number of Higher Education Institutions*. Retrieved from: <http://en.moe.gov.cn/Resources/Statistics/edu_stat_2014/2014_en02/201508/t20150831_204482.html>.

Cho, Moon-Heum. 2012. Online student orientation in higher education: A development study. *Education Tech Research Development*. 60(6): 1051–1069.

Choudaha, R., and L. Chang. 2012. *Trends in International Student Mobility*. New York: World Education Services.

Clark, N. 2012. Internationalizing the community college campus. *World Education News and Review*. October 1. Retrieved from: <wenr.wes.org/2012/10/wenr-october-2012-internationalizing-the-community-college-campus>.

Cohen, E.B., and R. Winch. 2011. Diploma and Accreditation Mills: New Trends in Credential Abuse. *Verifile Accredibase*. Available at: <www.esrcheck.com/file/Verifile-Accredibase_Diploma-Mills.pdf>.

College Data. 2015. Whats the Price Tag for a College Education? Retrieved January 1 from: <www.collegedata.com/cs/content/content_payarticle_tmpl.jhtml?articleId=10064>.

Conrad, M., and K. Morris. 2010. *Shifting from Retention Rates to Retention Risk: An Alternative Approach for Managing Institutional Student Retention Performance*. Toronto: Higher Education Quality Council of Ontario.

Constitute. *Mexico's Constitution of 1917 with Amendments Through 2007*. 2007. Oxford: Oxford University Press. Retrieved from: <www.constituteproject.org/constitution/Mexico_2007.pdf>.

Cope, J., and E. Black. 1985. New library orientation for international students. *College Teaching*. 33(4): 159–162.

Council for Higher Education Accreditation. *Diploma Mills: An Old Problem and a New Threat*. Washington, D.C.: CHEA. Available at: <www.chea.org/degreemills/frmPaper.htm>.

Council of Graduate Schools. 2015. Graduate Schools Report 3.5% Increase in First-time Enrollment (press release). September 17. Retrieved October 6, 2015 from: <www.cgsnet.org/graduate-schools-report-35-increase-first-time-enrollment>.

Council of Ministers of Education, Canada. 2013. *The Role of Education Agents in Canada's Education Systems*. Retrieved from: <www.cmec.ca/Publications/Lists/Publications/Attachments/326/The-Role-of-Education-Agents-EN.pdf>.

Cramer, J. 2004. *Diploma Mills: Federal Employees Have Obtained Degrees From Diploma Mills and Other Accredited Schools, Some at Government Expense*. Washington, D.C.: U.S. Government Accountability Office. Available at: <www.gao.gov/new.items/d04771t.pdf>.

Curtin, N., A.J. Stewart, and J.M. Ostrove. 2013. Fostering academic self-concept: Advisor support and sense of belonging among international and domestic graduate students. *American Educational Research Journal*. 50(1): 108–137.

Curtis, P. 2004. Overseas students 'not making British friends.' *The Guardian*. November 29.

Dalton, J.C. 1999. Beyond borders: How international Developments are changing student affairs practice. *New Directions for Student Services*. 86(1). San Francisco: Jossey-Bass.

Damtew T., and P.G. Altbach, 2003. *African Higher Education: An International Reference Handbook*. Indiana University Press.

Davis, G.P. 2014. *Creating Global Citizens: Challenges and Opportunities for Internationalization at HBCUs*. Washington, D.C.: American Council on Education. Available at: <www.acenet.edu/news-room/Documents/Creating-Global-Citizens.pdf>.

De la Luz Arriaga Lemus, M. 2014. The struggle to democratize education in mexico. *NACLA Report on the Americas*. 47(3): 31.

Di Maria, D.L. 2014. *Successful Relationships with Recruiting Agents: Essential Considerations*. Washington, D.C.: NAFSA: Association of International Educators.

Directgov. October 2, 2012. *Qualifications: What the Different Levels Mean.* Retrieved from: <http://webarchive.nationalarchives.gov.uk/20121015000000/www.direct.gov.uk/en/EducationAndLearning/QualificationsExplained/DG_10039017>.

Drewitz, M. 2011. Deciphering Chinese credentials for general admissions and transfer purposes. Workshop presented at the bi-regional I-XII NAFSA: Association for International Educators conference, Reno, NV.

EducationUSA. 2015. *Global Guide 2015.* Washington, D.C..

———. n.d. *Policy Guidance for EducationUSA Centers on Commercial Recruitment Agents.* Washington, D.C. Retrieved from: <www.educationusa.info/pdf/Policy_Guidance_for_EducationUSA_Centers.pdf>.

Elliott, J.D. 2014. Internationalizing the Curriculum. Seminar. The Gulf University of Science and Technology. West Mishref, Kuwait. March 5. Faculty Development Training.

Ellison, P. 2008. Graduate admissions issues. In *The College Admission Officer's Guide*, edited by B. Lauren. Washington, D.C.: American Association of Collegiate Registrars and Admissions Officers.

Elon University. 2015a. *The Elon Commitment: An unprecedented university commitment to diversity and global engagement.* Retrieved from: <www.elon.edu/e-web/administration/president/strategicplan2020/diversity.xhtml>.

———. 2015b. *Study Abroad: First Steps.* Retrieved from: <www.elon.edu/e-web/academics/international_studies/study-abroad/First%20Steps.xhtml>

Elwell, F. 1999. *An Essay on Higher Education.* Retrieved from: <www.faculty.rsu.edu/users/f/felwell/www/Theorists/Essays/Elwell1.html>.

ESL. *67 China Foreign ESL & TEFL Teachers Arrested for Fake Diplomas & TEFL Certificates in Scam Sting.* Retrieved April 8, 2016 from: <http://esl.com/jobs/446376/67-china-foreign-esl-tefl-teachers-arrested-for-fake-diplomas-tefl-certificates-in-scam-sting-beware>.

Euromaidan Press. 2014a. Ukraine brings peace to liberated territories. September 2. Retrieved from: <http://euromaidanpress.com/2014/09/02/ukraine-brings-peace-to-liberated-territories/>.

———. 2014b. Separatists preparing to seize schools for "referendum." May 10. Retrieved from: <http://euromaidanpress.com/2014/05/10/separatists-preparing-to-seize-schools-for-referendum/>.

Farrugia, C.A., and R. Bhandari. 2015. *Open Doors 2015 Report on International Educational Exchange.* New York: Institute of International Education.

Fee, E.J., W. Radford, S. Dench, and S. Marshall. 2011. Internationalization and SEM at Simon Fraser University. In *SEM in Canada: Promoting Student and Institutional Success in Canadian Colleges and Universities*, edited by S. Gottheil and C. Smith. Washington, D.C.: American Association of Collegiate Registrars and Admissions Officers.

Fischer, K. 2015. Foreign students aren't edging out locals, numbers show. *The Chronicle of Higher Education.* February 2. Retrieved from: <http://chronicle.com/article/Foreign-Students-Arent-Edging/151547/>.

Fitzgerald, V.F. 1998. The Identification of Problems in Academic and Social Support Systems by International Students. Unpublished Ph.D. Dissertation. University of Iowa, Iowa City.

Fletcher, A., and C. Aldrich-Langen. 1998. *The Milwaukee Symposium: Refining the Methodology for Comparing US and Foreign Educational Credentials.* Washington, D.C.: NAFSA, Association of International Educators.

Florcruz, M. 2013. China's diploma mills: Report reveals 100 fake universities. *IB Times.* Retrieved April 8, 2016 from: <www.ibtimes.com/chinas-diploma-mills-report-reveals-100-fake-universities-1328373>.

Frey, J. 2003. *Credit Practices in the United States, and Suggestions for Determining U.S. Credit Equivalents for Credit Systems Used in Other Countries.* Milwaukee, WI: Educational Credential Elevators.

———. 2014. *Evaluating Foreign Educational Credentials in the United States: Perspectives on the History of the Profession.* Milwaukee, WI: Educational Credential Evaluators, Inc.

Gallo., M. 2015. Personal communication, August 2.

Gardner, L., G. Barrett, and C. Pearson. 2014. African American administrators at PWIs: Enablers of and barriers to career success. *Journal of Diversity in Higher Education.* 7(4): 235–251.

Gareis, E. 2012. Intercultural friendship: Effects of home and host region. *Journal of International and Intercultural Communications.* 5(4): 309–328.

Garrett, R. 2014. *Explaining International Student Satisfaction: Initial Analysis of Data from the International Student Barometer.* Boston: I-graduate.

Geo TV. 2013. Around 620 Saudi gov't officials found using fake degrees: report. GeoTV Online. Retrieved February 20, 2016 from: <www.geo.tv/latest/62079-around-620-saudi-govt-officials-found-using-fake-degrees-report>.

Gibbs, P. 2007. Does advertising pervert higher education? Is there a case for resistance? *Journal of Marketing for Higher Education.* 17 (1): 3–11.

Goff, J., and M. Snowden. 2015. Emerging SEM organizations for graduate and international students. In *Handbook of Strategic Enrollment Management*, edited by B. Bontrager *et al.* San Francisco: Jossey-Bass.

Gonzales, R.G., and A.M. Bautista-Chavez. 2014. *Two Years and Counting: Assessing the Growing Power of DACA.* Retrieved September 9, 2015, from: <www.immigrationpolicy.org/special-reports/two-years-and-counting-assessing-growing-power-daca>.

Gov.UK. 2015. *New GCSE Grading Structure: A Postcard.* Retrieved August 15, 2015 from: <www.gov.uk/government/publications/new-gcse-grading-structure-a-postcard>.

Grasgreen, A. 2011. At home on campus, not in country. *Inside Higher Ed.* April 6. Available at: <www.insidehighered.com/news/2011/04/062/ohio_university_international_student_experience_survey>.

Green, M.F. 2015. *Mapping the Landscape: Accreditation and the International Dimensions of U.S. Higher Education.* Washington, D.C.: NAFSA: Association of International Educators.

Gresham, R., and V. Clayton. 2011. Community connections: A programme to enhance domestic and international students' educational experience. *Journal of Higher Education Policy and Management.* 33(4): 363–374.

Grimes, P.W., and J.P. Rezek. 2005. The determinants of cheating by high school economics students: A comparative study of academic dishonesty in the transitional economies. *International Review of Economics Education.* 4(2): 23–45.

Grolleau, G., T. Lakhal, and N. Mzoughi. September 2008. An Introduction to the Economics of Fake Degrees. *Journal of Economic Issues.* 42(3): 673–693.

Grove, J. 2011. International students do not use Facebook to choose their university. *Times Higher Education.* September 17.

Grubb, W.N. 2009. *OECD Reviews of Tertiary Education.* Paris: OECD.

Hamnett, B. 2004. *A Concise History of Mexico.* Cambridge: Cambridge University Press.

Hansen, M.E. 1993. *An Orientation and Leadership Training Handbook for International Students* (Beacon College Handbook). Edison, NJ: Middlesex County College.

Havergal, C. 2015. The cost of agents. *Inside Higher Ed*, February 20. Retrieved November 4, 2015 from: <www.insidehighered.com/news/2015/02/20/british-universities-are-spending-more-agents-recruit-international-students>.

Hawawini, G. 2011. *The Internationalization of Higher Education Institutions: A Critical Review and a Radical Proposal*. Fontainebleau: INSEAD. Available at: <www.insead.edu/facultyresearch/research/doc.cfm?did=48726>.

Hayhoe, R., and J. Lin. 2015. China's Private Universities: A Successful Case Study. *International Higher Education*. 51: 6–8.

He, A. 2015. Gaokao exam looks for wider acceptance. *China Daily*. Retrieved August 3, 2015 from: <usa.chinadaily.com.cn/epaper/2015–06/05/content_20918644.htm>.

Helms, R.M. 2014. *Mapping International Joint and Dual Degrees: U.S. Program Profiles and Perspectives*. Washington, D.C.: American Council on Education. Retrieved from: <www.acenet.edu/news-room/Documents/Mapping-International-Joint-and-Dual-Degrees.pdf>. (C10,13)

Herashchenko, Y. 2014. Kvit: There will be no simplified university transfer system for students from the ATO zone. *Euromaidan Press*. Retrieved from: <http://euromaidanpress.com/2014/08/16/kvit-there-will-be-no-simplified-university-transfer-system-for-students-from-the-ato-zone/>.

Hill, B. 2010. *The Internationalization Laboratory*. Washington, D.C.: American Council on Education.

Hoffman, I., and O. Popa. 1986. Library orientation and instruction for international students: The University of California-Davis experience. *RQ*. 25(3): 356–360.

Hollis, E.V. 1938. *Philanthropic Foundations and Higher Education*. Columbia University Press.

Hoover, E. 2015. Before overhauling that website, do your homework. *The Chronicle of Higher Education*. August 25. Retrieved November 4, 2015 from: <http://chronicle.com/article/Before-Overhauling-That/232571>.

Hovland, K. 2010. *Global Learning: Aligning Student Learning Outcomes with Study Abroad*. Washington, D.C.: NAFSA: Association of International Educators.

Hovland, K. 2014. *Global Learning: Defining, Designing, Demonstrating*. Washington, D.C.: NAFSA: Association of International Educators and the Association of American Colleges and Universities. Retrieved from: <www.aacu.org/sites/default/files/files/Global/global_learning_2014.pdf>.

Hudzik, J. 2011. *Comprehensive Internationalization: From Concept to Action*. Washington, D.C.: NAFSA: Association of International Educators. Retrieved from: <www.nafsa.org/uploadedFiles/NAFSA_Home/Resource_Library_Assets/Publications_Library/2011_Comprehen_Internationalization.pdf>.

Hussain, A. 2015. Axact harmed Pakistan and committed treason. *Pakistan Times*. Retrieved February 17, 2016 from: <www.pakistantimes.com/2015/05/20/axact-harmed-pakistan-and-committed-treason-altaf-hussain-368953.html>.

i-Graduate. 2011. *International Student Barometer Entry Wave: Ontario Results 2010*. Surrey, UK: i-Graduate.

ICEF Monitor. 2014a. OECD releases detailed study of global education trends for 2014. *ICEF Monitor*. September 17. Retrieved Nov 4, 2015 from: <http://monitor.icef.com/2014/09/oecd-releases-detailed-study-global-education-trends-2014/>.

———. 2014b. *High Performance, High Pressure in South Korea's Education System*. January 23. Retrieved August 17, 2015 from: <http://monitor.icef.com/2014/01/high-performance-high-pressure-in-south-koreas-education-system/>.

———. 2015a. U.S. community colleges stepping up international recruitment. July 29. Retrieved from: <http://monitor.icef.com/2015/07/us-community-colleges-stepping-up-international-recruitment>.

———. 2015b. China encouraging overseas universities to accept gaokao exam results. June 2. Retrieved July 27, 2015 from: <http://monitor.icef.com/2015/06/china-encouraging-overseas-universities-to-accept-gaokao-exam-results/>.

IIE. *See* Institute of International Education.

INEGI. *See* Instituto Nacional de Estadistica, Geogradia e Informática.

Ingram, T.N., D. Greenfield, J.D. Carter, and A.A. Hilton. 2015. *Exploring Issues of Diversity within HBCUs*. Charlotte, NC: Information Age Publishing.

Innova University. 2016. *Innova University Offers Presidential Scholarship*. Retrieved February 18, 2016 from: <http://innova.university/tuition/scholarship/index.html>.

Institute for Competitiveness and Prosperity. 2010. International Students: Presentation at CUPA-MTCU-HEQCO Day. Toronto: Institute for Competiveness and Prosperity.

Institute of Distance Education, Korea National Open University. 2010. *E-Learning in Lifelong Education*. Seoul: Korean National Open University.

Institute of International Education. 2009. *Three Year Bologna-Compliant Degrees: Responses from U. S. Graduate Schools*. Available at: <www.iie.org/~/media/Files/Corporate/Membership/Articles-and-Presentations/Survey-Bologna-Process-Briefing-Paper-2009.pdf?la=en>.

———. 2014a. *Open Doors Report on International Educational Exchange*. Retrieved from: <www.iie.org/Research-and-Publications/Open-Doors>. (C1,10,11,23)

———. 2014b. *Charting New Pathways to Higher Education: International Secondary Students in the United States*. Retrieved from: <www.iie.org/~/media/Files/Corporate/Publications/IIE-International-Secondary-Students-In-The-US.pdf?la=en>.

———. 2014c. International Students by Academic Level, 2012/13–2013/14. *Open Doors Report on International Educational Exchange*. Retrieved October 6, 2015 from: <www.iie.org/Research-and-Publications/Open-Doors/Data/International-Students/Academic-Level/2012–14>.

———. 2015a. *Open Doors Report on International Educational Exchange*. Retrieved from: <www.iie.org/Research-and-Publications/Open-Doors>. (C1,33)

———. 2015b. Project Atlas. Retrieved Nov 4, 2015 from: <www.iie.org/Services/Project-Atlas/China/International-Students-In-China>.

Instituto Nacional de Estadistica, Geogradia e Informática. 2001. *Indicadores Sociodemográficos de México, 1930–2000*. Aguacalientes, Mexico. Retrieved from: <www.inegi.org.mx/prod_serv/contenidos/espanol/bvinegi/productos/integracion/sociodemografico/indisociodem/2001/indi2001.pdf>.

International Qualifications Assessment Service. 2009. *International Education Guide for the Assessment of Education from South Korea*. Edmonton, AB: Government of Alberta.

Jamshaid, Y. Interview with the author. May 17, 2015.

Johnson, B.J., S.D. Hoskins, and T.E. Johnson. 2015. From another perspective: Perceptions of white faculty of the racial climate at black colleges. In *Exploring Issues of Diversity within HBCUs,* edited by T.N. Ingram, *et al.* Charlotte, NC: Information Age Publishing.

Joint Council for Qualifications UK. 2015. *Access Arrangements and Reasonable Adjustments 2015–2016.* Retrieved January 15, 2016 from: <www.jcq.org.uk/exams-office/access-arrangements-and-special-consideration/regulations-and-guidance/access-arrangements-and-reasonable-adjustments-2015-2016>.

Jordan, M. 2015. International students stream into U.S. colleges. *The Wall Street Journal.* March 24. Retrieved from: <www.wsj.com/articles/international-students-stream-into-u-s-colleges-1427248801>.

Joshee, J., M. Leventhal, and J. Weller. 2013. Closing the Loop: Funding Comprehensive Internationalization through Inbound Recruitment—A Performance-Based Reinvestment Model. AIRC Annual Conference. Miami, FL.

Kallur, R., and M. Reeves. 2006. *Guidelines for Ethical Practices in International Student Recruitment.* Washington, D.C.: NAFSA: Association of International Educators. Retrieved from: <www.nafsa.org/uploadedFiles/NAFSA_Home/Resource_Library_Assets/ACE/guidelines_for_ethical(1).pdf?n=2584>.

Kamal, F. A speech by Mr. Farhan Kamal, Vice President–Business Unit of Axact. *YouTube.* Retrieved May 17, 2016 from: <www.youtube.com/watch?v=yv64gH9Rg6I>.

Khan, W.S. 2015. The article nobody will publish. *Pak Tea House.* Retrieved April 3, 2016 from: <http://pakteahouse.net/2015/05/26/the-article-nobody-will-publish-by-wajahat-s-khan/>.

Khan, Z., and N. Toosi. 2010. Fake degree scandal toils Pakistan politics. *San Francisco Chronicle.* Retrieved February 16, 2016 from: <http://sfgate.com/cgi-bin/article.cgi?f=/n/a/2010/06/29/international/110240D24.DTL>.

Kingsbury, A. 2005. Hot on the trail of academic fraud. *U.S. News & World Report.* 138 (2): 76.

Knight, J. 2003. Updated internationalization definition. *International Higher Education* 33: 2–3.

———. 2004. Internationalization remodeled: Definition, approaches, and rationales. *Journal of Studies in International Education.* 8(1): 5–31.

Knowlton, E. 2012. 24 photos of China's insanely stressful college entrance exam process. *Business Insider.* June 12. Retrieved from: <www.businessinsider.com/24-stunning-photos-of-chinas-college-entrance-exams-2014-6>.

Kogan Page Ltd. 2014. *British Qualifications 2014: A Complete Guide to Professional, Vocational and Academic Qualifications in the United Kingdom.* London.

Kotler, P., and K.F. Fox. 2002. *Strategic Marketing for Educational Institutions.* Upper Saddle River, NJ: Prentice-Hall.

LaFleur, D. 2015. Administration and management of international joint and dual degrees. *International Briefs for Higher Education Leaders.* 5: 16–18.

Lane, J.E., K.C. Krebs, and L. Thompson. 2015. Leveraging system assets to strengthen campus internationalization: Strategic planning and the role of leadership. *International Briefs for Higher Education Leaders.* 5: 7–10.

Leary, T. 2012. Supporting International Students with First Year Transition into Canadian Universities: Recommendations from Atlantic Canada. Ph.D. Dissertation, University of Calgary.

Lee, J.M. 2015. Re(defining) the diversity of HBCUs beyond race. In *Exploring Issues of Diversity within HBCUs,* edited by T.N. Ingram, *et al.* Charlotte, NC: Information Age Publishing.

Lee, J.J., and C. Rice. 2007. Welcome to America? International student perceptions of discrimination. *Higher Education.* 53(3): 381–409.

Lee, S., and A. Shaikh. 2013. Multiple testing and heterogeneous treatment effects: re-revaluating the effect of progresa on school enrolment. *Journal of Applied Econometrics.* 29: 612–626.

Leedock, J., 2011. *Revamping Pre-Arrival Communications for International Students* (webcast). July 13. Denver: Academic Impressions.

Lher, N., G. Juneau, and S. Molstad. 2003. From the Southern Hemisphere to the rural South: A Mauritian students' version of coming to America. *College Student Journal.* 37(4): 564–569.

Lin, J. 2015. China: private trends. *International Higher Education.* 36: 17–18.

Livers, A., and K. Caver. 2003. *Leading in Black and White: Working Across the Racial Divide in Corporate America.* San Francisco: John Wiley & Sons.

Lucido, J. 2015. How admission decisions get made. In *Handbook of Strategic Enrollment Management,* edited by B. Bontrager *et al.* San Francisco: Jossey-Bass.

Luo, J., and D. Jamieson-Drake. 2013. Examining the educational benefits of interacting with international students. *Journal of International Students.* 3(2): 85–101.

Mallinckrodt, B., and W.E. Sedlacek. 1987. Student retention and the use of campus facilities. *NASPA Journal.* 24(3): 28–32.

Mamiseishvili, K. 2011. International student persistence in U.S. postsecondary institutions. *Higher Education.* 64(1): 1–17.

Margolis, A., S.K. Higashi, and R. Weaver. 1991. *The Educational System of the United Kingdom: The Admission and Placement of Students from the U.K. and Study Abroad Opportunities.* Washington, D.C.: American Association of Collegiate Registrars and Admissions Officers.

Mayhew, M.J., K. Vanderlinden, and E.K. Kim. 2010. A multi-level assessment of the impact of orientation programs on student learning. *Research in Higher Education.* 51(4): 320–345.

Mazzarol, T., and G.N. Soutar. 2002. "Push-pull" factors influencing international student destination choice. *International Journal of Educational Management.* 16(2): 82–90.

McFadden, C., C. Maahs-Fladung, and W. Mallett. 2012. Recruiting international students to your campus. *Journal of International Students.* 2(2): 157–167.

McGaskey, F.G. 2012. The potential benefits of attending Historically Black Colleges and Universities for black doctoral students. In *Black Graduate Education at Historically Black Colleges and Universities: Trends, Experiences, and Outcomes,* edited by R. Palmer, A. Hilton, and T. Fountaine. Charlotte, NC: Information Age Publishing.

McLemee, S. 2014. The Economics of Fake Degrees. *New Zealand Herald.* July 6. Available at: <http://m.n12zherald.co.nz/education-qualifications/news/article.cfm?c_id=186&objectid=11288575>.

Mendoza, G.S. amd N. Shaikh. 2015. *Tuition Benefits for Immigrants.* Retrieved September 1, 2015 from: <www.ncsl.org/documents/immig/InStateTuition_july212015.pdf>.

Ministry of Education and Human Resources Development, Republic of Korea. 2001. *Education in Korea 2001–2002.*

Mirwaldt, P. 2010. Health and wellness services. In *Achieving student success: Effective student services in Canadian higher education,* edited by D. Hardy Cox and C.C. Strange. Montreal and Kingston: McGill-Queen's University Press.

Mutual Educational and Cultural Exchange Act of 1961. United States code, Title 22: Chapter 33. Retrieved from: <www2.ed.

gov/about/offices/list/ope/iegps/fulbrigh-thaysact.pdf>.

NACAC. *See* National Association for College Admission Counseling.

NAFSA. 2007. *Internationalizing the Campus 2007. Profiles of Success at Colleges and Universities.* Washington, D.C.: NAFSA.

———. 2008. *Internationalizing the Campus 2008. Profiles of Success at Colleges and Universities.* Washington, D.C.: NAFSA.

———. 2011. *NAFSA's Contribution to Internationalization of Higher Education.* Washington, D.C.: NAFSA.

———. 2016. *NAFSA International Student Economic Value Tool.* Available at: <www.nafsa.org/Explore_International_Education/Impact/Data_And_Statistics/NAFSA_International_Student_Economic_Value_Tool/>.

National Association for College Admission Counseling. 2013. *Report of the Commission on International Student Recruitment.* Arlington, VA: NACAC. Retrieved from: <www.nacacnet.org/studentinfo/InternationalStudentResources/Documents/Intl-StudRecruitReport.pdf>.

———. 2015. *Trusted Sources: Seeking Advice on Applying to Universities in Another Country.* Arlington, VA: NACAC. Retrieved from: <www.nacacnet.org/International/InternationalInitiatives/Pages/Trusted-Sources-Applying-to-University-in-Another-Country.aspx>.

National Institute of Lifelong Education. 2014. *Recognition and Validation of Nonformal and Information Learning.* Retrieved December 30, 2015 from: <http://nile.or.kr/eng/contents/contents.jsp?bkind=basic&bcode=DACAAB&bmode=view&idx=BCJDFCECEBDJD&pageNo=1>.

———. 2015a. *About BDES.* Retrieved May 1, 2016 from: <http://bdes.nile.or.kr/nile/info/nInfo5_1.do>.

———. 2015b. *Survey of Koreans Participating in Lifelong Learning.* Lifelong Learning in Korea 2015.1. Seoul: NILE. Available at: <www.nile.or.kr/nile_web2/common/download.jsp?file_name=20150331191427792898139of.pdf>.

Navarette, D.G. 2013. Becas de posgrado para indigenas: un programa no convential en mexico. *Cadernos de Pesquisa.* 43(150). Retrieved from: <www.scielo.br/scielo.php?script=sci_arttext&pid=S0100-15742013000300012&lng=es&nrm=iso&tlng=en>.

NCAT. *See* North Carolina A&T State University.

Nerad, M. 2010. Globalization and the internationalization of graduate education: A macro and micro view. *Canadian Journal of Higher Education.* 40(1): 1–12.

NILE. *See* National Institute of Life Long Education.

Nordic National Recognition Information Centres. 2009. *The Educational System of Ukraine.* Stockholm: NORRIC. Retrieved from: <http://norric.org/files/education-systems/Ukraine2009/at_download/file>.

NORRIC. *See* Nordic National Recognition Information Centres.

North Carolina A&T State University. 2015. *Strategic Plan and Initiatives.* Retrieved October 18 from: <www.ncat.edu/about/strategic-plan-Initiatives.html>.

North Dakota University System. 2012. *Internal Transfer Agreement Review.* Retrieved from: <www.ndus.edu/uploads/reports/96/dsu-internal-review-ddj-final-draft-020912.pdf>.

Olson, C. 2010. *Internationalities of the Curriculum: American, Canadian, and Australian Perspectives.* AIEA Conference. Washington, D.C.

Organization for Economic Co-operation and Development. 2006. *Starting Strong II: Early Childhood Education and Care.* Paris: OECD Publishing. Retrieved from: <www.oecd.org/edu/school/37423645.pdf>.

———. 2014. *Education at a Glance 2014: OECD Indicators.* Paris: OECD Publishing.

———. 2015. *Economic survey of China 2015.* Paris: OECD Publishing. Retrieved from: <www.oecd.org/china/economic-survey-china.htm>.

Ortiz, A., L. Chang, and Y. Fang. 2015. International student mobility trends 2015: An economic perspective. *World Education News and Reviews.* February 2. Retrieved October 6, 2015 from: <wenr.wes.org/2015/02/international-student-mobility-trends-2015-an-economic-perspective/>.

Padlee, S.F., A.R. Kamaruddin, and R. Baharun. 2010. International students' choice behavior for higher education at Malaysian private universities. *International Journal of Marketing Studies.* 2(2): 202–211.

Passel, J., and D. Cohn. 2015. Unauthorized immigrant population stable for half a decade. *Fact Tank.* July 22. Retrieved from: <www.pewresearch.org/fact-tank/2015/07/22/unauthorized-immigrant-population-stable-for-half-a-decade/>.

Paton, G. 2013. GCSEs: 'Extra Time' rule overhauled to stamp out abuse. *The Telegraph.* Retrieved January 15, 2016 from: <www.

telegraph.co.uk/education/education-news/10254909/GCSEs-extra-time-rule-overhauled-to-stamp-out-abuse.html>.

Perna, L.W., D. Gerald, E. Baum, and J. Milem. 2007. The status of equity for Black faculty and administrators in public higher education in the South. *Research in Higher Education.* 48(2): 193–228.

Peterson, P. 2014. Time to check your GPS. *Inside Higher Ed.* October 28. Retrieved from: <www.insidehighered.com/views/2014/10/28/essay-international-education-initiatives-and-what-they-are-missing>.

Pezzini, M. 2012. An emerging middle class. *OECD Observer.* Retrieved from: <www.oecdobserver.org/news/fullstory.php/aid/3681/An_emerging_middle_class.html>.

Pollack, K. 2008. Faculty's role in recruitment. In *The College Admission Officer's Guide*, edited by B. Lauren. Washington, D.C.: American Association of Collegiate Registrars and Admissions Officers.

Pratt, A., J.D. Dalfonso, and R. Rogers. 2014. *Digital, Social, Mobile: The 2014 Social Admissions Report.* Uversity. Retrieved November 7, 2015 from: <www.uversity.com/downloads/presentations/2014-Social-Admissions-Report-Webinar.pdf>.

Rabinowitz, P. 1996. Promoting the adoption and use of best practices. In *Learn a Skill.* Community Tool Box. Retrieved Januarty 23, 2016 from: <http://ctb.ku.edu/en/table-of-contents/analyze/choose-and-adapt-community-interventions/using-best-practices/main>.

Raimo, V., C. Humfrey, and I. Huang. 2014a. Power and control: managing agents for international student recruitment in higher education. *Studies in Higher Education.* 41(8).

———. 2014b. *Managing International Student Recruitment Agents: Approaches, Benefits and Challenges.* Retrieved from: <www.britishcouncil.org/sites/britishcouncil.uk2/files/managing_education_agents_report_for_bc_2.pdf>.

Read, G. 1996. The International Education Act of 1966. *The Phi Delta, Kappan.* 47(8): 406–409.

Redden, E. 2014a. The younger international student. *Inside Higher Ed.* July 8. Retrieved from: <www.insidehighered.com/news/2014/07/08/new-research-provides-insight-growing-pool-international-high-school-students-us>.

———. 2014b. The ideal and the real. *Insider Higher Ed.* November 12. Retrieved from:

<www.insidehighered.com/news/2014/11/12/new-report-highlights-challenges-establishing-international-joint-or-dual-degree>.

———. 2015a. Fee for being foreign. *Inside Higher Ed.* May 8. Retrieved from: <www.insidehighered.com/news/2015/05/08/some-public-universities-are-charging-differentiated-tuition-rates-or-raising-fees>.

———. 2015b. Brazil expected to cut back on scholarship program. *Inside Higher Ed.* September 14. Retrieved March 24, 2016 from: <www.insidehighered.com/quicktakes/2015/09/14/brazil-expected-cut-back-scholarship-program>.

———. 2016. New rules for Saudi scholarship program approved. *Inside Higher Ed.* February 3. Retrieved March 24, 2016 from: <www.insidehighered.com/quicktakes/2016/02/03/new-rules-saudi-scholarship-program-approved>.

Removska, O. 2014. War and the right to education. *Euromaidan Press.* November 25. Retrieved from: <http://euromaidanpress.com/2014/11/25/war-and-the-right-to-education/>.

Rice, K.G., C. Choi, Y. Zhang, J. Villega, H.J. Ye, D. Anderson, A. Nesic, and M. Bigler. 2009. International student perspectives on graduate advising relationships. *Journal of Counseling Psychology.* 56(3): 376–391.

Ringer, J.B. 2000. *The People's Republic of China: A Workshop Report on the Education System and Guide to the Academic Placement of Students in Education Institutions in the United States.* Washington, D.C.: American Association of Collegiate Registrars and Admissions Officers.

Roberts, D.C. 2015. Internationalizing higher education and student affairs. *About Campus.* 20(2): 8–15.

Rogers, G. 2015. How students (really) decide: Class of 2015. *The Journal of College Admission.* 228: 42–43. Retrieved November 5 from <www.nxtbook.com/ygsreprints/NACAC/nacac_jca_summer2015/#/44>.

Roslyn Kunin & Associates. 2012. *Economic Impact of International Education in Canada—An Update Final Report.* Vancouver: RKA, Inc.

Ross, J. 2013. UNSW joins the gaokao band. *The Australian.* April 27. Retrieved from: <www.theaustralian.com.au/higher-education>.

Rui, Y. 2014. China's removal of English from gaokao. *International Higher Education.* 75: 12–13.

Sandeen, A. 2004. Educating the whole student: The growing academic importance of student affairs. *Change.* May/June: 28–33.

Saul, S. 2016. The Mideast came to Idaho State. It wasn't the best fit. *New York Times.* March 21. Retrieved on March 24, 2016 from: <www.nytimes.com/2016/03/22/us/a-middle-eastern-tension-point-pocatello-idaho.html>.

Schoorman, D. 2000. What really do we mean by 'internationalization?' *Contemporary Education.* 71(4): 5–11.

Schultheis, L. 2013. Strategic university partnerships for enrollment management. *Strategic Enrollment Management Quarterly.* (3)1: 194–203.

Schweitzer B., G. Morson, and P. Mather. 2011. *Understanding the International Student Experience.* Baltimore: American College Personnel Association.

Secretaría de Educación Pública. 2013. Comunicado 047.-Sep modifica acuerdo 648 para evaluación de educación básica. Retrieved from: <www.sep.gob.mx/es/sep1/C0470413>.

———. 2014. Anunció el presidente enrique peña nieto la transformación del programa oportunidades del programa. Retrieved from: <www.prospera.gob.mx/Portal/wb/Web/anuncio_el_presidente_enrique_pena_nieto_la_transf>.

———. 2014. Principales Cifras del Sistema Educativo National 2013–2014. First Ed. Mexico DF: Dirección General de Planeación y Estadística Educativa. 9–286. Retrieved from: <http://fs.planeacion.sep.gob.mx/estadistica_e_indicadores/principales_cifras/principales_cifras_2013_2014.pdf>.

Serban, A., C. Kozeracki, D. Boroch, L. Over, I. Malmgren, and B. Smith. 2008. *Transfer Issues and Effective Practices: A Review of the Literature.* Sacramento: The Research and Planning Group for California Community Colleges.

Shaikh, S.A. 2013. Team Meet 2013–14 Speech. Retrieved April 2, 2016 from: <https://vimeo.com/92325751>.

Shambaugh, D. 2014. *China at the Crossroads: Ten Major Reform Challenges.* Washington, D.C.: Brookings Institution. Retrieved from: <www.brookings.edu/research/papers/2014/10/01-china-crossroads-reform-challenges-shambaugh>.

Sharma, Y. 2012, Fake qualifications industry expands into lucrative new areas. *University World News.* Issue 219. Retrieved February 18, 2016 from: <www.universityworldnews.

com/article.php?story=20120426151308456>.

———. 2015. China pushes for foreign universities to use its college-entrance exam. *The Chronicle of Higher Education.* June 3. Retrieved from: <http://chronicle.com/article/China-Pushes-for-Foreign/230649>.

Sherry, M., P. Thomas, and W.H. Chui. 2010. International students: a vulnerable student population. *Higher Education.* 60(1): 33–46.

Simpson, K., and W. Tan. 2009. A home away from home? Chinese student evaluations of an overseas study experience. *Journal of Studies in International Education.* 13(1): 5–21.

Skinner, M., and J. Grier. 2006. *The Educational System of the United Kingdom.* Washington, D.C.: American Association of Collegiate Registrars and Admissions Officers.

Smith, C., and T. Demjanenko. 2011. *Solving the International Student Retention Puzzle.* Windsor, ON: University of Windsor.

Smith, C., B. Whiteside, S. Blanchard, and C. Martin. 2013. International Student Support Services at Ontario Universities. *Strategic Enrollment Management Quarterly.* 1(1): 55–66.

Snyder, T., and C. Hoffman. 2000. *Digest of Education Statistics, 1999.* Washington, D.C.: National Center for Education Statistics. Available at: <http://nces.ed.gov/pubs2000/2000031.pdf >.

Southern Association of Colleges and Schools. 2014a. *Agreements Involving Joint and Dual Academic Awards: Policy and Procedures.* Decatur, GA: SACSCOC Commission on Colleges. Retrieved from: <www.sacscoc.org/pdf/JointDualAwards.pdf>.

———. 2014b. *Advertising, Student Recruitment, and Representation of Accredited Status.* Decatur, GA: SACSCOC Commission on Colleges. Retrieved from: <www.sacscoc.org/pdf/081705/advertising.pdf>.

———. 2016. *Substantive Change for SACSCOC Accredited Institutions.* Decatur, GA: SACSCOC Commission on Colleges. Retrieved from: <www.sacscoc.org/pdf/081705/SubstantiveChange.pdf>.

Stateuniversity.com. n.d. *Consortia in Higher Education—Types of Consortia, Conclusions.* Retrieved from: <http://education.stateuniversity.com/pages/1881/Consortia-in-Higher-Education.html>.

Stephens, P. 2013. International students: Separate but profitable. *Washington Monthly.* October.

Stiegler, B.N. 2015. *Academics, Part 1: Structures and Policy*. Salisbury University. Washington D.C.: American Council on Education.

Strayhorn, T.L., and J.B. Hirt. 2008. Social justice at Historically Black and Hispanic-serving institutions: Mission statements and administrative voices. In *Understanding Minority-Serving Institutions*, edited by M. Gasman, B. Baez, and C.S.V. Turner. Albany, NY: State University of New York Press.

Sweeney, L. 1986. *PIER Workshop Report on South Asia, The Admission and Placement of Students from Bangladesh, India, Pakistan, Sri Lanka*. Washington D.C.: American Association of Collegiate Registrars and Admissions Officers, NAFSA.

———. 1997. *PIER World Education Series, India. A Special Report on the Higher Education System and Guide to the Academic Placement of Students in Educational Institutions in the United States*. Washington D.C.: American Association of Collegiate Registrars and Admissions Officers.

Tamez Guerra, R., J. Rubio Oca, B. Fuentes Lemus, M. Valdés Garza. 2006. *Disposiciones para la Operación de Estudios de Posgrado en el Sistema Nacional de Educación Superior Tecnológica*. First Ed. Mexico D.F.: Dirección General de Educación Superior Tecnológica.

Tas, M. 2004. Promoting diversity: Recruitment, selection, orientation, and retention of international students. Ph.D. Dissertation. University of the Incarnate Word. (UMI No. 3134700).

Taylor, M.C. 2012. On a wing and a prayer. In *Black Graduate Education at Historically Black Colleges and Universities: Trends, Experiences, and Outcomes*, edited by R. Palmer, A. Hilton, and T. Fountaine. Charlotte, NC: Information Age Publishing.

Techler, U. 2004. The changing debate on internationalisation of higher education. *Higher Education*. 48(1): 5–26.

Tekle, S., V. Quintal, and R. Taylor. 2005. Factors influencing international students' choice of an education destination—A correspondence analysis. *Journal of Marketing for Higher Education*. 15(2): 31–46.

Tempus. 2012. *Higher Education in Ukraine*. Retrieved from: <http://eacea.ec.europa.eu/tempus/participating_countries/overview/ukraine_tempus_country_fiche_final.pdf>.

Terriquez, V. 2015. Dreams delayed: Barriers to degree completion among undocumented community college students. *Journal of Ethnic and Migration Studies*. 41(8): 1302–1323.

The Chronicle Herald. 2011. N.S. turfs Dal fee hike plan. July 28, 2011.

The Information Database on Education Systems in Europe. *The Education System in the United Kingdom (England, Wales and Northern Ireland)—2003/04*. Retrieved from: www.eurydice.org.

The Observatory on Borderless Higher Education. 2014. *The Agent Question: Insights from Students, Universities and Agents*.

Thelin, J.R. 2011. *A History of American Higher Education* (2nd ed.). Baltimore, MD: The Johns Hopkins University Press.

The World Bank. *Mexico* (Data). Retrieved November 25, 2014 from: <http://data.worldbank.org/country/mexico>.

Tinto, V. 1975 Dropout from higher education: A theoretical synthesis of recent research. *Review of Educational Research*. 45(1): 89–125.

Tompson, H.B., and G.H. Tompson. 1996. Confronting diversity issues in the classroom with strategies to improve satisfaction and retention of international students. *Journal of Education for Business*. 72(1): 53–57.

Treat, T., and L.S. Hagedorn. Spring 2013. The community college in a global context. *New Directions for Community Colleges*. 161: 5–9.

Trebor, I. 2014. How education is being turned over in Donetsk. *Euromaidan Press*. September 24. Retrieved from: <http://euromaidanpress.com/2014/09/24/how-education-is-being-turned-over-in-donetsk/>.

Tsang, E.Y. 2013. The quest for higher education by the Chinese middle class: Retrenching social mobility? *Higher Education*. 66: 653–668.

Twain, M. 1869. *Innocents Abroad, or The New Pilgrim's Progress, Volumes 1–2*. Hartford: American Pub. Co.

Tyshchenko, Y. and O. Smirnov. 2015. *«Annexed» Education in Temporarily Occupied Crimea*. Monitoring Report. Kyiv: Ukrainian Center for Independent Political Research. Retrieved from: <www.ucipr.kiev.ua/userfiles/monitoring_report_education_ARC_Mar2015e.pdf>.

UCAS. *See* Universities and College Admission Service.

USCIS. *See* U.S. Citizenship and Immigration Services.

U.S. Citizenship and Immigration Services. 2015. *Number of I-821D, Consideration of Deferred Action for Childhood Arrivals by Fiscal Year, Quarter, Intake, Biometrics and Case Status: 2012–2015 (June 30)*. Retrieved from: <www.uscis.gov/sites/default/files/USCIS/Resources/Reports%20and%20Studies/Immigration%20Forms%20Data/All%20Form%20Types/DACA/I821d_performancedata_fy2015_qtr3.pdf>.

U.S. Department of Education. 2008. *Diploma Mills and Accreditation—Diploma Mills*. Available at: <www2.ed.gov/students/prep/college/diplomamills/diploma-mills.html>.

U.S. Department of State. n.d. *The Early Years: An Informal History of the Fulbright Program*. Washington, D.C.: Bureau of Educational and Cultural Affairs. Retrieved from: <http://eca.state.gov/fulbright/about-fulbright/history/early-years>.

UNICEF. *See* United Nations Children's Fund.

United Nations Children's Fund. 2014. Ukraine: Access to education for children affected by the crisis should be at the top of national agenda (press release). August 8. Retrieved from: <www.unicef.org/ceecis/media_26464.html>.

———. 2015. *The Children*. Retrieved from: <www.unicef.org/ukraine/children_26253.html>.

Ushe, A. 2014. *The Korean Academic Credit Bank: A Model for Credit Transfer in North America?* Toronto: Higher Education Strategy Associates. Available at: <http://higheredstrategy.com/wp-content/uploads/2014/08/Intelligence-Brief-8-Korea-Aug-17.pdf>.

Van Nelson, C., J.C. Nelson, and B.G. Malone. 2004. Predicting success of international graduate students in an American university. *College and University*. 80(1): 19–27.

VanDeventer Iverson, S. 2007. Camouflaging power and privilege: A critical race analysis of university diversity policies. *Educational Administration Quarterly*. 43(5): 586–611.

Verbik, L., and V. Lasanowski. 2007. International student mobility: Patterns and trends. *World Education News & Reviews*. October 1. Available at: <http://wenr.wes.org/2007/10/wenr-october-2007-feature/>.

Vlaardingerbroek, B. 2009. *Secondary School External Examination Systems Reliability, Robustness and Resilience*. Amherst, NY: Cambria Press.

Vyas, H. 2010. Over 51K fake degrees issued in state, CBI tells HC. *The Times of India*. October 28. Available at: <http://timesofindia.indiatimes.com/city/mumbai/Over-51K-fake-degrees-issued-in-state-CBI-tells-HC/articleshow/6825330.cms>.

Wait, I.W., and J.W. Gressell. 2009. Relationships between TOEFL score and academic success for international students. *Journal of Engineering Education.* 98(1): 389–398.

Walsh, D. 2015. Fake diplomas, real cash: Pakistani company Axact reaps millions. *The New York Times.* May 17. Retrieved March 31, 2016 from <http://mobile.nytimes.com/2015/05/18/world/asia/fake-diplomas-real-cash-pakistani-company-axact-reaps-millions-columbiana-barkley.html> .

Wang, L., and A.C.T. Dupigny. 2004. *Education in Sierra Leone,* Africa Human Development Series. Washington, D.C.: The World Bank.

Wasserstrom, J.N. 2014. Should we be optimists or pessimists on China? *The Chronicle of Higher Education.* October 1. Retrieved from: <http://chronicle.com/blogs/conversation/2014/10/01/should-we-be-optimists-or-pessimists-on-china>.

Watkins, R. 2013. International credential placement recommendations: An historical survey. *College and University.* 88(3).

Weiss, R. 1973. *Loneliness: The Experience of Emotional and Social Isolation.* Cambridge, MA: MIT Press.

West, E., and L. Addington. 2014. *International Student Recruitment Agencies: A Guide for Schools, Colleges and Universities.* Arlington, VA: National Association for College Admission Counseling. Retrieved from: <www.nacacnet.org/international/documents/intlstudentrecruitment.pdf>.

White, A. 2011. Chinese students' international study: Factors feeding the decision process. *World Education News & Reviews.* February 1. Retrieved from: <http://wenr.wes.org/2011/02/wenr-januaryfebruary-feature/>.

Wilkerson, J. 201.4 Session and live chat on knowing what data you need before you begin. Presentation.

Wilkins, S., and J. Huisman. 2011. International student destination choice: The influence of home campus experience on the decision to consider branch campuses. *Journal of Marketing for Higher Education.* 21(1): 61–83.

Willer, P., and I. Steglitz. 2011. Campus Internationalization: Whose Job Is It, Anyway? Annual conference of NAFSA: Association of International Educators, Kansas City, MO, June 2011.

Williams, D., R. Watkins, and M. Baxton. 2010. *The AACRAO International Guide.* Washington, D.C.: American Association of Collegiate Registrars and Admissions Officers.

Williams, K. 2008. Graduate enrollment management: Leading the way to EM's future. *College and University.* 83(4): 55–58.

Williamson, E.G. 1949. The Student Personnel Point of View. *American Council on Education Studies, Series, VI, Student Personnel Work, No. 13.* Washington, D.C.: American Council on Education.

Wodon, Q., B. De la Briere, C. Siaens, and S. Yitzhaki. 2003. *Mexico's Progresa: Innovative Targeting, Gender Focus and Impact on Social Welfare.* Washington, D.C.: World Bank Publications.

Wojciechowski, A., and L.B. Palmer. 2005. Individual student characteristics: Can any be predictors of success in online classes? *Online Journal of Distance Learning Administration.* 8(2).

World Bank. 2014. *Total Population Data.* Retrieved from: <http://data.worldbank.org/indicator/SP.POP.TOTL>.

World Education News & Reviews. 2007. The impact of the Bologna Process beyond Europe, Part I. April 1. Retrieved from: <wenr.wes.org/2007/04/wenr-april-2007-bologna-process-beyond-europe/>.

———. 2011. Admitting Chinese undergraduates. November 1. Retrieved from: <http://wenr.wes.org/2011/11/wenr-novemberdecember-2011-feature-admitting-chinese-undergraduates>.

———. 2015. New study: How international bachelor's students choose institutions. *World Education News & Reviews.* November 3. Available at: <http://wenr.wes.org/2015/11/new-study-international-bachelors-students-choose-institutions/>.

World Education Services, Inc. 2004. Practical Skills in International Credential Evaluation (workshop). New York, NY: World Education Services.

Xinhua News. 2015. Chinese universities face rising survival crisis. Retrieved from: <http://news.xinhuanet.com/english/2015-06/04/c_134298210.htm>.

Young, K.E., C.M. Chambers, and H.R. Kells. 1983. *Understanding Accreditation: Contemporary Perspectives on Issues and Practices in Evaluating Educational Quality.* San Francisco: Jossey-Bass, Inc.

Zhang, A., and G. Zhou. 2010. Understanding Chinese international students at a Canadian university: Perspectives, expectations, and experiences. *Comparative and International Education.* 39(3): 1–16.

Zhao, C.M., G.D. Kuh, and R.M. Carini. 2005. A comparison of international student and American student engagement in effective educational practices. *Journal of Higher Education.* 76(2): 209–231.